In this book, leading western specialists and Russian and Ukrainian feminists examine how gender has shaped Russian and Ukrainian history from the twelfth century to the present. In particular, they analyse the current backlash against women's emancipation. Using new archival materials and the insights of feminist theory, the contributors explore the relevance of gender equality and difference in Russian history. They find that women have not merely submitted to the patriarchal system, but instead have found creative ways of resisting it. Chapters focusing on contemporary Russia discuss abortion, pornography, sexual minorities, young women's lifestyles, the impact of economic reform on women and the development of the women's movement. This book will be of interest to students and specialists in Russian, Ukrainian and women's studies, as well as to historians, political scientists, sociologists and economists.

D0904301

Women in Russia and Ukraine

Women in Russia and Ukraine

Edited and translated by

ROSALIND MARSH

Centre for Women's Studies
University of Bath

CAMBRIDGE
UNIVERSITY PRESS

Published by the Press Syndicate of the University of Cambridge
The Pitt Building, Trumpington Street, Cambridge CB2 1RP
40 West 20th Street, New York, NY 10011–4211, USA
10 Stamford Road, Oakleigh, Melbourne 3166, Australia

© Cambridge University Press 1996

First published 1996

Printed in Great Britain at the University Press, Cambridge

A catalogue record for this book is available from the British Library

Library of Congress cataloguing in publication data

Women in Russia and Ukraine / edited and translated by Rosalind Marsh.
    p.   cm.
Includes index.
ISBN 0 521 49522 9 (hbk.). – ISBN 0 521 49872 4 (pbk.)
1. Women – Russia (Federation) – History. 2. Women – Ukraine –
History. 3. Feminism – Russia (Federation) – History. 4. Feminism –
Ukraine – History. I. Marsh, Rosalind J.
HQ1665.15.W663 1995
305.4'0947 – dc20   95–7639   CIP

ISBN 0 521 49522 9 hardback
ISBN 0 521 49872 4 paperback

WD

Contents

Part II: Women in the USSR and post-Soviet Russia: sexuality, identity, health and reproduction

Part III: Women and work

Part IV: Feminism and politics in Russia and Ukraine

Illustrations

Tables

Notes on contributors

Lynne Attwood is Lecturer in Russian Studies at the University of Manchester. She received her doctorate in Soviet Studies and Sociology from the Centre for Russian and East European Studies, University of Birmingham, and has taught Russian Studies and Sociology at the University of Texas at Austin and at the University of Humberside. She is the author of *The New Soviet Man and Woman: Sex-Role Socialization in the USSR* (Basingstoke: Macmillan, 1990; Bloomington: Indiana University Press, 1991); the editor of *Red Women on the Silver Screen: Soviet Women and Cinema from the Beginning to the End of the Communist Era* (London: Pandora, 1993); and has contributed to a number of other books on women and cinema in the Soviet Union and Russia.

Sue Bridger is Senior Lecturer in Russian Studies at the University of Bradford. She is the author of *Women in the Soviet Countryside* (Cambridge: Cambridge University Press, 1987) and numerous articles on women in Russia. With James Riordan, she edited *Dear Comrade Editor: Readers' Letters to the Soviet Press under Perestroika* (Bloomington and Indianapolis: Indiana University Press, 1992). She is currently editing a collection of essays on 'Women in Post-Communist Russia' for *Interface: Bradford Studies in Language, Culture and Society* (University of Bradford), and writing a book on the impact of market reforms on Russian women.

Mary Buckley is Reader in Politics at the University of Edinburgh. She is the author of *Women and Ideology in the Soviet Union* (Hemel Hempstead: Harvester Wheatsheaf, 1989; Ann Arbor: University of Michigan Press, 1989) and *Redefining Russian Society and Polity* (Boulder, Colo.: Westview Press, 1993); and the editor of *Perestroika and Soviet Women* (Cambridge: Cambridge University Press, 1992). She has written numerous articles on Russian women and is currently working on rural Stakhanovism.

Linda Edmondson is ESRC Research Fellow at the Centre for Russian and East European Studies, University of Birmingham. She is the author of *Feminism in Russia, 1900–1917* (London: Stanford University Press, 1984) and the editor of *Women and Society in Russia and the Soviet Union* (Cambridge: Cambridge

University Press, 1992). She is currently engaged in research on 'Gender and Citizenship in Russia, 1860–1920: Issues of Equality and Difference'.

Donald Filtzer is Senior Lecturer in European Studies at the University of East London. He recently completed the third volume of his historical study of industrial workers in the Soviet Union: *Soviet Workers and Stalinist Industrialization* (London: Pluto, 1986); *Soviet Workers and De-Stalinization* (Cambridge: Cambridge University Press, 1992); and *Soviet Workers and the Collapse of Perestroika* (Cambridge: Cambridge University Press, 1994). Part of his research has involved an analysis of the role of female labour in the political economy of the Soviet system.

Hilde Hoogenboom is finishing her doctoral dissertation, 'A Two-Part Invention: The Russian Woman Writer and Her Heroines, 1860–1917', at Columbia University, New York. She teaches Literature Humanities, part of Columbia's core curriculum. Her research interests include women's fiction, autobiography, theory and culture.

Lindsey Hughes is Reader in Russian History and Chair of the History Department at the School of Slavonic and East European Studies, University of London. She has a BA in Russian (Sussex, 1971) and a Ph.D from Cambridge (1976), and has taught in the Universities of Cambridge, Belfast and Reading. Her books include *Russia and the West: Prince Vasily Vasilevich Golitsyn (1643–1714), the Life of a Seventeenth-Century Westernizer* (Newtonville, Mass.: Oriental Research Partners, 1984); *Sophia, Regent of Russia, 1657–1704* (New Haven, Conn.: Yale University Press, 1990). She edited, translated and introduced volume 25 of S. M. Solov'ev's *History of Russia from Earliest Times* (Gulf Breeze, Fla.: Academic International Press, 1989); jointly edited *The Russian Chronicles* (London: Century, 1990); and edited *New Perspectives on Muscovite History: Selected Papers from the IV World ICSEES Congress* (New York: St Martin's Press, 1993). She has contributed to the *Modern Encyclopedia of Russian and Soviet History*, and written more than thirty articles. She is currently working on *Russia in the Reign of Peter the Great* for Yale University Press.

Janet Hyer is a doctoral candidate in the Department of Political Science at the University of Toronto. She has an MA from the Institute of Soviet and East European Studies, Carleton University, Ottawa, where she was research assistant to Professor R. C. Elwood on his book *Inessa Armand: Revolutionary and Feminist* (Cambridge: Cambridge University Press, 1992). She has contributed articles on Russian women to *Canadian Woman Studies/Les Cahiers de la femme* and was guest editor for the special issue of the journal entitled *Soviet Women*, vol. 10, no. 4 (Winter 1989). She is currently writing her dissertation on the medical profession and the regulation of women's fertility in Soviet Russia during the 1920s and 1930s.

Melanie Ilic is Senior Lecturer and Field Chair for Women's Studies at Cheltenham and Gloucester College of Higher Education, where she also teaches Russian and Soviet History. She is an Honorary Research Fellow and Research Consultant at the Centre for Russian and East European Studies, University of Birmingham, where she is also currently registered for a Ph.D on the protection of female labour in the Soviet Union in the 1920s and 1930s.

Catriona Kelly is Lecturer in Russian Language and Literature at the School of Slavonic and East European Studies, University of London, and was formerly a British Academy Post-Doctoral Fellow at Christ Church, University of Oxford. She is the author of *A History of Russian Women's Writing, 1820–1992* and the editor of *An Anthology of Russian Women's Writing, 1777–1992* (both published by Oxford University Press in 1994); author of *Petrushka, the Russian Carnival Puppet Theatre* (Cambridge: Cambridge University Press, 1990); and author of numerous articles on Russian women's writing and on popular culture. Authors whom she has translated from Russian include Leonid Borodin, Sergei Kaledin, and the poets Elena Shvarts, Anna Barkova and Ol'ga Sedakova.

Rosalind Marsh is Professor of Russian Studies and Director of the Centre of Women's Studies at the University of Bath. She was awarded an MA at Cambridge and a DPhil. at Oxford. She taught at the Queen's University of Belfast from 1977 to 1987, and at the University of Exeter from 1987 to 1991, where she was Director of the Centre for Russian, Soviet and East European Studies from 1989 to 1991. She is the author of *Soviet Fiction since Stalin: Science, Politics and Literature* (London and Sydney: Croom Helm, 1986), *Images of Dictatorship: Stalin in Literature* (London and New York: Routledge, 1989) and *History and Literature in Contemporary Russia, 1985–1994* (Basingstoke: Macmillan, 1995). Her articles on Russian women and women's literature include 'The Birth, Death and Rebirth of Feminist Writing in Russia', in Helena Forsås-Scott (ed.), *Textual Liberation: European Feminist Writing in the Twentieth Century* (London: Routledge, 1991). She has just completed editing *Gender and Russian Literature: New Perspectives* for Cambridge University Press.

Shane O'Rourke is Lecturer in the Department of History, University of York. He has a BA and an MA from the University of East Anglia, and a DPhil. from the University of Oxford. His doctoral thesis was entitled 'Warriors and Peasants: The Contradictions of Cossack Culture, 1861–1914'.

Solomea Pavlychko is a research associate at the Institute of Literature of the Academy of Sciences of Ukraine in Kiev. She is the author, in Ukrainian, of *Byron; His Life and Work* (Kiev: Dnipro, 1989) and *Labyrinths of Thought: The Intellectual Novel of Great Britain* (Kiev: Naukova Dumka, 1993); in Russian, of *Transcendental Poetry of American Romanticism: Emerson, Whitman, Dickinson* (Kiev: Naukova Dumka, 1988); and in English, of *Letters from Kiev* (New York: St Martin's Press,

1992). She has translated into Ukrainian *Lord of the Flies* by William Golding and *Lady Chatterley's Lover* by D. H. Lawrence, and has written numerous articles on English and American literature and the women's movement in Ukraine. She was a founder member of the Women's Community of Rukh.

Hilary Pilkington is Lecturer in Russian Politics and Society at the Centre for Russian and East European Studies, University of Birmingham. She teaches post-Soviet politics and Russian culture and society, and her research interests are in the area of changing socio-cultural relations and identities. She is author of *Russia's Youth and Its Culture: A Nation's Constructors and Constructed* (London: Routledge, 1994) and co-editor of *Women in the Face of Change: The Soviet Union, Eastern Europe and China* (London: Routledge, 1992).

Anastasiia Posadskaia (Anastasia Posadskaya) has a Ph.D in economics from the Institute of Economics of the former USSR. She has undertaken sociological research into women's employment and other issues at the KamAZ plant and in the town of Taganrog. She was one of the four founder members of 'Lotos' – the League for Emancipation from Sexual Stereotypes – and since 1989 has been a director of the Moscow Centre for Gender Studies at the Institute for Research into Socio-Economic Problems of the Population of the Russian Academy of Sciences. She has written a number of articles on the contemporary situation of Russian women, and is the editor of *Women in Russia: A New Era in Russian Feminism* (London: Verso, 1994).

James Riordan is Professor of Russian Studies and Academic Head of the Department of Linguistic and International Studies at the University of Surrey. He studied at the Universities of Birmingham and London and Moscow State University, and has taught at the Universities of Portsmouth, Birmingham and Bradford. He is the author of numerous publications on sport, youth and sexuality in the former Soviet Union. His many books include *Soviet Youth Culture* (Basingstoke: Macmillan, 1989); *Sport, Politics and Communism* (Manchester: Manchester University Press, 1991); and *Soviet Social Reality in the Mirror of Glasnost* (New York: St Martin's Press, 1992). With Igor Kon he is editor of the ground-breaking *Sex and Russian Society* (London: Pluto Press, 1993).

Marian Rubchak is Associate Professor of European and Russian History at the University of Valparaiso, Indiana. She has an MA from Rutgers University, New Jersey and a Ph.D from the University of Illinois, Chicago. She edited, translated and introduced volume 5 of S. M. Solov'ev's *History of Russia from Earliest Times,* and is the author of various articles on Ukrainian history and politics, the Ukrainian émigré community, and contemporary feminism in Ukraine and Russia.

Elena Sargeant (neé Kuz'mina) is Honorary Research Assistant in the History Department of the University of Aberdeen, where she has taught Russian language and modern and contemporary European history since 1992. She was born in Ukraine in 1966; and in 1988 graduated with Honours from the History Department of Moscow State University, where she became a Candidate of Historical Sciences (Ph.D) in 1991. She has published several articles in the field of Slavic history, including a study of a previously unknown manuscript about the Russian satirist M. E. Saltykov-Shchedrin (1826–89) by the Bulgarian writer Zakhari Stoianov, which she discovered in a Bulgarian archive. Her research interests lie in the areas of Russian, Soviet and post-Soviet history, women's studies and modern and contemporary European history.

Susan Gross Solomon is Professor in the Department of Political Science at the University of Toronto. She was co-editor of *The Social Context of Soviet Science* with Linda Lubrano (Boulder, Colo.: Westview Press, 1980), co-editor with John F. Hutchinson of *Health and Society in Revolutionary Russia* (Bloomington: Indiana University Press, 1990), and editor of *Beyond Sovietology: Essays in Politics and History* (Armonk, N.Y.: M. E. Sharpe, 1994). She is now completing a monograph on Soviet social medicine in the inter-war years.

Elena Stishova is Professor at the Russian Institute of Cinematography, Moscow, and a critic, publicist and author of books and articles on contemporary Russian cinema. She edited the special feminist issue of the journal *Isskustvo kino*, no. 6 (1991). Her publications in English include *Look Who's Here!*, published in English in Bombay, and 'The Mythologization of Soviet Woman: *The Commissar* and Other Cases', in Lynne Attwood (ed.), *Red Women on the Silver Screen*. Her other interests are feminist criticism, and the cinema and psychoanalysis.

Christopher Williams is Lecturer in European Studies at the University of Central Lancashire, Preston. He has an MSc. from University College, Swansea and a Ph.D from the University of Essex, and has published numerous articles on Russian social policy in *Irish Slavonic Studies, Revolutionary Russia, Sociology of Health and Illness* and *Journal of Urban History*. He has recently published *AIDS in Post-Communist Russia and the Successor States* (Aldershot: Avebury, 1995); and, with James Riordan and Igor Il´inskii, is completing a second book, *Young People in Post-Communist Russia and Eastern Europe*, for Dartmouth Press. He is currently engaged on a University-funded project on Polish politics since 1989.

Acknowledgements

I would like to acknowledge, gratefully, the financial support offered by the ESRC, the Ford Foundation, the British Academy, the British Council in Russia and Ukraine, South West Arts and the Council for Co-operation in Russian and Soviet Education for the conference on 'Women in Russia and the Former USSR' held at the University of Bath in March–April 1993, at which earlier versions of many of the chapters in this volume were presented. Special thanks are due to Celia Dyer for ensuring the efficient organization of the conference.

I should also like to thank the British Council for enabling me to do research in St Petersburg; the Kennan Institute for Advanced Russian Studies, Washington, D.C., for awarding me a research fellowship; St Antony's College, Oxford, for making me a Senior Research Associate; and the University of Bath for awarding me the study leave essential to complete this book.

The comments of Mary Buckley and Linda Edmondson have been of particular value in preparing this volume. Natasha Zhuravkina has helped with the finer points of Russian translation, and Marian Rubchak has provided invaluable assistance with the transliteration of Ukrainian according to a modified Library of Congress system. Thanks are also due to all the participants of the 'Women in Russia' conference, who helped to make the occasion so successful and to stimulate debate and further reflection on many issues discussed in this volume.

1

Introduction: women's studies and women's issues in Russia, Ukraine and the post-Soviet states

ROSALIND MARSH

Until the late 1960s, history had been predominantly regarded as the actions of great men and governments; the historians of every culture had largely ignored the female sex, and hence the history of over half the human race.[1] It was the 'second wave' of the feminist movement in the West in the 1960s and 1970s which stimulated interest in the history and experience of women,[2] who had previously, in the words of the new feminist historians, been 'hidden from history',[3] 'made to disappear'[4] by the unwitting or deliberate neglect of historians, who had been predominantly male. Although much interesting work in women's history has appeared in the last twenty-five years, there is still much scope for future research in this area. In many countries the discipline is still in its infancy; it is only in the United States that women's history has secured a widespread and stable institutional base in university and college curricula.

Russian women's history

In Russia, until very recently, the history and experience of women has not been regarded as a serious subject of study, partly because Russia and the USSR have always been irredeemably patriarchal societies, and partly because during much of the Soviet period, from the rise of Stalin to the late 1960s, the Communist Party had decreed that the 'woman question' (*zhenskii vopros*) – the Russian term for the whole range of issues concerning the legal, social, political, philosophical and cultural status of women – had been 'solved'.[5] At the same time, foreign historians and social scientists studying Russia continued to follow the agenda considered important in the USSR, focusing well into the second half of the twentieth century on political élites and economic forces, even after social history, which included a study of previously neglected groups such as women and the working class, had become a respectable, even fashionable discipline among historians of other countries.[6] The dilatoriness of Slavists in investigating Russian social history may partly, perhaps, be ascribed to the Soviet government's refusal to allow access to many vital archival sources, and partly to the intrinsic interest and political significance of a study of the origins and exercise of political power in Russia and the USSR, subjects about which many people in the West knew little,

1

and which in any case corresponded more closely to the interests of western historians and social scientists, the majority of whom were male. Although political history and high politics in Russia and the other states of the former Soviet Union have been, and still remain, fascinating and rewarding subjects of study, it has now become clear that the women's movement in the West and the growing influence of social history in university history departments have promoted some of the most exciting and productive research into Russian and Soviet society over the last two decades.[7] Western historians and literary critics began to discover, often with the force of a revelation, that 'In Russian history, there were women too.'[8] Works on Russian women's studies are now so numerous that it is impossible to list all the important research on this subject, although the output of research in this field is still not widespread in the former USSR itself, and is relatively small in comparison with the study of women's history and culture in Britain, the United States and Germany.

The historiographical context

From the mid-1970s, western historians of Russian women have begun to publish the fruits of their research, concentrating initially on the history of the women's liberation movement in Russia in the years 1860–1930,[9] and the lives of prominent revolutionary women and feminists, such as Aleksandra Kollontai, or her predecessors in the nineteenth-century radical movement;[10] then, as it became easier to gain access to Russian archives, examining the lives of less exceptional women, such as peasant women and factory workers.[11] More detailed subsequent research has focused on women rulers,[12] and on the experience of women of various classes and professional groups at different periods of Russian history.[13] At the same time, social scientists began to explore the problems attendant on the alleged 'emancipation' of women by the Soviet regime, which had come to public attention in the USSR in the late 1960s with the publication of Natal'ia Baranskaia's story *A Week Like Any Other:*[14] the double burden that women were obliged to bear, and the harmful consequences for society and the Soviet family.[15] If the first western research to some extent followed Soviet agendas, concentrating on women's struggle for political emancipation, subsequent research has been more concerned with showing how the patriarchal system shaped women's lives, and how women, living in a society which wished them to be powerless, responded creatively to its attempts to control them. Within the USSR, the public discussion in the press of issues which had formerly been taboo, and the influence of the western feminist movement, led Soviet women themselves to make tentative attempts to re-establish a native women's movement. At first, during the Brezhnev era, the small band of Soviet feminists could only operate underground;[16] but after the inception of glasnost, the women's movement began to take public, often very diverse forms.[17]

This volume is an attempt to continue the path-breaking work in Russian women's studies initiated by previous feminist historians and social scientists, filling in certain gaps which have appeared in the literature and extending previous research on the social and economic situation of women in Russia and the ex-Soviet Union during the Gorbachev era into the first three years of the post-communist period.[18] Many of these contributions are revised versions of papers first presented at a conference on 'Women in Russia and the Former USSR', held in the University of Bath in March–April 1993, but others have been offered specially for inclusion in this book.

The theoretical dimension

There is no unanimity of theoretical viewpoint in this volume, although the contributors all write from a feminist perspective, in that they take it for granted that a study of the role played by women in the history of the Russian and Soviet empires, and an analysis of the political, social and economic position of women in the ex-Soviet Union today, are subjects of interest and value in themselves – issues which would still be highly debatable in the former USSR, and even in some western departments of history and Slavonic studies. Work in Russian women's studies is far from being completely accepted by academic establishments in the West, although a measure of recognition is now evident from the occasional incorporation of chapters on women and the family in mainstream treatments of Russian history and society.

Linda Edmondson's essay, 'Equality and difference in women's history: where does Russia fit in?', directly engages with many important theoretical issues raised by feminist historians in the past twenty years, in the context of Russian women's history both before and after the Bolshevik Revolution. She demonstrates how at different times in history emphasis has been laid on women's equality or difference, questions conventional assumptions about sexual difference and rehabilitates the concept of egalitarianism in the teeth of the critique launched against it both by contemporary western feminist theorists and anti-feminist women in the post-Soviet states. She highlights the potential dangers posed by any political philosophy emphasizing gender difference, which tends to devalue individual identities among both men and women, especially in a society like Russia, with its long tradition of autocracy, arbitrary censorship and suppression of the individual.

This book aims to build upon some of the best traditions established by previous work in Russian women's studies and women's studies in general. Hitherto much research in Russian women's studies has focused either on history, literature or the social sciences;[19] but it has been decided to combine research in history, culture and contemporary society in this anthology, because in women's studies (and in Russian studies too), rigid boundaries between disciplines have come increasingly to be seen to be artificial.[20] Several contributors, notably Hughes, Hoogenboom and Kelly, use evidence from art and literature, demonstrating that such primary sources, and the literary and psychoanalytical theoretical approaches that cultural historians can bring to bear on them, can be valuable and illuminating, even though some historians may feel uncomfortable with this kind of evidence.[21]

In the last twenty years, a growing number of feminist historians have argued that it is important not only to reappraise women's situation in the past, but also to gain direct insight into the experience of women themselves. Many contributors to this volume attempt to recover women's own voices, through the use of memoirs, diaries, autobiographies and correspondence, wherever these may be obtained. Such an approach suggests that, while the political dimension of Russian women's *subjection* should not be lost, it is also vital to stress women's *subjectivity* and their own perceptions of their experience, and to explore the strategies they devised in accommodating to or resisting a patriarchal society. The contributors implicitly acknowledge that a simplistic appropriation of the term 'patriarchy', without an analysis of the specific historical contexts in which male oppression and female subordination or resistance may occur, is abstract and artificial.[22]

Another boundary now perceived as unhelpful is the former rigid division between the tsarist and Soviet periods of Russian history. Contemporary Russian and Ukrainian feminists regard their current situation as indissolubly linked with the history of women's oppression and the fate of the first-wave women's move-ment in their countries, which had been largely suppressed until the Gorbachev era. The rediscovery of this forgotten tradition through the works of western scholars proved to be a revelation for many Russian women groping their way toward a feminist consciousness during the 'period of stagnation' under Brezhnev.[23] Subsequently, glasnost and the burgeoning indigenous women's movement provided a stimulus for feminist scholars in Russia and the other post-Soviet states to initiate a serious reappraisal of women's contributions to their own history, society and culture.[24]

Many contributors interweave past and present, suggesting that contemporary trends in the post-Soviet states cannot be adequately analysed without an exploration of their origins in the Gorbachev era. *A fortiori*, the traditional values espoused by current leaders in Russia and Ukraine had their origin in the patriarchal, pro-natalist policies propagated in the Brezhnev era (and earlier, in Stalin's time). The post-Soviet states are still being governed by conservative men whose policies on women, like those of their predecessors, are largely determined by economic and demographic factors and who, while rejecting some aspects of their communist past, are now able to articulate with impunity more extreme patriarchal views than those propagated during the 'era of stagnation', since they no longer have any reason even to pay lip-service to idealistic Marxist notions of women's equality.

The juxtaposition of research into women's history and the situation of women in contemporary society renders it abundantly clear that, whatever the political system in Russia, it has always had predominantly negative consequences for women. The conservative values propagated in the perestroika and post-perestroika eras have their roots much further back, in long-standing patriarchal Russian and Soviet attitudes toward women. Under the rule of the tsars, the Soviet regime and the new democratic rulers of Russia and Ukraine, power has always rested in the hands of men who have legislated for women. It is not only the Russian state which has been patriarchal; reform movements in Russia, even those sympathetic to women's rights, have always been eager to instruct women that political issues other than those of primary concern to women are most important; that it is first necessary to struggle for a new society, and only then to address women's problems. Radical Russian men always seem to have been able to persuade prominent women to accept this point of view. This was true at the beginning of the twentieth century of the 'socialist feminist' Aleksandra Kollontai, who attacked the 'bourgeois feminist' movement because she believed that it was necessary to make the revolution first, before dealing with women's issues; and it was equally true of dissidents of the Brezhnev era like Elena Bonner. It has also been true of the new political parties and movements of the Gorbachev era: Russian democrats and Ukrainian nationalists have only been interested in liberating people from the communist system, and have little interest in women's rights; and these attitudes have been carried on into the post-communist governments. Some eastern European feminists have called the system which has developed since 1990 'male democracy'[25] and certainly, democratization in Russia and Ukraine does seem to have been a 'gendered concept',[26] granting men and women equal rights in the formal sense, but suggesting that their duties were to be very different: women's would be firmly rooted in the moral, spiritual and thus private sphere.

Most contemporary historians of women are researching the experience of women in their own countries; there have previously been comparatively few international or multi-national collections based on one country or one theme in women's history.[27] However, historians and social scientists in the former Soviet Union, fettered by political and patriarchal constraints,[28] have been slow to explore the history and contemporary situation of women in their own countries, so the work of foreign scholars in this field is still invaluable to women of the post-Soviet states in their efforts to reconstruct their own past. It is, nevertheless, also very gratifying that this volume (like the 'Women in Russia' conference itself)[29] is able to illustrate the new-found freedom of Russian and Ukrainian feminists to research their own societies and to exchange information and opinions with western researchers. The contributions by women active in the feminist movement in Russia and Ukraine, written in a highly charged, committed style which differs from the more dispassionate papers by western scholars, are important documents which focus on the problem of male power and female impotence in their societies; they seek to form and inform the contemporary women's movement in their countries, and remind us that the issues discussed here are of more than academic interest – indeed, they are matters of life and death to many women in the Soviet successor states.

Some of the early research in Russian women's studies was based on the paradox that many western scholars and feminists were attracted to this subject because they took at face value the Soviet government's claim to have emancipated women; but when they did further research, the exploitative, misogynistic nature of the Soviet regime emerged clearly. By the 1990s, however, it had become evident that western feminists would have to learn to be careful not to impose their own modes of thinking uncritically on women from the former USSR.[30] Many women in the post-Soviet states are highly suspicious of western *feministki* who, in their opinion, have an easy life and cannot possibly understand their problems.[31] There are a number of possible reasons why Russian and Ukrainian women have so little sympathy for western-style feminism: the general conservatism and misogyny of Soviet society inherited from the Stalin and Brezhnev eras; traditional communist hostility to 'bourgeois' feminism; the stereotypes presented in the media which make Russian women feel that to be a feminist inevitably means that they will 'lose their femininity' and cease to be attractive to men; the fact that Russian women are tired of ideological slogans about 'equal rights', which in practice mean that they are obliged both to work full time for negligible pay and to shoulder the bulk of the domestic chores; and, finally, the fact that Russian women simply do not know what feminism is, since western feminist ideas have been consistently misrepresented in the Soviet and post-Soviet press. Perhaps most importantly, in the post-communist period many Russian and Ukrainian women perceive 'feminism' as intimately linked with discredited Soviet socialism, as yet another 'ideology' which is hostile to the individual. Dialogue between scholars and feminists in the West and the East has demonstrated that it is not easy for the two sides to understand each other, but it is hoped that greater information will lead to greater tolerance of each other's point of view. The time has now come for western feminists, while continuing to point out the dangers of new forms of male exploitation in the post-Soviet states, to acknowledge, even to celebrate the cultural differences between women in the West and the former Soviet Union.

This book also differs from earlier studies in that it focuses on certain new issues which became topical in the Gorbachev era, and have grown even more important and controversial in the post-communist states, with the sexual revolution and the transition to a market economy: problems attendant on women's sexuality, health, reproduction and identity, and those related to women's work, unemployment and entrepreneurial activities. The disintegration of the Soviet empire and the rethinking of the colonial heritage have also raised new questions about the relationship between gender and ethnicity and their contribution to the formation of national identity. Hitherto much research has concentrated almost exclusively on *Russian* women, or has been devoted to women of specific countries or areas, such as Central Asia or the Baltic states; but this anthology juxtaposes essays on Russian women's history with a consideration of the unique position of Don Cossack women in the nineteenth-century Russian empire; and compares the contemporary situation of Russian and Ukrainian women, in an attempt to high-light the similarities and differences between the cultural traditions and position of women in two major areas of the Russian and Soviet empires. Marian Rubchak and Solomea Pavlychko point out that Ukrainian women are heirs to the same

Soviet cultural experience as Russian women, while stressing the inevitable dichotomy which exists between the perceptions of the colonizer and the colonized.

While focusing mainly on Russia and Ukraine, this volume also aims to emphasize the diversity of women's experience in the former Soviet Union. After the breakdown of the unitary state and the monolithic vision of the Communist Party, it is important to highlight the range of differences which can exist both within a national experience, and between the multi-national post-Soviet states. In the Russian Federation itself, pluralism is now the watchword: it has become clear that, contrary to the simplistic view frequently propounded by the Soviet Communist Party, there is no single collective entity which can be labelled 'Soviet women' (still less, 'post-Soviet women').[32] This volume suggests that there is a huge difference between the lives and opinions of young and old women, urban and rural women, professional and uneducated women, prostitutes, lesbians, religious women, radical feminists and women of all ages and nationalities who wish to return to the traditional values of home and family. Such richness and multiplicity remind us that it is impossible to universalize a particular pattern of experience for women, and also warn against the perils of Eurocentrism and westernism. In this connection, the juxtaposition of essays by western scholars, émigrés and feminists still living in Russia and Ukraine provides an interesting range of different views on the contemporary situation. Elena Sargeant's analysis of women's issues in post-Soviet Russia, for example, is written from the perspective of a woman who has lived for many years in the USSR, which differs in some respects from established western analysis, and also from some received opinions in Russia, notably her comments on the falsity of Soviet 'equality'. Another source of diversity is the inclusion of valuable contributions on women's issues by male scholars, and the quotation of opinions by men in the post-Soviet states, which illustrate the different views which can be adopted by men and women toward such issues as abortion and reproduction.

Women in Russian and Soviet history

In most countries, feminist historical research has concentrated heavily on modern history since 1800, but Lindsey Hughes helps to fill this lacuna, contributing to the rediscovery of the significant place women occupied in Russian culture long before the 'woman question' was put on the political agenda of the nineteenth-century Russian radical movement.[33] Her study of Peter the Great's two weddings is a subtle discussion of a culture in forced transformation and the effect that these profound social and political changes had on women's status. Whereas some previous research has tended to focus on the history of gender inequality, female oppression and male dominance in Russian and Soviet culture, the chapters by Rubchak, Kelly and O'Rourke, while by no means avoiding such issues, demonstrate that certain women in Kievan Rus´ and the Russian empire possessed more freedom and influence than we have hitherto been led to believe.[34] While adding to the documentation of women's marginalization and subordination in Russian and Soviet society, some contributors, notably Kelly, O'Rourke and Pilkington, also recover the private sphere of women's experience, yielding new insights into the role of sexual difference in Russian society and of patterns of female sociability, ritual and the history of private life. While not denying the reality of the patriarchal order, they emphasize that women have sometimes been able to use it to their best advantage.

To use terms coined by Gerda Lerner, the essays on women's history fall either into the categories of 'compensatory history', the history of notable women (for example, the studies of Peter the Great's wives and Vera Figner's autobiographical writings), or 'contribution history', which describes women's contribution to, and subjection in, a male-defined world (as in the essays analysing women's role in nineteenth-century merchant and Don Cossack communities, generally known for their quintessentially masculine pursuits).[35] Whereas Lerner regarded such developments as transitional, a stage in the growth of new conceptual frameworks, these and other papers in the volume corroborate the view that 'Such a process of recovery may take place alongside further theoretical developments and coexist with them. Indeed, the very process of recovery can yield important theoretical insights.'[36]

Such new insights are contained in the papers of Edmondson and Buckley, who rethink contentious historical debates, reappraising the role of male feminists in nineteenth-century Russia and of women Stakhanovites in Stalin's time. Now that it is fashionable among Russian intellectuals to disparage the radical and communist past, it is more necessary than ever for western scholars to pursue research in these areas. Edmondson presents an objective picture of the conflict between nineteenth-century male liberals and radicals, suggesting that their approach to 'the woman question' was largely determined by their own ultimate political interests; and Buckley focuses on the 1930s, a period for which sources in Russian women's history have been scarcer than for other periods. She highlights the genuine enthusiasm which some women demonstrated in contributing to the reconstruction of Soviet industry and agriculture in Stalin's time, and the considerable resistance provoked by female shock workers and Stakhanovites. Another new approach is employed in Donald Filtzer's essay, 'Industrial working conditions and the political economy of female labour during perestroika', which provides an interesting addition to the literature exploring the collapse of the Soviet regime in 1991, suggesting that the exploitation of women industrial workers under perestroika helped to destabilize the system as a whole.

This book also explores certain previously hidden aspects of Russian history, which form a fascinating background to current debates about women's work, sexuality and reproduction. In 'Teacups and coffins: the culture of Russian merchant women, 1850–1917', Catriona Kelly rediscovers the 'forgotten class' of merchant women, showing that many nineteenth-century women displayed considerable entrepreneurial talents, although they can hardly be regarded as models by either contemporary feminists or the new breed of businesswomen in post-communist Russia.[37] Sue Bridger, Elena Sargeant and Solomea Pavlychko highlight the re-emergence of such talents in contemporary Russia and Ukraine, sometimes directed toward surprising and unusual ends. Janet Hyer and Susan Gross Solomon reveal that even in the 1920s, generally considered to be a period of relative sexual freedom for Soviet women, the regime tried to control women's bodies and the reporting of sexual practices. In 'Managing the female organism: doctors and the medicalization of women's paid work in Soviet Russia during the 1920s', Hyer shows how the Soviet regime attempted to regulate women's fertility, adopting a rational approach to women's bodies based on economic factors; in 'Innocence and sexuality in Soviet medical discourse', Solomon demonstrates how sexuality and venereal disease were socially constructed: emphasis was laid on the alleged 'innocence' of the Russian rural peasantry in comparison with the depravity of city life, although the prevalence of nationalist, racist attitudes meant that free sexual practices and rampant venereal disease in Buriat-Mongolia could be acknowledged. Williams and Riordan suggest that regulation of fertility and sexuality has been a common practice in Russia, both before and after the 1920s. Williams's discussion of the reasons why a culture of abortion has grown up in Russia, which in 1994 still deserves the dubious accolade of 'absolute world leader' in abortion,[38] and Riordan's valuable overview of the position of sexual minorities in Russia and the former Soviet Union graphically illustrate the adverse effect which the policy of the Soviet government had over many years on the health and private lives of women, lesbians and homosexuals. The history of sexuality and reproduction in Russia reflects long-standing heterosexual male hostility to both homosexuality and women's sexuality, and a desire for the subordination of women.

Women in contemporary society

The essays focusing on the position of women in contemporary Russia and Ukraine assess the main implications of the perestroika and post-perestroika eras for women in the former USSR, concentrating on key issues such as women's role in politics, society and the economy, the intensifying demographic crisis[39] and the increase in pornography and violence against women. The discussion presented here makes no claim to be exhaustive, to duplicate other literature on women's issues or to present a unified point of view, but simply to update previous research and stimulate debate on many vital questions.

The contributions of western scholars and Russian and Ukrainian feminists graphically demonstrate that the perestroika and post-perestroika eras so far have had contradictory effects on the position of women. On the one hand, glasnost and the limited freedom of speech which followed it[40] have allowed the Russian press to discuss many issues affecting women's health and reproduction which could formerly only be discussed in *samizdat*, such as abortion, contraception, the terrible conditions in maternity hospitals, venereal disease and AIDS.[41] However, some issues which concerned male behaviour, such as domestic violence and rape, have only come lately to be discussed in the press, in the 1990s.

Another progressive development in the Gorbachev era was that some new concepts began to be used in discussions of women's issues, such as 'man's world', 'patriarchal relations of man to woman' and 'patriarchy'.[42] Some voices were raised suggesting that two parents should help in child-rearing, and that there were no 'women's problems', just problems of concern to society as a whole – views which were quite unusual in a Soviet context.[43] However, a 1989 article entitled 'How We Solve the Woman Question' by three women with feminist sympathies, including a contributor to this volume, Anastasiia Posadskaia,[44] based on draft recommendations on the status of Soviet women commissioned by the Council of Ministers,[45] provoked little public response, arousing more interest abroad than within Russia itself. Women's studies began to develop in Russia through the new Gender Studies Centre, established in Moscow in the spring of 1990, albeit with considerable resistance from the male academic establishment, which particularly objected to the unfamiliar concept of 'gender'.[46]

In the economic sphere, women obtained greater protection against heavy work and unhealthy working conditions (at least on paper), and were able for the first time to make choices about how to divide their working time: to do part-days or weeks in their paid jobs; to opt for flexi-time; or even to choose temporarily to give up paid work altogether. But although for many Russian women these options appear attractive, there is a danger that those who make such choices today will find that they are unable to rejoin the full-time workforce in the future. On a more positive note, the opportunity does now exist for women to engage in public discussion of economic problems that concern them, and to start up their own businesses, if they have the money and know-how.

On the negative side, the flood of words unleashed by glasnost in the perestroika and post-perestroika periods has led to little effective *action* on women's issues. By 1994, daily life was still as hard, or harder than ever, for many women; glasnost had exposed many problems in need of analysis, but horrific conditions still prevailed in abortion clinics and maternity hospitals,[47] and rape crisis centres had still not been established throughout the country (although two now exist in Moscow).[48] It was still true that 'given the backwardness of the country's pharmaceutical industry, the main method of terminating a pregnancy is abortion'.[49] Although by the post-communist period women's issues have come to be treated more frequently in the media,[50] formerly taboo issues such as lesbianism and contemporary feminism are still often treated in a superficial, sensational manner.[51] In the nascent Russian market economy, many laws concerned with the social protection of women have proved ineffective, or contain the hidden agenda of making women 'unprofitable employees' who can be made redundant with impunity.[52] New problems have been created by Yel'tsin's laws on the privatization of housing, which have encouraged criminal gangs to terrorize, even murder elderly women living alone.[53] In order for investigative journalism to achieve positive practical results, in 1994 there is still, as Mary Buckley argued in 1992, a need for 'more critical analysis, money and a political willingness to act'.[54] We can expect the first, especially from the Moscow Gender Centre, but in late 1994 the second and third are still highly unlikely, when in Russia President Yel'tsin is primarily concerned with the plummeting rouble, and in Ukraine President Kuchma is preoccupied with a new package of market reforms.[55] Women's issues do not represent a very high priority for the post-communist governments.[56]

Another problem is that, even with the introduction of the market system, the hopes that women would now have access to all the convenience products taken for granted by women in the West have not been realized. In Ukraine a joint venture producing tampons has been opened, but one factory cannot supply the entire population of women, and prices are very high. Similarly, although by 1993 a new factory mass-producing the coil had opened in Russia, sufficient supplies of the modern low-dose pill had been imported[57] and more information on contraception had been published, many women and couples still find contraceptives either psychologically unacceptable, unreliable, unavailable or too expensive. Perhaps it is unreasonable to expect the low priority accorded to consumer goods, or the high degree of prejudice and ignorance on sexual matters, which pertained for over half a century, to be corrected in such a short space of time.[58] This situation is, however, unlikely to improve in the foreseeable future, as Yel'tsin's government is trying to redress the catastrophic fall in the birth rate and encourage women to have children.[59] By 1994, fees had been introduced for abortions, and, according to Anastasiia Posadskaia, the state had 'virtually stopped buying in contraceptives'.[60]

Under Gorbachev and Yel'tsin, women have possessed even less political power than in earlier periods of Soviet history. Although Gorbachev called for the revival of the women's councils, and argued in 1988 for the opening of paths to women into the highest level of politics, his democratization reforms actually reduced the percentage of women at the highest level of government. The slackening of the party's control over the selection of candidates to the new USSR Congress of People's Deputies meant that the rough quotas based on social background and gender were no longer adhered to: female membership of the old USSR Supreme Soviet stood at around 33 per cent, whereas only 352 (that is, 15.7 per cent) of the new democratically elected Congress were women. Of these, 75 were elected from the official women's councils, so it was not surprising that when the reservation of seats for public bodies was abandoned, women's representation dropped to 5.4 per cent in the 1990 elections to the RSFSR Congress of People's Deputies. Under Gorbachev, almost two-thirds of women felt that women had not begun to play a more active role in public life since the advent of perestroika, although 42 per cent said they would like to participate in some way.

During 1989, women were highly visible on the streets in demonstrations, organizing meetings, electioneering and voting. In Lithuania, for example, they were seen as particularly important in the 'singing revolution', which led to the declaration of independence in March 1990. However, a highly symbolic episode occurred during the coup of August 1991, when women were requested to withdraw from the Russian Parliament building and leave its defence to men. Some women left, but the rest indignantly refused to go, arguing with the soldiers on their tanks and expressing their equal right to participate in the political life of their country.

When the new governments were being formed and people were taking their places in the new power structures, women seemed to disappear from view. Of the few women in Yel′tsin's government, Galina Starovoitova, his adviser on nationality issues, was dismissed in 1992; and Ella Pamfilova, the minister of social protection, resigned in January 1994 because she was unable to tackle social problems effectively, or even gain access to Prime Minister Chernomyrdin.[61] The reasons why women are not more prominent in politics in the post-Soviet states vary across countries, but two main factors are the still-current belief that politics is a 'man's world', and the fact that women have other priorities. One commonly articulated belief in Russia is that people will not vote for women: for example Larisa Vasil′eva, chair of the Council of Women Writers formed in 1989 under the Foreign Commission of the Writers' Union, declared after the 1989 elections: 'When a woman ran against a man she usually lost.'[62] Women are still much more acceptable as behind-the-scenes organizers, while men carry out often less onerous public duties. Even in the 1990s, women prominent in public life are often treated with patronizing sarcasm, as can be seen in a press report of 1994 about the failure of Irina Khakamada, who introduced the draft law 'On Non-Commercial Organizations' on behalf of the Economic Policy Committee, to secure its first reading in the State Duma. The journalist emphasizes her vulnerability, referring to 'the tears in Irina Khakamada's deep eyes'.[63]

At the Second Independent Women's Forum in Dubna in November 1992, there was no unanimity on whether women should form political parties, or simply act as an interest group lobbying the government. Many Russian women expressed reluctance to participate in the patriarchal power structures, but some Russian and western delegates argued that, unless women sought political power, their political influence would remain so weak that issues such as female unemployment, rape, contraception and abortion would either be kept off political agendas or, at best, be accorded low priority. After the suspension of the old Russian Supreme Soviet in September 1993, the 'Women of Russia' political movement was formed. It managed to achieve relative success in the December 1993 elections: the bloc took 8.1 per cent of the vote for the 225 Duma seats awarded on the basis of proportional representation from party lists, which meant that 21 candidates were elected; and at least two, perhaps up to four, of the 26 women candidates elected according to a system of first past the post in single-mandate districts were sympathizers.[64] Overall, the number of women candidates in the new Duma amounts to 60 (13.5 per cent); but it is only because of the moderately good showing of the 'Women of Russia' movement that the proportion of women is greater than in the old Congress of People's Deputies during the years 1990–3. This achievement suggests that some Russian women at least are prepared to vote for other women, and that women's issues will have some airing in post-communist Russia. However, the 'Women of Russia' bloc is by no means a radical feminist movement, but a descendant of the Committee of Soviet Women (the official women's organization under the communist regime) which concentrates on traditional female values of home and family.[65]

One of the proudest boasts of Soviet socialism was that over 90 per cent of women were in paid employment. However, as Sargeant, Filtzer and Ilic suggest, women have borne the brunt of the economic crisis in the former Soviet Union. Under perestroika it was they who spent most time in endless queues for food and clothes (in addition to their full-time jobs and domestic duties); and as they still do most of the shopping, they have been most affected by the deficits and hyper-inflation of the post-communist era. Since the price rises of April 1991 and January 1992, poverty and unemployment have had a disproportionate effect on women,[66] particularly among elderly women or those in low-paid service jobs. In 1993, according to Alevtina Fedulova of the 'Women of Russia' movement, 75 per cent of the unemployed were women (a higher proportion in rural areas), the average real pay was one-third lower for women than men, and women's pensions were only 70 per cent of men's.[67]

Rural women have suffered particularly badly. As Sue Bridger shows in 'The return of the family farm: a future for women?', the encouragement of 'family farms' after 1988 has created new problems for women, such as long working days, intensive non-mechanized labour and family conflicts. Under Yel'tsin's land reforms, the division of land has frequently been carried out in ways that violate women's rights and disregard the characteristic nature of their work, especially on the individual plots, which produce one-third of all agricultural output. Fears have been expressed that unless the situation changes, it will be mainly men, considered heads of the family, who will receive land during the land reform; and that a large proportion of the 'landless' will be women. Single mothers and elderly women, especially widows, who constitute the second largest group in the countryside and have spent their entire lives there, could be left socially unprotected.[68]

Many contributors suggest that, however imperfect women's emancipation was under the Soviet regime, the collapse of the Communist Party and the rise of nationalism have led to many results which are retrogressive from a western feminist point of view. The media campaign urging women to give up their jobs and go back to the home has been particularly insidious in the arduous economic circumstances of the 1990s, because overtired, overworked women in the former USSR regard staying at home as a tempting alternative; and many young women are eager to avoid the double burden which their mothers and grandmothers suffered. The St Petersburg feminist Ol'ga Lipovskaia has convincingly argued that the Russian mass media represent women's issues 'upside-down . . . The basic message is that the emancipation of women has harmed Soviet society, therefore woman must be returned to her traditional place at the domestic hearth.'[69] Indeed, since crèches and kindergartens either are insanitary, collapsing altogether for lack of funds, or prohibitively expensive for most families (because of the removal of state subsidies in January 1992, when ordinary and most special kindergartens raised their fees in panic when they were suddenly required to cover their own costs),[70] many women have little choice but to stay at home.

In the post-Soviet states, the former image of women and men as partners in the building of socialism is being replaced by that of the traditional family in which men work outside the home and women devote themselves to child care and domesticity. As Lynne Attwood argues in 'The post-Soviet woman in the move to the market: a return to domesticity and dependence?', the economic needs of the new post-Soviet states are now conveniently defined to coincide with the desire to return to traditional gender roles that was widely expressed in the Soviet media in the 1970s. Such views have been propagated by powerful Russian men in the late 1980s and 1990s, notably Gorbachev, Khasbulatov and Yel'tsin.

Attwood and Elena Stishova emphasize that, alongside this conventional stereotype of woman as wife, mother and servant to the Russian male, another more disturbing image of gender relations propagated by the media in the post-communist era is that of woman as sex object and victim of violence. Formerly, western feminists had praised the absence of such images in the USSR, which had stemmed from the ban on pornography and lack of advertising, contrasting Soviet restraint with the widespread denigration of women as sexual playthings, victims or temptresses in the West. However, this situation changed rapidly under glasnost, demonstrating that, as with national enmities, such feelings had simply been repressed, not eradicated. As many contributors show, the post-communist era has witnessed an intensification of the social problems that were discussed for the first time under perestroika: prostitution, pornography, rape and violence against women.[71] Since there are still very few positive sexual images of women in Russian culture, the freedom introduced by the 'sexual revolution' seems so far to have brought advantages mainly to men.

One factor which links the numerous ethnic groups, classes, professional groups and both sexes in the post-Soviet states is the search for new identities and values to fill the ideological vacuum created by the collapse of communism. The confusion sown by the sexual revolution is reflected in Elena Stishova's outspoken, highly personal account of the dilemma faced by a Russian liberal feminist torn between her support for artistic freedom and her dislike of sexual exploitation ('"Full frontal": perestroika and sexual policy'). Young people's search for identity through the adoption of various subcultural lifestyles is highlighted by Hilary Pilkington, who, in 'Young women and subcultural lifestyles: a case of "irrational needs"?', challenges the conventional Russian view that young women are motivated to join subcultural groups by personal or sexual deviancy, suggesting instead that they may be attempting to assert more control over their lives and identities.

Women and nationalism

One of the most difficult and painful results of democratization for women since the inauguration of glasnost has been the many national conflicts in the former

USSR, which have broken up families and created innumerable refugees, including many women and children. The other side of the coin is that many women have participated in nationalist movements too. Most prominent have been the group of women within the Lithuanian nationalist movement Sajudis, who, although they formed a separate group because they felt some women's issues could be best discussed without men, had no wish to challenge traditional gender roles or to effect a radical change in women's lives; as Mary Buckley has argued, 'they were reacting not against Lithuanian men, but against Russian power'.[72] Marian Rubchak and Solomea Pavlychko (a founder member of the Women's Community of the Ukrainian nationalist movement Rukh, who is still active in the Ukrainian feminist movement), suggest that if feminism played a part, albeit an ambivalent one, within the nationalist movement in Ukraine during the struggle for independence, it has largely been jettisoned in the new period of state-building, which requires the reassertion or invention of myths about the allegedly pure, maternal, self-sacrificial features of the traditional Ukrainian woman.

The former Soviet Union is an area of tremendous chaos, dislocation and disparity, although there are certain problems shared by many of the new states. Two common elements are the revival of nationalism and a situation of economic crisis during the period of transition to a market system. Both these factors — nationalism and economic crisis — seem historically to have been conducive to a conservative approach to the position of women. It seems to be true historically that a developing nationalism — whether German Nazism, Italian Fascism, Islamic fundamentalism or the national revival in contemporary eastern and central Europe and the Soviet successor states — is hostile to the idea of women's liberation. Emphasis is placed on women's reproductive and nurturing roles, rather than their role in the workforce; they are expected to stay at home and look after the children. If a period of national revival coincides with a serious economic crisis, women are the first to be driven out of the labour market; and the number of women in top professional positions and representative bodies decreases. Sometimes the issue of abortion is revisited, with some sections of society seeking to ban it in order to increase the indigenous population and prevent it from being overwhelmed by alien immigrants. Such debates have taken place in Russia and Lithuania; and, although abortion has not yet been banned in Russia, the 1994 directive to remove most abortions from medical insurance cover may lead to a greater number of illegal backstreet abortions.[73]

The disintegration of the USSR gave a tremendous impetus to nationalist activity in the new states, which immediately engendered more propaganda about women's traditional role. The new leader of Kalmykia, Kirsan Iliumzhinov, spoke for many men in positions of power in the Soviet successor states when he declared in 1993: 'Women shouldn't work at all; let them stay at home and bring up children.'[74] Ol'ga Lipovskaia has commented on such conservative attitudes: 'So the new role for women is already defined: they are supposed to be mothers; wombs to produce more children for their nation. Women themselves accept this responsibility to the state, as their gender identity is not recognized as being important in comparison with the growing national one.'[75] In Russia, the population decline in the 1990s, along with the diminishing proportion of ethnic Russians in the population, helps to reinforce this nationalistic message.[76] Similar sentiments are finding expression in other Soviet successor states, notably Georgia, Estonia, Lithuania and Ukraine. Estonia is concerned about its nation being on the verge of extinction, whereas the more militaristic Georgia feels it needs more soldiers both to defend its borders and establish national order within the country when dealing with ethnic minorities or fighting for political power. The national revival has been linked with the rise in the influence of national religions – the Russian Orthodox Church, the Catholic Church in Lithuania and Islamic fundamentalism in Central Asia – which provide further support for conservative attitudes toward women. In Lithuania, Catholic publications have promoted virginity and purity among young women, and warned them not to place too much emphasis on a career, or they will be in danger of not getting married (although, fortunately, it seems that the lives of women in Lithuania do not entirely conform to the stereotypes of conservative propaganda).[77]

In Central Asia, women in the newly independent states have been subjected to a confusing mixture of competing ideologies: 'nationalism, Muslim revivalism, post-Soviet idealism, and economic westernization'.[78] Kyrgyz women have spoken of a 'cultural vacuum' in which women have to manipulate contradictory messages about what they have been educated to expect as a Soviet woman, and what current political and economic demands expect of them as a good Kyrgyz woman. In many of the Central Asian states there has been a resurgence of such traditional practices as polygamy, wearing the veil, the payment of bride–price, and even female self-immolation. In one year in Uzbekistan alone, 450–500 women burnt themselves to death; some wives were 'helped' to commit suicide so that their husbands could marry again.[79] Although such practices are regarded with horror by Russian commentators, it should also be acknowledged that by no means all women in Central Asia are hostile to the revival of some aspects of their traditional culture. Self-immolation, however, is hardly likely to figure among these desirable customs.

Although it is impossible to generalize about women in all the countries of the former Soviet Union, Solomea Pavlychko's rueful remarks on Ukraine could apply to the position of women in many of the post-Soviet states: 'The so-called national revival is a revival of masculine culture . . . Women's views are not represented, their needs are not met, their problems are not addressed, their rights are not implemented.'[80] The collapse of socialism and the new emphasis on the male entrepreneur and the market mean that it is no longer necessary in the Soviet successor states even to pay lip-service to the notion of women's equality, which allows commitment to the patriarchal family to be revived with impunity. The new market system has given rise to what Lynne Attwood calls 'the aggressive re-masculinization of post-Soviet Russia'[81] – and this is equally true of many of the other independent states.

As Sue Bridger has argued, the huge omission in all the writing by the 'back-to-the-home lobby' is the figure of the husband. In the changed social climate of the post-Soviet states it is simply assumed that he is available and supportive, eager to help his wife to return to the home; but this is a highly misleading assumption to make.[82] Many men in post-Soviet Russia and Ukraine are unemployed or poorly paid, demoralized and unlikely to be either co-operative or sober, so many married women cannot afford to become full-time mothers. Moreover, as Elena Sargeant points out, there are also a large number of unmarried mothers who have no choice but to earn their own living.

The post-Soviet states now propagate a contradictory mixture of age-old traditional values and unprecedented, sometimes alarming new ideas on the role and status of women. Ol'ga Lipovskaia has noted with dismay that the image of women being promoted in the post-communist era is 'a model as old as the world: the dualistic image of Madonna and whore';[83] while Elena Stishova highlights the extraordinary reversal of values which has produced a modern variant of the image of the saintly prostitute characteristic of the nineteenth-century Russian literary tradition, allowing hard-currency prostitutes to enjoy great prestige in contemporary Russia.[84] It is hard to disagree with Attwood's disturbing conclusion: 'The domestication of women and the images of violence against women are two sides of the same coin: an attempt to reassert male dominance in post-Soviet Russia after decades of concern that women were challenging male supremacy.'[85] *A fortiori,* it could be argued that the efforts to establish control over women's bodies and the campaigns to return women to the home in post-communist Russia and Ukraine are an expression of men's newly acquired control over what they perceive as their own 'possessions', a reappropriation of male collective identity and a symbol of having won back freedom and power from the communist state.[86]

The women's movement in the former USSR

A more positive aspect of the present situation of women in the former USSR is that many new women's groups devoted to political, economic, educational, charitable, religious and artistic activities have sprung up spontaneously. Initially these were slow to form after democratization made it possible to establish informal groups independent of the Communist Party, but by 1990, largely because of the state's lack of interest in women's problems, a great diversity of women's groups had emerged.[87] At first all these organizations were unco-ordinated, but in the spring of 1990, a meeting of representatives of women's groups declared the beginning of a women's movement. Their most ambitious venture to date was to organize an Independent Women's Forum, held in Dubna, near Moscow, in 1991 and 1992. Insofar as the Dubna meetings are being seen inside Russia as historic in the development of the women's movement, Anastasiia Posadskaia's introductory speech at the Second Women's Forum is included here as a valuable historical document, and a perceptive analysis of the contemporary situation of Russian women by a prominent feminist actively trying to build up the women's movement in her country.

Hitherto the groups which have been most successful in influencing policy in both the perestroika and post-perestroika periods appear to have been the Committees of Soldiers' Mothers in both Russia and Ukraine,[88] the Group of Gender Expertise within the Supreme Soviet of the Russian Federation,[89] the Moscow Centre for Gender Studies and the 'Women of Russia' political movement. The soldiers' mothers demanded that their sons be obliged to serve in the Soviet army only within the borders of their own republic, that the widespread incidence of bullying be eliminated and that the number of soldiers killed in non-combat service be drastically reduced. In November 1990, Gorbachev issued a presidential decree on the implementation of the mothers' demands. More recently, women from the Moscow Gender Studies Centre can take much of the credit for the insertion of the 'paternity leave' clause into Yel´tsin's draft family legislation.[90] The most controversial provision of this draft law, 'For the Protection of the Family, Motherhood, Fatherhood and Children', introduced in 1992, was that a working week of no more than 35 hours should be established for all working mothers with children under the age of fourteen; since no enterprise, state-owned or private, would have wanted employees of this kind, women would, by law, have been pushed out of economic life altogether.[91] Fortunately, the influence of Ekaterina Lakhova, chair of the Commission for Women, Family and Demography attached to President Yel´tsin's office,[92] and of other members of the Group of Gender Expertise who later joined the 'Women of Russia' movement, along with the objections of liberal feminists, helped to get the draft law reconsidered and finally shelved, on the grounds that it violated the norms of the Russian Federation constitution, the European Commission of Human Rights and the United Nations Organization on the elimination of discrimination against women.[93]

In Ukraine, as Solomea Pavlychko shows, members of Rukh Women's Community successfully campaigned to get the issue of Chernobyl´ on the agenda of the Ukrainian parliament, to shut down the plant and give children holidays outside the contaminated area. On the whole, the more conservative women's groups have been the most successful: for example, after Lithuania gained its independence, the views of Sajudis women acquired the mantle of official ideology and were promoted in Parliament, in some sections of the media, and especially by the Catholic Church and the Catholic women's organization 'Caritas'.[94] Although some women are attempting to keep women's issues before the public through the 'Women of Russia' political movement and the Liberal Women's Foundation, established in February 1994,[95] these organizations are unlikely to wield much power at the national level. In both Russia and Ukraine, women have evinced more interest in supporting pressure groups on family problems or global issues, such as peace, the environment and human rights,[96] than in seeking to wield power in the mainstream, male-dominated political structures. Many women in Russia and Ukraine, however, currently appear to have lost faith in both the conventional political structures and the new organizations emerging from below, feeling powerless to change their situation.

At the 'Women in Russia' conference in Bath in 1993, most of the Russian and Ukrainian delegates emphasized that, with the single exception of the freedom of speech they now enjoy, the disadvantages of the current situation outweigh the advantages. Many spoke movingly about the increasing problems faced by women in their societies; all stressed the difference between the 'women's movement', as illustrated by the Dubna Forum, and the small band of feminists in the former USSR (they joked that in the whole of Russia there were only about fifteen feminists – eight in Moscow, seven in St Petersburg – and only six in Ukraine!). Perhaps the term 'family feminist' would be a more appropriate description of the majority of women activists in the post-Soviet states.[97]

Unfortunately, none of the delegates to the Bath conference was able to counter the disquiet expressed by western women about the disunity in the post-Soviet women's movement, and women's reluctance to strive to achieve political influence through the traditional power structures. It is to be hoped that the increasing prominence of the 'Women of Russia' political movement will force the mainstream parties to take up women's issues, and encourage women to become more active in politics.

All in all, the picture of women's situation in the ex-Soviet Union which emerged from the conference and is presented in this volume is a bleak one, although it is exhilarating to read contributions by Russian and Ukrainian women who take such a clear-sighted view of their own predicament, and are actively involved in trying to create a women's movement and a better society. In late 1994 political instability and economic crisis make it difficult to offer any definitive judgements on the prospects for women in Russia, Ukraine and the other post-Soviet states; but if it was possible during the early Gorbachev era to be ambivalent about the benefits and disadvantages of perestroika for women, by 1994 it has become clear that the economic crisis, nationalist revival and desire for de-Sovietization have led in most of the new states to a conservative reaction against women far greater than the current 'backlash' in the West.[98] As Ol'ga Lipovskaia has declared explicitly: 'Women are now losing those small achievements they had before perestroika.'[99] This opinion gained official support from the Tass information agency, which stated on 25 May 1993, reporting the conclusion drawn at a Supreme Soviet discussion on the social status of women: 'The position of women is deteriorating in all spheres of public life.'[100]

Conclusion

This volume aims to make a contribution to the growing body of scholarship on women in history and contemporary society in Russia and Ukraine, and to present to a western audience documents by Russian and Ukrainian feminists which vividly illustrate the problems affecting women in the post-Soviet states in the 1990s. The essays offered here demonstrate that the male experience should not be regarded as universal, and that Russian and Ukrainian women's studies are valuable and autonomous fields in their own right. It is, however, also to be hoped that this book will yield general insights into Russian history and post-Soviet society, and that such research will eventually be incorporated into revised studies of Russia, Ukraine and the former USSR, which will facilitate a fuller understanding of the past and present by including an analysis of sexual difference and gender relations.

Notes

1 Rosalind Miles, *The Women's History of the World* (London: Michael Joseph, 1988), p. xi; Gerda Lerner, 'Placing Women in History: Definitions and Challenges' (1975), in *The Majority Finds Its Past* (New York: Oxford University Press, 1981), pp. 145–53.
2 For further discussion, see Karen Offen, Ruth Roach Pierson and Jane Rendall (eds.), *Writing Women's History: International Perspectives* (Basingstoke and London: Macmillan, 1991), pp. xx–xxii.
3 Sheila Rowbotham, *Hidden from History* (New York: Pantheon, 1974).
4 Dale Spender, *Women of Ideas and What Men Have Done to Them* (London and Sydney: Pandora, 1982), p. 42.
5 Mary Buckley, *Women and Ideology in the Soviet Union* (Hemel Hempstead: Harvester Wheatsheaf, 1989; Ann Arbor: University of Michigan, 1989), pp. 108–60. After Stalin's death, statements about the 'solution' of the 'woman question' became more modest and qualified.
6 See, for example, E. P. Thompson, *The Making of the English Working Class* (London: Victor Gollancz, 1963); Keith Thomas, *Religion and the Decline of Magic: Studies in Popular Belief in Sixteenth- and Seventeenth-Century England* (London: Weidenfeld and Nicolson, 1971).
7 For further discussion, see Barbara Evans Clements, 'Introduction: Accommodation, Resistance, Transformation', in Clements, Barbara Alpern Engel and Christine D. Worobec (eds.), *Russia's Women: Accommodation, Resistance, Transformation* (Berkeley and Oxford: University of California Press, 1991), pp. 1–13; Linda Edmondson, 'Introduction', in Edmondson (ed.), *Women and Society in Russia and the Soviet Union* (Cambridge: Cambridge University Press, 1992), pp. 1–4; Barbara Alpern Engel, 'Engendering Russia's History: Women in Post-Emancipation Russia and the Soviet Union', *Slavic Review*, vol. 51, no. 2 (Summer 1992), pp. 309–21. For a useful bibliography of works in Russian women's history up to 1991, see Mary Zirin, 'Women, Gender and Family in the Soviet Union and East/Central Europe: A Preliminary Bibliography', in Offen, Pierson and Rendall, *Writing Women's History*, pp. 457–505.
8 Adapted from Miles, *Women's History of the World*, p. xi.
9 Richard Stites, *The Women's Liberation Movement in Russia: Feminism, Nihilism and Bolshevism* (Princeton, N.J.: Princeton University Press, 1978); Linda Edmondson, *Feminism in Russia, 1900–1917* (Stanford, Calif.: Stanford University Press, 1984). For a later 'revisionist' interpretation of the nineteenth-century radical movement, see Linda Edmondson, 'Women's Emancipation and Theories of Sexual Difference in Russia, 1850–1917', in Marianne Liljeström, Eila Mäntysaari and Arja Rosenholm (eds.), *Gender Restructuring in Russian Studies,* Slavica Tamperensia, vol. 2 (Tampere, Finland: University of Tampere Press, 1993), pp. 39–52.
10 See, for example, Barbara Evans Clements, *Bolshevik Feminist: The Life of Alexandra*

Kollontai (Bloomington: Indiana University Press, 1979); Beatrice Brodsky Farnsworth, *Aleksandra Kollontai: Socialism, Feminism and the Bolshevik Revolution* (Stanford, Calif.: Stanford University Press, 1980); Barbara Alpern Engel, *Mothers and Daughters: Women of the Intelligentsia in Nineteenth-Century Russia* (Cambridge: Cambridge University Press, 1983).

11 Beatrice Brodsky Farnsworth and Lynne Viola (eds.), *Russian Peasant Women* (Oxford: Oxford University Press, 1992); Susan Bridger, *Women in the Soviet Countryside* (Cambridge: Cambridge University Press, 1987); Rose L. Glickman, *Russian Factory Women: Workplace and Society, 1880–1914* (Berkeley: University of California Press, 1984).

12 Lindsey Hughes, *Sophia, Regent of Russia, 1657–1704* (New Haven, Conn.: Yale University Press, 1990).

13 See, for example, Mary Schaeffer Conroy, 'Women Pharmacists in Russia Before World War I: Women's Emancipation, Feminism, Professionalization, Nationalism and Class Conflict', in Edmondson, *Women and Society*, pp. 48–76; Catriona Kelly, 'Life at the Margins: Women, Culture and Narodnost', 1880–1920', in Liljeström et al., *Gender Restructuring in Russian Studies*, pp. 139–54.

14 N. Baranskaia, *Nedelia kak nedelia, Novyi mir*, no. 11 (1969); English translation: Natalya Baranskaya, *A Week Like Any Other: A Novella and Short Stories*, trans. by Pieta Monks (London: Virago, 1989).

15 Gail Warshofsky Lapidus, *Women in Soviet Society: Equality, Development and Social Change* (Berkeley: University of California Press, 1978); Lapidus (ed.), *Women, Work and Family in the Soviet Union* (Armonk, N.Y.: M. E. Sharpe, 1982); Barbara Holland (ed.), *Soviet Sisterhood* (Bloomington: Indiana University Press, 1985); Mary Buckley, *Women and Ideology in the Soviet Union*; Lynne Attwood, *The New Soviet Man and Woman: Sex-Role Socialization in the USSR* (Basingstoke: Macmillan, 1990; Bloomington: Indiana University Press, 1991).

16 For the first Russian feminist *samizdat* journal, see Tatyana Mamonova (ed.), *Women and Russia: Feminist Writings from the Soviet Union* (Oxford: Blackwell, 1984).

17 Ol'ga Lipovskaia, 'New Women's Organizations', and Solomea Pavlychko, 'Between Feminism and Nationalism: New Women's Groups in the Ukraine', in Mary Buckley (ed.), *Perestroika and Soviet Women* (Cambridge: Cambridge University Press, 1992), pp. 72–96. On the situation in 1992–4, see below, pp. 290–7.

18 For valuable studies of the Gorbachev era, see Buckley, *Perestroika and Soviet Women;* Chris Corrin (ed.), *Superwomen and the Double Burden* (London: Scarlet Press, 1992); Sue Bridger, 'Young Women and Perestroika', and Mary Buckley, 'Glasnost and the Woman Question', in Edmondson, *Women and Society*, pp. 178–226. There is some information on women in post-Soviet Russia in Barbara Einhorn, *Cinderella Goes to Market: Citizenship, Gender and Women's Movements in East Central Europe* (London and New York: Verso, 1993); and Nanette Funk and Magda Mueller (eds.), *Gender Politics and Post-Communism: Reflections from Eastern Europe and the Former Soviet Union* (London and New York: Routledge, 1993), pp. 274–302; see also the interviews with Russian women in William Millinship, *Front Line: Women of the New Russia* (London: Methuen, 1993), pp. 13–287; and Tatyana Mamonova, *Women's Glasnost vs. Naglost: Stopping the Russian Backlash* (Westport, Conn.: Bergin and Garvey, 1994), which contains an idiosyncratic introduction by the prominent émigré feminist.

19 Notable exceptions are Edmondson, *Women and Society*, Liljeström et al., *Gender Restructuring in Russian Studies*, and Jane T. Costlow, Stephanie Sandler and Judith

Vowles (eds.), *Sexuality and the Body in Russian Culture* (Stanford, Calif.: Stanford University Press, 1993), all of which combine papers in these three disciplines.

20 Linda Edmondson, *Women and Society* refers to women's studies as 'interdisciplinary' (p. xxi); Offen, Pierson and Rendall, *Writing Women's History*, allude to 'the multi-disciplinary field of women's studies' (p. xxi).

21 For a persuasive defence of this approach, see Joan Wallach Scott, *Gender and the Politics of History* (New York: Columbia University Press, 1988), pp. 8–9; see also Hoogenboom below, pp. 78–80.

22 For further discussion, see Sheila Rowbotham, 'The Trouble with Patriarchy' (1979), reprinted in her *Dreams and Dilemmas: Collected Writings* (London: Virago, 1983).

23 In a 1991 interview, the St Petersburg feminist Ol′ga Lipovskaia admitted that she had learnt about the feminist movement in Russia through the books by Richard Stites and Linda Edmondson; see Rosalind Marsh, 'Olga Lipovskaya and Women's Issues in Russia', *Rusistika*, no. 5 (June 1992), pp. 16–21.

24 Belated responses to glasnost include S. V. Polenina (ed.), *Trud, sem′ia, byt sovetskoi zhenshchiny* (Moscow: Nauka, 1990); N. M. Rimashevskaia (ed.), *Zhenshchiny v obshchestve: realii, problemy, prognozy* (Moscow: Nauka, 1991). Recent examples in the post-communist era include Irina Shcherbakova, 'The Gulag in Memory', in Luisa Passerini (ed.), *International Yearbook of Oral History and Life Stories*, vol. 1, *Memory and Totalitarianism* (Oxford: Oxford University Press, 1992), pp. 103–15; and the unpublished contributions of Ol′ga Demidova, Irina Shcherbakova, Elena Trofimova, Ol′ga Panchenko, Ol′ga Voronina and Tat′iana Klimenkova to the 'Women in Russia' conference in Bath, 1993. The most comprehensive study of contemporary Russian society by Russian feminists available in English is Anastasia Posadskaya (ed.), *Women in Russia: A New Era in Russian Feminism* (London: Verso, 1994).

25 This phrase was originally attributed to a Yugoslav feminist in Celestine Bohlen, 'East Europe's Women Struggle with New Roles, and Old Ones', *New York Times*, 23 November 1990, Section 4, pp. 1–2. See also Anastasiia Posadskaia below, p. 302.

26 Hilary Pilkington, 'Russia and the Former Soviet Republics', in Corrin, *Superwomen and the Double Burden*, p. 218.

27 Notable exceptions include Offen, Pierson and Rendall; Renate Bridenthal, Atina Grossmann and Marion Kaplan (eds.), *When Biology Became Destiny: Women in Weimar and Nazi Germany* (New York: Monthly Review Press, 1984); Judith Fridlander et al. (eds.), *Women in Culture and Politics: A Century of Change* (Bloomington: Indiana University Press, 1986); in Russian women's studies, see Buckley, *Perestroika and Soviet Women*; Liljeström et al., *Gender Restructuring in Russian Studies*.

28 There was some research on 'the woman question' in Soviet institutes before glasnost: see G. A. Tishkin, *Zhenskii vopros v Rossii v 50–60 gg. XIX v.* (Leningrad: Izdatel′stvo Leningradskogo Universiteta, 1984). On the general problems of Soviet historians and social scientists confronting the legacy of the past, see R. W. Davies, *Soviet History in the Gorbachev Revolution* (Basingstoke: Macmillan, 1989); Rosalind Marsh, *History and Literature in Contemporary Russia* (Basingstoke: Macmillan, 1995). It will take an immense psychological transformation for feminist analysis of women's history and women's issues to become acceptable and widespread in the ex-USSR.

29 Rosalind Marsh, 'Postscript: Report on the "Women in Russia" Conference in Bath', *Rusistika*, no. 7 (June 1993), pp. 20–1.

30 This case has recently been forcefully argued by Larissa Lissyutkina, 'Soviet Women

at the Crossroads of Perestroika', in Funk and Mueller, *Gender Politics and Post-Communism*, pp. 274–5; see also Edmondson below, pp. 104–5.

31 For a notorious example of this view, see Tatyana Tolstaya, 'Notes from Under-ground', review of Francine du Plessix Gray, *Soviet Women Walking the Tightrope* (London and New York: Doubleday, 1990), *New York Review of Books*, vol. 37, no. 9 (31 May 1990), pp. 3–7. For a more reasoned feminist case, see Ol'ga Lipovskaia, 'Sisters or Cousins: How Close is Sisterhood?', unpublished paper presented to 'Women in Russia' conference at Bath, 1993.

32 For further discussion, see Corrin, *Superwomen and the Double Burden*, p. 3.

33 Other notable works on Russian women's history and culture before 1800 include N. L. Pushkareva, *Zhenshchina drevnei Rusi* (Moscow: Mysl', 1989); Joanna Hubbs, *Mother Russia: The Feminine Myth in Russian Culture* (Bloomington: Indiana University Press, 1988); Eve Levin, *Sex and Society in the World of the Orthodox Slavs, 900–1700* (Ithaca, N.Y.: Cornell University Press, 1989); and the essays in Clements, Engel and Worobec, *Russia's Women*, pp. 17–94.

34 For an earlier work on this theme, see Ann M. Kleimola, ' "In Accordance with the Canons of the Holy Apostles": Muscovite Dowries and Women's Property Rights', *Russian Review*, vol. 51, no. 2 (April 1992), pp. 204–29.

35 Lerner, 'Placing Women in History'. O'Rourke's study of Cossack women is particularly interesting in the context of the contemporary Cossack revival in the former USSR, which still focuses primarily on men and their warlike activities: see, for example, Vladimir Seleznev, 'Bitter Line: How the Cossacks Are Getting Along in the Newly Foreign Countries', *Rossiiskie vesti*, 18 March 1993, p. 2; trans. in *Current Digest of the Post-Soviet Press* (hereafter *CDPSP*), vol. 44, no. 12 (1993), pp. 20–1.

36 Offen, Pierson and Rendall, 'Introduction', *Writing Women's History*, p. xxx.

37 Contemporary Russian businesswomen were discussed by Diana Medman, a Moscow businesswoman and president of the Women's Club 'Transfiguration', in her paper 'Delovaia zhenshchina, politiko-ekonomicheskii aspekt', presented at the 'Women in Russia' conference, Bath, 1993, which spoke of women entrepreneurs who display 'absorption in their work, a creative approach, optimism and independence'. For further discussion, see Zoya Khotkina, 'Women in the Labour Market: Yesterday, Today and Tomorrow', in Posadskaya, *Women in Russia*, pp. 105–8.

38 Andrei Baiduzhii, 'Demographic Catastrophe Has Become a Reality', *Nezavisimaia gazeta*, 2 February 1994, p. 1, report of a conference on 'Protecting the Health of Mothers and Children', held in January 1994; trans. in *CDPSP*, vol. 46, no. 5 (1994), p. 19.

39 In the 1990s, for the first time in post-Second World War Russia, the death rate exceeded the birth rate. The number of babies born in 1992 was 11 per cent fewer than in 1991; and there were 100 abortions per 1,000 women, twice the number of births. On the catastrophic situation by mid-1994, see A. Baiduzhii, 'The People of Russia Are Getting Sick a Lot and Dying Early: It Is Now a Fact That There Is a Demographic Catastrophe in Our Country', *Nezavisimaia gazeta*, 16 July 1994, pp. 1, 4; trans. in *CDPSP*, vol. 46, no. 28 (1994), pp. 8–11. For further discussion, see Williams and Sargeant below, pp. 143–6 and 271–6.

40 Stephen White, *After Gorbachev* (Cambridge: Cambridge University Press, 1993), pp. 94–101.

41 See Mary Buckley, 'Social Policies and New Social Issues', in Stephen White, Alex Pravda and Zvi Gitelman (eds.), *Developments in Soviet Politics* (Basingstoke: Macmillan,

1990), pp. 185–206. Such issues are still being discussed in 1994: on AIDS, see *Nezavisimaia gazeta*, 5 January 1994, p. 2; on maternity hospitals, see Elena Shafran, 'Expulsion of the Foetus: Why Women in Russia Are Afraid to Give Birth', *Izvestiia*, 26 January 1994, p. 8; trans. in *CDPSP*, vol. 46, no. 4 (1994), p. 23.

42 Ol′ga Voronina, 'Zhenshchina v "muzhskom obshchestve"', *Sotsiologicheskie issledovaniia*, no. 2 (1988), pp. 104–10.

43 See, for example, Larisa Vasil′eva, 'Post-Congress Reflections on Women's Role in Society', *Pravda*, 24 June 1989, p. 3; trans. in *Current Digest of the Soviet Press*, vol. 41, no. 25 (1989), pp. 33–34; for further discussion, see Sargeant below, p. 270. Similar views about the need for men to take greater domestic responsibilities had earlier been expressed at the All-Union Conference of Women in January 1987: see Mary Buckley, *Women and Ideology*, pp. 195, 203.

44 N. Zakharova, A. Posadskaia and N. Rimashevskaia, 'Kak my reshaem zhenskii vopros', *Kommunist*, no. 4 (1989), pp. 56–65. For further discussion of this article, see Ilic, pp. 234–5; Marsh, p. 288.

45 Waters, 'The Emergence of a Women's Movement', in Funk and Mueller, *Gender Politics and Post-Communism*, p. 289; on the genesis and impact of this article, see Posadskaya, 'Self-Portrait of a Russian Feminist', in Posadskaya, *Women in Russia*, p. 191.

46 Natal′ia Rimashevskaia, 'The New Women's Studies', in Buckley, *Perestroika and Soviet Women*, pp. 118–22; see also Marsh below, p. 288. Feminist research is also being conducted in the Institute of Ethnography and Anthropology and the Institute of Philosophy in Moscow. In Ukraine women's studies has been even slower to develop: see Pavlychko, p. 310.

47 For an account of the insensitive treatment of pregnant women in such establishments, see Elena Shafran, 'Expulsion of the Foetus'.

48 I am grateful to Lynne Attwood for the information that one rape crisis centre attached to the Moscow Gender Centre is mostly concerned with domestic violence and rape, including violence by *nouveaux-riches* against their wives, who have no work outside the home; while the other, known as 'Sestry' ('Sisters'), is mostly concerned with other forms of rape. 'Sestry', established by the new Moscow Sexual Assault Recovery Centre under Natasha Gaidarenko, was established in 1994, but the organization has little money: see James Meek, 'Russians Start First Rape Crisis Hotline', *Guardian*, 14 May 1994; Kira Iakubovskaia, 'Moscow Opens Centre for Sexual Abuse Victims', *Izvestiia*, 2 August 1994, p. 7; trans. in *CDPSP*, vol. 46, no. 31 (1994), p. 15.

49 Baiduzhii, 'Demographic Catastrophe Has Become a Reality', p. 19. He reveals that 3.5 million abortions are performed annually, and there are 216 abortions for every 100 births. Vladimir Borzenko, 'Abortion in Russia: In the Light of Public Opinion', *Segodnia*, 10 March 1994, p. 9; trans. in *CDPSP*, vol. 46, no. 10 (1994), pp. 16–17, cites a higher figure of 4 million officially registered abortions, and claims that the real figure is much higher.

50 See, for example, the discussion section of the journal *Sotsiologicheskie issledovaniia*, no. 5 (1992). According to Susan Hardy Aiken and Adele Marie Barker, 'Afterword: Histories and Fictions', in Aiken, Barker et al. (eds.), *Dialogues/Dialogi: Literary and Cultural Exchanges Between (Ex)Soviet and American Women* (Durham, N.C., and London: Duke University Press, 1994), pp. 385–6, the popular magazine *Ogonek* agreed to start up a column on women's issues entitled 'Zhenskii ugol' (Women's

Corner'), but in 1993–5 women's issues appear to have been subsumed under the rubric 'Nravy' ('Manners', or 'Customs').

51 On lesbianism, see, for example, Galina Toktal′eva, 'Olia i Iulia', *Sobesednik*, no. 46 (Nov. 1989), p. 11; and the account of lesbianism in a prison camp in Aleksandr Alenin, 'My Husband's Name is Tanya', *Trud*, 16 February 1994, p. 4; trans. in *CDPSP*, vol. 46, no. 7 (1994), p.15. For a more accurate picture, see the interview with Evgeniia Dobrianskaia in Millinship, *Front Line*, pp. 57–63; Ol′ga Zhuk, 'The Lesbian Subculture: The Historical Roots of Lesbianism in the Former USSR', in Posadskaya, *Women in Russia*, pp. 146–63. For the sensationalist treatment of feminism, see Posadskaya, 'Self-Portrait of a Russian Feminist', p. 193.

52 Professor Vladimir Terekhov, 'Russia's Farm Women Can't Raise the Crops on Their Own', *Nezavisimaia gazeta*, 12 August 1993, pp. 1–2; trans. in *CDPSP*, vol. 45, no. 32 (1993), p. 26; for further discussion, see Ilic below, pp. 230–7.

53 James Meek, 'Weakest Are Sacrificed on Altar of Privatised Homes', *Guardian*, 1 June 1994, p. 10, claims that two separate gangs have killed 22 vulnerable people in this way; Anastasia Posadskaya, 'Introduction', in Posadskaya (ed.), *Women in Russia*, p. 7, states that the Moscow Gender Centre has received many letters on this subject, but the press has refused to investigate it.

54 Mary Buckley, 'Glasnost and the Woman Question', p. 223.

55 'Rouble Collapse Pushes Yeltsin Towards U-Turn', *Guardian*, 12 October 1994, p. 1, relates that on 'Black Tuesday', 11 October 1994, the rouble slumped to 3,926 to the dollar; Julian Borger, 'Kuchma Gives Ukraine "Last Option Reforms"', *Guardian*, 12 October 1994, p. 11, cites President Kuchma as saying that much of Ukraine's industry was idle, and a quarter of the workforce unemployed.

56 See also Sargeant below, pp. 279–82.

57 Larissa Remennick, 'Patterns of Birth Control', in Igor Kon and James Riordan (eds.), *Sex and Russian Society* (Bloomington: Indiana University Press, 1993; London: Pluto, 1993), p. 56.

58 Personal observation of a session on family planning at the Second Independent Women's Forum at Dubna, November 1992, revealed that there is considerable ignorance, but a great desire for knowledge, on the part of young Russian girls in the provinces. Mamonova, *Women's Glasnost vs. Naglost*, p. xvii, claims that only 18 per cent of the population has access to birth control; see also interview with gynaecologist Svetlana Zotova, in Millinship, *Front Line*, pp. 23–30, which suggests that many Russian girls will not go to a gynaecologist for fear of being called prostitutes. For fuller discussion, see Larissa Remennick, 'Patterns of Birth Control', in Kon and Riordan, *Sex and Russian Society*, pp. 45–63, which cites statistics to show that condoms and *coitus interruptus* are the most widely used forms of contraception. For further discussion, see pp. 147–9.

59 Tat′iana Khudiakova, 'We Could Turn into a Country of Pensioners', *Izvestiia*, 2 February 1994, p. 3; trans. in *CDPSP*, vol. 46, no. 5 (1994), p. 19, states that in 1993 the birth rate in Russia was one of the lowest in the world: 9.2 per 10,000 population, while the mortality rate increased from 10.5 per 10,000 in 1987 to 14.6 in 1993. These issues are discussed further by Sargeant below, pp. 271–6; Williams, pp. 143–6.

60 Cited in Kate Clark, 'Translator's Preface', in Posadskaya, *Women in Russia*, p. xiii.

61 For Pamfilova's explanation of her resignation, see Galina Valiuzhenich, 'Why Ella Pamfilova Resigned', *Argumenty i fakty*, no. 5 (February 1994), p. 3, and 'Ella Pamfilova Really Is Leaving', *Izvestiia*, 17 February 1994, p. 1; trans. in *CDPSP*, vol. 46, no. 7,

p. 18; and Sargeant below, p. 279. See also the interview with Pamfilova in Millinship, *Front Line*, pp. 186–92. In May 1994 Pamfilova was appointed to head a public Council for Social Policy under the president. See Tat'iana Khudiakova, 'Ella Pamfilova Revives the Idea of Social Reform. And Hopes for the President's Support', *Izvestiia*, 24 May 1994, p. 2; trans. in *CDPSP*, vol. 46, no. 21 (1994), p. 20.

62 Vasil'eva, 'Post-Congress Reflections', p. 33.

63 Aleksei Kirpichnikov, 'Social Sphere Left "With a Hat but No Pants"', *Segodnia*, 21 April 1994, p. 2; trans. in *CDPSP*, vol. 46, no. 16 (1994), p. 18.

64 There is some doubt about the exact figures, since the allegiance of some deputies is difficult to classify: the list of candidates in *Rossiiskaia gazeta*, 12 November 1993, states that two candidates from the single-member constituencies were members of the 'Women of Russia' movement; *Novaia ezhednevnaia gazeta*, 18 January 1994, refers to a 'Women of Russia' bloc of 23; but Wendy Slater, 'Female Representation in Russian Politics', *Radio Liberty/Radio Free Europe Bulletin*, vol. 3, no. 22 (3 June 1994), p. 27, calculates that there is probably a voting bloc of between 24 and 26 seats.

65 It was formed from the Union of Women of Russia (the renamed Committee of Soviet Women), the Association of Businesswomen of Russia and the Union of Women in the Navy. For fuller discussion, see Slater, 'Female Representation in Russian Politics', pp. 27–33.

66 On female poverty and the effect of inflation, see the interview with a single woman pensioner, Alla Emel'ianova, in Millinship, *Front Line*, pp. 25–9; after the 1992 price increases, even the relatively well-off film director Tania Petrenko could not afford fruit and vegetables: ibid., p. 227.

67 Marina Pankova, 'Alevtina Fedulova: "Women are People Too"', *Nezavisimaia gazeta*, 6 March 1993, p. 6; trans. in *CDPSP*, vol. 45, no. 10 (1993), pp. 23–4; discussed by Sargeant below, p. 269. However, Fedulova complains that there are no reliable statistics on women. Medman, 'Delovaia zhenshchina', refers to data from the Russian Federation Employment Service which suggest that on 1 January 1993, women constituted 412,500, or 85 per cent of the unemployed.

68 Terekhov, 'Russia's Farm Women', p. 25.

69 Ol'ga Lipovskaia, unpublished manuscript of speech at an unofficial Human Rights Conference held in Moscow, December 1987.

70 Millinship, *Front Line*, pp. 4–5.

71 For statistics on the great increase in reports of rape and violent sex crimes, see Valerii Iakov, *Izvestiia*, 12 August 1993, p. 8. Almost 14,500 were reported in Russia in 1993, but this was probably only a fraction of the real number. See Attwood below, p. 266.

72 Mary Buckley, 'Glasnost and the Woman Question', p. 218; see also Mary Buckley, 'Gender and Reform', in Catherine Merridale and Chris Ward (eds.), *Perestroika: The Historical Perspective* (London: Edward Arnold, 1991), pp. 70–2.

73 Dmitrii Frolov, 'Bureaucrats Show Concern for Multiplying the Nation: By Making All Abortion Clinics Charge Fees', *Segodnia*, 10 March 1994, p. 9; trans. in *CDPSP*, vol. 46, no. 10 (1994), pp. 16–17; for further discussion, see Sargeant below, p. 281.

74 A. Evtushenko, 'Local Elections on the Eve of a Decisive Battle', *Komsomol'skaia pravda*, 13 April 1993, p. 1; trans. in *CDPSP*, vol. 45, no. 15, p. 2.

75 Ol'ga Lipovskaia, 'Gender Bender', *This Magazine*, no. 25 (May 1992), p. 24.

76 Vadim Pervyshin, 'Unichtozhenie', *Molodaia gvardiia*, no. 8 (1993), pp. 3–8.

77 Nijole White, 'Women in Post-Independence Lithuania: The Slow Road to Gender Consciousness', paper presented to 'Women in Russia' conference, Bath, 1993.

78 Kathleen Kuehnast, 'Representing Gender: Political Ideologies, Ethnicity and Islam in Post-Soviet Kyrgyzstan', unpublished paper presented to 'Women in Russia' conference, Bath, 1993.

79 Timur Kadyr, 'Woman of the East – the Age of Freedom is Nowhere to Be Seen', *Megapolis-Ekspress*, 7 October 1993, p. 7; trans. in *CDPSP*, vol. 44, no. 40 (1992), pp. 30–1.

80 See p. 313 below.

81 See p. 255 below.

82 Discussed by Sue Bridger, 'Young Women and Perestroika', p. 197; Larisa Kuznetsova, 'Val i Valentina', *Rabotnitsa*, no. 9 (1988), p. 22; see also Bridger, p. 246; Sargeant, p. 270.

83 Lipovskaia, 'Gender Bender', p. 24.

84 The most striking example of this is Petr Todorovskii's film *Interdevochka* (*International Girl*, 1989), discussed by Stishova below, p. 192; and by Lynne Attwood, 'Sex and the Soviet Cinema', in Kon and Riordan, *Sex and Russian Society*, pp. 71–3. Although *Interdevochka* could be interpreted as a moral tale warning women against prostitution, in the press high-class prostitutes were characterized as 'independent businesswomen': see 'Eshche odna "zakrytaia" tema', *Argumenty i fakty*, no. 16 (1990), p. 7; see also 'Interdevochka', *Sovetskii ekran*, no. 3 (1989), p. 33; *Literaturnaia gazeta*, 8 February 1989; *Izvestiia*, 24 March 1990.

85 See below, p. 264.

86 A similar view is expressed in Nanette Funk, 'Introduction: Women and Post-Communism', in Funk and Mueller, *Gender Politics and Post-Communism*, p. 2.

87 Lipovskaia, 'New Women's Organizations'; Marsh, '"From Problems to Strategy"?', p. 17; for further discussion, see Marsh below, pp. 286–94.

88 The Committee of Soldiers' Mothers was founded in 1989 to aid invalided victims of the war in Afghanistan. For the influence of the committees in Ukraine, see Pavlychko, pp. 308–9.

89 See Sargeant below, p. 278.

90 For a sceptical view of this achievement, see Attwood, p. 258.

91 For further discussion, see Ilic, p. 233; Attwood, p. 256; Sargeant, p. 278.

92 Posadskaya, *Women in Russia*, p. 192, refers to Lakhova's 'relatively positive' role: her influence with Yel'tsin, her dislike of the old Soviet Women's Committee, and the fact that, although she is not a feminist, she has commissioned the Centre for Gender Studies to produce a report on the current situation of Russian women.

93 Some of these issues are discussed in Gabi Liuka, 'Russian Authorities Decide to Concern Themselves with Children and Parents', *Nezavisimaia gazeta*, 5 June 1992, p. 6; trans. in *CDPSP*, vol. 44, no. 23 (1992), p. 25; Tat'iana Khudiakova, 'The State Could Suffocate the Family in Its Loving Embraces', *Izvestiia*, 25 November 1992, p. 2; trans. in *CDPSP*, vol. 44, no. 47 (1992), p. 28; for further discussion, see Ilic, Attwood and Sargeant below, pp. 235–6, 258 and 278.

94 White, 'Women in Post-Independence Lithuania'.

95 Gleb Cherkasov, 'New Challenge to Russian Foundations: Liberal Women's Foundation is Created', *Segodnia*, 15 February 1994, p. 2; trans. in *CDPSP*, vol. 46, no. 7 (1994), p. 17; discussed below in Sargeant, pp. 278–9.

96 See Valentina Kostantinova, 'No Longer Totalitarianism, But Not Yet Democracy: The Emergence of an Independent Women's Movement in Russia', in Posadskaya, *Women in Russia*, p. 69, for women's membership of the Green Party, Transnational

Radical Party, the Blue Movement ('for human ecology') and the Andrei Sakharov Union of Democratic Forces. On women's interest in green issues in Ukraine, see Pavlychko below, pp. 308–9.

97 For the use of this term in relation to Northern Ireland, see Joyce McCartan, the director of the Women's Drop-in Information Centre on the Ormeau Road, Belfast, cited in Amanda Mitchison, 'Ulster's Family Feminists', *New Society*, vol. 83, no. 1312 (19 February 1988), pp. 17–19. I am grateful to Rick Wilford for this reference. For the appropriateness of this definition, see Pavlychko's comment about 'concerned mothers' below, p. 308.

98 Susan Faludi, *Backlash: The Undeclared War Against Women* (London: Vintage, 1992).

99 Ol'ga Lipovskaia, speech during 'Voices of Russian Women' tour of southern England, March 1993.

100 *Summary of World Broadcasts*, SU/1700, B/5 (28 May 1993), p. 8.

PART I
Women in history: from the seventeenth to the twentieth century

2

Peter the Great's two weddings: changing images of women in a transitional age

LINDSEY HUGHES

Count Burkhard Munnich once observed that it was 'thanks to Peter I that the fair sex began to appear in society'.[1] Upper-class Muscovite women were driven from the seclusion of the *terem*, or women's quarters, divested of their old-fashioned robes, squeezed into western corsets and low-cut gowns and transformed into suitable companions for their 'decent beardless' spouses. Peter's attitude toward the 'fair sex' was characteristically pragmatic, although not explicitly formulated. It was no use creating a new breed of men to run the army, navy and government departments without at the same time reforming their wives and mothers on the model observed in the West in 1697–8 and closer at hand in Moscow's Foreign Quarter (for example, in the home of Peter's German mistress, Anna Mons). Women were expected to socialize with men, clad in 'German' dress and equipped with appropriate social skills, including the ability to make small talk in French. Everyone was required to do his or her bit for the cause of reform.

The rapid and sometimes brutal transformation of élite women in Peter's reign has few parallels in history, but investigation of the process is hampered by the failure of women themselves to leave much in the way of written evidence of their experiences. This is also true, although to a lesser extent, of Russian men. There is a dearth of early eighteenth-century memoir literature.[2] Social and cultural historians are therefore obliged to piece together the evidence from a variety of sources, not least from the art of the period. This paper is structured around two items of graphic evidence. Both feature the nuptials of Peter I (reigned 1682–1725), who helpfully provided cultural historians with invaluable material by marrying twice, first in Moscow in 1689 to the good Russian noblewoman and virgin Evdokiia Lopukhina (a bride chosen by his mother), secondly in St Petersburg in 1712 to his own choice, the illiterate Livonian peasant Ekaterina Alekseevna (the future Catherine I, formerly Martha Skavronskaia), who had already borne him as many as five children and may have been the mistress of one or more of his generals before they met. When set against related materials on the legal and social aspects of marriage, these two occasions provide striking evidence of cultural change, not only in the realm of male–female social relations but also in such diverse areas as dress, architecture, music and society mores in general.

Marriage no. 1: Evdokiia Fedorovna Lopukhina, 27 January 1689

Like all Russian royal marriages, Peter's first had political implications. It was arranged by Peter's mother, Natal'ia Naryshkina, and her relatives in order to distract Peter from his 'juvenile' pursuits and to underline his coming of age as a challenge to the authority of Peter's half-sister, the regent Sophia, and her circle.[3] It was also hoped (and it proved to be the case) that Peter's wife would produce a male heir before Praskov'ia, wife of Peter's elder half-brother and co-tsar Ivan, who had been married off in 1684. As had become usual during the seventeenth century, the tsar's bride was selected from a lesser boyar clan with the aim of minimizing power struggles among the more prominent families. Little is known about the preliminaries to the choice. Groom and bride – aged seventeen and twenty respectively – were married in the Kremlin palace chapel of SS Peter and Paul on 27 January 1689 in a 'modest' ceremony.[4] Prince Boris Kurakin, who was married to Evdokiia's sister, wrote that the tsar's bride was 'fair of face, but of mediocre intellect and no match for her husband in character, which led to the loss of her happiness and the downfall of her clan'.[5] Kurakin claims that for the first year of marriage Peter was in love with his bride, and that estrangement came later, but Peter's return to his favourite pursuits of sailing and boat-building less than a month after the wedding would suggest otherwise.

Evdokiia's conventional upbringing in the *terem* is reflected in a handful of letters written to Peter in the early years of their marriage. These are set formulae texts, laced with standard terms of endearment – *batiushka, svet moi* – and larded with the subservient tones required of a royal bride: 'Your wretched little wife Dun'ka greets you' ('*Zhenishka tvoia Dun'ka chelom b'et*'). 'Write to me, *batiushka*, about your health, so that I, hearing about your health, may rejoice.' 'Write to me, *svet moi*, about your health, and make poor wretched me happy in my sadness.'[6] It is not known whether Peter deigned to write about his health: no letters from him to Evdokiia survive. The marriage produced two sons (possibly a third) between 1690 and 1693.[7] It ended, as we shall see, in 1699.

I know of no surviving account of the 1689 wedding ceremony (the *venchanie* or 'crowning' of Orthodox ritual) or of the festivities which preceded and followed, but we may assume – given the traditional attitudes of Peter's mother and her ally Patriarch Joachim who were both alarmed by Peter's unconventional behaviour – that they followed the general outline described in Grigorii Kotoshikhin's account of Russia in the reign of Tsar Aleksei.[8] The section on royal weddings is based on Aleksei's marriage to his first wife Mariia Miloslavskaia in 1647, the excessively pious tone of which, it should be noted, was influenced by a group of religious purists at court known as the Zealots of Piety.[9] Before the *venchanie* the tsar prayed in the cathedral, was sprinkled with holy water by the patriarch and visited the tombs of his ancestors. A ceremonial meal was taken before the wedding, the guests eating and drinking 'not in order to satisfy their hunger but because it is required by ritual'. After the church ceremony a priest delivered a homily: the bride was to be obedient to her husband, to give him no cause to chastise her, to live in piety, to observe fasts, all in the manner prescribed in the sixteenth-century *Domostroi* or *Book of Household Management*.[10] Straight after the *venchanie* the couple would go to the wedding feast, thence to the bedchamber. After about an hour relatives and guests would go to 'enquire after the health' of the couple, in order to ascertain whether the marriage had been consummated. If it had not, the procedure would be repeated until confirmation was received, whereupon the wedding guests would visit the tsar and his bride in their bedchamber and be entertained to drinks. The following morning the newlyweds visited the bathhouse separately, during which time the bride's nightgown was inspected for the relevant stains. After they dressed they were greeted by the patriarch and feasting was resumed. On the third day the bride's relatives were honoured with a feast. On the fourth day there was a banquet for the patriarch and church hierarchs. The royal couple visited monasteries, almshouses and prisons. Secular entertainments were minimal: music played on trumpets, fifes and drums was acceptable, 'but there are never any other games, music or dancing at royal weddings'.[11] Alien elements crept in – after the *venchanie* the couple drink from a cup of red French wine, the hall is decked with Persian and Turkish carpets – but overall the tone is restrained and seemly, all carried out according to strict protocol or *chin*.

The assumption that Peter's wedding to Evdokiia observed similar conventions is endorsed by *Kniga liubvi znak v chesten brak*, a presentation booklet on the 'honourable state of marriage', hand-copied and illustrated by scribes and artists in the Moscow Press (*Tipografiia*) with verses by the poet Karion Istomin.[12] The frontispiece (Figure 2.1) depicts Peter and his bride in traditional garb: the tsar wears his coronation robes and holds the orb and sceptre (as indicated in Kotoshikhin's description);[13] Evdokiia is clad in an almost identical jewelled brocade gown and the distinctive tsaritsa's crown. In this religious allegory, which is closely related in style to panegyric engravings and *conclusiones* which reached Moscow from Poland and Ukraine in the 1670s–80s,[14] the earthly plane is linked to the heavenly sphere through the patron saints Evdokiia and Apostle Peter, who with Christ and the Mother of God are guests at the wedding, as indicated by the text above the drawing: 'There was a marriage in Cana of Galilee and the mother of Jesus was there; and Jesus also was bidden and his disciples to the marriage' (John 2:1). Appropriate biblical texts from the marriage service – strings of words reminiscent both of scroll texts in icons and baroque shaped-poetry – issue from the mouths of the couple and their patrons.[15] A vertical text from earth to heaven reads: 'And God created man in his own image, male and female created he them' (Genesis 1:27).

Thus the life of the royal court appears as religious drama, reflecting the divine events of the Old and New Testaments. The role of the bride in the Orthodox tradition is indicated both by Evdokiia's pious and submissive pose and by the verses which follow – she is devout, mild, obedient, a *prechestnaia deva*, destined to produce children to perpetuate the glory of the dynasty and of Russia. The tsar is the sun, she is the moon. But the miniatures, for all their stereotyped features, also hint at new trends in portraiture, notably in the moulded shading of the faces and the three-dimensional quality of the bodies. Elements of the so-called Moscow Baroque style are even more evident in the verses. Syllabic poetry (*virshi*) on the Polish model was popularized at the Muscovite court by the monks Simeon Polotskii, and his pupil Silvester Medvedev, who enjoyed the favour of the regent Sophia. Both wrote occasional verses (see, for example, Polotskii's ode on the wedding of Tsar Fedor in his *Rifmologion* collection). Istomin, too, had mastered the genre. His verses for *Kniga liubvi znak v chesten brak*, a series of contemplations on the role of parts of the body and the senses in human life and divine worship, intermingle Christian with pagan references (for example, Orpheus and Amphion) and include such modern images as astronomers observing the heavens. *Kniga liubvi znak v chesten brak* is thus itself a product of a transitional age. It is contemporaneous with the first realistic Russian female portraits, those of the regent Sophia Alekseevna, in which for the first time a Russian woman is depicted as a ruler in her own right, rather than as a performer of pious acts in devotional settings to which images of living Russian women had hitherto mostly been confined.[16] The novelty of this genre is indicated by the fact that there are no surviving portraits of Tsaritsa Evdokiia as a young woman, although there are several later paintings of her as a nun. It is thus impossible to determine whether the 1689 miniature is a likeness or a notional depiction of the 'pious tsaritsa'. One suspects the latter: Evdokiia's individual personality and features were much less important than her idealized attributes.

Transition: the end of seclusion

Peter's first visit to the West with the Grand Embassy in 1697–8 proved crucial for the fate of Evdokiia in particular and upper-class Russian women in general. Shortly after he returned to Moscow, Evdokiia was consigned to a nunnery, a decision influenced by a combination of Peter's boredom with a wife who compared unfavourably with women he had met abroad and Evdokiia's association with conservative groups, including her own kinsmen, who opposed reform. (In 1710 Peter told a Danish envoy that he had divorced Evdokiia in order to allow her to live a life of piety!)[17] For other Russian women, however, it was a case of coming out rather than being shut away, as attempts were made to reform the life of the Russian court in imitation of models observed in Germany, Holland, England and Austria. We learn from Filippo Balatri (1684?–1756), a young Italian castrato singer brought to Russia by Prince Petr Alekseevich Golitsyn, that in 1699 a group of Muscovite ladies was invited to a concert and ball in the palace of Peter's favourite Franz Lefort. The tsar went out to greet them, 'like a gallant cavalier', but the women were very timid and entered the hall 'in confusion, having quite lost their composure'. The tsar danced with them, but according to Balatri the ladies danced very badly, with convulsive movements. He adds that they were the wives of boyars whose husbands had been ordered to bring them to the ball; they had been 'forced to obey the tsar's will'. Guards were posted at the doors to stop the

2.1 Frontispiece of *Kniga liubvi znak v chesten brak*
(K. Istomin, facsimile edn., Moscow, 1989)

guests leaving early, a practice that Peter later employed regularly in St Petersburg.[18] The observations of the Austrian envoy Johann–Georg Korb coincide with Balatri's. At Lefort's palace in February 1699 he saw Peter the Great's sister Natal'ia peeping through a curtain from an adjoining room, escorted by a group of married ladies. This was 'a great departure from Russian manners, which up to now forbade the female sex from appearing at public assemblies of men and from festive gatherings'.[19] But old manners died hard even among the highest government officials. A few months later at the house of Lev Naryshkin, Peter's uncle, Korb and other guests were taken to the chamber of Naryshkin's wife, who dispensed small glasses of brandy. To catch a mere glimpse of a boyar's wife in this fashion was deemed a great honour, according to the old custom. Unmarried daughters were not seen at all.[20]

Men had to change their appearance and behaviour, too. In 1698 Peter shaved off selected boyars' beards. From 1700 men and women in towns were forced by decree to adopt western dress.[21] Dummies wearing examples of 'French and Hungarian' outfits were displayed at the city gates.[22] Women of all classes, even the wives of the clergy, dragoons, infantrymen and musketeers and their children, were to wear dresses, hats and coats, German overskirts, petticoats, and shoes. Fines were imposed on anyone caught wearing the old fashions: forty copecks for people on foot, two roubles if on horseback.[23]

Naturally there was resistance to such innovations, and Peter responded in characteristic fashion with force and mockery. Weddings were one of his favoured models for teaching his reluctant subjects a lesson in modern manners. In January 1702, for example, traditional nuptials on the model of the tsar's first wedding were parodied in the arrangements for the wedding of Peter's jester Filat (Feofilakt) Shanskii.[24] The festivities, held in the Lefort palace, lasted three days, the first two of which were celebrated in Old Russian style, with men and women in separate rooms, men presided over by the mock sovereign Fedor Romodanovskii and the mock patriarch Nikita Zotov, women by a mock tsaritsa. The Dutch artist Andrei Schoenbeck engraved the two scenes.[25] The Dutch painter Cornelius de Bruyn reports: 'All that were invited were ordered to dress after the ancient manner of the country, more or less richly, according to the regulation in that case prescribed . . . The third and last day it was resolved to appear in the German dress, and everybody did so, except some of the Russian Ladies. The men and the women sat at table together, as the custom is with us; and there was dancing and skipping about, after the entertainment, to the great satisfaction of the Czar himself, as all his guests.'[26] The message was clear: old Muscovite customs, including the separation of men and women at social gatherings, were an object of ridicule. Another of these old/new wedding feasts was held in February 1704 for the nobleman Ivan Kokoshkin and his bride. Muscovite robes were described by a Russian contemporary as 'fancy dress' (*ubornaia*): 'people wore old-fashioned garments, long robes and caftans'.[27] Weddings continued to provide a butt for the tsar's mocking of traditional sensitivities, the most notorious being the dwarf wedding of 1710, celebrated shortly after the marriage of Peter's niece Anna Ioannovna.

Once Peter's mixed parties and assemblies started to bring men and women together, the reform of betrothal procedures became desirable, for strict traditions of arranged marriages were more easily maintained under the *terem* system when young unmarried men and women (officially, at least) led separate lives. In addition, the tsar believed that marriage based on choice rather than compulsion would be conducive to higher birth rates. In Muscovite Russia marriage contracts were made between the parents, or if they were dead, close relatives of the bride and groom, who usually did not set eyes upon each other until the contract had been sealed. The husband was supposed to see his new bride only after the wedding ceremony when her veil was lifted. A law of 1702 stipulated a six-week betrothal period (*obruchenie*) before the wedding (*venchanie*), during which time the engaged couple should meet and the betrothal could be broken at the request of either party. Grooms could refuse to marry an ugly, sick or disfigured bride (including one with damaged sex organs) if these handicaps had been concealed at the betrothal or if a healthy girl had been shown in the place of the real bride (but the same clause is not specified for girls thus tricked.)[28] An edict of 1724 specifically forbade forced marriages, including those arranged for 'slaves' by their masters.[29] Other laws allowed the marriage of Orthodox Christians to partners of other faiths.[30] Peter observed the new conventions in the betrothal and marriage of his own children and nieces. A foreign observer noted that in arranging the marriage of his daughter Anna, 'although he was her father, Peter deemed her consent essential'.[31]

Wedding no. 2: Ekaterina Alekseevna, 19 February 1712

These cultural changes, along with reforms in many other areas of political, economic and social life, form the background to Peter's second wedding. The story of the future Catherine I's rags-to-riches courtship and marriage has been told often, although many details remain obscure.[32] The couple probably met in 1704 (Martha, as she then was, was a refugee of the Great Northern War) and their first child was probably born toward the end of that year. As Ekaterina Alekseevna, Catherine assumed the status of unofficial mistress. She never learned to read and write, but her dictated letters to Peter are in sharp contrast to the few surviving items from Evdokiia, chatty, uninhibited, often crude.[33] Other children followed, of whom two daughters were alive when the pair were betrothed in secret on or before 6 March 1711, when it was announced that 'her majesty (*gosudarynia*) Tsaritsa Ekaterina Alekseevna is [now] the true and legal sovereign lady'.[34] Peter gives the reason for this step in a letter to Aleksandr Menshikov written in Poland on 12 May 1711: 'Thank you for your congratulations about keeping my word, which I am obliged to do on account of this hazardous journey [to the war against Turkey], to ensure that if they [his daughters Anna and Elizabeth] are left orphans, they will be more secure. If God brings this affair [the war] to a happy conclusion, we shall complete the business in St Petersburg'.[35]

The war was lost, but the couple returned. Their union was finally solemnized on 19 February 1712 in the church of St Isaac of Dalmatia in St Petersburg. Peter was anxious to emphasize that they were already man and wife. He wrote: 'Yesterday we completed our old wedding [ceremony].'[36] According to the British ambassador, Charles Whitworth, guests were expressly invited to his majesty's *old wedding*.[37] After the ceremony the couple paid a visit to Aleksandr Menshikov's palace on Vasil'evskii island, then drove in sledges to the newly built Winter Palace across the river.[38] Menshikov supervised proceedings as marshal or master of ceremonies, carrying a diamond-studded cane. Peter's choice of dress and attendants emphasized a naval theme:[39] the tsar wore the uniform of rear-admiral (his current rank); the proxy fathers, brothers and other attendants were mostly naval officers, including the Dutchman Vice-Admiral Cornelius Cruys. Cruys's wife acted as proxy mother to Catherine.[40] The naval motif is one of many examples of Peter's temporary abandonment of his royal role in exchange for another rank, thereby allowing himself to circumvent traditional protocol. In this case the subterfuge may have been inspired by awareness of Catherine's unsuitability in the eyes of the Church and traditionalists: it could be argued that it was not the tsar marrying his bride but a naval officer wedding his sweetheart. There were no official announcements of Peter's wedding to foreign rulers. A ceremony along the lines of 1689, with the tsar in coronation robes and the tsaritsa in traditional royal apparel, was eschewed, as was the traditional location in the Moscow Kremlin. Only in 1724 was Catherine allowed to don the royal regalia for her own coronation as empress-consort in the Moscow Cathedral of the Dormition.

The foreign community was well represented at the wedding, in sharp contrast, one may suppose, to the 1689 proceedings, when Patriarch Joachim would surely have objected violently to the presence of 'heretics'. Charles Whitworth and the Polish, Danish and Dutch ambassadors and envoys occupied places of honour at the banquet, these and lesser foreigners and their wives comprising a third of the 180 guests present. In a parody of the honouring of leading churchmen at seventeenth-century weddings, Peter's reception was graced by selected members of the All-Drunken Synod, described in the guest list as 'ecclesiastical personages' (*dukhovnye persony*): Nikita Zotov, Peter Buturlin and Iurii Shakhovskoi sat at their own small table in the middle of a larger circle of guests, while female members of the Synod, 'abbesses' Dar'ia Rzhevskaia and Anastasiia Golitsyna, were seated at the women's table. Regular Orthodox clergy and choristers were relegated to the seventh (and last) side-chamber. The couple's daughters, Anna and Elizabeth, appeared for a short while as bridesmaids, but left early.[41]

The festivities, as captured in the engraving by Aleksei Zubov, were totally in the spirit of the new capital[42] (Figure 2.2). The setting is the ballroom on the first floor of the first Winter Palace (completed in 1711, but demolished in 1726 to make way for a new version), hung with what look like fabrics and tapestries (although they may well have been painted canvas sheets) and mirrors. Men and women sit in the same room (albeit at separate sections of the table, a custom which continued to be observed on occasions to the end of the reign).[43] Yet all is not as

2.2 Aleksei Zubov, engraving of Peter the Great's wedding to Catherine I
(M. A. Alekseeva, *Graviura petrovskogo vremeni*, Leningrad, 1990)

it seems: in reality (according to information in the official court record or *pokhodnyi zhurnal*) the main hall accommodated just forty-five guests, while the rest were distributed in six adjoining chambers, but Zubov crams over a hundred figures into one room, the proportions of which are distorted. Apart from Peter, Catherine I and Menshikov, the figures are notionally portrayed (there is no attempt at individual likenesses). It is even possible that the engraving was made before the wedding took place.[44] In other words, Zubov's picture is just as stylized and idealized as Istomin's 1689 tribute to the newlyweds. Zubov, no less than Istomin and his draughtsmen, strove to emphasize the grandeur of the occasion, but if the first was a marriage blessed quite graphically in heaven, the second was decidedly of this world, even though icons of the Crucifixion and the Ascension can be glimpsed in the corners of the room. According to descriptions, toasts were followed by gun salutes from the Admiralty and Peter–Paul fortress, the signal given by Menshikov through a window. There was dancing from six p.m. until eleven p.m., accompanied by musicians (clearly visible in the lower left corner of the complete version of Zubov's engraving), after which fireworks and shells were let off (Peter was fond of noisy entertainment) and a firework tableau formed the word *Vivat*. The following day the guests reassembled for fruit and sweets and more dancing.

The contrast between this occasion and the first wedding in 1689 is evident: the naval theme, the gun salutes, ladies (*damy*) in low-cut gowns and exaggerated French wigs, gentlemen (*kavalery*) in fashionable tunics and breeches in the setting of the baroque Winter Palace, designed by Domenico Trezzini, the tsar's Swiss-Italian architect. Far from composing himself in prayer and performing oblations to his ancestors before his wedding, as his predecessors had done and as he himself may have been required to do in 1689, Peter dictated three letters, none of which mentioned the wedding at all.[45] In the engraving the bride glances knowingly over her shoulder at the observer – no downcast gaze, no pious pose.

The question which the engraving and descriptions of 1712 cannot answer is to what extent those present, particularly the women, who not so long ago had been hidden from the male gaze, were fully acclimatized to their new surroundings and role. Cultural westernization was invariably accomplished with a degree of compulsion, be it decrees on shaving and dress, the transfer of the nobility to St Petersburg or the law on public assemblies. To quote Iurii Lotman, a nobleman of Peter's time was 'like a foreigner in his own country: even when fully grown up he had to learn artificially what people usually absorb from direct experience in infancy'. European manners, transposed to Russian soil, acquired a new significance. 'One did not have to become a foreigner, just behave like one . . . Thus, daily life took on the attributes of theater.'[46] It may be useful to envisage Peter's second wedding in these terms, as a public spectacle in which the new manners were acted out in the fancy dress of naval uniform and French wigs against a backdrop of classical architecture. One of the acutest observers of Petrine women, the young German noble F. W. von Bergholz, observed: 'The Russian woman, until recently coarse and uneducated, has changed for the better to such a degree that now she concedes little to German or French ladies in subtlety of manners and good breeding and in some respects is even superior to them.'[47] He pronounced the gowns of Peter's daughters, Anna and Elizabeth, at the coronation anniversary celebrations in June 1721 to be of the latest French fashion and their elaborately bejewelled coiffeurs 'of an elegance which would have done credit to the best Parisian hairdresser'.[48] Even so, he noted some tell-tale signs. On seeing the royal women in full evening dress on the anniversary of Poltava in 1721 he remarked that he had 'never seen so many precious gems at one go, except perhaps at an audience of the Turkish envoy in Paris'.[49] 'In general the ladies here adore precious gems, with which they try to outdo each other.'[50] Peter Henry Bruce noted: 'The Russian women are of a middling stature, generally well proportioned, and might pass for handsome in any part of Europe; their features are far from despicable, were it not for that preposterous custom of painting their faces, which they lay on so abundantly, that it may truly be said they use it as a veil to hide their beauty.'[51]

Had the curtains and veils of the seventeenth-century *terem* merely been exchanged for another form of concealment? A nineteenth-century commentator on such matters evidently thought so when he wrote that the Petrine noblewoman 'stood on the threshold of two eras, two moral codes – old Russian and modern European – unable to reject either one, but tending in externals in the direction of the latter, but in beliefs and superstitions to the former'.[52] Sadly, a fuller study of the beliefs of Petrine women is severely hampered by lack of sources. In the matter of externals, Peter's court differed markedly from that of his predecessors, not least in breaking down the barriers between men and women by ending female seclusion. But in other ways, for example by introducing compulsory military service for life for many noblemen, it kept men and women apart, separating husbands from their wives and daughters for years on end and discouraging early marriages, while the new military ethos shifted the balance of public ceremonial from all-male religious rites to all-male military and naval parades, in which women remained passive onlookers. Women may have gained access to public occasions and more of a say in their choice of husband, but it is clearly premature to speak of the emancipation of women in Petrine Russia.

Notes

This chapter is dedicated to the memory of the Russian historian Lidiia Nikolaevna Semenova, who died in March 1993. It stems from a chapter on Petrine women in my forth-coming book *Russia in the Reign of Peter the Great* (New Haven, Conn.: Yale University Press, 1996).

1 B. C. Minikh (Munnich), 'Ocherk daiushchii predstavlenie ob obraze pravleniia Rossiiskoi Imperii', *Bezvremen'e i vremenshchik. Vospominaniia ob epokhe dvortsovykh perevorotov (1720e–1760e gody)* (Leningrad, 1991), p. 37. (The memoir was written for Catherine II.)

2 See B. A. Gradova, 'Rukopisnye memuary petrovskogo vremeni', *Issledovanie pamiatnikov pis'mennoi kul'tury v sobraniiakh i arkhivakh otdela rukopisei* (Leningrad, 1987).

Istoriia dorevoliutsionnoi Rossii v dnevnikakh i vospominaniiakh. T. I: XV–XVIII veka (Moscow, 1976) lists not one work of the period written by a woman.

3 On the political background, see Lindsey Hughes, *Sophia, Regent of Russia, 1657–1704* (New Haven, Conn.: Yale University Press, 1990). In 1682, following the death of Tsar Fedor and a rebellion of the Moscow musketeers, a diarchy was established, with Ivan Alekseevich as 'senior' and Peter as 'junior' tsar and Sophia as regent.

4 *Polnoe sobranie zakonov rossiiskoi imperii*, vol. III (St Petersburg, 1830), pp. 10–11 (hereafter *PSZ*); *Drevniaia rossiiskaia vivilofika*, vol. XI (St Petersburg, 1891), p. 194; M. M. Bogoslovskii, *Petr I. Materialy dlia biografii*, vol. I (Moscow, 1940), p. 66.

5 B. A. Kurakin, 'Gistoriia o tsare Petre Alekseeviche', in *Rossiiu podnial na dyby*, vol. I (Moscow, 1987), p. 369.

6 *Pis'ma russkikh gosudarei i drugikh osob tsarskogo semeistva*, vol. III (Moscow, 1861), pp. 68–9 (both letters 1694, otherwise undated).

7 See L. A. J. Hughes, 'A Note on the Children of Peter the Great', *Study Group on 18th-Century Russia Newsletter*, no. 21 (1993), pp. 10–16.

8 G. Kotoshikhin, *O Rossii v tsarstvovanie Alekseia Mikhailovicha* (St Petersburg, 1906; The Hague, 1969), pp. 6–14.

9 For references to descriptions of earlier royal weddings, see Daniel Kaiser, 'Symbol and Ritual in the Marriages of Ivan IV', *Russian History*, vol. 14 (1987), pp. 247–61. Written descriptions of Tsar Mikhail's wedding to Evdokiia Streshneva in 1626 were accompanied by drawings (ibid., p. 248, note 3), but unfortunately it was not possible to locate these before the completion of this chapter.

10 For a new edited translation, see Carolyn Pouncy, *The Domostroi: Rules for Russian Households in the Time of Ivan the Terrible* (Ithaca, N.Y. and London: Cornell University Press, 1994). The *Domostroi* provisions on marriage are detailed and discussed in Kaiser, 'Symbol and Ritual'.

11 Kotoshikhin, *O Rossii*, p. 13. It should be noted that at lower levels of society, weddings were usually occasions for drunken carousing and singing. As Kaiser notes in 'Symbol and Ritual', p. 254, traditional, pagan symbolism 'overshadowed Christian ritual'.

12 K. Istomin, *Kniga liubvi znak v chesten brak* (facsimile edn., Moscow, 1989). (The title alludes to: 'Let marriage be had in honour among all': Hebrews 13:4). Istomin (1640s–1720s) was an editor and translator in the Moscow Press, as well as author of sermons and educational works. See L. L. Sazonova's introduction in ibid., pp. 43–64.

13 Kotoshikhin, *O Rossii*, p. 8.

14 M. A. Alekseeva, 'Zhanr konkliuzii v russkom iskusstve kontsa XVII v.', in T. V. Alekseeva (ed.), *Russkoe barokko. Materialy i issledovaniia* (Moscow, 1977), pp. 7–29.

15 The texts read: Christ: 'In blessing I will bless thee and in multiplying I will multiply they seed' (Genesis 22.17); Mother of God: 'Behold and visit this vine' (Psalm 80); Peter: 'Bless us, O God, bless us' (Psalm 66); Evdokiia: 'Heavenly virgin, help us.'

16 See, for example, the portrait of Tsaritsa Mariia Miloslavskaia bearing a scroll with religious text in Ushakov's icon *Tree of the Muscovite State* (1668). On portraits of Sophia, see Hughes, *Sophia*, pp. 139–44.

17 J. Juel, 'Iz zapisok datskogo poslannika Iusta Iuliia', *Russkii arkhiv* (Moscow, 1892), p. 6.

18 Iu. U. Gerasimova, 'Vospominaniia Filippo Balatri. Novyi inostrannyi istochnik po istorii Petrovskoi Rossii (1698–1701)', *Zapiski otdela rukopisei*, vol. 27 (1965), p. 178. Balatri is especially informative on his master's wife, Dar'ia [Liapunova], who went to Vienna with her husband in 1701. At home in Moscow Dar'ia seemed 'nun-like',

pious, reserved, fearful of mixing with foreigners. Once she got used to Vienna, however, she enthusiastically took to socializing and visiting theatres and balls, despite the dire warnings of their Russian priest (p. 187).

19 J.-G. Korb, *Diary of an Austrian Secretary of Legation at the Court of Czar Peter the Great*, trans. and edited by Count Mac Donnell, vol. I (London 1863/1968), pp. 264–5.

20 Korb, *Diary*, vol. II, p. 37.

21 *PSZ*, vol. IV, no. 1741, p. 1.

22 I. A. Zheliabuzhskii, 'Zapiski' (26 August 1700), in A. B. Bogdanov (ed.), *Rossiia pri tsarevne Sof'e i Petre I*, (Moscow, 1990), p. 286.

23 *PSZ*, vol. IV, no. 1887, p. 182 (1701, n.d.); P. N. Petrov, 'Korennoe izmenenie russkogo byta pri Petre Velikom', *Severnoe siianie*, vol. 2 (1863), no. 78, pp. 441–3.

24 On Shanskii, see A. A. Golombievskii, *Sotrudniki Petra Velikogo* (Moscow, 1903), p. 58.

25 For captions, see *Pridvornaia zhizn': 1613–1913* (St Petersburg, 1913), pp. 57–8. A third print has not survived. See M. A. Alekseeva, *Graviura petrovskogo vremeni* (Leningrad, 1990), pp. 34–5.

26 C. de Bruyn, *Travels into Muscovy, Persia, and Part of the East Indies; containing an Accurate Description of what is most remarkable in those Countries*, vol. I (London, 1737), pp. 25–6, 28. Zheliabuzhskii also mentions it, but only the old-fashioned dress, 'Zapiski', pp. 305–6.

27 Zheliabuzhskii, 'Zapiski', p. 307.

28 *PSZ*, vol. IV, no. 1907, pp. 191–2 (3 April 1702). On marriage contracts in general, see L. N. Semenova, *Ocherki istorii byta i kul'turnoi zhizni Rossii. Pervaia polovina XVIII v.* (Leningrad, 1982), pp. 15–62.

29 *PSZ*, vol. VII, no. 4406, p. 197.

30 Semenova, *Ocherki*, p. 42.

31 H. F. de Bassewitz, 'Zapiski grafa Bassevicha, sluzhashchie k poiasneniiu nekotorykh sobytii iz vremeni tsarstvovaniia Petra Velikogo (1713–1725)', *Russkii arkhiv*, vol. 3 (1865), p. 133.

32 Catherine has aroused little scholarly interest in her own right and some of the older studies are still the best. See, for example, N. I. Kostomarov, 'Ekaterina Alekseevna, pervaia russkaia imperatritsa', *Drevniaia i novaia Rossiia* (1872), no. 2, pp. 129–70. A recent popular study of Catherine's background and the prelude to her marriage to Peter is T. Martem'ianov, 'Malan'ina svad'ba', *Smena*, 1992, no. 9, pp. 154–66.

33 See *Pis'ma russkikh gosudarei i drugikh osob tsarskogo semeistva*, vol. I (Moscow, 1861).

34 *Pokhodnyi zhurnal 1711 goda* (St Petersburg, 1854); second edn. (St Petersburg 1910–13), p. 308.

35 *Pis'ma i bumagi Petra I*, XI (i) (Moscow, 1962), pp. 230, 496 (hereafter *PiB*). (Menshikov's reference to 'keeping your word' is probably an allusion to Peter's insistence that Menshikov keep his, a few years earlier, by marrying Dar'ia Arsen'eva.)

36 *PiB*, XII (i), p. 86 : '*my staruiu svoiu svad'bu vchera okonchili*' (letter to Gavriil Menshikov).

37 Whitworth, in a dispatch to London written the day after the wedding: *Sbornik Imperatorskogo Russkogo Istoricheskogo Obshchestva*, vol. 61 (St Petersburg, 1888), p. 144. Whitworth also wrote that the service was held in Menshikov's chapel, but one is more inclined to accept the version of Peter's secretary Aleksei Makarov (see next note).

38 For Makarov's description of proceedings, see *Pokhodnyi zhurnal 1712 goda* (Moscow, 1854). The relevant passages are reprinted in A. Bychkov, 'O svad'be imp. Petra

Velikogo s Ekaterinoi Alekseevnoi', *Drevniaia i Novaia Rossiia*, 1877, no. 3, pp. 323–4. See also Whitworth, *Sbornik*, pp. 142–6.

39 See list of attendants drawn up in Peter's own hand, *PiB*, XII (i), p. 83.

40 The custom of choosing proxy or adopted mothers, fathers, brothers and sisters at weddings, even if the authentic relatives were still alive, was traditional.

41 This detail is from Whitworth, *Sbornik*, pp. 144–5.

42 See Alekseeva, *Graviura petrovskogo vremeni*, pp. 122–4. For a detailed analysis of the engraving, see G. V. Mikhailov, 'Graviura A. Zubova. Svad'ba Petra I. Real'nost' i vymysl', *Panorama iskusstv*, vol. 2 (1988), pp. 20–55.

43 See the detailed description of the wedding of Count Pushkin in September 1721: F. W. von Bergholz, *Dnevnik kammer-iunkera Berkhgol'tsa, vedennye im v Rossii v tsarstvovanie Petra Velikogo s 1721–1725 g.* (Moscow, 1857–60), part 1, pp. 179–81. Tables were mixed only after the wedding night. In January 1710 Just Juel described a New Year banquet at which Catherine and other women were entertained in a separate room, 'so that on this occasion, *contrary to the normal practice*, they were apart from the men' (Juel, 'Iz zapisok datskogo poslannika', p. 135).

44 Alekseeva, *Graviura petrovskogo vremeni*, p. 122.

45 *PiB*, XII (i), pp. 83–6 (to the kings of Poland and Prussia and V. L. Dolgorukii).

46 Iu. Lotman, 'The Poetics of Everyday Behaviour in Russian Eighteenth-century Culture', in Iu. M. Lotman, B. A. Uspenskii, *The Semiotics of Russian Culture*, edited by Ann Shukman, Michigan Slavic Contributions, no. 11 (Ann Arbor: University of Michigan Press, 1984), pp. 232–4.

47 Bergholz, *Dnevnik*, part 1, p. 101.

48 Ibid., p. 54.

49 Ibid., p. 69.

50 Ibid., p. 193.

51 P. H. Bruce, *Memoirs of Peter Henry Bruce Esq. A military officer in the service of Prussia, Russia and Great Britain* (London, 1782), p. 85.

52 A. S—tskii, 'Russkaia preobrazovannaia zhenshchina v epokhu Petra Velikogo', *Russkii mir*, 1859, no. 30, p. 675.

3

Women in a warrior society: Don Cossack women, 1860–1914

SHANE O'ROURKE

The studies of women in Russian peasant society that have been completed to date present a dismal picture of women's lives under a particularly brutal and harsh patriarchal regime.[1] The peasantry as a whole was an oppressed and exploited class, but within it women were deprived of the few privileges male peasants enjoyed. Despite massive contributions to the survival of the peasant farm and family, their role was systematically devalued and demeaned. Peasant women could not be the head of their household and neither could they participate in the public life of the community, apart from the exceptional circumstance of there being no adult male to fulfil these functions. Throughout their lives peasant women were subject to the authority of a male, first their fathers, then their husbands and finally their sons.[2]

Peasant culture, however, was not monolithic and there were many variations of it throughout imperial Russia. What is applicable to one group of peasants living in a particular area with a particular historical experience cannot necessarily be assumed to apply to all other peasants. One distinct cultural group within the peasantry was the Cossacks, who had a history and tradition very different from those of the peasants of the central provinces. This chapter will focus on the Don Cossacks, the oldest and largest of all the Cossack communities, to see how their distinctive tradition shaped the lives of the women within that community and how the women shaped that tradition.

The Cossacks were warriors who lived in anarchic and egalitarian communities that had grown up in the steppe frontiers of Muscovy and imperial Russia. Over the course of time they had been brought back under the control of the imperial state. The imperial state had always viewed the anarchic Cossack social order with intense suspicion, since it posed an implicit and on occasion an explicit challenge to its own autocratic order. At the same time, the state valued the martial abilities of the Cossacks and sought to preserve them. Throughout the seventeenth and eighteenth centuries, the control of the state gradually tightened until the independence of the Cossacks had vanished.[3] The state granted the Cossacks land in return for military service, and it was this that gave the Cossacks their dual identity as warriors and peasants.

Before examining the status of women within that community, it would seem that their position would be at least as bad as that of the Russian peasant women who have been the focus of several recent studies. In many ways the Cossacks epitomized the values of a patriarchal society. Great emphasis was placed on qualities such as physical strength, aggression, resourcefulness, courage and cunning: all of which are traditionally associated with males.[4] Given this, it is logical to expect that women would occupy a very subordinate position within Cossack communities. This chapter, however, will argue that Cossack women enjoyed significantly more status and power over their own lives than appears to have been general among peasant women.

Cossack women had a long tradition of taking decisions and acting independently of their men. Just as much as their menfolk, Cossack women were products of the frontier which the steppe remained until the first years of the nineteenth century. In the middle of the seventeenth century Cossack women had played an active role in the defence of Azov alongside their men.[5] Due to the onerous military commitments of the Cossacks, Cossack settlements were frequently deprived of all active males.[6] In such a situation the responsibility for the defence of the communities fell by default on to women. At the very least, these responsibilities involved defensive measures such as securing the livestock within the stockade if an attack was imminent,[7] but if the need arose women were expected to engage the Tatar nomads in battle. An essay in the provincial newspaper *Donskaia Rech'* in 1888 described the situation as it had existed up to the first quarter of the nineteenth century:

> Cossack women in the absence of their husbands and fathers put on male clothes and repulsed attacks of enemies and also formed cavalry units, etc. Even as recently as sixty years ago, going into the fields to work with their scythes, pitchforks and rakes, the women also took weapons. In case of need, at least one detachment of women transformed themselves into men and defended themselves courageously.[8]

The frontier caused the collapse of a sexual division of labour not only in the agricultural sphere, to which I will return, but also in that most quintessentially male sphere, armed combat. In these circumstances, Cossack women were accustomed to making decisions in the absence of men and taking responsibility in all aspects for the security and well-being of their families and communities. The exigencies of the frontier would not allow the luxury of a rigid demarcation of roles along sexual lines, but demanded that Cossack women play a very assertive role within their communities. Having said this, one would expect that as the Don ceased to be a frontier, the position of women would slowly but steadily become more debased. However, this was not the case. The terms of Cossack military service meant that responsibilities continued to devolve on to women in a way that simply did not happen in the central Russian provinces until the last decades of the nineteenth century.

Under the obligations of Cossack military service, all Cossack women had to accept the loss of their men at various points in their lives. As a community, the Cossacks had to develop methods of coping with the constant flow of men leaving

3.1 Surikov, *Kazachka: Portrait of L. Motrina*
(V. S. Kemenov, *Surikov* (Leningrad, 1991), plate no. 53)

and returning to their homes and families. In contrast, before the introduction of universal military service in 1874, only peasant women who had the misfortune to be married to a man selected for the draft would experience the loss of a husband through military service. These women were few in number and, as Beatrice Farnsworth has shown, peasant communities had no way of coping with them.[9] In 1835 three basic categories of military service for the Cossacks were laid down: preparatory, active service and reserve. After completing preparatory service, the Cossack spent twelve years on the active service list. Of these, only the first four were spent away from the Don, but Cossacks remained liable for mobilization at any time during the subsequent eight years which were termed 'privileged service'. On completion of these twelve years, Cossacks entered the reserves for five years. After this they were transferred into the militia, which would only be mobilized as a last resort.[10]

As a child growing up in a Cossack family, a girl would have experienced the absence of her father and brothers at various times. As a married woman, her first experience of it would be either right at the start of her marriage or not long after it.[11] Then each year all the men on 'privileged service' were called up for one month in the summer, the busiest time of the agricultural year. In addition there was always the possibility of a general mobilization which removed all the active men at a stroke. In short, Cossack women had to get used to the absence of their men both at the start of their marriage and to expect it throughout their married lives. This had profound consequences for the position of women in Cossack society.

Russian peasant agriculture had traditionally had a very strict sexual division of labour. Peasant society regarded male labour as much more valuable than female labour, although women did at least as much as men, if not more, in terms of the labour they contributed to the farm and family.[12] It was felt that women as a group were incapable of performing these traditional male tasks, although individual women might in certain circumstances perform them adequately enough.[13] Similarly, among the Cossacks more value was placed on labour that was regarded as male.[14] In this Cossacks were no different from peasants. What was different, however, was that the sexual division of labour was of necessity much less rigid among the Cossacks. Because of the frequent absence of not just husbands but on occasion of all able-bodied men, Cossack women had to have an intimate knowledge of all aspects of farm life. A journalist noted in 1868: 'Cossack women are not afraid of the scythe, the axe, the rake or the plough. In a word, of anything that relates to the farm.'[15] This was not just an idle survey of farm implements. Of the four tools listed, only the rake was traditionally associated with women. The scythe, the plough and above all the axe were steeped in male sexual symbolism. The official gazette of the *Voisko* [Cossack Host] related a similar story:

> During the whole period the man finds himself on service, all the male work and duties around the farm are carried out by the young wife who remains behind and is now mistress. The majority of Cossack women of the TransDon *stanitsas* [self-

governing Cossack communities, comprising either one large village or several smaller ones] work the land themselves. They sow the grain, they cut the hay with their own hands and manage the fisheries. Many of the women practise trades such as the making of fishing nets and agricultural tools, e.g., ploughs, harrows, carts and the other small tools necessary in an agricultural economy.[16]

The fact that women carried out male work routinely and not just in exceptional circumstances demonstrated how traditional sexual roles could be merged at need, and this could not but have an effect on the status of Cossack women. Many contemporary commentators remarked upon this. Mikhail Kharuzin, an anthropologist who visited the Don in the 1870s, believed that men were obliged to acknowledge, however grudgingly, that a woman was as capable of running a farm as a man, and that through her hard work and experience was often able to win a position of near equality with a man.[17] Another believed that it enabled women to establish their essential humanity in the eyes of men.[18]

Women had a very prominent and very public role in the Cossack economy. The publicity aspect is very important. The labour of other peasant women was equally vital to the survival of their farms and families, but its value could be denied by men as simply being women's work. This could not happen in Cossack society. The structure of Cossack life demanded that women play a very visible, public role in the economy; this could not be denied by men, since every man had to serve and was therefore acutely aware that anything that he did, his wife had to be able to do at least as well, especially when he was away. This in turn meant that Cossacks as a community could not deny the value of female labour, nor the absolute dependence of their way of life upon it. It is in this sense that the value of women was publicly acknowledged and their status raised accordingly.[19]

The property rights that women enjoyed in Cossack society provided a tangible expression of their status and power within it. In any society, control of property is a source of power, and the closer that society is to subsistence level, the greater the power. One of the ironies of imperial Russia is that peasant women possessed substantial property rights that could be enforced against outsiders and, more importantly, relatives, rights that English women did not gain until the late nineteenth century.[20] While peasant women retained control of whatever property they brought with them, they were always excluded from controlling the common family property unless exceptional circumstances pertained.[21] Cossack custom, however, placed the wife of the master second in the family hierarchy.[22] The only difference between having a woman as head of the household rather than a man was that a woman could not represent her household in the communal assembly if she had an adult son. In all other ways she was regarded by the community as the head of the household if her husband died before her. Authority passed not to her sons, whatever their age, but to her. She then gained control over the common family property, which was hers to bequeath as she wished.[23]

When she married, a Cossack woman could take with her what by the standards of the time was a quite substantial amount of property. The value of her trunk gathered by her mother over several years might range from only a few roubles to several hundred.[24] Fathers likewise would frequently give additional presents to their daughters, such as livestock, tools or vines, depending on the wealth of the family.[25] Gifts such as livestock might be used jointly by a couple, but there was no ambiguity over ownership. Kharuzin cited the decision of one of the *stanitsa* courts in 1879: 'Both spouses make use of the dowry, but the wife preserves exclusive ownership over it.'[26]

Women's right to their own property gave them considerable power in their relationships with the men in their lives, whether husbands or sons. A woman's power over the male members of her family increased when she became the head of the household after the death of her husband. As well as retaining her own property, she also inherited all the family property which she then had the power to bequeath to whomsoever she wished and in whatever proportion. The following extract from a will makes this clear:

> 1880, October 29. I, the Cossack woman M.Z. with two sons, S. and P.Z., and since my husband's death a widow, have drawn up the following will. I possess the following common moveable and immoveable property which is to be divided. In the *khutor* [small Cossack village] I have a three-walled storeroom with a garden. I also possess the following livestock: three cows; three pairs of bulls; ten sheep; and some domestic lumber. This property which I have inherited is mine to manage as I see fit. Therefore I bequeath it forever to my son P.Z. and to his children. My other son, S., and his children must not in any circumstances take legal action over my property, since I have deprived him of his share on account of his disrespect for me. If after my death he begins legal action, then I request the court and the authorities not to hear his case or give him any satisfaction. This will becomes valid on the day of my death, but until then I remain in control of all the property I possess.[27]

Evidently, therefore, women were accorded considerable property rights by Cossack custom and, importantly, ones that could be enforced. In many ways women's property rights were much more clearly defined than men's and were consequently much more secure. Men remained vulnerable to the caprice of their parents up to the day of their death. A woman, once she had received her share at the time of her marriage, no longer had any financial obligations to her parents. Neither her natal nor her husband's family could touch the property which she brought with her into the marriage. These property rights gave Cossack women significant power in their relationships with the men in their lives. What they could not do, of course, was guarantee that all women would receive decent treatment from their husbands and other male relatives.

Outside observers of Cossack life seem to have been split between those who believed that Cossack women had managed to achieve some sort of parity with men and those who believed that they suffered violence as a matter of routine from their husbands. A report in the official gazette of the *Voisko* believed that high levels of violence against women were the norm for half the women in the *Voisko*.[28] Others pointed out that while the structure of Cossack life allowed women more freedom as a whole, it did render those women who remained in the families of their in-laws more vulnerable to the crime of *snokhachestvo* (incest between a Cossack woman and her father-in-law, generally forced by the father-in-law), as the following report makes clear:

> In the April session of the Kamenskaia *stanitsa* court, two cases were heard which are characteristic of one of the common features of Cossack family life, i.e. the relationship of the father-in-law to his young daughter-in-law, particularly during the period when her husband was away on service. The account of the daughter-in-law is particularly interesting. In her own words, she resisted her father-in-law for a long time, but eventually, under the constant pressure of her father-in-law and his cruel threat to denounce her to her husband, she finally gave in and entered into a criminal liaison with her father-in-law. This affair continued for twelve years, both while the husband was at home and while he was absent on service. Her husband coming home suspected this relationship and tormented and harassed his wife greatly until she finally confessed her sin before the husband and the community. After this the unhappy woman and her father-in-law were committed for trial accused of incest.[29]

Happily, in this case the woman was cleared of any misconduct, while the father-in-law was jailed for three years. It is impossible to know how widespread *snokhachestvo* was, since like all crime committed within the family it was notoriously difficult to detect. The absence of the husband for the first three years of his marriage did increase the opportunity for the crime to take place, but it is clear that *snokhachestvo* was not a right and that if it was discovered, it was punished. In Razdorskaia *stanitsa*, for example, a survey of local customs discovered that the Cossacks regarded *snokhachestvo* and rape as serious crimes, while in contrast adultery was not seen as a terribly serious matter.[30] Violence by men against women is present in many societies, and Cossack society was and is not unique in this sense. Clearly, women did suffer violence from the men they married, but it is far from clear that this was the norm. The image of a self-confident, self-reliant woman emerges much more strongly from the sources than a demoralized and broken victim. A further source of strength for Cossack women was their ability to form relationships outside the family. They were able to rely on a network of female friends to help them cope with the vicissitudes of a difficult life.

The very close and institutionalized friendships that existed among Cossack men had their parallels among Cossack women. The Cossack custom of *odnosumstvo*, literally 'one bag', was probably the most important of these friendships. It derived from a tradition whereby a group of men departing for service would place all their belongings in one bag as a sign of their trust and dependence on each other. Just as the men formed intimate and enduring relationships with their service comrades, so the wives of these men also forged friendships out of their common experiences, as the following report makes clear:

> It is well known that when Cossacks leave for service, they are sent off at the same time to a particular regiment and by an ancient custom refer to each other as *odnosumki*. Similarly, their wives, when seeing off their husbands, by the same custom also address each other as *odnosumki*. From this time they are closely acquainted and for many this acquaintance began as a young woman little by little is transformed into a

close friendship for life . . . When travelling from the *khutor* to the *stanitsa*, a Cossack woman counts it her greatest pleasure to catch sight of her *odnosumki*, usually as they come out of church after the service. Here on the porch they question each other closely. Has anyone received a letter from the men on service? Who and when exactly? Are the men in good health? Is the service hard or easy, etc., etc.? It goes without saying that the mothers of the men participate happily in this questioning and answering session . . . [31]

Women in Cossack society did not enjoy equality with men. Cossack women carried vast burdens and received unequal rewards. However, their status within that society was significantly higher than was the norm for the wider peasant community. Cossack women were accorded a value and respect that were systematically denied to peasant women. This was an expression of the distinct historical experience of the Cossacks. The exigencies of life in a frontier society produced women who were self-reliant, tough, confident and accustomed to exercising authority. Even though the Don ceased to be a frontier society in the nineteenth century, the structure of Cossack life ensured that women continued to display these same traits. Cossack military service meant that women continued to have responsibilities thrust upon them, regardless of traditional conceptions of gender roles. This was most obvious in the domestic economies of the Cossacks, where the sexual division of labour was eroded to the extent that all women had to be able to do anything a man could do around the farm. Because this blurring of a division of labour was rooted in the very fabric of Cossack life, military service, it could not be dismissed by the community as exceptional, as in the case of peasant women who were widows, or as an isolated phenomenon without any wider relevance. Cossack women out of necessity had to combine in their own persons all the skills that had traditionally been divided along gender lines. This gave women a moral authority within that society and within their families. The moral authority of Cossack women was backed by property rights that were substantial and explicit, which they could and did use to ensure that they received a necessary level of respect from their men. Of course, women as individuals could still suffer enormously at the hands of their men, either through beatings or being raped in the guise of *snokhachestvo*, but as a group they enjoyed a level of prestige and power altogether unusual in the context of imperial Russia.

Notes

1 Rose L. Glickman, 'Peasant Women and Their Work', in Beatrice Brodsky Farnsworth and Lynne Viola (eds.), *Russian Peasant Women* (Oxford: Oxford University Press, 1992), pp. 54–72; Christine D. Worobec, 'Temptress or Virgin? The Precarious Sexual Position of Women in Post-Emancipation Ukrainian Peasant Society', *Slavic Review*, vol. 49, no. 2 (Summer 1990), pp. 227–38; Christine D. Worobec, 'Victims or Actors? Russian Peasant Women and Patriarchy', in Esther Kingston-Mann and Timothy Mixter (eds.), *Peasant Economy, Culture and Politics of European Russia* (Princeton, N.J.: Princeton University Press: 1990); Christine D. Worobec, *Peasant*

Russia: Family and Community in the Post-Emancipation Period (Princeton, N.J.: Princeton University Press, 1991). Slightly more positive views are Beatrice Brodsky Farnsworth, 'The Litigious Daughter-in-Law: Family Relations in Rural Russia in the Second Half of the Nineteenth Century', *Slavic Review*, vol. 45, no. 1 (Spring 1946), pp. 49–64; and Barbara Alpern Engel, 'The Woman's Side: Male Outmigration and the Family Economy in Kostroma Province', *Slavic Review*, vol. 45, no. 2 (Summer 1986), pp. 257–71.

2 Glickman, 'Peasant Women and Their Work', p. 55.
3 For the fullest account of this process, see S. G. Svatikov, *Rossiia i Don (1549–1917: issledovanie po istorii gosudarstvennago i administrativnago prava i politicheskikh dvizhenii na Donu* (Belgrade, 1924).
4 V. Bronevskii, *Istoriia Donskogo voiska*, 3 vols., (St Petersburg, 1834), vol. 3, p. 94. See also S. Nomikosov (ed.), *Statisticheskoe opisanie oblasti donskogo* (Novocherkassk, 1994), p. 313.
5 A. I. Rigel'man, *Istoriia o Donskikh kazakakh* (Moscow, 1846: facsimile edition, Rostov-on-Don, 1992), pp. 82–3.
6 M. Seniutkin, *Dontsy: istoricheskie ocherki voennykh deistvii. Biografii starshin proshlogo veka, zametki iz sovremennago byta i vzgliad na istoriiu voiska donskago* (Moscow, 1886), p. 2.
7 Bronevskii, *Istoriia Donskogo voiska*, vol. 3, p. 95.
8 *Donskaia rech'*, 3 July 1888.
9 Beatrice Brodsky Farnsworth, 'The *Soldatka*: Folklore and Court Record', *Slavic Review*, vol. 49, no. 1 (1990), pp. 58–73.
10 Nomikosov, *Statisticheskoe opisanie oblasti donskogo*, pp. 342–3.
11 M. Kharuzin, *Svedenie o kazatskikh obshchinakh na Donu: materialy dlia Obychnago Prava* (Moscow, 1885), p. 180.
12 Glickman, 'Peasant Women and Their Work', p. 56; Worobec, 'Victims or Actors?', p. 184.
13 Worobec, *Peasant Russia*, p. 71.
14 Nomikosov, *Statisticheskoe opisanie oblasti donskogo*, pp. 250–1.
15 *Donskoi vestnik*, 18 April 1868.
16 *Donskiia oblastnyia vedomosti*, 9 July 1876.
17 Kharuzin, *Svedenie*, pp. 169–72.
18 Nomikosov, *Statisticheskoe opisanie oblasti donskogo*, p. 322.
19 A similar situation appeared to be developing among peasant women whose husbands were absent for long periods in the cities toward the end of the nineteenth century. See Engel, 'The Woman's Side', p. 270.
20 Farnsworth, 'The Litigious Daughter-in-Law', p. 55.
21 Glickman, 'Peasant Women and Their Work', p. 55.
22 Kharuzin, *Svedenie*, p. 218; *Donskoi vestnik*, 4 August 1869.
23 Nomikosov, *Statisticheskoe opisanie oblasti donskogo*, p. 321; Kharuzin, *Svedenie*, p. 205; *Donskoi vestnik*, 4 August 1869.
24 Kharuzin, *Svedenie*, p. 194; *Donskoi vestnik*, 18 March 1868.
25 Kharuzin, *Svedenie*, p. 197; *Donskoi vestnik*, 18 March 1868.
26 Kharuzin, *Svedenie*, p. 197.
27 Ibid., p. 241.
28 *Donskiia oblastnyia vedomosti*, 14 March 1879.
29 *Donskoi golos*, 6 June 1882.

30 *Donskoi vestnik*, 4 August 1869; *Donskoi golos*, 6 June 1882. Contrast this with Rose Glickman's claim that 'the patriarch's authority over the household's life from the smallest detail to the largest included the right to sexual intercourse . . . ': Glickman, 'Peasant Women and Their Work', p. 55.

31 *Donskiia oblastnyia vedomosti*, 14 May 1880.

4

Teacups and coffins: the culture of Russian merchant women, 1850–1917

CATRIONA KELLY

Feminism in Europe, and in western culture more generally, has had a long and distinguished history of association with left radicalism. Mary Wollstonecraft and Germaine Greer are only two of the better-known Anglophone figures at either end of an enduring historical tradition. It is no surprise, therefore, that feminists, including feminist historians, have shared the traditional tendency of radicalism and socialism to regard capitalism with suspicion, if not actual hostility. Studies of women's history everywhere have given a great deal more weight to the victims of capitalism (prostitutes, factory workers) than to its beneficiaries (women factory owners, employers or traders). In Britain at least, consideration of the latter group of women until recently would have seemed a tribute to what was known, from the title of a middle-brow and enthusiastically success-oriented Conservative newspaper, as 'Daily Mail feminism'. In the field of Russian history, where feminism's international inclination to left radicalism has been still further reinforced by Soviet internal politics, it would have seemed – indeed, to some extent still does still seem – almost indecent to compose a serious study of women selling anything other than themselves.[1] Yet there are a number of reasons why analysis of female merchants (*kupchikhi*) and traders is not only justified, but requisite. Though the idea that women may benefit from capitalist systems is uncomfortable, it must be confronted if we are to understand why at least some women should be supporters of such systems. Whilst trading and factory owning made the fortunes of few women, they appear to have provided a number with a reasonable living; and though the proportion of women traders, and indeed of *kupchikhi* generally, in city populations was far lower than that of factory workers or servants, the mercantile élite no less deserves description than those other élites (for example, women writers or women revolutionaries) whose activities have already been chronicled *in extenso*. Furthermore, the study of merchant women has immediate relevance to our comprehension of the woman question as debated in nineteenth-century Russia. The many satirical representations of merchant women that appeared in fiction and painting between about 1840 and the Russian Revolution differ neither in tone nor in substance from representations of 'unenlightened' women (whether aristocrats or peasants) everywhere in nineteenth-century fiction and journalism, and so indicate once more the close connection between Russian radical discourse and misogynist rhetoric.[2] Finally, over and above such feminist considerations, understanding of the fact that some Russian women belonging to the merchant class did trade in their own right, and apparently with some success, has value as a corrective to the widely favoured, but misleading, opinion that all merchant families remained stalwart bastions of medieval patriarchal values right up until the early twentieth century.

My discussion of merchant women (I have concentrated on those of St Petersburg and Moscow for reasons of space) falls into two parts. In the first part, I shall be looking at some key fictional representations of metropolitan merchant women – representations which changed remarkably little between the 1840s, when they first made their appearance, and the Russian Revolution. The second part of the chapter, by contrast, will move beyond imaginative representations to more obviously 'factual' sources (guild handbooks and memoirs), in order to indicate that in actuality Russian merchant women seem to have led rather different lives from those upon which writers and painters loved to expend their bile.

First of all, then, let us consider one of the latest, but also one of the most famous, images of a *kupchikha* ever constructed: Kustodiev's 1918 painting 'The Merchant's Wife Drinking Tea' (Figure 4.1). The nameless 'wife' in question, an impassively seductive woman of thirty something, sits, as overdecorated as her own tea-service, before a table laden with delicacies, next to a shining samovar, with a saucer of tea frozen halfway to her Mona Lisa smirk. The picture's apparent drama is undercut by the fact that the main actress herself seems as unreflective as any prize cow; as she sits in the shade of her garden, any thoughts she has, one may assume, are green ones. And so the discreet eroticism which the image radiates lies less in the *kupchikha*'s own smooth décolletage, reflected in the opulent lines of the samovar, than in the flaring red interior of the sliced watermelon placed in the centre of the table, and the purring cat who rubs up to one of the *kupchikha*'s shoulders, inviting the viewer to do likewise.

Kustodiev's painting, whilst rather fussily overillustrative for its substantial dimensions (the canvas is roughly four-feet square), is all the same an infectiously enthusiastic celebration of kitsch objects. It is also an extraordinarily powerful evocation of a past not so much vanished as imaginary. The costume and table-setting suggest a date considerably before that of the painting's composition, perhaps in the 1840s or 1850s – as does Kustodiev's own handling of the relationship between figure and panoramic background – but the exact historical moment is as unclear as is the precise whereabouts of the location. The backdrop could depict Moscow, but it could equally well represent a vista of almost any other of the old Russian cities with which merchants were associated (Kaluga, Nizhnii Novgorod, Saratov, Rostov or Yaroslavl', to name only the most famous).[3] Devoid of exact historical content, Kustodiev's representation is also empty of moral commentary. His painting suggests that the woman whom we are viewing is indolent; that she exists for a life of pleasure; that she eschews ratiocination; but it also suggests that there is something almost admirable in that state. Composed

4.1 Boris Kustodiev, 'The Merchant's Wife Drinking Tea', 1918
oil on canvas, 120.5 cm × 121.2 cm, Russian Museum, St Petersburg

at one of the very rare moments in Russian history when the decorative
was appreciated for its own sake, this picture is able to take the fundamental
traits of the *kupchikha* as established by seventy years of previous representations,
and strip them of the satirical and critical content that had formerly been
requisite.

Writers and painters working before Kustodiev who produced generalized
representations of 'the merchant woman' (as we shall see later, portraits of actual
merchant women were crafted according to different conventions) had generally
agreed with him that merchant women wore their wealth on their backs. For
example, in his 1864 study of the Apraksin market traders, N. A. Leikin
described one rich merchant's wife parading in a white hat with a feather, and a
pomegranate-coloured brocade *salop* (padded coat) with fur lining. Leikin went on

to assert that a 'good coat' was considered such an important item of merchant women's dress that it would often form part of their dowries.[4] Ostentatious attire was, we learn, also the rule indoors, provided the occasion merited it. An 1874 guidebook to St Petersburg describes the Merchants' Club as 'one of the grandest and dullest institutions in the capital', filled with 'self-important [*sanovitye*] individuals from wealthy merchant families, come to show off their dazzling costumes – in the case of the fair sex, or, in the case of the other sex, to play cards for high stakes'.[5]

Like Kustodiev, nineteenth-century commentators were wont to observe that fine clothes were only one of merchant women's many self-indulgences. Once retired to their brash, tasteless houses, men and women would separate; whilst the men played billiards, or talked business in the *zala* (salon, or formal drawing-room) with its rows of hideous smeary oils capturing the likenesses of beetroot-cheeked, pompous ancestors, the women would retire to their parlour, and sit by the hour gossiping and drinking tea, or tippling on madeira. Left to themselves, merchant women would flick through French novels in translation, or scan various kinds of chapbooks, or copy out 'sensual poems' in their albums (*tetradki*), or occasionally exert themselves so far as to bully one of the horde of servants. But their veneer of gentility was always ready to peel off, laying bare the cheap underlay of vulgar hussydom, as the following case of a hen-party on its way back from the bathhouse on the day before a wedding purports to illustrate:

> The shamelessness and amorality of these brazen trollops [*baby*] sometimes transcends all boundaries. They not only bawl out songs at the tops of their voices, so that the whole street resounds, but sometimes lean out of their carriage windows to taunt and abuse passers-by, or to bombard them with birch-besoms and empty bottles.[6]

During the first three-quarters of the nineteenth century, male merchants were uniformly perceived by writers and journalists as licensed thieves, cheating their weary and defenceless customers, harassing them and baying at them 'like packs of dogs'.[7] Though ostentatiously pious, they had seldom absorbed the tenets of the religious literature to which they so frequently applied themselves in leisure hours; their acts of charity were intended to raise their own social profile, rather than to conform with the dictates of the Gospels.[8] For their part, women of the merchant class functioned in reportage and fiction as metaphors for the amoral nature of trading practice. Occasionally represented as the cowering victim of male tyranny, a married women was more often seen as an accessory to her husband's greed and narrow-mindedness, chivvying her daughters into financially advantageous liaisons, or more often into status-enhancing alliances with members of the gentry, such as superannuated civil servants. The *kupecheskie smotriny*, or premarital rituals in which nubile young women were presented to prospective husbands, were seen as a reflection of the readiness of merchant parents to sell anything, even their own daughters, so long as they could turn a profit.[9] Unmarried girls might be seen either as innocent fledgling beauties in white dresses, hounded into marriage by their ambitious parents, or as apprentices to their mothers, honing the rapacity that they would later exercise to perfection. P. Fedotov's famous painting 'The Major's Courtship' (Figure 4.2) hovers between these two possibilities. Set in a merchant *zala*, from whose walls rows of stiffly painted whiskery ancestors frown down on their descendants, the painting makes the most of the melodramatic possibilities of the *smotriny*. The reluctant, or more likely mock-reluctant, female protagonist rushes from the sight of her elderly suitor; her bearded father looms disapprovingly, whilst her mother snatches at her crinoline in an attempt to retrieve her. At the bottom of the canvas, a smugly corpulent black-and-white cat sits and cleans its face; the sexual symbolism is just as blatant as in Kustodiev's painting, but it is introduced to very different effect.

Representations of merchant women, and representations of merchants in general, are most frequently to be found in texts and pictures dating from between 1840 and 1870. This was a period in which Russian social commitment was generally expressed in rather lurid fictions of class antagonism and exploitation, and also one at which members of the gentry were struggling to assert their authority in urban local government against the rival claims of the merchant class.[10] Thereafter, the merchants' collaboration in creating a new civic environment, and the increasing convergence of their lives with those of the gentry, meant that the electricity of hatred prickled less painfully in journalism and literature, but its charge could still be felt. In Sof'ia Smirnova's melodramatic story 'A Personal Insult', written in the 1890s, a merchant factory owner, 'despite having studied abroad at three universities, had for all that remained a real Russian *muzhik*'. A similar message is conveyed by Petr Boborykin's *Kitai-gorod*, a fictional study of the depraved merchants in whose stranglehold Moscow languishes, which argues that contact with 'abroad' can instil in Russian tradesmen only a love of costly footwear and expensive mistresses.[11] Just as in earlier years, women characters in later fiction act either as representatives of merchant culture's self-serving commercialism, or, more frequently, as the broken victims of that commercialism. Ol'ga Shapir's *She Came Back* shows a *kursistka* (a student of the university-equivalent courses of higher education for women) returning home to her provincial town, and gradually realizing that her engagement to the dullard owner of a local business runs the risk of turning her into a fretful, underemployed marital hostage like her fiancé's sister, whilst in Chekhov's *A Doctor's Case-Notes*, the protagonist observes a merchant household where wealth and cultural impoverishment go hand-in-hand, and where the daughter of the house has to be rescued, by his sympathetic bedside sermon, from the hysterical neurasthenia to which her parasitic, but wretched, existence has reduced her.[12]

For certain Slavophile and neo-Slavophile commentators, who saw Russian merchants as the necessary agents of a peculiarly Russian popular commercialism, these merchants' female appendages might exceptionally be seen as the representatives of a quintessentially Russian energetic uprightness.[13] But otherwise, views that Russian traders were repugnant both in ethical and aesthetic terms displayed a remarkable longevity. As so often in Russian culture, texts and paintings contributed to the construction of the reality which they purported to express. The

4.2 Pavel Fedotov, 'The Major's Courtship', 1848
oil on canvas, 58.3 cm × 75.4 cm, Tret'iakov Gallery, Moscow

merchant memoirist Petr Buryshkin lamented that rich Russians were far less likely to be lionized than their counterparts in France, and snobbery against merchant families does seem to have been all but ubiquitous.[14] Although Russian merchants had been marrying into the aristocracy since at least the late eighteenth century, and although the richest magnates, such as the Shchukins, Morozovs and Riabushinskiis, were amongst the most notable Russian patrons of the arts, the Russian merchant community remained beyond the pale of aristocratic and especially intelligentsia values. Officialdom, too, was inclined to treat merchants with hauteur; the state was sensitive to the possibilities of traders as milch-cows for revenue, but the regulation of trading always retained a sense of the ascetic distaste for money-making evident in Russian Orthodox Christianity. Where a British clergyman of the early twentieth century might happily have supplemented his stipend by means of private investment, a Russian clergyman was expressly forbidden from contact of any kind with trade.[15]

Merchants themselves could not, of course, help being influenced by their social positioning; the fact that trading was next to taboo helped reinforce the special character of the merchant estate as self-absorbed in its apartness, yet at the same time gnawed by doubt as to its rightful place in society. But Russian commerce, though it might look to tradition as legitimation, was for all that not totally inflexible in its attitudes. As the cities expanded over the course of the nineteenth century, so too did the opportunities for trade, and these did not go unremarked and unexploited by city merchants. Immigration, as foreigners and provincial merchants moved into the metropolitan centres, was another important factor of change. Finally, shifts in the character of the merchant hierarchy were ensured by alterations to the legal status of the guild system, whose power was weakened by measures of 1864 and 1865, and more or less ended in 1898 by the introduction of 'trading certificates' as an alternative to membership of the guilds themselves.[16] Few indeed of those registered as 'merchants' and 'traders' in the early nineteenth century could still state, in the biographies that they gave to the guilds, 'from an old merchant family'; the numbers of such 'trading aristocrats' had been diluted by large numbers of outsiders, some of them former peasants, and others from ethnic minorities (most particularly Germans and Jews), and in any case many of the magnates had switched to holding 'trading certificates'.[17]

The new and less exclusive character of commercialism after 1865 was reflected in the increasingly mercantile flavour of urban culture: by the late nineteenth century, the streets of Moscow and St Petersburg bristled with bright advertisements, on which wares were temptingly displayed; street songs, jokes and popular comedies placed an ever-greater emphasis on the necessity of making money. In the fairground shows of the 1890s and 1900s, merchant women's status as a metaphor for the character of Russian trade in general began to be positively coloured. Marriage to a 'merchant's daughter' was seen as an excellent way of bettering oneself, and women's financial rapacity now attracted collusive approval, as in the following tale of a sharp-witted adventuress from the street markets:

A vot i peterburgskaia dama,
Tol'ko ne iz Amsterdama,
Priekhala iz Rigi
Prodavat' figi.
Kupecheskikh synkov obstavliaet,
Da seti im rasstavliaet.
Kar'eru nachala s prachki
Da davali ei mnogo potachki.

(Here's a lady for to greet yer
Not from Amsterdam, she's from Peter,
She came from Riga a while back
To sell figs, green and black,
She has the merchants' sons eating out her hand,
And she's making her marriage plans.
She started out doing the washing and scrubbing,
But got paid well for her trouble.)[18]

Even before these changes, the character of Russian trade, at any rate in the capitals and in such harbour towns as Odessa, was not as monolithic as some commentators, especially the authors of realist fiction, might lead one to believe. In actual fact, even the restricted terms of fictional stereotype suggest some potential for change: the notorious conservatism of Russian merchants was at obvious variance with their equally notorious desire to make money by all possible means, the latter being surely doomed to erode the former. It is also clear from all accounts that the term 'merchant', even in the first half of the nineteenth century, embraced a multitude of divergent activities, from the small traders of the *Gostinyi dvor* – who are reliably reported to have been as importunate as their counterparts in the *suqs* of Arabia and North Africa, and to have driven as hard a bargain – up to the polished and respectable owners of substantial trading firms and industrial enterprises.[19] This diversity of scale and occupation is reflected in the directories (*spravochnye knigi*) that were published by the metropolitan Russian guilds at intervals throughout the nineteenth century, and regularly from the 1860s. These directories likewise indicate the multiethnic nature of Russian trade in the capitals, and, most importantly for us, the fact that trade was by no means solely a masculine occupation. The numbers of women merchants listed ran into hundreds, and between 1858 and 1915 they made up something between 8 and 15 per cent of registered first, second and third guild traders in Moscow and St Petersburg.[20]

The existence of these women traders has gone unrecognized not only by traditional stereotypes of the *kupchikha*, but also by academic studies. The Russian merchant class has generally been analysed from the perspectives of economic and social history; the extent of change and stasis in trading patterns over the course of the nineteenth century has been traced, and the question whether or not a true Russian bourgeoisie on the western pattern ever came into being debated.[21] Neither of these two approaches has facilitated sophisticated study of the mentality of Russian merchants; the brief discussions of merchants' domestic existence that have appeared have reproduced the conventional view that merchant life consisted of a perpetual dramatization of the *Domostroi*, in which men dominated every aspect of domesticity, the only existence allowed to their womenfolk.[22] Our picture of how Russian merchant women lived still comes to us courtesy of the playwright Aleksandr Ostrovskii and other sources whose overt satirical purpose has apparently not made them seem less trustworthy in the eyes of many readers. A recovery of the lives of actual merchant women for history seems requisite.

In the rest of this essay, I attempt to trace the outlines of merchant women's lives in the second half of the nineteenth and early twentieth centuries, basing my observations mostly on the entries for women registered in a selection of the Moscow and St Petersburg guild address books published during that period. Exemplary rather than exhaustive, my survey can be only the beginning of retrieval and analysis of merchant women's biographies. It deals with a fairly small sample of material, views merchant women from the outside, not through their own words, and is synchronic rather than diachronic in character, not concerning itself in any depth with historical developments in merchant women's existence.[23]

To avoid misunderstanding, it might be as well to clarify further my purpose in devoting attention to merchant women in the first place. This is, as will have become clear already, very much a 'myth and reality' study. Elsewhere in my work, I have been concerned to problematize historical sources, and question the possibility of finding absolute answers in apparently transparent materials.[24] In this chapter my analysis will be relatively straightforward, though I should register one or two problems with the material. The guild directories by no means supply us with a full picture of Russian women's involvement in trade. Like all reference sources, these directories have a sprinkling of faults: pages are sometimes missing from extant copies, and individual entries occasionally give incomplete or misleading information. Besides, the directories recorded only those women traders who had sufficient capital to be eligible for the guilds, as well as sufficient financial resources to pay their dues, and who themselves felt that their businesses were of a size to benefit from legal recognition. There were undoubtedly far more *torgovki* (female traders) in Moscow and St Petersburg than there were merchants, or even, after 1898, holders of 'trading certificates'.[25] All the same, the information given in the address books about types and locations of businesses, as well as home addresses, ages and dependent relatives, does allow us to begin considering merchant women as individuals, rather than as colourful stereotypes. These books, and the informative memoirs of such merchants as Petr Shchukin and Petr Butyrkin, also suggest that merchant women, even if they did not run their own businesses, did not have to be tailors' dummies, waste disposal units for liqueurs and candy, over-upholstered termagants or terrified, anaemic virgins: there is evidence for a 'hidden' class of wives and daughters who helped the family business along.

My interest in women's involvement in trade does not of course mean that I advocate treating female traders as heroines by whose entrepreneurial spirit we might all do well to be inspired. Certainly, as the former Soviet Union marketizes, there is some direct contemporary relevance in the very existence of women traders during the pre-revolutionary period, but the women about whom I shall be writing are, for various reasons, not obvious models for modern businesswomen, let alone for modern feminists. If contemporary commentators were perhaps unduly inclined to dwell on the exploitative nature of trade in Russia, that does not mean that their comments were entirely without foundation. One of the occupations that the address books attribute to a number of women is 'lace seller', for example. Since traders of this kind bought in piece-work in bulk from Russian peasant manufacturers working solo, it is more than likely that any trading success achieved by female entrepreneurs was achieved at the cost of their exploitation of other women, the peasant out-workers who actually made up the lace.[26] Women were also involved in the ultimate money-grubbing merchant profession, usury. So much is clear not only from Dostoevskii's chilling fictional portrait of Raskol'nikov's first and intended victim in *Crime and Punishment*, but also from the more disinterested information given in the address books: in 1885, for example, there were twelve such women registered as active in Moscow (and undoubtedly many more working outside the boundaries of the law).[27]

In another sense, too, merchant women of the nineteenth century were very much products of their own time: they were marginal figures in a business culture that was dominated by men. True, there was no legal barrier to trading by women, including married women, and *kupchikhi* could benefit from Russia's comparatively liberal property and inheritance laws, according to which wives disposed over their own property, and daughters had rights to shares in their parents' estates. Indeed, as the address books made clear, women had often inherited their businesses (from a husband or father, or even a brother), rather than having built them up single-handedly. Women could vote in the elections of the merchants' representative bodies, the *kupecheskie obshchestva*, and in theory even hold office in these.[28] But the social and cultural circumstances of the Russian merchantry were rather less permissive than the enlightened letter of the law might suggest. The guilds, in St Petersburg and Moscow at least, were entirely run by male officers, and other aspects of merchants' public life were also dominated by men. The lengthy ritual courtesies of formal negotiations, usually beginning with a merchant accosting a buyer, survived well into the twentieth century; even in the 1880s, wholesalers and retailers would meet to debate prices and deals over a glass of tea, or more stimulating liquid, in a *traktir* (tavern and tea-room), as they had done since at least the beginning of the nineteenth century. All this made women conspicuous: accosting buyers in the street would have been just as detrimental to the reputation of a 'respectable' woman as visiting the male-dominated environment of the *traktir*. Dress was also a problem. Though 'German clothing' had been worn by metropolitan merchants since the early nineteenth century, some traders would still, in the 1880s, put on caftans in order to go about their daily business, affect long beards, and wear their hair long and caught back in top-knots – an authoritarian masculine uniform that had no female equivalent.[29]

Such deterrents no doubt lay behind the fact that the greatest business successes of the nineteenth century involved men. The great Moscow dynasties, the Mamontovs, the Morozovs, the Riabushinskiis and the Poliakovs, were Europeanized and self-consciously 'modern'; accordingly, they tended to believe that their daughters should have as good an education as money could buy. But only occasional women in these dynasties made notable careers in business. Timofei Savvich Morozov, the founder of the first modern Russian textile mill (*khlopchatobumazhnaia fabrika*), was succeeded as director after his death by his wife, Marfa Fedorovna, who is remembered by Buryshkin as 'a very tough woman indeed, highly intelligent, full of *savoir-vivre*, with her own opinions on all subjects. The genuine head of the family.' As Buryshkin also recalls, another Morozova, Varvara Alekseevna, was born into another big merchant family, the Khludovs, from whom she inherited her own business interests; after her husband's death, she took over his factories too. For her part, Savva Mamontov's daughter Aleksandra is registered by the 1915 guild directory as the owner of a craft pottery works.[30] By far the majority of working women in these dynasties, however, moved out into more genteel professions such as medicine, teaching or writing, according to a pattern of social mobility that had been established in the 1820s and 1830s.[31] The founders of the major Moscow dynasties, such as Savva Mamontov and Savva Morozov themselves, had no female equivalents. Though a number of Moscow magnates' wives had 'married up', sometimes from the factory floor, there were apparently no cases of women rising by their own skills and efforts from the peasantry to the commercial élite.[32]

According to the guild directories, the average registered woman merchant was no magnate, but the owner of a small business, or at most a string of small businesses, such as a chain of grocery shops. The proportion of women traders increases markedly as one goes down the guild system. The number of women listed in the first guild was tiny both absolutely and proportionately. In St Petersburg in 1858 and 1865, for example, the figures were 4 women, or about 2 per cent, and 11 women, or about 3 per cent, respectively. The second guild had a substantially higher proportion of women than the first – around 10 per cent; before the third guild was abolished (in the mid-1860s), women were still better represented here (the figure for St Petersburg in 1858 was about 15 per cent). After 1898, women merchants proportionately held their own, though their overall numbers declined in accordance with the general decline in the importance of the guild system. They made up 16 per cent of the St Petersburg first guild in 1915, and 9 per cent of the second, whilst the corresponding figures in Moscow were around 17 and 12 per cent respectively; in addition, women now made up around 17 per cent of those holding 'trading certificates'. (The rise in first guild numbers at this date is largely explained by an influx of Jewish traders, for whom the acquisition of guild status was an important prerequisite of settlement rights outside the Pale.)[33]

If the small scale of their operations is a unifying factor, in other ways the situation varied a good deal. It is, indeed, the variety of women merchants' occupations which is the most striking first impression. Women seemed to make and sell just about anything: from bricks to fish, from tobacco to paintings, from snuff-boxes to steel buckets, from harnesses to cosmetics. They ran haulage businesses and cab firms, owned grain-importing businesses and warehouses, hotels, money exchanges and rooming-houses. Bizarre combinations of goods abounded: one woman trader in Moscow during 1885 is registered as a vendor of 'soap and fish' (not at the same counter, one hopes), whilst a St Petersburg small trader was recorded, in 1915, as a seller of 'herbs and hen coops'. On at least three occasions (one in Moscow 1885, two in Moscow 1915), there are entries for shopkeepers selling 'china and coffins' in the same establishment (hence the title of this essay). Numerous women also owned factories: tanneries, vodka distilleries, iron foundries, textile manufactures and sugar refineries are all recorded. Some worked as building or road transport contractors, or occasionally even as water transport contractors. In the early twentieth century, a surprising number of them branched out into new businesses: electrical goods, undertaking, electric theatres and car hire being four types of activity that were registered to women merchants and trade certificate holders in Moscow during 1915.[34]

One has to bear in mind, of course, that a woman's ownership of a business might have given her a merely titular role; the guild directories are not specific on this point. I earlier mentioned some of the aspects of traditional merchant life which might have been discouraging to women; is there any way of telling whether the women listed as traders in the directory were actually involved in their businesses or not? The presence of a number of listings for women who are declared to have 'no trade' is interesting in this respect. It was possible to retain the passport and status advantages of the merchant estate (such as protection against corporal punishment, harassment about the *propiska* [the permit to reside in a Russian city], and, before 1874, against conscription), even if one were not commercially active. Women to whom business was uncongenial could and did sell their businesses, living thereafter on unearned income.[35]

If women's failure to sell a business may be negative evidence that they did work in that business, a positive pointer to their working may be evident in the fact that the majority of women in the lower guilds lived on the premises of their business. This suggests that they would have had difficulty in detaching themselves completely from the activities of that business. (A striking number of women from the first guild, on the other hand, were wealthy widows who lived at a considerable distance from the city where their business was registered, and in some cases outside Russia altogether.) The propinquity of women's living quarters and their trading establishments may not have dictated that they be much involved with the day-to-day organization of businesses that were heavily dependent on 'masculine' skilled labour (such as forges or foundries). But even here they may have overseen the financial side of the business. Numerous merchant women were literate (in the extremely conservative Old Believer merchant communities, it was generally women who acted as elementary literacy teachers, or *masterichki*), and there was nothing to stop those who were not from employing clerks and assistants (*prikazchiki*) to help with the accounting systems that were legally required.[36]

The most conclusive supporting evidence for the actual involvement of women in business comes from the large numbers of the businesses registered to women that were compatible with traditional 'feminine' domestic activities, such as housework, childcare or sewing. There were vastly more women traders than there were industrialists, and the majority of traders were engaged in three broad areas of activity. The most popular of these was textile and fashion sales; in second place came sales of food, drink and liquor; and in third followed service sector businesses such as cookshops, restaurants, inns and hotels (how many of the women registered as owners of the last were in fact brothel-keepers is a question on which the directories maintain absolute discretion). These three areas of activity absorbed more than half of all registered women merchants. By no means all the rest conformed to easy classifications of 'femininity' (there were, for example, slightly more women selling ironmongery, harness and fodder than there were selling furniture and china); but it is noticeable that widows who discarded some of the businesses that they had inherited from their husbands tended to keep on, say, food and clothes shops, rather than brick works or haulage companies.[37]

The guild directories suggest, then, that the 'typical' merchant woman during the second half of the nineteenth century, and the first fifteen years of the twentieth, would have been a trader with a small business selling food or clothes, or else a restaurant or tavern keeper, somewhere within travelling distance of, if not actually at, her home address. As far as more personal details go, she would have been a widow, aged somewhere between her late thirties and her late sixties, with at least three children. Though possibly a moonlighting member of the *dvorianstvo* (gentry) she was more likely to be a merchant's daughter, a *meshchanka* (petty bourgeoise), or a peasant holding guild papers. Like her male counterparts, she could well be a non-Russian (Jewish, French, German, Swedish or British, in roughly descending order of probability), rather than a Russian; if a Russian, she might belong to an Old Believer sect rather than mainstream Orthodoxy. The directories give no details about the denomination to which Christian merchants belonged, but a number of women traders were registered in the Rogozha district of Moscow, where there was a concentration of Old Believers.[38]

The presence of women traders in Rogozha did not, however, signify a preference amongst women for this traditional merchant district, or indeed for any other traditional 'merchant' district in either capital. All the indications are that women merchants were quite widely scattered through both Moscow and Petersburg, a situation which is attributable to the fact that many of them sold goods (food, clothes, utensils) of the kind that city-dwellers would have purchased close to their homes. The only notable concentrations − which are again attributable to the particular profile of women merchants − were in the central shopping districts of both St Petersburg and Moscow: around Tverskaia Street and Kitai-gorod in Moscow, and Nevskii Prospekt in St Petersburg. Here lived communities of milliners and dressmakers, often of foreign origin, who supplied high-quality clothing; market traders; and also jewellers and perfumers. Until the early twentieth century, the main other clusters in St Petersburg were on the Vasil'evskii island and around the Kalashnikovskaia pristan' with its corn warehouses; from about 1900, the new commercial district of the Petersburg (now Petrograd) Side began to be a popular place of settlement. In Moscow, the development, also around 1900, of the Arbat, Meshchanskaia and Presnia districts as new residential quarters (haut-bourgeois, petit-bourgeois and proletarian respectively) was similarly accompanied by the formation of clusters of women shopkeepers in each place.[39] The 1915 Moscow directory also gives some indications that a few women trading in the centre of the city were beginning to move out to peripheral areas (Mar'ina Roscha, Lefortovo and others), perhaps because of improvements in public transport; but separation between work and home was still by no means the norm.

The directories also give some information on women's living conditions in a more private sense. Most women lived either in a rented flat over a rented shop or other trading premises, or in their own house or flat next to the business that they owned. Given the size of women's businesses, accommodation was likely to be relatively modest: a medium-sized flat, or a one- or two-storey house in wood, brick or stone, of the kind still to be seen on the Fontanka or off the Ligovskii Prospekt in St Petersburg, or around the Taganka and in the back streets off Prospekt Mira (formerly the Bol'shaia Meshchanskaia) in Moscow. These were not the grandiose *style moderne* palaces inhabited by the likes of the Riabushkinskiis or the Morozovs, or the eighteenth-century aristocrat's residence purchased by Sergei Shchukin; they did not have space for armies of servants. Unlike women from the aristocracy, or magnates' wives, who generally had housekeepers to organize the servants, an ordinary *kupchikha*, like the wife of a country landowner, usually had to supervise domestic labour herself. We can get a good idea of what that might involve from Sof'ia Soboleva's 1865 story *The Good Old Days*, which, for all its ironic title, in fact gives quite a sympathetic portrait of a woman from the merchant classes who has married into the civil service hierarchy. Soboleva's story suggests that merchant households had a strong self-sufficiency ethic; housekeeping, therefore, demanded that a good deal of time be spent on putting food by.[40]

Merchant housekeeping was by no means merely a matter, then, of keeping servants busy. In addition to its demands, some *kupchikhi* who did not have their own businesses would help out in their husband's, or other male relation's, firm. These women slipped through the net of guild directories, which did not acknowledge their existence. However, an example that has been recorded, because her descendants' house in St Petersburg was turned into a 'museum of daily life' during the 1920s, was Elena Gerasimovna Kovrigina who was hard at work in her husband's tallow business as early as the 1820s. Before settling in St Petersburg, the Kovrigins had led an itinerant life, travelling together to make purchases at the trade fairs that remained centres of the wholesale trade right up to the 1930s.[41] Another and later instance of a wife who acted as a concealed business partner was Elizaveta Grigor'evna Mamontova, who, with her husband Savva, was the instigator and organizer of the famous Russian art and craft movement workshops at Abramtsevo.[42]

As for *kupchikhi* who had no part in business, they, like many aristocratic women before the Revolution, tended to devote themselves to good causes, a decision fostered not only by their possession of wealth and leisure, but also by the merchant class's traditional attachment to charitable causes. One famous example of a philanthropic woman merchant was A. A. Abrikosova, who founded, in the early twentieth century, a lying-in hospital on Miusskaia Square in Moscow at a cost of 100,000 roubles. (After the Revolution it was, ironically enough, re-named [after Lenin's wife] the Nadezhda Krupskaia Lying-In Hospital.) E. I. Beklemisheva, née Prokhorova, another Moscow merchant woman, set up a soup kitchen and typhus hospital in the Chernigov region during the famine year of 1892; in this particular case, personal charity extended to working in the sponsored institutions too, and she herself became infected with typhus. Several women of the Khludov family were noted patrons of the arts, and as such seem to have combined generosity with hard-headedness in selecting the projects that they wished to sponsor. For example, the theatrical director Nemirovich-Danchenko found himself receiving an early lesson in business management when his request to V. A. Morozova for funds met with a polite, but rather frosty, refusal.[43]

If even *kupchikhi* who were apparently unemployed sometimes had full lives, *kupchikhi* who had businesses probably on occasion resembled the tireless eighteenth-century British entrepreneur Elizabeth Raffald, who had managed to organize four catering businesses, two newspapers, a street directory, a domestic servants' agency, a useless husband and sixteen children before her early death at the age of forty-eight.[44] Surviving portraits of individual merchant women, as opposed to evocations of 'the merchant woman' in general, also represent a rather different *kupchikha* to the one ridiculed in satire. Vasilii Tropinin's portrait of Anna Fedorovna Mazurina, for example (the version of 1844 is reproduced as Figure 4.3) shows a canny, sensible woman, her gaze both amused and shrewd, sitting in her good black silk dress, starched lace cap and sable stole as though she were impatient to be finished with the sitting. For all the uncoarsened skin of her hands, she looks like a woman who has spent her life working, not gossiping over cups of tea.[45] It is not only Tropinin's own influences that make one think of the Dutch School: it is the emphasis on plain values, on undramatic, but solid, quality, that is evident both in the chair that Mazurina is sitting on, and in her own clothes. Tropinin's portrait suggests a woman who, like the mother described by Shchukin, was the ultimate authority in her own house, not crossed by anyone.[46] Indeed, it makes sense to suppose that in many Russian merchant households, as in the households of the urban working class, interior space was dominated by women. That explains why few women were interested in running their own businesses unless they had to: there were other, and more direct, routes to authority and power. But it also explains why they could make a go of running businesses if they tried.[47]

This chapter has established the standard merchant woman of literature, journalism and realist painting as a bored, flighty and greedy drone of the female gender; it has argued that the merchant woman of Russian actuality was just as likely to be a

4.3 Vasilii Tropinin, 'Portrait of Anna Fedorovna Mazurina', 1844
oil on canvas, 100 cm × 80 cm, private collection, UK

worker bee. Because domestic duties, and trade, were activities which the written
culture of Russia during the nineteenth and early twentieth century despised, the
lives of such women have gone almost unrecorded in fiction and journalism,
including even that produced by women. The only fictional depiction of an
entrepreneurial merchant woman that appears to reflect the toughness and energy

of its real-life original is Boborykin's Anna Serafimovna Stanitsyna. Stanitsyna's demand that her husband cede overall control of the family business to her – 'There's nothing to be afraid of, mine's the only factory that's properly run' – strikes a new note, not merely in the toy-theatre atmosphere of this novel, but also in Russian literary tradition at large.[48] Uniquely, in a literary culture that has reduced the 'distaff side' of commercialism to silence, we hear the voice of a merchant woman herself, a woman making full use of her economic power, and quite well aware of this, and of her professional competence. It is clear that in real life also, at least some merchant families valued the financial acumen and industriousness of their womenfolk; the fact that male merchants married women from merchant families, and on at least one occasion from the peasantry, rather than rich aristocratic ladies, is sufficient indication that decorative idleness was little appreciated. The money-making drive certainly supported gender constraints – one may suppose that, as in peasant families, women's productive capacities, like their reproductive capacities, were often taken for granted, and therefore under-valued. But in some circumstances, this drive could also wear down gender constraints: the emphasis on success which characterizes all trading communities is finally, after all, no respecter of persons. 'Feminism? How is that sold? In bags or whole wagons?' These words, put into the lips of an early twentieth-century businesswoman by *Gazeta-kopeika*'s woman columnist, Ol'ga Gridina, are entirely adequate to the money-making, gender-blind character of Russian commercialism not only at that time, but in the nineteenth century as well.[49] And if, as Gridina's businesswoman also implies, women traders were most unlikely to be concerned with bettering the lot of their sex in a general sense, and had little interest in the mainstream feminism of their day, whether socialist or 'bourgeois' (which also had little interest in them), their activities, seen in historical perspective, did make a contribution of their own to the momentous changes that overtook Russian women's lives between 1880 and 1920.

Notes

I would like to express my gratitude to the British Academy, which funded the research on which this paper was based; and to thank Al'bin Konechnyi, St Petersburg, for his help with bibliographical sources.

1 The representation of women as economic victims *passim* is evident, for example, in such an otherwise-balanced collection as Barbara Evans Clements, Barbara Alpern Engel and Christine D. Worobec (eds.), *Russia's Women: Accommodation, Resistance, Transformation* (Berkeley: University of California Press, 1991). My introductory remarks admittedly ignore the existence of a right-wing feminist counter-tradition, from the moral, family- and conscience-centred strictures of, e.g., Stéphanie de Genlis and Jane Austen, to the libertarian polemics of, e.g., Kate Millett or Camille Paglia, which has exerted a particular influence upon the literary and artistic representations produced by women; but there is no doubt that action and reaction within intellectual debate as such, both feminist and anti-feminist, has generally been shaped by the

association of feminism with left-tending collective radicalism, rather than with right-wing individualism.

2 On this see particularly Barbara Heldt, *Terrible Perfection: Women and Russian Literature* (Bloomington: Indiana University Press, 1987), and Catriona Kelly, *A History of Russian Women's Writing, 1820–1992* (Oxford: Clarendon Press, 1994), chap. 1.

3 Another of Kustodiev's paintings of a *kupchikha* shows a less racy lady standing in front of a fanciful view of Nizhnii Novgorod: see *Russian and Soviet Paintings 1900–1930: Selections from the State Tretiakov Gallery, Moscow, and the State Russian Museum, Leningrad* (Washington D.C.: Smithsonian Institution, 1988), p. 133. Kustodiev himself was brought up in the eastern merchant town of Astrakhan'.

4 N. A. Leikin, *Apraktsintsy: stseny i ocherki dopozharnoi epokhi* (St Petersburg, 1864), p. 42. The *Entsiklopedicheskii slovar' Brokgauza i Efrona*, edited by I. Andreevskii (80 vols. and 4 supp. vols., St Petersburg, 1890–1907), describes Leikin as 'a humourist', but commends the hidden seriousness in his portraits of the 'dark kingdom', i.e., merchant life. Many of Leikin's sketches were originally published in the 'boulevard newspaper' *Peterburgskaia gazeta*; on this see Louise McReynolds, *The News under Russia's Old Regime: The Development of a Mass-Circulation Press* (Princeton, N.J.: Princeton University Press, 1991), pp. 64–9; however, I would question McReynolds's view (ibid., p. 69) that Leikin's work was enjoyed by merchants laughing at themselves; I suspect, rather, that he was presenting comforting visions of vulgar 'new money' for other members of the middle ranks, such as minor civil servants, who considered themselves more cultivated, if less wealthy, than the traders of the Apraksin market.

5 Vladimir Mikhnevich, *Peterburg ves' na ladoni*, 2 vols. (St Petersburg, 1874), vol. 1, p. 231.

6 Leikin, *Apraktsintsy*, p. 64. On merchants' home life, see ibid., pp. 91–100, 116–7; on their reading tastes, see also P. I. Bogatyrev, 'Moskovskaia starina', in N. S. Anushkin (ed.), *Ushedshaia Moskva: vospominaniia sovremennikov o Moskve vtoroi poloviny XIX veka* (Moscow, 1964), p. 115.

7 A. Sh—n, *Griaz' i zoloto torgovli* (St Petersburg, 1865), p. 7.

8 Ibid., pp. 36–7; Alfred J. Rieber, *Merchants and Entrepreneurs in Imperial Russia* (Chapel Hill: University of North Carolina Press, 1982), pp. 30–1. For churches founded by merchants, see, e.g., *Ukazatel' Moskovskikh tserkvei*, compiled by M. Aleksandrovskii (Moscow, 1915), no. 3, no. 215. On the disinterested side of merchant philanthropy, see Mark D. Steinberg, *Moral Communities: The Culture of Class Relations in the Russian Printing Industry, 1867–1907* (Berkeley: University of California Press, 1992), pp. 38–62, and also the second part of this essay.

9 The down-trodden merchant wife appears, for example, in Mariia Zhukova's story *The Monk* (1837): see *Vechera na Karpovke* (Moscow, 1986); the harridan in Ostrovskii's *A Family Affair* (*Svoi liudi – sochtemsia*). On the *kupecheskie smotriny*, see particularly Gogol's play *The Marriage*, and Leikin, *Apraktsintsy*, pp. 54–6. Public *smotriny* were held in Moscow at Sokol'niki, and in St Petersburg in the Summer Garden, on May 1.

10 On the contest over civic leadership, see Daniel R. Brower, *The Russian City: From Tradition to Modernity, 1850–1917* (Berkeley: University of California Press, 1990), pp. 98–9.

11 S. A. Smirnova, *Povesti i rasskazy* (St Petersburg, 1896), p. 356; P. D. Boborykin, *Sobranie romanov, povestei i rasskazov v 12 tomakh*, vol. 1 (Moscow, 1896).

12 O. A. Shapir, *Sobranie sochinenii* (St Petersburg, 1910), vol. 4, pp. 335–436; A. P. Chekhov, *Polnoe sobranie sochinenii i pisem v 30 tomakh* (Moscow, 1974–1982), vol. 10,

pp. 75–85. Chekhov's own view of enterprise was, of course, less cut-and-dried than his narrator's: see particularly his handling of the peasant-boy-made-good Lopakhin in *The Cherry Orchard*.

13 On the Slavophiles, see Rieber, *Merchants*, pp. 138–40; see also Petr Buryshkin, *Moskva kupecheskaia* (New York, 1954: reprinted Moscow, 1991), p. 98, which quotes an early twentieth-century article from *Novoe vremia* hymning the virtues of Russian merchants, and especially the 'innumerable spiritual qualities' of their womenfolk.

14 Buryshkin, *Moskva*, p. 113.

15 Recent studies of merchant patrons of the arts include Beverley Whitney Kean, *All the Empty Palaces: The Merchant Patrons of Modern Art in Pre-Revolutionary Russia* (London: Barrie and Jenkins, 1983), and Christina Burrus, *Art Collectors of Russia: The Private Treasures* (New York: Tauris Park Books, 1994). On the state's contradictory attitudes to merchants, see Rieber, *Merchants*, pp. xx–xxi, 3–4; on the religious view of trade, see, e.g., the massively popular medieval text 'The Virgin's Descent into Hell', trans. from the Greek in the twelfth century, in which horrible punishments are visited on usurers and the avaricious. (An accessible edition is N. K. Gudzii, *Khrestomatiia po drevnerusskoi literature* (Moscow, 1973), pp. 92–7.) On the trading prohibitions extended to priests (including Protestant ministers) see *Entsiklopedicheskii slovar' Brokgauza i Efrona*, vol. 16, *Gil'dii*, p. 680.

16 On the legal status of the guilds after 1898, see I. D. Mordukhai-Boltovskii (ed.), *Svod zakonov Rossiiskoi Imperii*, 21 vols. (St Petersburg 1912), vol. 9, *Zakony o sostoianiiakh*, arts. 530–60, and *per index*. The legislation history is summarized in *Entsiklopedicheskii slovar' Brokgauza i Efrona*, vol. 16, *Gil'dii*, pp. 679–80; vol. 33, *Kuptsy*, pp. 57–8; *Novyi entsiklopedicheskii slovar' izdaniia Brokgauza i Efrona*, ed. K. K. Arsen'ev (29 vols., St Petersburg, 1911–19, never completed), vol. 23, *Kuptsy*, cols. 680–2.

17 On the guild biographies, see the sources listed in note 20 below.

18 On shop signs etc., see P. I. Shchukin, 'Iz vospominanii', *Shchukinskii sbornik*, vol. 10 (Moscow, 1912), pp. 141–2; A. Bakhtiarov, *Briukho Peterburga: obshchestvenno-filologicheskie ocherki* (St Petersburg, 1888), pp. 266–74. A superb selection of commercial signs is now on show in the Museum of the History of St Petersburg at the Peter and Paul Fortress. The text quoted comes from a peep-show recorded by Bakhtiarov, *Briukho Peterburga*, p. 315. A fuller study of commercialism in turn-of-the-century Russian culture is S. A. Smith and Catriona Kelly, 'Culture and the Market-place, 1881–1921', in Catriona Kelly and David Shepherd (eds.), *An Introduction to Russian Cultural Studies* (Oxford: Oxford University Press, forthcoming).

19 An interesting indication of mobility in the merchant community even at a relatively early stage is given by A. I. Aksenov, *Genealogiia moskovskogo kupechestva XVIII veka: iz istorii formirovaniia russkoi burzhuazii* (Moscow, 1988), which demonstrates that many important merchant families of the early eighteenth century had moved outside the *kupechestvo* by 1800. On sales techniques in Russian bazaars, see Robert Lyall, *The Character and History of the Russians, and a Detailed History of Moscow* (London, 1823), pp. cxxix–cxxx, 272–96; E. B. Lanin, *Russian Characteristics* (London, 1892), pp. 177–88. On the Moscow industrialists, see, e.g., Rieber, *Merchants*, pp. 285–332; Buryshkin, *Moskva*, passim; Harvey Pitcher, *The Smiths of Moscow* (Cromer: Swallow House Books, 1984), especially pp. 60–70.

20 Pre-1860 publications include *Spisok gg. kuptsov, inostrannykh gostei i birzhevykh maklerov, proizvodivshikh dela na Sankt-Peterburgskoi Birzhe s 1836 na 1837* (St Petersburg, 1837); *Kniga adresov Sanktpeterburgskogo kupechestva i inostrannykh gostei, s*

oboznacheniem roda ikh torgovli . . . (St Petersburg, at intervals, 1844–1880); *Spisok Moskovskim vsekh gil'dii kuptsam* . . . (Moscow, 1828, 1829). The post-1860 series of directory annuals are as follows: 1860–98 (St Petersburg): *Spravochnaia kniga o litsakh Peterburgskogo kupechestva, poluchivshikh na* . . . *god soslovnye svidetel'stva*; (Moscow) *Spravochnaia kniga o litsakh, poluchivshikh na* . . . *god iz Moskovskoi kupecheskoi upravy kupecheskie svidetel'stva*; 1898–1917 (St Petersburg) *Spravochnaia kniga o litsakh, poluchivshikh na* . . . *god kupecheskie i promyslovye svidetel'stva* and (Moscow) *Spravochnaia kniga o litsakh, poluchivshikh na* . . . *god iz Moskovskoi kupecheskoi upravy kupecheskie i promyslovye svidetel'stva*. For the full list of such books, see P. A. Zaionchkovskii (ed.), *Spravochniki po istorii dorevoliutsionnoi Rossii*, second edn. (Moscow, 1978), pp. 495, 525.

21 Despite the similarity in name, the Russian gil'dii had nothing in common with western 'guilds'. They were set up in 1721 as a system of administrative divisions (this later became a system of fiscal divisions), in which privileges (e.g., the right to foreign trade in the first guild, to wholesale trade in the second) were linked to the level of capital (later, of turnover). See Rieber, *Merchants*; Gregory Guroff and Fred V. Carstensen, *Entrepreneurship in Imperial Russia and the Soviet Union* (Princeton, N.J.: Princeton University Press, 1983); A. N. Bokhanov, 'Rossiiskoe kupechestvo v kontse XIX–nachale XX veka', *Istoriia SSSR*, vol. 4 (1985), pp. 106–18; M. L. Gavlin, 'Moskovskii torgovo-promyshlennyi kapital v kontse XIX veka', in *Russkii gorod*, part 4 (Moscow, 1981), pp. 43–65.

22 See, for example, Rieber, *Merchants*, pp. 24–31.

23 The assertions about women's lives that follow are based on the *Kniga adresov* for 1858 and the *Spravochnye knigi* for 1865 and 1915 for St Petersburg, and the *Spravochnye knigi* for 1885, 1910, and 1915 for Moscow. My observations are largely based on guild merchants, though I have included some facts about trading certificate holders for Moscow in 1915, because of the drop in the numbers of genuine merchants observable at this date. (See notes 34, 37; on the declining numbers of Moscow merchants, see Bokhanov, 'Rossiiskoe kupechestvo', p. 112.) In due course, I hope to flesh out the scheme that I have constructed here by using material from such archival sources as divorce-court records and passport petitions. Women traders in modern post-Soviet Russia require separate investigation; they have so far only been the subject of journalistic ephemera. (See, e.g., the article on 'Russian businesswomen' published in *Marie Claire*, June 1994; I owe this reference to Galina Aplin.) [Editor's note: for further information on Russian and Ukrainian businesswomen, see p. 23, note 37, pp. 312–13.]

24 See especially Catriona Kelly, 'Life at the Margins: Women, Culture and Narodnost' in Russia, 1890–1920', in Marianne Liljeström, Eila Mäntysaari and Arja Rosenholm (eds.), *Gender Restructuring in Russian Studies*, Slavica Tamperensia, vol. 2 (Tampere, Finland: University of Tampere Press, 1993), pp. 139–54.

25 The total number of women traders outside the guilds is difficult to calculate, because town-dwellers were in fact forbidden to trade without certificates, and hence were reluctant to declare themselves in censuses. But the ubiquity of street and square markets in both Moscow and Petersburg suggests that their numbers must have run into thousands. One unofficial source (Lyall, *The Character*, pp. 530–1), gives an estimate of 9,000 female street hawkers and traders (as against around 14,000 men) for Moscow in 1805.

26 On women peasant piece-workers, see Minna Gorbunova, 'Zhenskie promysly v Moskovskoi gubernii', in *Sbornik statisticheskikh svedenii po Moskovskoi gubernii*, vol. 7,

p. 4, and Judith Pallot, 'Women's Domestic Industries in Moscow Province, 1880–1900', in Clements, Engel and Worobec (eds.), *Russia's Women*, pp. 163–8.

27 See *Spravochnaia kniga* for 1885: the surnames of the women concerned were Rybakova, Andronova, Baicher, Bobyleva, Brylina, Geikhtman, Goliziter, Moskvich, Nakir'er, Poplavskaia, Sapozhnikova and Tutektal.

28 See *Novyi entsiklopedicheskii slovar' Brokgauza i Efrona*, vol. 17, *Zhenshchiny v torgovle*, cols. 823–4; Mordukhai-Boltovskii, *Svod zakonov*, vol. 9, *Zakony o sostoianiiakh*, arts. 589–96, and *per index*.

29 On the guild officers, see the lists published annually in the *Spravochnye knigi*; on trading customs, see especially Bakhtiarov, *Briukho*, pp. 129–30.

30 Buryshkin, *Moskva*, p. 124, pp. 131–2; a photograph of some of the Morozov women is reproduced in Burrus, *Art Collectors of Russia*, p. 27, plate 20. On Mamontova, see the Moscow *Spravochnaia kniga* for 1915.

31 See Buryshkin's comments on his own sister, who trained as a medical student: *Moskva*, pp. 212, 216. Women writers from the merchant classes included the 1830s poet Nadezhda Teplova, the 1860s writer A. Kobiakova-Studzinskaia (see her 'Vospominaniia', *Russkoe slovo*, no. 7 (1860), pp. 1–17), and the late nineteenth-century journalist and memoirist Anna Volkova (see her *Vospominaniia* (Moscow, 1913)). Information about all these women is available in Marina Ledkovsky, Charlotte Rosenthal and Mary Zirin (eds.), *Dictionary of Russian Women Writers* (Westport, Conn.: Greenwood Press, 1994).

32 One woman who had risen greatly through marriage was Zinaida Grigor'evna, the wife of Savva Timofeevich Morozov, on whom see Buryshkin, *Moskva*, p. 130; Pitcher, *The Smiths of Moscow*, pp. 64–5.

33 I have calculated these figures from *Kniga adresov* (for 1858), and the *Spravochnye knigi* for 1865 and 1915 (St Petersburg) and 1885 and 1915 (Moscow). There were 14 Jewish women in the Moscow 1915 first guild, and 25 in the St Petersburg first guild (i.e., around a half and two thirds respectively of women guild members). On Jewish merchants in general, see Arcadius Kahan in Guroff and Carstensen (eds.), *Entrepreneurship*.

34 The spread of occupations listed here includes the holders of 'trading certificates' in Moscow, who were sometimes more adventurous in their choice of business than the merchants proper.

35 The numbers of non-trading women merchants were, for Petersburg, about 170 in 1858, and 39 in 1915, and for Moscow, 31 in 1885, and 54 in 1915. They seem to have included the owners of apartment blocks as well as those living off income invested in companies: a number are stated to be inhabiting apartments 'in their own houses' (i.e., apartment blocks).

36 On the *masterichki*, see Bogatyrev, 'Moskovskaia starina', p. 137. The official accounts system involved keeping separate books for cash and credit receipts and outgoings, and for goods and materials bought and sold: see Mordukhai-Boltovskii, *Svod zakonov*, vol. 11, *Ustav torgovyi*, articles 669–91.

37 The figures for trading sectors were as follows:

Clothing, accessories, fabrics: St Petersburg, 1858: 55, 1915: 21, Moscow, 1885: 66, Moscow, 1915: 28 [trading certificates: 195].

Food, drink, tobacco, flowers: St Petersburg, 1858: 56, 1915: 11; Moscow, 1885: 69, 1915: 14 [trading certificates: 131].

Hotels, traktirs, bathhouses etc.: St Petersburg, 1858: 25, 1915: 11; Moscow, 1885: 58, 1915: 12 [trading certificates: 99].

Ironmongery, builders' supplies, harness, etc.: St Petersburg, 1858: 35, 1915: 11; Moscow, 1885: 24, 1915: 11 [trading certificates: 54].

Domestic goods: furniture, utensils, etc.: St Petersburg, 1858: 19, 1915: 9; Moscow, 1885: 36, 1915: 6 [trading certificates: 41].

'Manufactured goods', jewellery: St Petersburg, 1858: 3, 1915: 9; Moscow, 1885: 49, 1915: 10 [trading certificates: 68].

The total of women trading in cultural items, drugs and perfumes, monumental masonry or miscellaneous goods, was 60, 37, 54, 10 and [84] over the different years. Factory owners numbered 21, 4, 11, 17 and [33] respectively; financial and contracting services were provided by 14, 11, 31, 3 and [33]; laundries and dye-works occupied -, -, 7, 2 and [18]: a tiny number also provided such services as horse-dealing or knackers' yards, hairdressers and (in 1915, 13 trading certificate holders) electric theatres. As for women's tendency to shed certain businesses, see, e.g., the Moscow merchant E. A. Gal'mina, whose husband ran a flour wholesaling business in 1910, and who is herself listed as keeping a bread shop in 1915; A. Mart'ianova, whose husband had a string of businesses in 1910, had kept on only a restaurant in the city centre and a food-shop at her home; E. Oldenburg had a habadashery (*galantereinaia*) at her home in 1915, and had given up her husband's businesses elsewhere.

38 There were 42 women merchants in the Rogozha district in 1885, and 11 in 1915 [and 41 traders].

39 The figures for the central Moscow shopping areas (Tverskaia, Miasnitskaia and Kitai-gorod) were 113 in 1885, and 35 in 1915. This represents about a quarter of the total population of women merchants in each case. In 1915, the Arbat, Meshchanskaia and Presnenskaia districts had 24 women merchants, or around a sixth of the total population. In Petersburg in 1858, 112 merchants, again about a quarter, inhabited the Moskovskaia and Liteinaia districts. The 1915 directory does not give district numbers, but the street names indicate that the streets to both sides of the middle of the Nevskii were still popular, and that numerous women lived on the Bol'shoi Prospekt, Petersburg Side.

40 Sof'ia Soboleva, 'Dobroe staroe vremia', *Russkoe slovo*, no. 4 (1865) pp. 38–72; no. 5 (1865), pp. 1–40. See also Buryshkin on his own mother, *Moskva*, pp. 207–9.

41 See T. Sapozhnikova, 'Dom Kovriginykh', in *Obshchestvo "Staryi Peterburg" 1921–1923* (St Petersburg, 1923), pp. 47–74. The museum was closed in the 1930s.

42 See Buryshkin, *Moskva*, p. 171.

43 Ibid., pp. 151, 171. These women unfortunately do not appear in such standard biographical guides as the *Russkii biograficheskii slovar'*.

44 On Elizabeth Raffald (1733–81), see Jane Grigson, *English Food* (Harmondsworth: Penguin, 1977), pp. 215–16.

45 Tropinin also painted Mazurina's husband and daughter: the latter's portrait is reproduced in E. Petinova, *Vasilii Andreevich Tropinin* (Leningrad, 1990), plate 93.

46 Shchukin, 'Iz vospominanii', p. 273; cf. Kobiakova's recollections of her fearsome Kostroma grandmother: 'Vospominaniia', pp. 3–4.

47 Not all merchant women did dominate the home: the traditional *Domostroi* stereotype was sometimes evident in real life. See, for example, Buryshkin's account of Petr

Alekseevich Bakhrushin (*Moskva*, p.135), who kept the whole household, including his widowed mother, in terror.

48 Boborykin, *Kitai-gorod*, p. 56. Interesting, too, is Boborykin's reference (p. 55) to Stanitsyna's effortless command of business language. A comparable figure is Gor'kii's Vassa Zheleznova, in the 1936 play of the same title: the earlier version, of 1910, true to its subtitle (*A Mother*), presents the heroine as the lynchpin of a naturalist family drama of disintegration and degeneration, rather than as an entrepreneur first and foremost. (See M. Gor'kii, *Polnoe sobranie sochinenii: khudozhestvennye proizvedeniia v 25 tomakh* (Moscow, 1968–76), vol. 19, pp. 127–70, and vol. 13, pp. 179–235.)

49 As Buryshkin relates (*Moskva*, chap. 2), male members of the Tret'iakov family were married to Mamontovas and Botkinas; other important merchant families connected by marriage included the Prokhorovs (male line) and Khludovs (female line), the Iakunchikovs (male line) and Mamontovs (female line) and the various branches of the Morozov family. On a male merchant who 'married down', see note 32. The Gridina quotation is taken from McReynolds, *News under Russia's Old Regime*, p. 231.

5

Vera Figner and revolutionary autobiographies: the influence of gender on genre

HILDE HOOGENBOOM

Many revolutionaries who were active between the 1860s and the 1880s wrote and published after 1905; a second wave of material, including autobiographies, came out in the 1920s as part of a wider movement to establish a revolutionary history. In 1921 Vera Figner began publishing memoirs about the People's Will and her twenty-two years in prison; in 1926 she selected and edited a collection of forty-four autobiographies by populists for the *Granat Encyclopedia*.[1] These eyewitness accounts of a dwindling group known as *stariki* (the elders) are used as primary sources by historians, and their authors certainly wrote them for that purpose. In addition to providing information about the populist movement, populists also strove to justify why they had become revolutionaries, as is suggested by such titles as: 'Why I Became a Revolutionary' or 'How I Became a Revolutionary'.[2] But they were only able to guess why. Vera Figner, for example, altered interpretations of her early motivations as her circumstances changed. Populists rarely explain this aspect of their lives satisfactorily in terms of the evidence of cause and effect that a historian would find convincing.

At the time of publication, these historical documents were valued as 'unmediated', 'eyewitness' accounts, and the same is true today, although historians might quibble about their accuracy and tendentiousness.[3] But, in fact, populist memoirs were mediated by several factors – time, the teleological nature of hindsight and the process of writing itself – as populist writers themselves were well aware. Vera Figner described this phenomenon: 'I could not find a language right away . . . [T]he historical perspective prevented me from speaking the language of a participant and eyewitness.'[4] She was aided by her own primary source, found in police archives in 1917 – her pretrial testimony written in prison in 1883: 'In this testimony I found precisely that language which would not come to me in 1913–14 for the description of People's Will.'[5] Her admission is striking: she had to work at writing as a participant and eyewitness, which on the surface might seem a most natural activity.

I propose to use literary analysis of autobiographical texts in order to illustrate how populists wrote about becoming revolutionaries as a means of thinking through their lives and giving them a coherent shape or meaning. They made choices about what to include and exclude, and in the process their lives became less random, more purposeful. Populists felt that writing about the experience (as many did, some at great length in a variety of genres, including poetry) was part of the experience. Populist autobiographies as a genre grew out of earlier short activist pieces that began to appear after 1905: the portrait, or short biography in memory of dead friends and comrades, histories and poetry. The Society of Former Political Prisoners and Exiles required short autobiographies from members in 1921; its journal *Prison and Exile* (*Katorga i ssylka*) included the pieces listed above. Collections by *Granat* and the Society followed.[6] The portraits from the early years were also a rehearsal for full-length autobiographies, started at that time, but finished and published in the 1920s.

At a distance of thirty or forty years, revolutionaries tried to justify their ideas and lives, and came up against the problem of time and memory. As writers, they filtered experience through what they read, often each others' memoirs, which focused their memory. Moreover, like other autobiographers, they read the evolution of their path in life back into their childhood and youth. They chose information to fit models that already existed both in life and on paper. Figner thought that fiction had no connection with real life: 'Life in the hands of writers becomes more purposeful and whole, minus many details, than it is.'[7] This could also have been a description of revolutionary autobiography – more purposeful and whole than life. A literary approach will be used to analyse how revolutionaries created their lives on paper, and to examine their presentation of cause and effect on the written page.

How can this essay change the way a historian might use these autobiographies? This chapter will show that the episodes justifying why they became revolution-aries demonstrate a remarkable cohesiveness among themselves and form a genre with conventions. Genre conventions create a relationship of parts to the whole, affording a perspective from which to decide what is typical or unusual in a revolutionary autobiography. Conventions also provide an artistic structure that places demands on both writer and reader in the form of expectations, which must be fulfilled or accounted for in some way. Just as the saints' lives depict stages in the development of religious consciousness, these autobiographies aim to portray the revelation of social consciousness. The episodes that populists recognized as common for the development of social consciousness in their generation reflected their sense of who they were, of what one had to know about them in order to judge their revolutionary activity in the proper light. Their justifications at some level served to defend themselves against accusations of cold-blooded violence and murder, by emphasizing the depth of their convictions and overall moral goodness.

The cohesiveness of these memoirs makes them a good sample to use in studying the effects of gender on self-representation. Why does gender matter in these memoirs, other than the fact that it is there, and how does it change our reading of them? Gender, in addition to time, hindsight and the act of writing, mediated these memoirs, shaping experience and conventions, or representations of experience. Did it matter to Figner and others that they were women? Her feminism, shared by her generation, assumed that, once women showed that they could perform like the best of men, the woman question had been solved in theory.[8] They emphasized that they were worthy of an education and that they were fired by ideological zeal, evidenced by self-sacrifice. Yet their attempts at gender-neutral autobiographies expose the stereotypes they tried to counter, and contain evidence of the circumstances particular to this generation of Russian women.

Childhood and other conventions

Many found the most potent justification for the path they had taken in childhood impressions. In a period when representations of childhood had shifted from the depiction of little adults to a view of childhood as a separate sphere of existence, revolutionaries evoked their pure, instinctive, moral sense of right and wrong. Andrew Wachtel has written about the influence on gentry memoirs of Tolstoi's depiction of childhood, with its emphasis on happiness, a mother's love and closeness to nature. By contrast, unhappy childhoods appear in works by non-gentry or gentry who had revolutionary sympathies.[9] This correlation might suggest that all revolutionaries, gentry and non-gentry, had unhappy childhoods, but some did in fact have happy childhoods complete with nature and loving mothers.[10] Yet, as Wachtel argues, childhood had political connotations. In a possible subgenre of gentry autobiographies, populists emphasized the future potential of the child's moral experience.

Childhood shaped the conventions of the genre of revolutionary auto-biography, which included references to family background, historical events, education, booklists and religion. Revolutionaries used this list of formative influences to organize their perceptions of revolutionary consciousness into conversion scenes, the heart of the genre. Many populists created a formative triad that connected deep feeling, life experience and purposeful reading in order to write about the development of their consciousness of injustice. In addition, their childhoods coincided with Alexander II's Great Reforms, and possessed social and historical, as well as personal, significance.

The writing of populist autobiography existed in at least two historical time-frames: the time when they had been united, and their position at the time of writing in the post-1917 period, when they felt themselves to be in political opposition to the Bolsheviks. Their moral justifications of why they became revolutionaries in the 1870s had new relevance under the Bolsheviks, who tried to co-opt the status of their predecessors to create a revolutionary history, thereby adding legitimacy to the new regime. The split between the two generations of revolutionaries was reflected in the journal *Prison and Exile*, as well as in two letters which populists, led by Figner, sent to the Presidium in 1925 and 1927 protesting against such examples of communist immorality as political prisoners, forced emigration and the death penalty without a trial.[11] Figner understood these differences in terms of the relations between the individual and the organization: the People's Will (the terrorist wing of the populist movement, formed in 1879) had supplanted the individualist revolutionary of the 1860s with a structure that maintained a balance between the individual and the collective; the Socialist Revolutionaries introduced violence for its own sake, while the Bolsheviks erased the individual.[12] By contrast, the populists, with Figner at their head, emphasized in their memoirs the formation of a deeply moral character and solid political convictions, a process that often began in childhood.[13]

Although populists and Bolsheviks were writing their autobiographies for *Granat* at the same time in the mid-1920s, there are striking differences between the two genres in their depiction of early influences that led to the development of political consciousness. In contrast to the populists, who emphasized the growth of their feelings and ideas through early contact with the people and/or books, Bolsheviks depicted rough, even violent childhood scenes with sex, drinking and child labour, to show that they *were* the people – the peasants and urban proletariat. Populists, with only a handful of exceptions, wrote about their development through reading, while the reverse was the case for Bolsheviks: only a handful out of the 245 autobiographies and biographies included their reading. Between these generations the cultural connotations of reading had changed, from self-help, upward mobility and social consciousness to a class marker of gentility, the opposite of the cruel world that Bolsheviks wished to depict.

What do we make of the fact that nine of the thirty male revolutionaries in the *Granat* collection omitted childhood altogether and began with their formal education, while all fourteen women wrote about their childhood?[14] Childhood for revolutionaries who came of age in the 1870s coincided with the Great Reforms, and memories of events such as the emancipation of the serfs in 1861, the Polish rebellion of 1863 and Karakozov's attempt to assassinate Tsar Alexander II in 1866 provided a means of inserting themselves into the course of history. They were eyewitnesses of the injustices of the old system. Women more often had personal experience of injustice within their family as they were growing up. The patriarchal family was seen as symbolic of the tsarist regime, so this injustice had not only personal, but also social, political and historical relevance. Liberal thinking compared the oppression of women to that of serfs, so women's childhood and family were regarded as playing a role in the development of their revolutionary consciousness of injustice and oppression. Some male populists treated this theme too, developing it through a mother or sister, to show their early awareness of injustice.[15]

In addition to differences based on gender, this chapter will suggest that some men, like women, felt themselves to be in a disadvantaged position; such men used similar strategies of justification to women. Lower-class men, like most women, wrote about both their childhood and education in order to show that they deserved an education. Since a formal education was not a given for them, their desire for an education was radical in itself. Moreover, the difficulties they encountered in acquiring an education had the potential to radicalize them. Women likewise tried to show why they were worthy of an education, using as evidence their early love of reading and learning as children. The greater the difficulties, the more evidence they gave. Lower-class men, like women, associated their early reading with their mothers.[16] Self-education, widely practised and *de rigueur* for this generation, revealed that class hindered men, while both gender and class were obstacles for women.

Vera Figner's influence

Vera Figner's influence on populist autobiographies was both direct and indirect, a combination of her ideas and activities as leader and writer. As editor of *Granat*, figurehead for the populists and an extensively published memoirist over nearly thirty years, what did Figner look for in a revolutionary autobiography? Literary evidence includes not only what populists wrote about their own lives, but how they wrote about other revolutionaries and their writings, which together exposed conceptions about how ideally one should become a revolutionary. She gave her most complete reading of the genre, which, like many others, could be subtitled, 'Why I Became a Revolutionary', in an essay on Lev Tikhomirov's pamphlet, 'Why I Ceased To Be a Revolutionary'. While Tikhomirov (1852–1923) might not have been a significant figure – a propagandist, he became a member of the executive committee of People's Will in 1879 and emigrated to Europe in 1883 – the treachery he represented still upset former comrades and reverberated in their minds thirty years later.[17] Tikhomirov warned Russian youth away from radical books and ideas, which had corrupted him as a youth because he had been unable to think critically, and had no experience with which to compare what he read in books. Not only was his youth to blame, but radicalism itself demanded passive minds: it 'castrated his mental capacity'.[18] Tikhomirov converted to Russian Orthodoxy and supported the autocracy.

By contrast, Figner found an answer to Tikhomirov's decision in what she knew about his childhood and family, as well as what his autobiography revealed about his character. She connected a conservative, religious background with his return to Russian Orthodoxy and autocracy; he did not. Tikhomirov blamed an education in the world of ideas before he could think critically. She agreed that he could not think, but found the reason in his character rather than his youth: 'Nothing is said in his notes about family relations and the circumstances of his upbringing: no mention is made of a single incident that would mark some kind of stage in his spiritual life, nor of a single "lesson of life" as a child which would have a moral influence on him.'[19] He lacked a stable moral reference point in his upbringing, and, more importantly, did not even think in those terms – he did not perceive, or look for, a moral vacuum.

To Figner, critical thinking was a product of childhood influences that prepared heart and mind for later reading. 'Essentially, he had neither a childhood with clear memories and sharp incidents which put their stamp on his whole life, nor an adolescence or youth with mistakes and passions, when he was in conflict with himself and his surroundings – that inner life which enables a personality to develop.'[20] In Figner's analysis, Tikhomirov failed to remain a revolutionary because he never truly became one, except as an accident of history. Figner did not regard herself as a profound psychologist, but she, like other revolutionaries, had to be a careful judge of human nature, because in the business of revolution one was forced to trust others with one's life. An unstable personality was therefore dangerous to everyone. Not surprisingly, she did not take Tikhomirov's conversion seriously either, because his nature, in her opinion, was that of a *poseur*, as evidenced by his lack of a firm moral foundation in childhood.

P. Granat, however, did not share the faith Figner put in the formative influence of childhood, and the differences between them illustrate a larger pattern of disagreement which has been indicated above. Like Tikhomirov, Granat was interested in exposure to ideas, while Figner saw childhood as the beginning of the road to consciousness, because it brought together early emotional and moral experience. Granat outlined the project in the general terms of populism's ideology and class: 'the evolution of ideas and the shift in the social strata feeding the revolutionary ranks'.[21] In correspondence with Figner over populist auto-biographies, he discounted the formative influence of childhood as irrelevant to populism and not historically representative, and cut this material.[22]

Figner, on the other hand, elided the reasons for becoming a revolutionary with moral development in childhood. When inviting potential contributors to his collection, Granat mentioned Figner's participation as bait, and made her contact some populists.[23] They knew they were writing for her, which in part accounted for their decision to include long sections on their childhood, similar to those in her own memoirs published a few years previously. Nikolai Morozov dedicated the first volume of his full-length memoirs to Figner.[24] We can see her influence in the published *Granat* autobiographies: some contain extensive descriptions of childhood, although nine entries have none at all. The correspondence between Figner and Granat reveals an undercurrent of polite disagreement. He limited her control by suggesting she should footnote differences of opinion with the memoirs under her name, rather than making editorial corrections.[25] However, Granat granted her some control when he offered her the manuscripts with proofs, and in one case asked her to review extensive cuts in A. I. Kornilova-Moroz's entry, which in published form remained the longest, containing an extensive description of childhood and adolescence.[26] Figner's editorial views evidently prevailed.

The soft revolutionary

The foundation of future social consciousness in many memoirs was a childhood memory of an event or something read that produced emotion, perceived as evidence of innate, moral knowledge. In her analysis of Tikhomirov's auto-biography, Figner had in mind a particular childhood 'lesson of life' that she summed up in a poem 'To My Sister' (*Sestre*, first published as 'To a Child' [*Rebenku*, 1906]).[27] Her depiction of an ideal childhood moment early on in the publication of revolutionary memoir material reverberated in other populist memoirs. In the process, she unwittingly showed that the display of emotion, not in and of itself either masculine or feminine, had different implications for male and female populists: the latter had to balance emotion with their wish to be taken seriously.

In Figner's poem, reading and feeling produce a memory, the affective triad at the heart of a number of representations of childhood. She also emphasized her sister's intelligence and literacy; her emotion is serious, induced and even controlled by tendentious, not lightweight, literature. A little girl with an inquisitive mind and a big heart is happy to play and be outside in nature. But she also wants to be clever, so she reads and learns to write. She listens to a story about a child who dies of poverty and the narrator carefully observes her reaction: 'And I hear, with a child's grief,/How you began to sob.' Her metaphor for knowledge is tears; evidence of moral knowledge is depth of emotion. While empathy and tears might appear culturally more appropriate for a girl, to whom Figner addressed the poem, they also played key roles in male childhoods. Indeed, Figner looked for just such a scene in Tikhomirov's childhood, an indication that she saw it as fitting for both boys and girls.

Men shared her view, but did not depict themselves weeping or emphasize their intelligence and literacy in the same breath as their emotional responsiveness. Lev Deich began his memoir with an equally ideal scene, very much like Figner's poem, containing a story, tears and empathy for the oppressed. But the roles are reversed: his nanny shed the tears and he, like Figner, observed her, in effect distancing himself from the emotions. Deich, who was born in 1855, depicted a scene on the swings with his little sister, under the care of their nanny. As the bells began to ring, their nanny explained the occasion: the proclamation of the emancipation of the serfs. This dramatic opening echoes the beginning of *My Past and Thoughts*, which describes Herzen's nanny carrying him out of burning Moscow in 1812. Deich saw the significance of this episode as emotional and historical, rather than intellectual: 'although at the time we could understand very little. But possibly, her story, in conjunction with her tears and the whole situation . . . was the first thrust toward the development in my character of sympathetic responsiveness and the yearning to ease the heavy burden of the oppressed and persecuted.'[28] Despite the fact that the tears were not his, Deich attributed to himself the same emotional response as Figner's girl.

Populists later saw themselves as a generation that had practised emotional self-restraint and generally selfless behaviour, a view that women found more comfortable than men, in part because emotions and selflessness were identified with their sex. For example, Nikolai Morozov regretted that he had held his emotional nature in check when young. But he identified his feelings with the grand romantic ideas that motivated his generation, not with his sex. In contrast, Figner continued to think that one should repress egotistical impulses for the greater good, despite the realization that this had gone out of moral fashion.[29] What she saw as true for herself and her generation in fact had particular relevance for women. Sof'ia Perovskaia, famous for her restraint and selflessness, was portrayed by E. N. Olovennikova as a hard-core revolutionary who nevertheless possessed

feminine softness (*Granat*, p. 323), an indication that despite the positive connotation of restraint, a lack of emotion amounted to an absence of femininity.
Emotions implied excess, and these autobiographies favoured an ascetic, ostensibly
gender-neutral life.

Saints' lives, the obvious literary model for the exemplary, ascetic life in
opposition, were used by women rather than men, although the saints were mostly
men. For example, N. A. Golovina reveals that she read saints' lives as a child,
adding that she herself later had a chance to suffer for the truth (*Granat*, p. 72). In
particular, populist women depicted their childhood as a serious time spent in
isolation, when they did not play with other children, in an attempt to limit their
association with society and its implications of feminine excess. By contrast, men
did not need to dissociate themselves from their gender in order to be taken
seriously. Girls showed how they differed from other girls when they read instead
of playing, dancing or enjoying clothes. Figner stated: 'I did not like playing with
dolls, and imperceptibly learned to read and write . . . '[30] A. P. Pribyleva-Korba
considered her rejection of music lessons to be the first exercise of her will. Like
Figner, she refers in the next sentence to her reading, in this case a suitcase of
tendentious literature brought home by her brother (*Granat*, p. 366). A. I.
Kornilova-Moroz compared herself to Perovskaia, whose asceticism made her a
positive role model: 'First and foremost, we both grew up in an isolated, simple
family situation, were never attracted by clothes, did not go out in the evenings or
go visiting, and did not like dances even as children' (*Granat*, p. 207). One man
showed his seriousness by distancing himself from his sister because she did care for
these things. N. K. Bukh created a key childhood scene from his sister's wedding
to a playboy in the provinces: he was disgusted by the contrast between her
society pretensions, learned in Moscow, and the poor peasants who came to wish
them well in exchange for a little food (*Granat*, p. 42).

These women rejected the female attributes of their class and adopted male
models, but the significance of adopting male models lay precisely in their
rejection of feminine (not necessarily female) models. Kornilova-Moroz described
the influence on women populists of Chernyshevskii's *What Is To Be Done?* and of
his elusive, ascetic revolutionary Rakhmetov, rather than of his heroine Vera
Pavlovna: 'As a personality, Vera Pavlovna was not interesting to young people, but
her activity found many female followers. Rakhmetov's rigorous behaviour made
a strong impression, and his influence was very noticeable in the best representatives of our generation' (*Granat*, p. 207). In contrast to women ascetics, who
rejected the excesses associated with their class and gender, men rejected only the
comforts of class; their asceticism made them more masculine. A. K. Kuznetsov
described how Nechaev's brand of asceticism won him followers: he slept on the
floor and ate only bread and milk. His toughness impressed his wealthier followers
(*Granat*, p. 228).

In addition to saints' lives, Russian women took the Decembrists and their
wives as models of exemplary, ascetic opposition. Perovskaia's situation possessed
the added drama of her father's position as governor of St Petersburg; her rejection

of rank and privilege recalled their earlier sacrifices. In her article on the Decembrist wives, Figner used the religious significance of the reversal of social hierarchy
embodied in Jesus's 'Sermon on the Mount', with its tenet that the last shall be first,
and in the process created on paper a model of the female revolutionary.[31] Women
at the pinnacle of Russian society became lower than the lowest woman: they gave
up titles, inheritance and other privileges, children and the right to return to
Russia, which wives of ordinary prisoners had. Once in Siberia, they lived in
poverty, at times without food or adequate clothing, which they gave to the men,
and did menial household tasks, not very successfully. When the men were moved
to the Petrovsk prison, the women asked to live with them. Figner read her own
experience into their lives: 'They demonstrated a strong will and a daring deter-
mination to move unswervingly to their projected goal, with indefatigable energy
and active love.'[32] In fact, she turned the Decembrists' wives into imprisoned
revolutionaries, as when she noted that these women had been caught completely
unprepared, unlike later women revolutionaries.

By contrast, men associated sacrifice with loss of a career. For Lev Deich, a
consistent revolutionary was expected to sacrifice everything, leaving school and
career: 'As is well known, it was even considered reprehensible to graduate from
school, because that gave one the possibility of taking a "privileged position". A
true revolutionary had to burn his bridges behind him and after some preparation
"go to the people".'[33] Deich hints with light irony that he played his role. Nikolai
Morozov used heavier irony to describe his sleepless week spent deciding between
revolution or science, friends or career (*Granat*, p. 307). Abandoning science was
his main concern, although he worried about his parents' reaction. He compared
the appeal of danger to 'the spirit of Fenimore Cooper'.[34] He imagined himself
returning from prison after being given up for dead and showing the wound in
his hands and feet, in a dramatic, heroic, Christ-like image that was the male
equivalent of female self-sacrifice. Many men continued their careers during and
after prison, suggesting that their self-sacrifice was a youthful phase (as they themselves thought it was, to judge by the irony above), not integral to their identity as
men.

Childhood in history

Revolutionaries whose childhood coincided with the Great Reforms inserted
historical events into their childhoods, making them at once historical and personal.
Twelve out of the forty-four autobiographies refer to the emancipation of the
serfs in 1861; some also noted their reaction to the Polish rebellion of 1863 and
Karakozov's attempt on Alexander II's life in 1866. The emancipation, which
represented an attempt by the system to reform itself, opened the door to doubt
and inspired children to sense that the system was wrong.

These events not only gave populists a historical connection with their cause,
but also a physical and emotional relationship with poor and oppressed people. For
example, in 1861, A. F. Mikhailov saw soldiers marching by to put down a

peasant revolt (*Granat*, 251). A. V. Pribylev recounted two memories that he felt had future consequences: he saw a woman and man driven past his house in a cart for a public beating; and in 1863 he witnessed daily marches of Polish prisoners at noon, because the town lay *en route* to Siberia (*Granat*, pp. 349–50). A. A. Filippov remembered factory explosions in 1861 and 1862 (*Granat*, p. 481). In 1861, N. F. Tsvilenev remembered feeling sorry for house serfs without land skills (*Granat*, p. 514). V. I. Chuiko remembered women crying in 1863 as Polish prisoners in irons were led past in carts (*Granat*, p. 604). G. F. Cherniavskaia-Bokhanovskaia lived near a prison for Poles, and remembered them being sentenced to hard labour in public (*Granat*, p. 579). E. N. Koval'skaia (*Granat*, p. 491), O. K. Bulanova-Trubnikova (*Granat*, p. 30) and L. G. Deich had Polish teachers.[35] Moments that unite memory and feeling in childhood dot these autobiographies, though none are as fully developed as the fictional scenes in Figner's 'To My Sister' or Deich's autobiography.

Some women who responded to 1861 saw the source of their experience of injustice as personal, within their family. E. N. Koval'skaia, an illegitimate serf on her father's estate, celebrated the emancipation because she could no longer be sold – although in theory, for her father had freed her and her mother long before (*Granat*, p. 191). Figner and O. K. Bulanova-Trubnikova claimed that after 1861 their fathers, who were not serf owners, changed from autocrats into better fathers and husbands. Figner wrote: 'a deep moral revolution took place in father: a landlord advocating serfdom, which he was in relation to the servants, to mother and to us, became a liberal; an uncontrollable man became restrained'.[36] As children, both women had found solace with their nannies before their fathers reformed, as if to emphasize the coldness of family life under a despotic parent. Some men also had despotic fathers, but they described the effect on their mothers, not on themselves, unlike Figner and Bulanova-Trubnikova, who noted the effect of their fathers on both their mothers and themselves. N. K. Bukh's mother, an uneducated, religious woman, was very afraid of his father (*Granat*, p. 43). N. F. Tsvilenev's mother claimed to have restrained her husband, who had tyrannized serfs and servants (*Granat*, p. 514). This is not to say that these despotic fathers had no effect on their sons, but these populists made a connection between despotism and oppression which was gendered.

In some autobiographies, the connections between memory and feeling are so vague as to suggest that these moments have been inserted because they should be there, as a matter of form rather than a real reason, an indication of genre conventions at work. O. V. Aptekman read something about serfdom, which jogged his memory, and he recalled a childhood scene that he had forgotten. He connected the beating a soldier gave his father with serfdom, concluding that the attack made him sensitive to oppression in general. In other words, any memory of serfdom was as important as the feeling it was supposed to evoke: sympathy and the hatred of oppression. A more obvious use of memory as a structuring convention without any real meaning occurs in V. K. Debogorii-Mokrievich's autobiography. Born in 1848, he claimed to have had his first memory at the age of six, and to have become conscious at nine, but oddly, did not say what he remembered or of what he became conscious. The facts of a first memory and consciousness were important enough in the genre for them to be included, even though they contained no relevant material. The only early (but no longer childhood) memory he shared was of 1861: 'I retained intact a vivid impression from that time of the unusual unanimity that reigned among peasants' (*Granat*, p. 87). His observation is not vivid – nothing happened to the peasants or to him – but he included it for formal reasons, because populists felt a need to establish a physical as well as emotional connection with the peasants, and emphasized any actual contact with them in their childhood.

The bookish revolutionary

Literature, together with feeling and memory, formed the third leg of the affective triad that Figner described in 'To My Sister'. Revolutionaries read widely, if uniformly, to judge by their booklists, another convention of the genre: Pisarev, Dobroliubov, Chernyshevskii, science, philosophy, economics, statistics, history and fiction. They equated ideas with physically obtaining the books, which changed the worldview of some, while confirming that of others. Radicals consistently thought of their conversion to revolutionary consciousness in terms of books. Only three autobiographies omitted the booklist. O. K. Bulanova-Trubnikova was a blue-blooded revolutionary: her mother was the daughter of the Decembrist V. P. Ivashev, and her nanny had accompanied Ivashev's wife, Camilla Le Dantu, to Siberia. She neither had to acquire, nor display the necessary knowledge; moreover, she was rich and could afford whatever education she chose. V. K. Debogorii-Mokrievich overwhelmingly believed in experience of life as opposed to reading about it, and the absence of the booklist was a matter of principle. S. F. Kovalik, born in 1846, left school before reading circles came into fashion. Only four booklists appear in autobiographies by Bolsheviks, but they contain the same books as those cited by the populists, which gives them an anachronistic flavour, and further shows the heavy use of booklists to be a generational marker.[37]

The separation of reading into fiction and non-fiction was a standard way of dividing their lives before and after conversion. M. M. Chernavskii grew up a conservative, until he read Pisarev. An extreme example, he literally saw in reading a process of self-definition, the glue that held him together as he constructed a new worldview (*Granat*, pp. 564–8). Nikolai Morozov experienced no change: 'When I first read Pisarev and Dobroliubov, it seemed to me that they merely expressed my own thoughts.'[38] He also claimed that Fenimore Cooper fired his imagination and made danger appealing when he went 'to the people'.[39] By contrast, Figner converted during discussions with Sof'ia Bardina about Marx,[40] not unlike G. F. Cherniavskaia-Bokhanovskaia: 'These readings completed what had been begun by the historical situation and impressions of early childhood, by the echoes of the Polish rebellion, the civic motifs of Nekrasov. My personality had been formed. Lavrov's *Historical Letters, Das Kapital* and progressive Russian literature met prepared ground' (*Granat*, pp. 582–3). The stages in the development of her social consciousness echo Figner's ideas.

A comparison of two autobiographies, by a brother and sister, shows how gender affected writing about similar childhoods and education. Mikhail Moreinis and Fanni Moreinis-Muratova, from a wealthy orthodox Jewish family opposed to formal education, prepared in secret for the gymnasium, and were radicalized by their tutor. Fanni detailed her childhood isolation, broken when someone first gave her books; booklists and the structure of her course of study followed. Mikhail, however, omitted why or how he went about getting his education and what he learned – apparently he assumed that it was his right as a male, a right granted by society, denied by his parents. Fanni wrote that she had followed the example of an aunt (not her brother or tutor) who had left her family to study medicine; she showed that she deserved an education, and how she got it. Their father refused to let them leave the house when he discovered their studies. Fanni then left home, which was an agonizing decision because her mother had died and her father was going blind; her brother also left, but we know this from her memoir, not his.

Evidence of Fanni's seriousness, like that of the women mentioned above who emphasized their reading when rejecting feminine pursuits, was the extent of her reading; and some women went into extraordinary detail. E. N. Koval´skaia, a former serf, even quoted the poems she learned as evidence of her education (*Granat*, p. 190). A. P. Pribyleva-Korba secretly read German literature in the original, and like Figner, stressed that she never read bad literature (*Granat*, p. 367).[41] N. A. Golovina contrasted her early reading, directed by her father, a man of the 1840s, with her poor education in a girls' gymnasium (*Granat*, pp. 72–3). When men complained, it was about what they learned (especially classical languages), not about whether they learned at all.

Men who took education for granted (not all did) did not write about their childhoods, but focused on the next step, the access that educational institutions gave them to people and books. A. A. Filippov was inspired by a teacher who made history come alive: 'perhaps completely unconsciously, love for the people and hatred for enslavers was born in my soul' (*Granat*, p. 481). But men who struggled for their education went into more detail about it, like women. M. F. Frolenko was an exception among men: poor, without expectations, he missed opportunities, assuming he did not have them. But even his hotchpotch education, average marks and poverty accidentally landed him in the Petrovsk Academy, where he ran the illegal library. V. I. Chuiko was poor too, but managed to get a gymnasium education where the literature teacher had great influence on him and gave him access to all progressive literature (*Granat*, p. 606). Children of serfs, such as S. P. Bogdanov and Nikolai Morozov, stressed early reading and formal education (*Granat*, pp. 26–7, 305). These men faced obstacles of class rather than gender; the need and desire for self-education began early, in childhood, and like women, they wrote about it.

Conclusion

Literary conventions in revolutionary autobiographies are ways in which the writer chose to describe why she or he became a revolutionary. They do not explain what the writers themselves frequently failed to understand, what led to consciousness – the problem Richard Stites puts at the centre of his work on Russian women.[42] Consciousness happened in stages, suddenly or imperceptibly, but a representation of its development through conversion scenes is not an explanation.

Despite attempts to break down her revolutionary development into stages, Figner still did not understand why she and her sisters became revolutionaries while her two brothers had conventional careers.[43] She initially saw her actions as reactions to current events, depicting her personality in action.[44] Figner subsequently recounted an argument which she had had in prison with Novorusskii about the main influence on revolutionaries in the 1870s: she thought it was literature (in a broad sense), while he argued that 1861 had caused a complete change in economic relations.[45] She subsequently readjusted this picture to include her family, deciding now that heredity was the key to a person's character.[46] After prison she worked with the Socialist Revolutionaries, but felt the difference a generation made, realizing that her ethics of self-sacrifice were of another era.[47] The Bolshevik Revolution forced her to think about the role of the individual activist and revolutionary organizations in history.[48] Finally, she received a letter from F. I. Sedenko-Vitiazev (1933), for whose release from exile she had interceded, who argued that her experience was now irrelevant, a historical exception, because people were suffering for nothing.[49]

Her autobiographies show a pattern of continuous reinterpretation; super-imposed on each other, they form a palimpsest of stories and histories, not unlike the genre taken together as a whole. The populists' lives overlapped; they built up an oral history and wrote for each other. These autobiographies give a sense of the incredible speed with which their lives changed. Many kept silent about the ostensible conclusion of their life's work, a successful revolution. This essay has concentrated on the beginning of their lives, but that was precisely the period which for them, over time, came to define who they were.

Notes

This chapter has benefited from comments on earlier versions by Robert Belknap, Barbara Alpern Engel, Robert Maguire and Richard Stites. Research for this article was supported in part by a grant from the International Research and Exchanges Board (IREX), with funds provided by the National Endowment for the Humanities, the United States Information Agency and the US Department of State, which administers the Russian, Eurasian and East European Research Program (Title VIII). In addition, the Harriman Institute at Columbia University supported archival research in 1992–4.

1 V. N. Figner (ed.), *Avtobiografii revoliutsionnykh deiatelei russkogo sotsialisticheskogo dvizheniia 70–80kh godov, Entsiklopedicheskii slovar'* Granat, vol. 40 (Moscow, 1927). Further references will be in the text as *Granat*. It and the companion three-part volume, *Deiateli Soiuza Sovetskikh Sotsialisticheskikh Respublik i Oktiabr'skoi revoliutsii (Avtobiografii i biografii), Entsiklopedicheskii slovar'* Granat, vol. 41 (Moscow 1927–9), were kept in special restricted collections of Soviet libraries and republished in a single volume, *Deiateli SSSR i revoliutsionnogo dvizheniia Rossii: Entsiklopedicheskii slovar'* Granat (Moscow, 1989). For a history of the enterprise of the Granat encyclopedia, see S. V. Belov, 'O brat'iakh Granat i ikh entsiklopedicheskom slovare', in *Deiateli SSSR i revoliutsionnogo dvizheniia Rossii: Entsiklopedicheskii slovar'* Granat (Moscow, 1989), pp. 799–801. Aleksandr (1861–1933) and Ignatii (1863–1941) Naumovich Granat were the publishers; P. Granat (who is not mentioned by Belov) was probably the editor. The Granat brothers were liberals; Aleksandr took part in revolutionary activities as a student, and Ignatii was formerly a history professor.
2 L. G. Deich, *Pochemu ia stal revoliutsionerom* (St Petersburg, 1921), and Nikolai Morozov, *Kak ia stal revoliutsionerom: povesti moei zhizni*, vol. 1 (Moscow, 1928).
3 See, for example, such comments as: 'They are human documents, valuable for their unmediated observations and experiences': '1917–1921 gg. Ot redaktsii', *Katorga i ssylka*, vol. 1 (1921), p. 6. The foreword to the 1989 reprint of *Granat* calls them 'living proof from living participants in events', while admitting that it is necessary to take into account the time when they were written (p. 5).
4 Vera Figner, *Zapechatlennyi trud, vospominaniia v dvukh tomakh* (Moscow, 1964), vol. 1, p. 42.
5 Ibid., p. 44.
6 *Deiateli revoliutsionnogo dvizheniia v Rossii: Bio-bibliograficheskii slovar' ot predshestvennikov dekabria do padeniia tsarizma* (Moscow, 1927–35).
7 Vera Figner, 'Mat'', *Polnoe sobranie sochinenii v semi tomakh* (hereafter PSS), vol. 5 (Moscow, 1932), p. 27.
8 Figner, 'Studencheskie gody', PSS, vol. 5 (Moscow, 1932), p. 82.
9 Andrew Baruch Wachtel, *The Battle for Childhood: Creation of a Russian Myth* (Stanford, Calif.: Stanford University Press, 1990), pp. 92–4.
10 For happy childhoods in nature, see M. I. Drei (*Granat*, p. 126), N. A. Charushin (*Granat*, p. 540) and N. M. Salova (*Granat*, p. 393). For loving, influential mothers, see E. M. Sidorenko (*Granat*, p. 414), V. I. Sukhomlin (*Granat*, pp. 423–4), M. I. Drei (*Granat*, pp. 126–7), M. F. Frolenko (*Granat*, p. 498), O. K. Bulanova-Trubnikova (*Granat*, p. 29), N. M. Salova (*Granat*, p. 394), V. I. Chuiko (*Granat*, p. 604) and G. N. Dobruskina (*Granat*, p.120).
11 RGALI (Russian State Archives of Literature and Art), fond 1185, opis' 3, delo 1, listy 3–6. Figner's first letter, dated 15 April 1926, got a response from the Presidium dated 7 May 1926; the second letter in response to the Central Executive Committee's manifesto dated 16 October 1927. These documents were recently published: Ia. V. Leont'ev and K. S. Iur'ev, 'Nezapechatlennyi trud: iz arkhiva V. N. Figner', *Zven'ia: Istoricheskii al'manakh*, no. 2 (Moscow and St Petersburg: Feniks Atheneum, 1992), pp. 424–88.
12 Vera Figner, PSS, vol. 5 (Moscow, 1932), p. 131. N. A. Morozov called the People's Will executive committee 'dictatorial', a description Figner denied in a footnote (*Granat*, p. 312).
13 RGALI, f. 1185, op. 3, d. 1, listy 3–6. The journal *Katorga i ssylka* (1921–35) belonged

to the Society of Former Political Prisoners and Exiles, initially founded by Figner in 1917 as the Committee to Help Freed Convicts and Exiles. In 1921 the Bolsheviks took over the committee and started the journal; Figner and some 40 per cent of the older revolutionaries refused to join: see Margaret Maxwell, *Narodniki Women* (New York: Athene-Pergamon Press, 1990), p. 293. At its sixth anniversary meeting, the Society chastised the populists for not supporting the 'present regime': 'Iz deiatel'nosti Obshchestva b. polikatorzhan i ss. poselentsev', *Katorga i ssylka*, vol. 6 (1923), pp. 325–6.

14 The men who omitted childhood were Ashenbrenner, Bakh, Feokhari, Kovalik, Kuznetsov, Mainov, Moreinis, Sidorenko, and Sukhomlin.

15 Mikhail Frolenko attributed his 'more conscious relationship to his surroundings and his memory of things seen' to family circumstances. His mother's parents had married her off for 50 roubles, but at 18 she demanded that her parents take her back because of ill-treatment; with two children, she married a second time for financial support. Both husbands were alcoholics.

16 Nikolai Morozov's father educated his mother, a former serf, and encouraged her to read his library of 300 books; she in turn educated her son (*Granat*, p. 305). Vasilii Sukhomlin's father also directed his mother's reading. Vladimir Chuiko's mother taught him to read and write; later she opened a boarding house for gymnasium students and he read their latest books (*Granat*, pp. 604–5). Women were also taught by their mothers: Vera Figner (*Granat*, p. 459), G. N. Dobruskina (*Granat*, p. 119), and Anna Pribyleva-Korba, who found in a neighbour a mother-substitute who also provided her with a library (*Granat*, p. 367).

17 Populists used this title, in reaction to Lev Tikhomirov, *Pochemu ia perestal byt' revoliutsionerom* (Moscow, 1895), for longer autobiographies: L. G. Deich, *Pochemu ia stal revoliutsionerom* (St Petersburg, 1921), and Nikolai Morozov, *Kak ia stal revoliutsionerom: povesti moei zhizni*, vol. 1 (Moscow, 1928). Tikhomirov, arrested in 1873, was part of the trial of 193 (1877–8), which freed him; he became an editor for *Land and Will* in 1878.

18 Tikhomirov, *Pochemu*, p. 23.

19 Vera Figner, 'Lev Tikhomirov', in *PSS*, vol. 5 (Moscow, 1932), p. 285.

20 Ibid, p. 287.

21 RGALI, f. 1642, op. 1, d. 84, list 1: letter from Granat to I. I. Popov, dated 17 November 1925.

22 RGALI, f. 1185, op. 1, d. 47, list 7: letter dated 10 April 1926.

23 RGALI, f. 1642, op. 1, d. 84, list 1: letter from Granat to I. I. Popov dated 17 November 1925. RGALI, f. 1185, op. 1, d. 47, list 3: letter from Granat to Figner dated 30 January 1926.

24 Morozov, *Kak ia stal revoliutsionerom*.

25 RGALI, f. 1185, op. 1, no. 47, list 5: letter from Granat to Figner dated 23 March 1926.

26 RGALI, f. 1185, op. 1, d. 47, list 7 and 8: letters dated 10 April 1926 and 12 May 1926.

27 Vera Figner, 'Sestre', *Stikhotvoreniia*, *PSS*, vol. 4, pp. 256–7; Figner, *Stikhotvoreniia* (St Petersburg, 1906), pp. 26–7.

28 Deich, *Pochemu ia stal revoliutsionerom*, p. 4.

29 Vera Figner, *Posle Shlissel'burga*, *PSS*, vol. 3, pp. 191, 194.

30 Figner, *Zapechatlennyi trud*, *PSS*, vol. 1, p. 31.

31 Figner, 'Zheny dekabristov', *PSS*, vol. 5, pp. 369–83.

32 Ibid., p. 383.

33 Deich, *Pochemu ia stal revoliutsionerom*, pp. 41–4.

34 Morozov, *Kak ia stal revoliutsionerom*, pp. 52–6.

35 Deich, *Pochemu ia stal revoliutsionerom*, p. 4.

36 Vera Figner, *Zapechatlennyi trud*, *PSS*, vol. 1, p. 24.

37 V. L. Kopp, *Granat*, vol. 41, pp. 211–12; P. A. Krasikov, *Granat*, vol. 41, pp. 218–19.

38 Morozov, *Kak ia stal revoliutsionerom*, p. 30.

39 Ibid., p. 55.

40 Figner, 'Studencheskie gody', *PSS*, vol. 4, pp. 80–2.

41 Figner, 'Mat'', *PSS*, vol. 5, p. 26.

42 Richard Stites, *The Women's Liberation Movement in Russia: Feminism, Nihilism and Bolshevism, 1860–1930* (Princeton, N.J.: Princeton University Press, 1978), pp. 3, 151.

43 See Figner, 'Mat'', pp. 30–1.

44 Figner, 'Predislovie', *Zapechatlennyi trud*, part 1: *Kogda chasy zhizni ostanovilis'*, *PSS*, vol. 2.

45 Figner, ibid., p.187.

46 Figner, 'Rodoslovnaia', *PSS*, vol. 5, p. 13; written in 1910–14.

47 Figner, *Posle Schlissel'burga*, *PSS*, vol. 3, p. 194.

48 Figner, 'Vtoraia vstrecha s Lesgaftom', *Zapechatlennyi trud*, part 1 (Moscow: Zadruga, 1921), pp. 329–32.

49 Ia. V. Leont'ev and K. S. Iur'ev, 'Nezapechatlennyi trud: iz arkhiva V. N. Figner', *Zven'ia: istoricheskii al'manakh*, no. 2 (Moscow and St Petersburg: Feniks Atheneum, 1992), p. 452; citation from RGALI, f. 1185, op. 3, d. 21, listy 12–18 ob.

6

Equality and difference in women's history: where does Russia fit in?

LINDA EDMONDSON

The history of women's emancipation and the nature and significance of feminism have been disputed territory from the very beginnings of organized women's movements in the middle of the nineteenth century. Conflict has focused on a number of fundamental issues, such as whether the solidarity of women is possible or desirable across class, ethnic and religious boundaries, or whether women's emancipation can be achieved without a full-scale social revolution. Disagreements have also arisen over a host of smaller, strategic issues: for instance, in the early decades, whether the campaign for female education should concentrate on access to university or on girls' secondary education; whether campaigns on sexual issues jeopardized the more 'respectable' work of philanthropy, education or women's suffrage; or whether women's suffrage itself was a viable demand in the prevailing political conditions. All these conflicts – the large and the small – affected women's movements variously in different countries, but were relevant everywhere, not least in Russia.

More persistent and pervasive than any of these, however, has been the issue of 'equality and difference', a cryptic phrase encapsulating the collision of ideas and multiplicity of aspirations and motives inherent in the women's movement since its inception and now occupying the attention of feminist historians and political and cultural theorists.[1] The argument revolves around the proposition that there is a fundamental incompatibility between a feminism that aims to make women and men social equals and a feminism that 'celebrates' women's difference from men. On the face of it the proposition seems to make sense, because what are involved are two contradictory positions on the issue of sexual difference.[2] Those who have argued that women and men are first and foremost human beings with common needs transcending gender have placed greatest emphasis on the striving toward equality – sometimes with the explicit aim of breaking down gender differences and stereotypes to encourage a more androgynous culture. Those who have seen sexual difference as an unbridgeable binary opposition have been suspicious of the emphasis on equality, believing that even if it could be achieved (which they doubt), it would be an equality dictated by male norms, reflecting a culture made by men and eradicating or devaluing those positive qualities perceived to be quintessentially female. I hope it will become clear in the course of this chapter that although this argument has a long history and unquestionably has affected the politics of women's liberation to a profound degree over a century and a half, the concept of a dichotomy between equality and difference is rather misleading.

To start with, the notion of a dichotomy is based on the false assumption that equality is a synonym for sameness.[3] The philosophy of universal human rights does not rest on the proposition that all individuals are identical, but rather that all should have equal standing before the law and that no one should suffer discrimination on the grounds of sex, nationality, religion, class or any other factor. The impulse behind egalitarian feminism has been to remove the legal, socio-economic and cultural barriers that have discriminated against women and have assigned them an inferior – an unequal – status in society. As Joan Scott points out (and it really should be quite obvious), the antithesis of equality is inequality. Posing a dichotomy between equality and difference shifts the ground and allows the problem of inequality to remain unresolved.[4]

The dichotomy is a misleading one also in the sense that it suggests that feminist strategies were determined in directly opposing ways, according to the individual's adherence to one or the other position. This may be true in current debates within feminism, and was certainly present in the feminism of the 'first wave'. But it oversimplifies the relationship of egalitarianism and difference within the women's movement. Many feminists at the turn of the century supported the suffrage campaigns (which some feminists nowadays regard as the epitome of misguided egalitarianism) precisely because of their belief in women's unique ability as mothers to transform national and international politics. Here a perception of difference underpinned, not undermined, support for equal citizenship.[5]

Without underestimating the real divisions between feminists on this issue, it might be worth reflecting that between the two poles lies a middle ground occupied by a variety of opinions combining elements of both and, hardly surprisingly therefore, revealing considerable ambivalence and inconsistency. In fact, one could say that in everyday discussion of feminism, sexual difference, sex roles and personal relations between men and women, people demonstrate very much more fluidity in their views than is reflected in the notion of a dichotomy. It hardly matters whether this fluidity is a result of a failure to think through the issues involved. What is significant is the great diversity in thinking about gender relations, even among those who consider themselves feminists.[6]

For all this diversity and inconsistency, however, the contest between 'equality' and 'difference' is vigorous and enduring, not least in east-central Europe. In post-communist societies the very concept of equality has been subjected to a sustained onslaught – and not only from exponents of the free market. The re-emergence of an active women's movement in Russia, following seventy years of denial and repression, has contributed to the dismantling of the phoney Soviet ideology of sexual egalitarianism, already under attack in Brezhnev's time.[7] But at the same time a strong resistance to western feminism has emerged. Here 'feminism' is understood to be a competitive ideology which aims to sacrifice all that is 'feminine' in women, in a mad pursuit of equal rights and opportunities with men;

feminism is seen as an ideology which ignores the special responsibilities that women bear as mothers and disregards the bitter experience of women's 'double (or triple) burden' in communist systems. Consequently, the 'equality–difference dichotomy' has a particular connotation in the post-communist context in eastern Europe generally and, more specifically, in the context of Russia's history before and after 1917.[8]

As the issue of equality and difference has recently become so embroiled in cultural politics, in the West as much as in eastern Europe, it may be worth trying to separate the two concepts and examine their significance to the women's movement in the nineteenth and early twentieth centuries. I shall try to show how intertwined the two are in reality and how difficult it is not only to disentangle them, but even 'to arrive at a relatively stable and shared understanding of their meanings'.[9] In the conclusion I shall turn specifically to Russia to see how the current debates on feminism fit in with the Russian experience of women's emancipation before 1917. Inevitably, the discussion will be brief and may seem far too abstract; a satisfactory treatment of the subject would require a book, or at the very least an extended essay. What I am attempting to do here is to set out the issues and question some of the assumptions that have been made in the past, and are currently being made, about gender and feminism. In particular, I hope it will become clear that the arguments against egalitarianism have been heavily dependent on perceptions of essential sexual difference that are by no means proven.

The historical debate

At the root of the struggle to achieve equal rights, status and opportunities for both sexes was, and still is, the conviction that women cannot begin to realize their own potential until all the impediments to their autonomy – legal, cultural and economic – have been removed. Thus, quite apart from its function as a basic philosophical principle of human rights, egalitarianism in the women's movement can be interpreted historically as a profoundly energizing force, offering the prospect of female liberation from legal subjection, economic dependence and cultural disparagement. It is not surprising, then, that egalitarian feminism derived its intellectual legitimation from the Enlightenment and its political rhetoric from the French Revolution, nor that the women's movements in the United States and Britain in the middle of the nineteenth century employed the imagery of the anti-slavery movement.[10] Equally telling is the fact that the brief few years of relatively open debate in Russia in the late 1850s and early 1860s saw the end of serfdom coinciding with the beginnings of Russian liberal feminist organization and a flourishing radical ideology of sexual equality, which was absorbed into the populist and Marxist revolutionary ethos and enabled women to play a notable role in revolutionary politics in late nineteenth- and early twentieth-century Russia.[11]

The campaigns of women's movements internationally in the second half of the nineteenth century had as their immediate goals the extension of secondary and higher education to women, the opening of employment in middle-class professions and the dismantling of laws restricting women's legal capacity. All three were critically important for breaking down the physical barriers and cultural stereotypes that restrained women within the ideology of a private, female sphere (even when thousands already worked in factories and sweatshops) and that reinforced long-held views about the biological incapacity of women to use and produce knowledge.

The drive to gain access to the public and hitherto exclusively male world (that is, formal education and training for professional employment, the institutions of civil society, and politics, local and national) was matched by campaigns to give women the authority within 'their' private realm to make decisions affecting themselves, their children and the welfare of the family. It was well understood by feminists in the middle of the nineteenth century and later that both private and public spheres were governed by men, that decisions relating to one area impinged directly on the other and that the designation of the former as 'woman's realm' was largely a self-deluding idealization or a hypocritical stratagem, in either case defusing the issue of equality and female autonomy. Before the long process of reform of family law was initiated in the middle of the nineteenth century, the power of a husband or father over his family was more immediately threatening and disabling to women than their formal exclusion from public life. The most obvious examples here were the virtual prohibition on divorce in many countries and the inability of a woman to gain custody of her children if a marriage broke down. Although a man's legal power was often not invoked, there were many recorded instances in which male authority in the home very effectively barred women from the public realm (even when this had been legally opened up to them) and prevented them from gaining secure legal protection against physical or psychological abuse.[12]

The existence of legislation on the statute book does not reveal the extent to which it was effective, of course. In societies where public lobbying was a central part of the political process, the degree of pressure exerted by particular groups – in this case, feminists and their supporters – to repeal that legislation may be a better indicator of its effectiveness, though equally it may indicate no more than that the law was ripe for repeal. Without doubt political rights for women became a central issue only where there was some possibility of success. In countries like Britain and the United States, where a representative system of government was well established, access to politics was quickly incorporated into the aims of the women's movement. By contrast Russia, an autocracy lacking any form of national legislature or rights of assembly and association until 1906, did not permit the open discussion of women's suffrage until after the turn of the twentieth century. The Russian women's movement did not become involved in the suffrage issue at any point until 1905, when the political crisis propelled demands for a constitution to the centre of the stage, and again in 1917 when the campaign for female suffrage enjoyed a brief moment of glory in the weeks following the February Revolution.[13] The suffrage histories of other countries were very varied, and the reasons for the variation are still disputed. In France, for example, women did not gain the vote until after the Second World War (as in Italy, Greece, Yugoslavia and Hungary).[14]

From our perspective at the end of the twentieth century, it has become hard to comprehend the enthusiasm and conviction (not to mention the willing physical self-sacrifice, in the case of the British suffragettes) that fuelled the suffrage movement eighty or ninety years ago. The history of how women won the vote has become a deeply unfashionable subject for feminist historians in recent years, and several have questioned the entire value of the suffragist enterprise.[15] We know from experience that an equal entitlement to vote and stand for office has not resulted in women's equal participation in politics or the dismantling of male privilege and dominance in social institutions, let alone the transformation of the political process and social relations predicted by the more utopian suffragists before 1914. But this is a criticism with the benefit of hindsight. At the time the most sustainable critique (apart from outright misogyny) came from socialists, from a class standpoint. The liberal campaign for women's suffrage was indefensible, they argued, because it assumed the perpetuation of the existing exploitative class system. Women's liberation, in the socialist view, could be won only with the liberation of society from capitalist relations. Even from this perspective, however, they supported universal suffrage without distinction of sex as a basic democratic principle, and Russian socialist parties (Marxists and populists) adopted the demand very soon after their formation.

Feminist claims for women's suffrage around the turn of this century were thus based in part on thoroughly egalitarian and pragmatic arguments: that women and men were intrinsically of equal worth to society, that women were, increasingly, being educated to the same level as men, that they were contributing to the national economy and paying taxes, and that, if they did not bear arms for their country, they bore children for the nation's future. Equal access to politics would give women the legal and formal status of full citizenship and would endow them with the practical means to influence and draft legislation.

But the history of women's suffrage reveals how interrelated concepts of equality and difference are in practice, and also how the one may be emphasized at the expense of the other by contemporary feminist historians when they write about earlier feminist movements. Feminists of the 1960s and 1970s, who were consciously retrieving a past that had been consigned to oblivion for two generations, tended to stress the egalitarian and rationalist content of the women's movement of fifty and a hundred years earlier, especially in their accounts of the campaigns for higher education, economic independence and suffrage. Historians over the past fifteen years have been more inclined than before to diminish the importance and value of the egalitarian motif, laying emphasis instead on the discourse of difference that some feminists employed when arguing the cause of women's emancipation.[16] This discourse was enclosed in the idealized nineteenth-century imagery of sexual difference (whose sentimental vision of 'Woman' as redeemer became a feminist target in the late 1960s). It claimed equal rights on the grounds of women's 'unique mission' as natural conciliators to regenerate a world corrupted by men's violence and greed; it argued that the female capacity to bear children gave women a special understanding and morality that men lacked, and that women were endowed with an intuitive intelligence that should be prized more highly than the cold, egotistic rationality of men. In other words, women, by virtue of their innate moral superiority and unique intelligence, would transform society once they were at last admitted to it as full citizens.[17]

Without questioning the sincerity of the essentialist feminist claim for women's special nature, I think one should bear in mind that it was also a highly expedient strategy. The contest over women's emancipation in the nineteenth century was closely related to contemporary debates about human nature and social relations, which turned on the issue of equality and difference. While socialist and liberal political philosophies were founded on the concept of civil equality, they were developed in societies where class, race and gender relations were unashamedly unequal. Moreover, egalitarian political theory did not invariably overturn essentialist ideas about gender – it might still take for granted 'the naturalness of the *categories* of "women" and "men", and indeed the conventional attributes of women and men'.[18] In this period, too, ideas of essential difference became virtually unassailable by being appropriated as scientific doctrine. In such a culture a feminist argument for equality might well be more persuasive if the egalitarian rhetoric were wrapped up in a reassuring parcel of maternalist discourse. To stress women's natural compassion, their nurturing skills, their capacity for self-sacrifice, their new role of understanding wife and companion, was an obvious way to disarm hostility. I do not mean that this was a cynical and calculating strategy; rather that it was a response to, a reflection of, the cultural norms and demands of the period.

The contemporary debate

Unlike the debates over women's emancipation a century ago, in which the issue of intelligence and brain size was vigorously disputed, current feminist writing tends to side-step the question of whether gender differences have their origins in genetically determined sexual difference. With some justification it has been argued that neurological research into brain size and structure, in pursuit of the 'truth' about sex-related differences in intelligence and aptitude, is irrelevant to the debate about gender. Whatever the actual physiological differences or similarities between the sexes, social relations in widely differing cultures and in all known historical epochs have been organized on the basis of gender, though gender has not been the only organizing category and the forms that gender distinctions have taken have been neither uniform nor static.

The current critique of egalitarian feminism, being (at its best) far more theoretically sophisticated than late nineteenth-century feminist metaphysics, is no longer couched in the discourse of self-sacrifice, salvation and spiritual redemption. Indeed it is in self-abnegation that Carol Gilligan identifies the incapacity of women to speak, quite literally, in an authentic voice.[19] Yet in arguing (convincingly, in my view) that women are socialized to suppress their own personalities in a patriarchal culture, it is dangerously easy to take one step further to the conviction that there is an intrinsically female mode of experiencing and interpreting the world. If we live now in a culture that has been defined and dominated by men, can we really be certain that it would be fundamentally different if women had had an equal or even dominant role in its evolution? There is a logical inconsistency in the assertion that the personalities of women (and there-fore the culture that they will then freely create) will be noted for certain qualities that are considered to be uniquely female, when those very qualities have been fostered in women in a culture that has actively oppressed them.[20]

Not only does this rhetoric use an unrealistic image of the female psyche, presenting a stereotype of femininity rather than a recognition of the great diversity of women's personalities, it also contains assumptions about male behaviour that are as stereotyped and mutually contradictory as the standard misogynist claims about women. While we can recognize that people will often employ rationality to make their irrational and possibly violent impulses and desires acceptable to themselves and others, or to avoid confronting painful and disturbing emotions, I cannot see how men can be, for example, by nature both 'uncon-trollably' aggressive and 'coldly' rational, and I find it highly improbable that either of these would be the dominant personality traits of any individual, unless he or she were suffering from a severe psychological disorder. Men (like women) may be brought up to think and behave in certain ways commensurate with their gender, but under the thick layer of conformity and adaptation that defines much human behaviour, they remain individuals, not clones of masculinity.

If we were to accept the argument that women are less egotistic than men and more attuned to the needs of others, less aggressive and competitive, more emotionally expressive and less trusting in rationality, would we have to accept that these qualities are immutable? If a man is nurturant and uncompetitive, is he 'effeminate' (pejorative) or 'feminine' (possibly approbatory), or is he instead an individual who for a complex of reasons has developed a personality that evades rigid gender stereotyping? If a woman 'fails' to develop the appropriate nurturing qualities, is she therefore 'masculinized' or (even worse) 'unsexed'? And if a person is, let us say, nurturant and rational, competitive and emotionally expressive, is this a balance of male and female, of animus and anima, or (as I would argue) a normally complicated individual, impossible to categorize? In proposing that a female culture would give women the conditions in which to develop their potential, we are in danger of imposing new norms of behaviour and emotional response that would be every bit as constraining for many as past cultures have been, and as the culture we live in now so lamentably is. The manifest desirability of a world in which co-operation and conciliation are the predominant character-istics lends appeal to the idea of a female culture, but it should not blind us to the fact that it depends on an unproven if pervasive assumption about sexual difference. As Toril Moi has argued:

it is necessary at once to deconstruct the opposition between traditionally 'masculine' and traditionally 'feminine' values *and* to confront the full political force and reality of such categories. We must aim for a society in which we have ceased to categorize logic, conceptualization and rationality as 'masculine', not for one from which these virtues have been expelled altogether as 'unfeminine'.[21]

One of the principal problems, it seems to me, with the present-day critique of egalitarianism is that it fails to address the question of power in the world as it is and as it has been, rather than as it might have become if 'feminine' values had been absorbed into the political development of human societies from their beginnings. It is hard not to deplore the brutality, opportunism and cynicism that permeate the political systems of the world we live in. As these are man-made and as women have been excluded or kept (with a few remarkable exceptions) firmly in subordinate positions, it is all too tempting to dissociate oneself from politics by claiming that it embodies masculine values, that women will never be admitted to the club on an equal basis and that even if they were, they would be forced to speak in the language of men and use the institutions of male authority. This response rests, of course, on the assumptions about sexual difference that I have been questioning in this chapter.

Unfortunately the interrelationship of gender and power still evades elucidation. Disputes about intelligence and aptitude have been partially resolved by experience: women have demonstrated by their own achievements that their intellects are undamaged by female hormones (though there is no consensus about the 'nature' of female intelligence), and men have turned out to be perfectly capable of nurturing small children. But the argument over the exercise of authority and the use of force remains unresolved. It is considerably more difficult – even for an egalitarian feminist – to detach violence from masculinity than it is to argue that intelligence is not dependent on sex. All the evidence from societies past and present seems to point to an inborn capacity for aggression in men that is either absent or reduced in women. It is claimed that an indissoluble link exists between male sexuality and aggression; from that claim it is possible to build an entire edifice of appropriate gender roles and thus explain the course of human development from the most primitive hunter-gatherer societies to our own 'postmodern' culture.

Holding testosterone and the Y chromosome responsible for the triumphs and tribulations of the world does, however, raise a number of serious objections. While men are statistically much more likely than women to commit acts of violence, against other men and against women and children, they certainly do not have a monopoly of aggression. Women can kill and inflict serious injury, even on their own children; society understandably regards this as abnormal behaviour, indicating genetic, hormonal or psychological disturbance.[22] Men's capacity for violence, however, is considered 'natural' and classified as pathological only if it has not been socially sanctioned, when it is then treated as a major social problem.[23]

But while women's capacity for violence is generally either underestimated or pathologized, it has at the same time been a subject of fascination and legend, from the mythical Amazons of antiquity to the 'Russian Amazons' of the 1870s, who achieved fame and notoriety for their roles in planning and carrying out the tsar's assassination. Such women become heroic not only because they are prepared to die for a cause, but also because they defy the established codes of gender.[24] Yet precisely because they are legendary and self-sacrificing heroines, they are not taken completely seriously; they are larger than life, rather than part of it. Moreover, in some situations when women take on male combatant and political roles – perhaps particularly when they are not isolated (and therefore unthreatening) actors, but instead groups engaged in a common purpose – they can be ridiculed and diminished, as the women's battalions were during the last months of Russia's involvement in the First World War (and by most historians ever since), or the female partisans in occupied Europe during the Second.[25]

Contrary to popular representations and, it must be said, much serious feminist theory, there is no irrefutable connection between male sexuality and violence. All men may be technically capable of rape, for example, but its incidence depends far more on culture and circumstance than on men's 'uncontrollable' sexual drives. The urge to kill is also severely limited: if it were not, there would be no need to conscript men into war or shame them out of their fear of violence and pain by the command to be 'real men'. What strikes one, in stark contrast to the popular glorification of war, is the testimony of so many veterans, whose recollections dwell less on the lust to kill than on the horrors and terrors of fighting, the consciousness of 'duty' and loyalty, the brutal loss of their comrades and, often, compassion for their adversaries.[26] While there is plenty of evidence, in history and in the immediate present, of men engaging with total commitment in the most horrifying massacres, tortures and rapes, I think it is mistaken to assume that these are 'natural' ways for men to behave and that the majority would do so if they were not constrained by society's inhibitions.[27]

These comments are necessarily subjective. The question is explosively controversial and unlikely ever to be settled conclusively one way or the other. But if, as I am arguing, physical aggression (along with other 'masculine' characteristics such as competitiveness and assertiveness) are neither the exclusive property of men nor observable in all men, then the question of power cannot be reduced to sex, chromosomes or muscular build. Whatever the origins of male supremacy, however, the systems of power at present constituted throughout the 'developed' world are indisputably controlled by men. A few female prime ministers and company directors have done nothing to redress the weighty gender imbalance, not only in 'high' politics but equally in all forms of social organization, including the family. Although it is too glib, and revealing of sexual stereotypes, to dismiss the few women who do rise to the top of the hierarchy as honorary men in personality and ambition, none the less it is true that willingly or not their presence there has not shifted public perceptions of the relationship between gender and power. While many feminists (not only those espousing difference) wish to see women, and men, empowered within social structures based on more co-operative principles than the present systems of domination and subordination, the hierarchical, male-dominated model continues to prevail in the 'real' world. It is not clear, however, that hierarchical structures are intrinsically male; all we can say is that until now men have created and dominated them.

The Russian experience

So far this discussion of the debates over egalitarianism and sexual difference, though expressing strong personal views, has addressed theoretical issues and only tangentially the particular situation of women in Russia, before and after 1917. It remains now to ask briefly how current theorizing about feminism relates to the Russian experience.

As I noted toward the beginning of this chapter, a resistance to egalitarianism has been one of the most striking features of the response to western feminism among women in the former Soviet Union and east-central Europe. If some of this resistance is clearly a reaction against the shortcomings of communist theory and practice (though some of it is itself a hangover from communist ideological hostility to western liberalism), it also owes a great deal to much older ways of thinking about female emancipation. In Russia these date back to the middle of the nineteenth century, when the 'woman question' first became an issue, and derive partly at least from Russian ambivalence toward the West, toward liberal consti- tutionalism and the worship of material progress. While one strand of the Russian women's movement enthusiastically embraced western constitutional ideals of equality and citizenship, others were less convinced that these offered solutions to Russia's crisis. The schism between liberals and radicals on the 'woman question', as on everything else, centred on the issue of 'Russia's path' to social justice, with the radicals insisting that only a complete social revolution would resolve the crisis.

Throughout this dispute the question of sexual difference became submerged: whereas in Britain, North America or France conflict within the women's move- ment was likely to focus on some version of the equality–difference debate, in Russia (and to a certain extent Germany, where the socialist women's movement became very strong) the collision focused on the directly 'political' issue of reform versus revolution. In Russia from the 1860s radicals championed sexual equality in theory and often by example, though they were by no means unaffected by essentialist ideas.[28] At the same time, having 'solved' the woman question in the 1860s, they and their populist and Marxist successors wished to put it aside as a distraction from the political struggle against autocracy and capitalism, with the result that the underlying tensions between egalitarianism and a belief in difference remained unaddressed until well after 1917.

In the radicals' rejection of western liberalism, however, there is much that is familiar from the current feminist deconstruction of liberal theory. Their criticism is not simply that theories of equal rights and opportunities fail to overcome the cultural influences and established power structures barring many individuals and groups from their legal entitlement. The problem, seen from the radicals' perspective, lies deeper: the very values of the liberal tradition are flawed. There is no inherent virtue, they argue, in individualism; it is socially divisive, breeding competitiveness and social isolation. In the essentialist feminist critique, individualism is a masculine obsession; feminine values incorporate 'relatedness' and community – precisely the values espoused in Russian populist and (within a strict class framework) Marxist thought.

Karen Offen claims that 'relational', as opposed to 'individualist' feminism, 'dominated European continental debate on the woman question until very recently', arguing that the Anglo-American emphasis on individualism had obscured the strength of the relational outlook, not only in Europe but in Britain and the United States too. Here the quarrel with liberalism is less concerned with equality than with individualism: relational feminists had an egalitarian concept of society, but based on the centrality of gender difference.[29] One may disagree with her conclusion that it 'dominated' the European debate at the expense of egalitarianism, yet concur that its influence was strong. How far can this analysis be applied to Russia?

In certain respects it is highly relevant to our understanding of the widespread Russian ambivalence toward western liberalism and Russians' accusation – before 1917 and again now, in the debate over philosophical replacements for socialism – that 'the West' has no spiritual values, no communal traditions to bind society. It also fits in well with the interpretation of Russian history which emphasizes the egalitarian (though, it must be said, heavily patriarchal) structure of the peasant commune as an essential cultural counterweight to the authoritarian hierarchy of the state. It is less easy, at first sight, to fit a gender-based theory of equality into radical politics, with its analysis of society founded on class exploitation. Yet Offen's argument that relational feminism based itself on the recognition of gender difference and co-operation between men and women (within the family and society) seems quite well suited to the radical vision of a new society in which sexual equality would be a central feature, but in which there was little rethinking of the concepts of masculinity and femininity.

Yet I think it is reasonable to be suspicious of all political philosophies that emphasize gender difference, especially in a context where individual identities are submerged in the collective – whether that collective be the peasant commune, the nuclear family or the nation-state. It is striking how closely the essentialist feminist critique of 'masculine' society resembles the Slavophile rejection of 'western' culture. In both discourses rationality, individualism and independence are denigrated, while intuition, spirituality, connectedness and community are given unquestioned value.

Motherhood is a central preoccupation in both discourses; while this comes as a welcome change from a cultural tradition that regards maternity as a reason for disqualifying women from membership of the 'human race', it may also become a trap, returning women to their separate sphere in the name of emancipation. A common response of Russian women to western feminism has been to claim that, unlike women in the West, Russians have no need of emancipation, because they already control the realm which really matters – the world of the family and the private space.[30] Whether this is accurate or not (in a world where the man is the chief or only breadwinner, the legendary domestic power of women may quickly evaporate), it is a great self-delusion to imagine that the public world of state power does not impinge directly on the private. This has been particularly true in authoritarian state structures such as imperial Russia or the Soviet Union, when the state has possessed almost unlimited formal and at times actual powers over the individual and the family.

Finally, one may question a political philosophy that accords so little value to the autonomy of the individual. The western feminist critique of liberalism focuses almost entirely on societies with a long-established tradition of representative government and the theoretical recognition of the rights of the individual. Despite its pretensions, the mighty edifice of constitutional democracy has excluded women, either deliberately or by default. But to argue, therefore, that the building should be demolished because women have been left outside or, at best, admitted by the back door, seems to me very dangerous. It suggests that there is no awareness of the real fragility of constitutional systems. A critique of individual autonomy may be very attractive in a society that has made a fetish of individualism. When such a critique is applied to societies such as Russia's, which have endured a centuries-long tradition of arbitrary government, heavy censorship and suppression of individual rights, it strikes me as far more questionable.

There can be no last word on this subject. Disagreements over the aims and means of feminism are unlikely ever to be resolved, although one might dream, utopian fashion, that one day there will no longer be a need for feminism of any variety. In the meantime the arguments will doubtless continue, with the 'equality–difference dichotomy' occupying a central place, as it has done in women's movements worldwide for the past century and a half.

Notes

This chapter forms part of my research on 'Women's Emancipation and Theories of Sexual Difference in Russia, 1855–1917', a project funded by the Economic and Social Research Council at the Centre for Russian and East European Studies, University of Birmingham.

1   Among the most influential and provocative critiques of egalitarian feminism and the liberal tradition have been Carole Pateman, *The Sexual Contract* (Cambridge, England: Polity, 1988) and *The Disorder of Women: Democracy, Feminism and Political Theory* (Cambridge, England: Polity, 1989); Carol Gilligan, *In a Different Voice: Psychological Theory and Women's Development* (Cambridge and London: Harvard University Press, 1982; reprinted 1993); Catherine A. MacKinnon, *Towards a Feminist Theory of the State* (Cambridge and London: Harvard University Press, 1989).

2   In recent discussion 'gender difference' has tended to replace 'sexual difference', but it is sometimes unclear whether perceived differences are understood to be biologically or culturally determined. In the meantime the scientific search for the ultimate proof

continues. For a recent attempt (the primary purpose of which is to demonstrate that there are structural differences between the brains of homosexual and heterosexual men), see Simon LeVay, *The Sexual Brain* (Cambridge, Mass.: MIT Press, 1993); for an informed debunking of this quest, see Stephen Jay Gould, *The Mismeasure of Man* (Boston: W. W. Norton, 1981; reprinted Harmondsworth, 1992).

3 Carol Lee Bacchi partly avoids this problem by posing the question as a choice between sameness and difference: *Same Difference: Feminism and Sexual Difference* (Sydney: Allen and Unwin, 1990).

4 See Joan Wallach Scott, *Gender and the Politics of History* (New York: Columbia University Press, 1988), p. 172.

5 Bacchi (*Same Difference*, p. 2) argues, incorrectly in my view, that before 1918 all feminists took this stand.

6 I choose the word 'feminist' with caution, as its use has always been contentious; moreover, it was not in general circulation until the 1890s. Many women avoided the term, for complex reasons, but there really is no adequate alternative that encompasses all the activities of women's movements from the 1850s to 1918. For the origin of the word and the problems of definition, see Karen Offen, 'Defining Feminism: A Comparative Historical Approach', *Signs: Journal of Women in Culture and Society*, vol. 14, no. 1 (1988), pp. 119–57.

7 See Lynne Attwood, *The New Soviet Man and Woman: Sex-Role Socialization in the USSR* (Basingstoke: Macmillan, 1990; Bloomington: Indiana University Press, 1991).

8 The literature on and from women in the former Iron Curtain countries is expanding rapidly. For a recent compendium of experiences and viewpoints, see Nanette Funk and Magda Mueller (eds.), *Gender Politics and Post-Communism: Reflections from Eastern Europe and the Former Soviet Union* (London and New York: Routledge, 1993). S. G. Aivazova points out that 'equality' and 'feminism' have become unacceptable concepts to many women in the former Soviet Union. S. G. Aivazova, 'Ideinye istoki zhenskogo dvizheniia v Rossii', *Obshchestvennye nauki i sovremennost'*, no. 4 (1991), p. 133. See also M. T. Stepaniants (ed.), *Feminizm. Vostok. Zapad. Rossiia* (Moscow, 1993). Gisela Bock and Susan James suggest that feminist hostility to the emphasis on difference is strongest in countries where eugenics and racialist theories have had the most dangerous impact in the past, notably Germany: Gisela Bock and Susan James (eds.), *Beyond Equality and Difference: Citizenship, Feminist Politics and Female Subjectivity* (London and New York: Routledge, 1992), p. 2.

9 Bock and James, *Beyond Equality and Difference*, pp. 1–2.

10 For an interesting discussion of the participation of women in the anti-slavery campaign and the links with the developing women's movement, see Clare Midgley, 'Anti-Slavery and Feminism in Nineteenth-Century Britain', *Gender and History*, vol. 5, no. 3 (1993), pp. 343–62. Nineteenth- and early twentieth-century feminists sometimes revealed a misplaced faith in the philosophers' attachment to sexual egalitarianism. It was the idea of equality itself, rather than the uses to which it was put, that inspired the early women's movement. Recently feminist historians have been arguing that the significance of the French Revolution for women was negative, not positive. See, for example, Joan B. Landes, *Women and the Public Sphere in the Age of the French Revolution* (Ithaca, N.Y. and London: Cornell University Press, 1988).

11 For the most comprehensive account of the Russian women's movements, see Richard Stites, *The Women's Liberation Movement in Russia: Feminism, Nihilism and Bolshevism, 1860–1930* (Princeton, N.J.: Princeton University Press, 1978).

12 For example, a woman in Russia before 1917 needed her father's or husband's permission to live separately; until the law was reformed in the 1870s and 1880s, a woman in England had no right to her own property or income; until 1991 in Britain marital rape was not recognized as a crime.

13 See Stites, *Women's Liberation Movement*, chaps. 7 and 9; Linda Edmondson, *Feminism in Russia, 1900–1917* (Stanford, Calif. and London: Stanford University Press, 1984).

14 New Zealand was the first country to enfranchise women (1893); Australia followed nine years later. Women in Finland (though the country was still a Grand Duchy of the Russian tsar) were the first Europeans to win the vote, in 1906. Germany, like Britain, capitulated after the First World War, along with Poland, Czechoslovakia and Austria.

15 Carroll Smith-Rosenberg was among the first historians to do so. See 'The New Woman and the New History', *Feminist Studies*, no. 3 (1975), p. 186.

16 See Lynne Segal, *Is the Future Female? Troubled Thoughts on Contemporary Feminism* (London: Virago, 1987), p. x, for a discussion of the turnaround in feminist thinking about difference in the late 1970s.

17 The use of the (often capitalized) singular noun, 'Woman', a mythologized represen-tation of all women, was a favoured device of Anglo-American writers. Other languages employed similar figures of speech: 'la femme', 'die Frau', and so on. In Russian the absence of definite and indefinite articles leads to some ambiguity, which is usually removed by the context, especially when '*zhenshchina*' is modified by the emotionally loaded adjective 'Russian' ('*russkaia zhenshchina*') – a further complication in the use of 'woman' to express cosmic (or national) significance. For doubts about the use of 'Woman' or 'women' as a category, see Denise Riley, *Am I That Name? Feminism and the Category of 'Women' in History* (Basingstoke and London: Macmillan, 1988).

18 Robert W. Connell, *Gender and Power: Society, the Person and Sexual Politics* (Cambridge, England: Polity, 1987), p. 26.

19 Gilligan, *In a Different Voice*, introduction to 1993 edn., p. xi. She claims to be uninterested in the debate about essential difference (p. xiii) and even disturbed by it (p. xix).

20 John Stuart Mill, an egalitarian who did believe there were innate sexual differences, none the less denied 'that any one knows or can know, the nature of the two sexes, as long as they have only been seen in their present relation to one another'. Quoted by Lea Campos Boralevi, 'Utilitarianism and Feminism', in Ellen Kennedy and Susan Mendus (eds.), *Women in Western Political Philosophy: Kant to Nietzsche* (Brighton: Wheatsheaf, 1987), p. 167. Mill's feminism greatly influenced Russian radicals' thinking on the 'woman question' during the 1860s.

21 Toril Moi, *Sexual/Textual Politics: Feminist Literary Theory* (London and New York: Routledge, 1985), p. 160.

22 The subject of female criminality and its relationship to women's sexuality provided rich pickings for doctors, psychiatrists and criminal anthropologists in the late nineteenth century. For a detailed analysis of the experts' debates in Russia, see Laura Engelstein, *The Keys to Happiness: Sex and the Search for Modernity in Fin-de-Siècle Russia* (Ithaca, N.Y. and London: Cornell University Press, 1992), especially chaps. 3 and 4.

23 It is sanctioned pre-eminently in war, but also (according to the local cultural attitudes) in wife-beating, marital rape, physical punishment of children, certain sports and so on.

24 Barbara Alpern Engel, *Mothers and Daughters: Women of the Intelligentsia in Nineteenth-Century Russia* (Cambridge: Cambridge University Press, 1983).

25 For a rehabilitation of the women's battalions and a trenchant critique of the ways in which women soldiers have been represented by historians, see Richard Abraham, 'Mariia Bochkareva and the Russian Amazons of 1917', in Linda Edmondson (ed.), *Women and Society in Russia and the Soviet Union* (Cambridge: Cambridge University Press, 1992), pp. 124–44. For a comparable deconstruction of the hostile stereotyping of female partisans and postwar activists, see Glenda Sluga, 'No Man's Land: The Gendered Boundaries of Post-War Trieste', *Gender and History*, vol. 6, no. 2 (1994), pp. 184–201.

26 For reassessments of stereotyped gender roles and attitudes to war, see Margaret R. Higonnet et al. (eds.), *Behind the Lines: Gender and the Two World Wars* (New Haven, Conn. and London: Yale University Press, 1987). For testimony to men's fear and depression in the First World War, see Paul Fussell, *The Great War and Modern Memory* (New York and Oxford: Oxford University Press, 1975), and Eric J. Leed, *No Man's Land: Combat and Identity in World War One* (Cambridge: Cambridge University Press, 1979). Reassessments of the Second World War are more complex. It is hard to deny its status as a 'just war'; moreover, it has exerted a strong influence on postwar politics to this day. There has been a greater tendency recently, however, to deglorify it. For the particular situation of Soviet writing on the war, and its 'deheroization' during the Khrushchev thaw and again in the Gorbachev period, see Frank Ellis, *Vasiliy Grossman: The Genesis and Evolution of a Russian Heretic* (Oxford: Berg, 1994), especially pp. 36–40. [Editor's note: Such sentiments are even more in evidence in memoirs and fiction about the Soviet–Afghan War; see, for example, Artem Borovik, *The Hidden War* (London: Faber and Faber, 1991); Svetlana Aleksievich, *Zinky Boys: Soviet Voices from a Forgotten War*, trans. by Julia and Robin Whitby (London: Chatto and Windus, 1992); Oleg Ermakov, 'Znak zveria', *Znamia*, no. 6 (1992), pp. 6–86; 'Afganskie rasskazy', *Znamia*, no. 10 (1989), pp. 83–128.]

27 In the face of a storm of belligerent nationalist discourse enveloping the combatant nations of former Yugoslavia, pacifist statements and articulate critiques of the current war are reaching a sympathetic audience. In Serbia, for example, besides women's verbal and written protests against the fighting, there has been no shortage of works by men, including a volume of essays edited by Aljoša Mimica and Ivan Čolović, *Druga Srbija* (Belgrade: Plato, 1993); a novel by Slobodan Selenić, *Ubistvo s predumišljajem*, (Belgrade: Prosveta, 1993); and a soldier's diary, Aleksandar Jasović, 'Ratni dnevnik 1991', in *Književnost* (Belgrade) no. 3–4 (1992) pp. 404–37. I am very grateful to Wendy Bracewell and Dušan Puvačić for these references.

28 I discuss this in 'Women's Emancipation and Theories of Sexual Difference in Russia, 1850–1917', in Marianne Liljeström, Eila Mäntysaari and Arja Rosenholm (eds.), *Gender Restructuring in Russian Studies*, Slavica Tamperensia, vol. 2 (Tampere, Finland: University of Tampere Press, 1993), pp. 39–52.

29 Offen, 'Defining Feminism', p. 135.

30 For a highly provocative version of this response, see Tatyana Tolstaya, 'Notes from Underground', *New York Review of Books*, vol. 37, no. 9 (31 May 1990), pp. 3–7.

PART II

Women in the USSR and post-Soviet Russia: sexuality, identity, health and reproduction

7

Managing the female organism: doctors and the medicalization of women's paid work in Soviet Russia during the 1920s

JANET HYER

A fundamental theme in the modern history of women is the regulation of women's fertility by the state. Different types of states – Weimar and Nazi Germany, Britain, the Soviet Union – have pursued policies designed to shape the choices which women make with regard to motherhood. These varying political systems (fascist, liberal-democratic, state socialist) were all concerned with the direction of the birth rate and ensuring a larger/better future supply of workers and soldiers.[1] Very few states formulated policies without using experts, and the early 1900s witnessed growing efforts to bring the area of human reproduction under the supervision of the medical profession.

This essay addresses the essential role which the medical profession played in defining the parameters of Russian women's reproductive lives during the 1920s. As studies of the growing medicalization of women's lives in other countries have shown, doctors have not confined themselves to passing judgement on purely medical matters.[2] They have also addressed moral, ethical and social issues. Given the profound implications which reproduction has for structuring both male and female gender roles, such issues were never far from the surface. How doctors have determined the definition of 'purely medical' is also a large part of the research problem.

Aspects of medicalization

Soviet doctors were no less inclined than their colleagues elsewhere to ruminate on motherhood and population. They commented on the nature of women, the suitability of contraception and abortion and the relationship between women's paid work and motherhood. And they combined science and ideology in order to buttress their arguments about woman and motherhood. While the medicalization of abortion and contraception is not a surprising phenomenon, what is less well known is the attempt by doctors to establish a degree of authority over women's participation in the paid workforce.[3] Just such an attempt is the focus of this essay.

There are two predominant aspects to the medicalization of women's paid work in Soviet Russia. As in the case of other countries during the early decades of the 1900s, Soviet doctors were attracted to the ideology of rationalization.[4] Experts sought to subject human reproduction to the same principles of scientific management that had come to govern the work process.

Rationalization is typically associated with economic activity. It contributed to the transformation of capitalist industrial systems in the early 1900s, and was also important in the new socialist system of the USSR. During the mid-1920s, in reaction to the 'scissors crisis' (the disparity between low agricultural prices and high prices of manufactured goods), the Soviet leadership became intent on making workers more productive. The Party launched a massive economization drive in 1926 to reduce industrial costs and improve labour discipline. The following year witnessed a vigorous campaign aimed at the rationalization of production (the improvement of the technology and organization of production, including the efficient organization of labour).[5]

As scholars of women's history have shown, the principles of rationalization were not confined to the workplace, but were also brought to bear on the organization of domestic labour. Atina Grossmann has argued in the case of Weimar Germany that 'the rationalization of everyday life meant the extension of assembly line techniques into housework and the bedroom . . . the same criteria set up for effective rationalization in industry were applied to sexuality: uniformity, standardization, reliability, reproducibility, and predictability'.[6] The domestic labour of women includes maternity as well as sex, and, as we shall see, Soviet doctors were caught up in a campaign to rationalize maternity.

The second feature of the medicalization of women's paid work offers a contrast between the Soviet socialist and western capitalist systems: Soviet doctors validated women's work outside the home. That this validation was evident during the transition to a centrally planned economy, when women were drawn into the workforce in unprecedented numbers, is not so remarkable. It is noteworthy, however, that doctors did not question the right of women to work during the period of the New Economic Policy (NEP), a time when female unemployment reached significant proportions.[7]

Doctors analysed the impact of industrial work on women's ability to have children, and, while the results were not always positive, they did not recommend that women leave the factory to become full-time housewives. Indeed, their research reflects the clash of goals and values which has shaped the lives of Soviet women: women have been required for economic production, but at the same time increased fertility has been promoted; status has been derived through participation in social production, yet having children has also been glorified.[8] An examination of how doctors studied women's paid work and the conclusions they drew indicates how doctors squared such conflicts.

The main sources for culling doctors' opinions on fertility regulation are Soviet specialized journals on obstetrics and gynaecology, paediatrics, the protection of motherhood and infancy and the protection of labour. General medical and public health journals are also informative. What emerges from a review of this literature is the social dimension of women's fertility. The ideology of rationalization provided a mechanism whereby decisions about childbearing could be placed squarely within the public domain. This was buttressed by the public nature of the production process in the factory, which offered ample research opportunities.

The interconnection between economic and medical discourses

In many ways, the most striking example of the application of rationalization to women's fertility is in the very language which doctors used. It is a vocabulary replete with economic terms and images.

As Anna Davin has observed in the case of Britain, the population was viewed as a national resource and was evaluated by some medical officers in economic terms. For example, one officer wrote in 1907 about infant mortality rates in this manner:

> Over-production lessens, under-production enhances the value of commodities. Considering the life of an infant as a commodity, its money value must be greater than thirty-five years ago. It is of concern to the nation that a sufficient number of children should annually be produced to more than make good the losses by death; hence the importance of preserving infant life is even greater now than it was before the decline of the birth rate.[9]

In the Soviet case, the interconnection of economic and medical discourses tended to focus on the productivity of mothers rather than the commodity value of children. According to A. S. Gofshtein, pregnancy could be productive or unproductive (*produktivnost'/neproduktivnost' beremennosti*), depending on whether or not it ended in a miscarriage, abortion, or if the baby died during birth or while still being nursed.[10] Mothers were described as producers (*proizvoditel'nitsy*). Producers, like pregnancies, came in two types – productive and unproductive.

Elsewhere in the literature, it is necessary to differentiate between efficient labour (*proizvoditel'nyi trud*) and productive capacity (*proizvoditel'naia sposobnost'*), the former referring to a worker's job performance at the factory and the latter to a woman's ability to become pregnant and bear healthy babies.[11]

In short, having babies was conceptualized as 'work'. It was then possible to evaluate this type of work in terms similar to that of industrial work. For example, the production of babies could be governed by tempo, with a heightened tempo (*uchashchennyi temp*) deemed by Gofshtein to be unproductive.[12]

Using the language of economics allowed doctors more readily to submit reproduction to analysis in terms of rationalization. However, it is important to remember that doctors were working and writing in a system which based itself on Marxist ideology. Thus, according to a Marxist theoretical framework, the language of economics also helped to boost the analytical status of fertility from unproductive domestic labour to productive labour in the economy. The emphasis in Marxism on the economic structure of society tended to ignore or downplay phenomena seen as part of the legal and political superstructure. The family, and hence women's domestic labour, was typically seen as part of the super-structure.

Aleksandra Kollontai, the foremost Bolshevik theorist on the 'woman question', had approached the problem of upgrading the status of women's issues in the early 1920s by asserting the invaluable nature of women's work in building the new economy and in providing future workers. The result is the social obligation of motherhood:

> As soon as one adopts this point of view, the question of the emancipation of women from the burden of maternity is solved. A labour state establishes a completely new principle: care of the younger generation is not a private family affair, but a concern of society and the state. Maternity is protected and provided for not only in the interests of the objectives of the national economy, but still more in the interests of the objectives of the national economy during the transition to a socialist system: it is necessary to save women from an unproductive expenditure of energy on the family so that this energy can be used efficiently in the interests of the collective; it is necessary to protect their health in order to guarantee the labour republic a flow of healthy workers in the future.[13]

Kollontai probably did not envisage the application of the principles of scientific management to motherhood, but it is instructive that both she and the medical profession brought fertility into the public sphere in order to make recommendations.

Fieldwork in the factories and mills: generating data

In 1931, the Soviet government gave doctors an official role in determining women's participation in the paid workforce. According to a March resolution of the Central Executive Committee, the Commissariats of Labour and Public Health were called on to conduct a more detailed study of women's paid work, with a view to increasing the number of fields into which women would be encouraged to move.[14] Yet the medical profession had been making inroads into the factories and mills since the mid-1920s, examining the impact of work on female sexuality and reproduction (or, as they phrased it at the time, the sexual sphere of women).

Dr G. A. Batkis, from the State Institute for Social Hygiene, argued in 1930 that the question of the impact of work on the reproductive function of women was far from settled.[15] According to Batkis, the main reason for this was the poor methodology employed by researchers. Whether or not they were methodologically sound, the doctors' studies reveal great enthusiasm for measurement and classification. Clearly, there was a belief that numbers were the progenitors of scientific rigour. Two examples will give some indication of the ways in which doctors organized their findings to draw reproduction into an increasingly dense net of scientific analysis.

N. N. Pis'mennyi compared the pelvises of women who were in the maternity wing of a Serpukhov hospital some time from 1925 to 1928.[16] The numbers led him to conclude that 'the best pelvises belong to the wives of professional workers and the female intelligentsia; after them come unskilled women workers and peasants; then the wives of workers and then the women factory workers'.[17] Pis'mennyi reasoned that factory workers were at the bottom of the pelvic hierarchy because working in a standing position, particularly for young women, contributed to the formation of a narrow pelvis. He did not indicate why a narrow pelvis is bad, but the implication is clear – a narrow pelvis may make delivery of a baby more difficult.

Dr A. A. Shepetinskaia gathered statistics on the 155 women workers of the Leningrad Elektrik factory, looking at everything ranging from menses through pelvic organs to pregnancy and birth.[18] What is unusual in her work is the marriage of anthropometry with obstetrics and gynaecology: the factory women were classified according to an anthropometric system of measurements and sized as wide, average, narrow or hypoplastic. The measurements of variables having to do with menses and pelvic organs were then categorized by physical type. This methodology led Shepetinskaia to conclude that 'the link between the constitution of a woman, her ability to work and rate of sickness is beyond doubt'.[19]

Regardless of how the researchers organized their work, there was a fairly standard repertoire of objects to be studied. The most obvious variables were pregnancy and birth. For their 1925 study of 800 working women from four factories in Moscow, A. V. Bartel's and D. M. Ginodman calculated the average number of pregnancies to be 4.1.[20] Iu. E. Gitel'son found an average of 3.6 pregnancies for his sample of 175 workers from a Moscow tobacco factory. Gitel'son also calculated that the average number of births was 2.7.[21]

Sometimes, but not invariably, the doctors commented on the rates of pregnancy and birth. Gitel'son, for example, described the average number of both pregnancies and births for his tobacco workers as very low and noted that 'according to the calculations of Grasse, in order to maintain population growth, each woman must bear 3.39 children. According to L. L. Okinchits, even more – from 4 to 5.'[22] Shepetinskaia, also evoking Okinchits, reported that the average of 2.4 births for women at the Elektrik factory was 'not enough to maintain population growth'.[23] Bartel's and Ginodman, on the other hand, do not comment on the social significance of the rate of pregnancy for their group of Moscow working women.

Some doctors calculated desirable birth rates based on their samples. For example, Gofshtein analysed 400 case histories of pregnant women and nursing mothers gathered at the Fourth Odessa Regional Consultation for the Protection of Maternity and Infancy. He determined, based on the number of live births, abortions and miscarriages to the number of pregnancies, that women should limit their families to three children and that they should space them four years apart.[24]

Gofshtein offered two reasons for establishing a regimen of three children at intervals of four years. First, frequent pregnancies not only weakened the 'female organism', they also diminished a woman's value in the workforce. According to the doctor, studies had shown that pregnant women and nursing mothers performed significantly below average at their jobs. Furthermore, the economy suffered when the state had to make enormous expenditures for frequent maternity leave. Clearly, Gofshtein was convinced that women could resolve the conflict between the goals of economic production and human reproduction by following his advice.

Questions of quality control

Gofshtein's second reason for regulating childbirth was a eugenic one. He argued that the eugenic value of babies which were the result of unremitting pregnancies was low both in physical and psychological terms. Limiting family size and spacing births was the way to rationalize the protection of the health of future generations.[25]

The question of hereditary traits was alluded to by some doctors: Shepetinskaia, for example, noted that 31.4 per cent of the women workers at the Elektrik factory had unfavourable heredity (*neblagopriiatnaia nasledstvennost'*), but that the percentage did not vary significantly from the norm.[26] Others, such as Z. O. Michnik, dealt with the question of eugenics in more detail.[27] Michnik argued that, in the interests of society, not only should the hereditarily sick not reproduce (in this category fell the mentally retarded, epileptics, 'idiots', alcoholics, criminals and people with psychiatric problems), but that women who were overburdened, who worked in hazardous conditions or who were living below the poverty line should not have large families.[28] On the other hand, 'the gifted, healthy and strong are obliged to pass their natural resources [*prirodnye bogatstva*] along to the next generation.'[29]

In order to ensure that future generations were of the best possible quality, 'the business of reproduction should be rationalized, orderly and regulated. Social control should be established over reproduction.'[30] Michnik recommended that already existing maternity clinics extend their mandate – doctors should decide, based on social, medical and eugenic criteria, whether or not to advise a woman to become pregnant.

Studying labour standards

Michnik's eugenic solution did not address factors which she had identified such as poverty and hazardous working conditions. Legislation had been passed in the early years of the new Bolshevik regime to protect women's labour. According to the first (1918) and subsequent labour codes, women were not allowed to have jobs which involved particularly large amounts of heavy physical labour or which took place in especially dangerous working conditions.[31] The Commissariat of Labour stipulated in a number of resolutions which hazardous jobs women would not be allowed to take. Finally in 1932, a list of jobs formally off-limits to women was drawn up.[32]

As for the scientific research, most studies were done on lifting and moving heavy objects and on body positions (such as standing at a work bench for an eight–hour shift) rather than problems such as toxic chemicals. This may have been the result of a problem with measurement. For example, in his study of Moscow tobacco workers (an industry dominated by female labour), Gitel'son noted that he could not find 'objective clinical data' to explain the majority of miscarriages: 'Therefore, the question unintentionally arises: perhaps the miscarriages could be explained by hazardous conditions in the tobacco factories.'[33] Unfortunately, he wrote, he could not demonstrate this clinically. The hazardous conditions were not spelled out, but probably referred mainly to toxic substances in tobacco dust.

Lifting heavy objects had been regulated by legislation since 1921. However, as researchers from the State Scientific Institute for the Protection of Labour noted, the established norms were unrealistically low.[34] In 1925, the Commissariat for Labour instructed the Institute to review the situation. Doctors found, with variation by age and length of work record, that lifting heavy objects was a factor in menstrual disorders, uterine haemorrhaging, prolapse of pelvic organs and problems with pregnancy (such as miscarriage, premature birth, stillbirth).[35] In one instance, that of a sugar refinery in Odessa, a conveyor belt was introduced into the production process in order to reduce the amount of heavy lifting.[36]

Conclusion

As NEP gave way to the centrally planned economy, industry developed even closer ties with the medical profession with maternity clinics being established in factories. In addition to providing obstetrical and gynaecological services, clinic staff were also to reduce morbidity among women workers, to promote increased productivity and to facilitate the rational use of female labour resources.[37]

The rational use of women workers for rapid industrialization was more complex than during NEP. Common to both periods was the desire for women to bear healthy children, but the economic strategy embodied in the five-year plan introduced two new wrinkles. Not only did it require the mobilization of every labour unit available, but it also emphasized the development of industrial sectors which had traditionally been dominated by men. Thus, doctors were now to consider both how women workers performed in new types of jobs and if such work could affect childbearing.

Regulating women's fertility through the medicalization of paid work was part of a pro-natalist agenda. Setting this agenda took into account both quantitative and qualitative considerations. The constant emphasis on childbearing stemmed primarily from a conviction that the declining birth rate had to be reversed.[38] Not only was there a concern that the population lost as a result of the First World War should be replaced, but a large and growing population was also equated with national security. For example, K. K. Skrobanskii believed that the First World War was evidence of the need not only for industrial and cultural development, but also for numerical superiority in terms of population in order to win military conflicts. He compared the prewar and postwar population of Russia with that of western Europe and concluded that there was little room for optimism about Russian superiority.[39] Indeed, Skrobanskii was convinced, despite acknowledging the lack of solid statistical evidence, that Russia had embarked on a course of depopulation.[40]

Even those doctors interested in eugenics did not suggest sacrificing quantity for quality. For example, Gofshtein's formula of three children over eight years was based on the greater productivity of women who had had three or four pregnancies in comparison to women who had had five or more. The end result in both cases was the same – three surviving children.[41] Perhaps in some instances, official ideology along with scientific orthodoxy (neither of which approved of neo-Malthusianism) silenced dissenting voices. For example, Professor P. I. Liublinskii noted that 'The state is by no means interested only in the growth of its population; the qualitative improvement of the population has significantly greater value and it can be achieved through eugenic birth control and through cutting back disorderly reproduction.'[42] Yet he would not commit himself to a position on overpopulation, merely noting in his extensive article on contraception that '[the question of overpopulation] demands original and thorough examination and in this work does not play a substantial role'.[43]

Doctors did not acknowledge the conflicting demands made on women. On the one hand, pro-natalism called for an increase in the birth rate and, thus, an increase in the amount of domestic work. On the other hand, the Bolshevik vision of women's liberation and the labour policy of the 1930s assumed the participation of women in the paid workforce. When neither a sweeping socialization of domestic work nor a redivision of the sexual division of labour were realized, the double burden fell squarely on the shoulders of women. In contrast, the medical profession attempted to facilitate the achievement of both goals by working to minimize the impact of industrial work on women's ability to bear children and to rationalize reproductive work. Yet, as official concern over the demographic situation throughout the history of the Soviet Union illustrates, women have largely resisted attempts to regulate their fertility and have used the limited means at their disposal to determine the number and spacing of children.

Notes

1 Cornelie Usborne differentiates between the quantitative population policy of Wilhelmine Germany and the qualitative policy of Weimar Germany: Cornelie Usborne, *The Politics of the Body in Weimar Germany: Women's Reproductive Rights and Duties* (Basingstoke: Macmillan, 1992).

2 See, for example, Wendy Mitchinson, 'The Medical Treatment of Women', in Sandra Burt, Lorraine Code and Lindsay Downey (eds.), *Changing Patterns: Women in Canada* (Toronto: McClelland and Stewart, 1988), pp. 237–63; Barbara Ehrenreich and Deirdre English, *For Her Own Good: 150 Years of the Experts' Advice to Women* (Garden City, N.Y.: Anchor Press/Doubleday, 1978); Linda Gordon, *Woman's Body, Woman's Right: Birth Control in America* (New York: Penguin Books, 1974), chap. 8.

3 In my dissertation, 'The Medical Profession and the Regulation of Fertility in the

Soviet Union During the 1920s and 1930s' (University of Toronto), I will deal equally with the medicalization of abortion, contraception and paid work.

4 Anna Davin, 'Imperialism and Motherhood', *History Workshop*, no. 5 (Spring 1978), pp. 9–63; Atina Grossmann, 'The New Woman and the Rationalization of Sexuality in Weimar Germany', in Anna Snitow, Christine Stansell and Sharon Thompson (eds.), *Powers of Desire: The Politics of Sexuality* (New York: Monthly Review Press, 1983), pp. 153–71.

5 See E. H. Carr and R. W. Davies, *Foundations of a Planned Economy, 1926–1929*, vol. 1, part 1 (Basingstoke: Macmillan, 1969), pp. 340–4.

6 Grossmann, 'New Woman', pp. 163–5.

7 Compare this situation with the postwar experience of women in many countries. See, for example, Alison Prentice et al., *Canadian Women: A History* (Toronto: Harcourt Brace Jovanovich, 1988), chap. 12.

8 In addition to the Order of the Glory of Work, there are the honorary titles of Mother-Heroine, the Order of Maternal Glory and the Maternity Medal, which were established in 1944.

9 Davin, 'Imperialism and Motherhood', p. 11.

10 A. S. Gofshtein, 'Ratsionalizatsiia materinstva', *Vrachebnoe delo*, no. 19 (1927), pp. 1401–6.

11 A. V. Bartel's and D. M. Ginodman, 'Materialy k voprosu o vliianii proizvodstvennogo truda na polovuiu sferu zhenshchiny', *Ginekologiia i akushertsvo*, no. 3 (1927), p. 253.

12 Gofshtein, 'Ratsionalizatsiia materinstva', p. 1404.

13 Alix Holt, *Selected Writings of Alexandra Kollontai* (New York: W. W. Norton, 1977), p. 142.

14 G. Serebrennikov, 'Itogi nauchno–issledovatel'skoi raboty po izucheniiu zhenskogo truda', *Voprosy truda*, nos. 2–3 (1933), p. 63.

15 Doktor G. A. Batkis, 'K metodologii izucheniia vliianiia professii na proizvoditel'nuiu funktsiiu zhenshchiny', *Okhrana truda*, no. 2 (1930), pp. 53–8.

16 N. N. Pis'mennyi, 'Akusherskie razmery taza v fabrichnom naselenii', *Okhrana truda*, no. 12 (1930), pp. 57–60.

17 Ibid., p. 60.

18 Doktor A. A. Shepetinskaia, 'Polovaia sfera rabotnits fabriki "Elektrik"', *Okhrana truda*, no. 9 (1929), pp. 101–4.

19 Ibid., p. 104.

20 Bartel's and Ginodman, 'Materialy', p. 255.

21 Iu. E. Gitel'son, 'Polovaia sfera u rabotnits tabachnoi promyshlennosti', *Ginekologiia i akusherstvo*, no. 3 (1929), p. 319.

22 Ibid., p. 320. L. L. Okinchits was an eminent figure in the field of obstetrics and gynaecology. He was based in Leningrad and occupied, among other posts, the chair of the Leningrad Obstetrical-Gynaecological Society.

23 Shepetinskaia, 'Polovaia sfera', p. 104.

24 Gofshtein, 'Ratsionalizatsiia materinstva', p. 1406.

25 Ibid.

26 Shepetinskaia, 'Polovaia sfera', p. 102.

27 Z. O. Michnik, 'Soznatel'noe materinstvo i regulirovanie detorozhdeniia', *Zhurnal po izucheniiu rannego detskogo vozrasta*, no. 1 (1928), pp. 70–6.

28 Ibid., p. 71.

29 Ibid., p. 72.

30 Ibid.

31 A. I. Denisov (ed.), *Trudovoe pravo: entsiklopedicheskii slovar'* (Moscow, 1959), p. 439. Protective labour legislation came to be more honoured in the breach than in practice.

32 N. G. Aleksandrov, *Sovetskoe trudovoe pravo* (Moscow, 1963), p. 293.

33 Gitel'son, 'Polovaia sfera', p. 318.

34 Doktora I. I. Okuneva, E. E. Shteinbakh and L. N. Shcheglova, 'Opyt izucheniia vliianiia pod"ema i perenoski tiazhestei na organizm zhenshchiny', *Gigiena truda*, no. 8 (1927), p. 12.

35 Ibid., pp. 12–18. See also Z. Izrael'son and V. Petikov, 'Zhenskii trud v Orlovskoi gubernii', *Voprosy truda*, nos. 8–9 (1926), pp. 220–30; Doktor D. G. Berger, 'K voprosu o vliianii truda rubshchits sakhara na otpravleniia ikh polovoi sfery', *Gigiena truda*, no. 9 (1928), pp. 72–7.

36 Berger, 'K voprosu o vliianii truda', p. 77.

37 Z. Michnik, 'Opyt organizatsii iacheek OMM na proizvodstve', *Voprosy strakhovaniia*, no. 34 (1932), p. 26. See also Dotsent Z. O. Michnik, 'Rabota iacheek OMM (zakrytykh zhenskikh konsul'tatsii) na predpriiatiiakh g. Leningrada', *Voprosy pediatrii, pedologii i okhrany materinstva i detstva*, no. 2 (1934), pp. 130–40.

38 Declining birth rates have long been of concern to the Soviet Union's political leaders and demographic 'crisis' has been a constant companion. The 1970s crisis has been well documented. See, for example, Ellen Jones and Fred W. Grupp, *Modernization, Value Change and Fertility in the Soviet Union* (Cambridge: Cambridge University Press, 1987). In the 1990s, the press has carried stories about the severity of the most recent crisis. See, for example, 'Demograficheskaia katastrofa stala real'nost'iu', *Nezavisimaia gazeta*, 2 February 1994, p. 1, and 'Izgnanie ploda', *Izvestiia*, 26 January 1994, p. 8. In both instances, the importance of the family and the centrality of motherhood to the definition of woman have been emphasized. For the 1920s, see Susan Gross Solomon, 'The Demographic Argument in Soviet Debates over the Legalization of Abortion in the 1920s', *Cahiers du Monde russe et soviétique*, vol. 33, no. 1 (January–March, 1992), pp. 59–82.

39 Prof. K. Skrobanskii, 'Abort i protivozachatochnye sredstva', *Zhurnal akusherstva i zhenskikh boleznei*, vol. 35, no. 1 (1924), pp. 2–3. Skrobanskii produced statistics which showed a marked decline in Russia's population vis-à-vis western Europe. In 1912, Russia, including Finland and Siberia, had 171,759,000 people. Territorial losses and deaths from the First World War, the Civil War and famine reduced the population of the USSR to around 90 million. On top of that, western European countries were threatening to overtake the USSR in population; Germany, for example, had a population between 75 and 80 million.

40 Ibid., p. 5.

41 See tables in Gofshtein, 'Ratsionalizatsiia materinstva', pp. 1402–3.

42 Prof. P. I. Liublinskii, 'Protivozachatochnye sovety i okhrana materinstva', *Leningradskii meditsinskii zhurnal*, no. 5 (1926), p. 76.

43 Liublinskii, 'Protivozachatochnye sovety', p. 78.

8

Innocence and sexuality in Soviet medical discourse

SUSAN GROSS SOLOMON

Introduction

The 1920s in Russia saw an explosion of empirical research on sex by physicians of different medical specialities. Gynaecologists, assessing a woman's entitlement to a cost-free abortion on social grounds, asked questions;[1] specialists in sex education, concentrating on the habits of young people, asked questions;[2] specialists in forensic medicine conducting research on prostitution asked questions;[3] sexologists studying the sexual habits of different social groups asked questions;[4] and venereologists examining the spread of sexual disease asked questions.[5]

In this corpus of literature, the venereological writing stands out for its attention to the tension between sexual activity and innocence. That tension animated discussions of the transmission of syphilis. To historians of medicine, this might be surprising: by the early twentieth century, in most of Europe the connection between sexual licence and syphilis had been firmly entrenched. But in Russia, in the 1920s as indeed before the Bolshevik Revolution, there was a lively discussion of non-venereal syphilis. The Soviet physicians who wrote about non-venereal syphilis routinely referred to the Russian peasantry and to the residents of the non-Russian hinterland, the national minorities (*natsmeny*). Thus, the discussion of non-venereal syphilis provides us with a fascinating instance of the way in which sexuality is socially constructed.[6]

The social construction of venereal disease

The Russian legacy

The roots of the Russian discussion of non-venereal syphilis stretch back into the tsarist period. As Laura Engelstein has pointed out in an important article, the nineteenth century recognized several distinct modes of the transmission of syphilis: in addition to congenital syphilis, there was venereal or sexual trans-mission; non-venereal transmission which occurred as a result of non-sexual body contact; and endemic syphilis which was 'the second writ large'.[7] Non-venereal transmission was widely considered to prevail in the countryside, venereal transmission in the city.

Most Russian venereologists writing before 1917 were convinced that the syphilis which plagued their country was primarily non-venereal in nature: the disease was spread from person to person as a result of shared eating and drinking vessels, lack of sanitation and ignorance about personal hygiene. The pervasiveness of the disease and the fact that it was hardly ever rooted out led venereologists to see syphilis in the Russian countryside as an endemic illness.[8]

It was, Engelstein argued, difficult to distinguish venereal from non-venereal syphilis on an evidential basis; the categorizations were driven by the cultural pre-conceptions of physicians about the innocence of the peasantry and sexual licence in the city.[9] The image of the pure peasant succumbing innocently to endemic syphilis was part of a myth of the purity of the countryside that served Russia well.[10]

After the Revolution

Discussion of Russian syphilis as both non-venereal and venereal continued into the Soviet period. Some of the most prominent venereologists persisted in arguing that the disease was spread among the peasantry primarily through non-sexual contact.[11] Like their Russian predecessors, Soviet physicians included among the main causes of that spread such social factors as poverty, cultural backwardness and lack of sanitation.[12] The focus on social factors fits well both with the nurturist philosophy that was widespread after the Revolution and with the sort of class analysis that became increasingly popular in Soviet social hygiene in the 1920s.[13]

But alongside the continuities, the 1920s saw interesting shifts in the Russian medical thinking about the spread of syphilis. In medical writing on urban syphilis, prostitution – traditionally seen as the main source of spread – was now said to account less than before for the transmission of the disease.[14] Surveys revealed that an increasing proportion of syphilitics identified people they knew as the source of their infection; questionnaires conducted on the sexual behaviour of a variety of social groups gave ample evidence of what researchers termed 'disorderly' sexual conduct.[15] In response to this new information, researchers began increasingly to ascribe the transmission of syphilis to the freer sexual mores that followed the Revolution.

In the writing about rural syphilis, the long-held view about the prevalence of non-venereal over venereal syphilis was watered down. It is interesting to speculate about the origin of the changed view. In the Soviet period, the persistence of non-venereal syphilis in endemic form became an embarrassment; it was seen as living proof of what the reigning expert on rural syphilis, Dr S. Gal'perin, called 'our wildness and our lack of culture'.[16] Not surprisingly, as the myth of peasant innocence or ignorance became an irritant, there emerged 'data' on the increasing venereal transmission of syphilis. In the mid-1920s, at the very time when fresh cases of syphilis seemed to be declining in the cities, there were fresh reports of syphilis in the countryside.[17] By 1928, the official position as reflected in the entry on venereal disease in the *Bol'shaia meditsinskaia entsiklopediia* was that, whereas prior to the war 70–85 per cent of rural syphilis was non-venereally transmitted, a decade later that figure had dropped to 50.3 per cent.[18] That official position was reflected in instructions issued in 1928 to Soviet syphilis researchers to register the disease as non-venereal *only* if the chancre were located in a clearly 'non-venereal' location, if the patient were too young to have had sexual intercourse or if the woman were a virgin. If none of the above conditions obtained, but the respondent still insisted that the source of the infection was non-venereal, researchers were instructed to list the cause as 'uncertain'.[19] These instructions reflected a willingness, previously absent among Soviet syphilis researchers, to consider the possibility that, even where there was evidence of non-venereal infection, there could also be venereally-transmitted infection.[20]

Today we might ascribe the new view of the spread of rural syphilis to changes in the way in which the disease was constructed, but Soviet researchers writing at the time ascribed the changing patterns to modernization. The city, they said, was impinging on the countryside. The demobilization of soldiers, the increasing movement between the town and country, and the process of urbanization combined to make the isolated village a thing of the past.[21]

The modernization explanation was patent as early as 1925. In a study of rural syphilis in three small settlements in Saratov guberniia, a research detachment (*otriad*) not only counted cases, but tracked the economic and social lifestyle of the peasantry, paying particular attention to the absence of hygiene. The case histories taken by researchers supported the conventional portrait of rural syphilis as primarily non-venereal, but the clinical examinations conducted suggested that rural syphilis was looking increasingly like urban syphilis: the ratio of gummous lesions (considered a hallmark of endemic syphilis) to condyloma (an accepted indicator of venereal syphilis) was lower than that reported by previous research on the rural sector.[22] But the researchers also noted that among both women and men, most of the syphilis cases occurred during the period of greatest sexual activity (18–29 years of age) and that most cases of fresh syphilis occurred in the three high risk groups: bachelors, divorced people and adolescents.[23]

The dynamics of peasant sexuality

In a curious way, the modernization argument was used to preserve the notion of the innocence of the peasantry. Venereal syphilis was referred to – even by enlightened physicians – as 'city or urban syphilis' as though to suggest that casual sexual relations were confined to the city. The countryside was pictured as the victim of the 'disorderly' sexual life of the city, with its early onset of sexual life, recourse to prostitution and instability of marriage.[24] Although evidence of 'disorderly sexuality' in the countryside was certainly present, as late as 1928 the prevalent view among venereologists, as expressed by Rossiianskii, was that 'the sexual life of sparsely settled places and tiny rural settlements until now differs significantly from the sexual life of people in huge cities. The homogeneity of population, the fact that people all know one another – all this helps the stability of relations.'[25]

There was evidence that could be interpreted as supporting the opposite view. The 1925 Saratov study referred to earlier described a set of rural habits that had clear sexual overtones. In the harvest season, a gathering (*posidelka*) of young girls and their male guests would take place. At the end of such gatherings, the male guests often stayed the night. Also common was the practice of poor peasants inviting their better-off neighbours to help them with the harvest and then urging them to stay for gatherings (*pirushki*).[26]

The venereologists who went to Saratov did not draw out the implications for sexuality of the habits described. But social hygienists adducing similar evidence did press the implications of those findings for peasant sexuality. For example, in 1926 I. Taradin of the Voronezh Social Hygiene department published an article on the sexual habits of Ukrainian rural youth. Taradin described the time-honoured habits of *dosvitki* or evening gatherings of young people. These gatherings (or their variants termed *vechernitsy, vechernushki, sidelki, posedki* or *posidelki*) brought together all the non-Party youths in the village. The evenings were marked by drinking, loud singing and random acts of hooliganism.[27] Not untypically, such evenings culminated with the time-honoured custom of *nochevanie* (overnights), according to which the young men stayed over and slept near the young women. The incidence of sexual relations that occurred during such evenings was very high. The questionnaire Taradin administered revealed that more than 69 per cent of young men reported becoming sexually aware for the first time after 'games with girls'; 73.4 per cent of the respondents reported having their first sexual relations during such overnights.[28]

And yet even the social hygienists continued to picture peasant sexual life as innocent. In 1929, the Sexology Laboratory of the Division of Social Pathology of the Ukrainian Psycho-Neurological Institute conducted a study of the sexual lives of peasant women. The detailed two-part article on this research, published in German, referred to the long-standing custom of *Probenächt* (trial nights). Typically after evening gatherings, 10 to 16 young people would lie in pairs on the straw. Shying away from the implications of the custom, the sexologists who wrote the article declared that rural sexual life was not characterized by the same 'lust' as in the city; it was more natural.[29]

What seems to have changed was only the grounds of the argument for peasant innocence: the hapless peasant who was the victim of urban sexuality gave way to the peasant engaging in sex without lust. As further support for the notion of peasant innocence, the researchers underscored the extent to which sexual habits were deeply embedded in rural culture. The habit of young people spending the night became widespread, so ran the argument, because it was felt necessary from an economic point of view to introduce young people to sexual life before marriage.[30]

To be sure, the correlation between the sexual customs of the peasantry and the spread of disease did not escape notice. But often, it was the city that was blamed for 'disorderly sexual relations' leading to disease in the countryside. A 1926 article by a venereologist describing the weakening of traditional rural norms concluded, 'The most disorderly sexual relations go on there and, as a consequence of the town, there is also prostitution.'[31]

By 1929, discussions of rural syphilis had reached something of an impasse: research had revealed sexual practices among the peasantry that were conducive to the spread of syphilis, but many venereologists seemed reluctant to revise their image of peasant sexuality. The logjam was broken by research on syphilis among the Buriat-Mongols.

Studying syphilis in Buriatiia

The Soviet government mandated research on syphilis in Buriatiia beginning in 1924, just one year after the region became an ASSR (Autonomous Soviet Socialist Republic).[32] Between 1914 and 1929, a series of research detachments were sent out to the area to map the extent of venereal disease.[33] Of that series, the one that was significant for our purposes was the 1928 joint Soviet–German venture to Kul'skoe, a remote region of Buriat-Mongolia 200 kilometres from the capital, Verchne Udinsk. The area of the expedition was saturated with syphilis: for Buriat-Mongolia as a whole, the rate of syphilization was 42 per cent, but in some parts of the autonomous republic, as much as 63 per cent of the population was infected with syphilis.

The Soviet physicians who came to Kul'skoe in 1928[34] were concerned to ferret out the aspects of Buriat lifestyle which made for the spread of the disease.[35] In keeping with the prevailing assumption that the endemic syphilis here was the result of non-venereal transmission, the Soviet team conducted a thorough study of the lifestyle and hygiene habits of the Buriats. Their study concluded, the researchers acknowledged that the pattern of disease was certainly affected by the Buriats' lack of sanitation and lifestyle. But the researchers placed far more weight on the sexual habits of this small people. On this issue, Dr. Okun', who wrote up the results of the expedition for publication, took the bull by the horns. 'In contrast to our predecessors', he declared, the 1928 Soviet team concluded that syphilis among the Buriats was spread primarily through sexual contact. As evidence, he cited the age distribution and marital status of syphilitics: most of the syphilis cases occurred among people in the age bracket 15 to 39; a disproportionate number were bachelors, adolescents or divorced.[36] The Soviet researchers did not reach their conclusion solely by inference. Questionnaires on the topic of sexual life were administered to the Buriats[37] – one form for women, another for men.[38] Then, using translators, 'intimate conversations' (read interviews) were conducted with respondents on a variety of issues such as the onset of sexual life, sexual life before and after marriage and alcoholism. (The intimacy of these conversations should not be exaggerated: these were not sexual confessions in the sense described by Foucault, but rather personal interviews designed to get around the fact that many of the Buriat respondents were illiterate and therefore could not handle the forms on their own.) The data collected by the Soviet researchers showed that sexual life among the Buriats was casual and began early; that ties were multiple and not enduring.

The 1928 expedition and mainline Soviet venereology

The 'outlying areas' had been the *a fortiori* case of non-venereal or, as it was called, lifestyle (*bytovoi*) syphilis. Indeed, in late 1927, Dr Volf Bronner wrote that among the small peoples, the overwhelming form of transmission of syphilis was non-venereal. The example Bronner used was Buriat-Mongolia.[39] In his 1928 entry on syphilis in the *Bol'shaia meditsinskaia entsiklopediia*, Rossiianskii declared: 'the prevalence of non-venereal spread of syphilis has a place only among those groups of the population that find themselves on the lowest level of cultural development'. As examples, he cited residents of remote agricultural places and the small nations.[40] In examining Buriat sexual habits as a factor contributing to the spread of syphilis, the 1928 Soviet research team intended to set in motion a reconsideration of the problem of venereal disease among the *natsmeny*.[41]

But the 1928 expedition had even more important implications for the study of syphilis in Russia as a whole. The expedition highlighted the issue of virtue and vice that is always latent in the question of sexual disease. Here, after all, was a primitive population so saturated with syphilis that the disease was declared to be 'endemic'. And yet at the same time, at least half of the cases of syphilis here were found to have been transmitted through sexual contact. On the face of it, the case of the Buriats challenged the image of the innocence of populations afflicted by endemic syphilis.

The fact that the population under study was non-Russian made it possible to side-step such a challenge. Invoking a form of cultural relativism, researchers acknowledged that the Buriats were engaged in extensive sexual contacts at an early age, but they explained that behaviour as part of 'lifestyle'. More to the point, the Russian researchers declared that Buriat sexual life suffered from 'disorganization' (*dezorganizatsiia*) without invoking a moral judgement.[42]

By focusing on the indigenous sexual customs of the Buriats, the social hygiene researchers undermined the notion that the sexual behaviour among the 'peoples of the East' was a function of the impact of the city. By stressing the impact of local socio-cultural habits on the transmission of disease, the researchers made a case for cultural change that was in keeping with the work of the regime in the outlying areas in the period 1929–31.[43]

The findings from Buriatiia were refracted back into the understanding of sexuality in the Russian countryside. In a 1929 article on sexual behaviour among university students 'from the East', a team of Soviet social hygiene researchers developed a typology of sexual conduct.[44] To the category of 'primitive' behaviour, researchers assigned peoples who engaged in extensive pre-marital sexual relations. The researchers were quite clear about the range of people who fitted that category:

What we have described occurs frequently enough not only among the so-called small peoples; in today's great Russian countryside one may also find the customs of gathering young people in specially rented little huts (*izba*); the underlying tone of these gatherings has a clear sexual character.[45]

Equally important, the researchers raised the issue of moral evaluation:

One should not approach the evaluation of these phenomena with an absolute yardstick, talking about the amorality of sexual behaviour, sexual promiscuity. One should seek the roots of these things in the traditions of the people . . . which grew up on the basis of completely absent marital and family relations. The traditions have outlasted the conditions which gave rise to them.[46]

Conclusion

The Russians who came to Kul'skoe concluded that syphilis among the Buriats was primarily transmitted through sexual contact. The finding was not surprising in itself. What was noteworthy was the ease with which the Russian venereologists, who had agonized over the relative weight of venereal and non-venereal transmission among the Russian peasantry, concluded that syphilis among the Buriats was spread primarily through sexual contact. The paper demonstrates the extent to which Russian venereologists constructed both sexual disease and sexual innocence differently in the Russian countryside and in Buriatiia. It also suggests the liberating effect upon disputes in medical science of the examination of a 'foreign' example. But of course, what is deemed a 'foreign' as opposed to an 'indigenous' example is also a function of social construction.

Notes

This chapter is a substantially revised version of the author's article 'The Soviet–German Syphilis Expedition to Buriat Mongolia, 1928: Scientific Research on National Minorities', *Slavic Review*, vol. 52, no. 2 (Summer 1993), pp. 205–32.

1 See Susan Gross Solomon, 'The Demographic Argument in Soviet Debates over the Legalization of Abortion in the 1920s', *Cahiers du monde russe et soviétique*, vol. 33, no. 1 (January–March 1992), pp. 59–82.

2 For example, see D. Lass, *Sovremennoe studenchestvo* (Moscow and Leningrad, 1928). For an analysis of some of the writings in this genre, see Sheila Fitzpatrick, 'Sex and Revolution: An Examination of Literary and Statistical Data on the Mores of Soviet Students in the 1920s', *Journal of Modern History*, no. 50 (June 1987), pp. 252–78.

3 See, for example, V. M. Bronner and A. I. Elistratov, *Prostitutsiia v Rossii* (Moscow, 1927), pp. 63–9. For the surveys by legal scholars, see D. P. Rodin, 'Iz dannykh o sovremennoi prostitutsii', *Pravo i zhizn'*, no. 5 (1927), pp. 63–9; A. Uchevatov, 'Iz byta prostitutsii nashikh dnei (po materialam, sobrannym studentami I M.G.U.)', *Pravo i zhizn'*, no. 1 (1928), pp. 50ff, as cited in John Quigley, 'The Dilemma of Prostitution Law Reform: Lessons from the Soviet Russian Experiment', *American Criminal Law Review*, vol. 29, no. 4 (1992), pp. 1206–7.

4 For a discussion of this corpus of writing, see Susan Gross Solomon, 'Soviet Sexology:

128   *Susan Gross Solomon*

Between the Scylla of Domestic Concerns and the Charybdis of the International Arena', paper presented at the Second Annual Symposium on Soviet–German Medical Relations Between the Wars, Berlin, 14 May 1993.

5 For some of the best examples of this literature, see M. I. Kozhevnikova, 'K voprosu o polovoi zhizni i istochnikakh zarazheniia venericheskikh bol'nykh', *Sotsial'naia gigiena*, vol. 6 (1926), pp. 111–23; B. B. Geft, 'Materialy izucheniiu polovoi zhizni sovremennoi molodezhi', *Venerologiia i dermatologii*, no. 8 (1927), pp. 748–58; M. S. Shamina, 'Nekotorye cherty iz polovoi zhizni uchashcheisia zhenshchiny', *Venerologiia i dermatologiia*, no. 3 (1930), pp. 82–94.

6 In all societies, medical discussions about the etiology and spread of syphilis reflect cultural preconceptions about sexuality and about virtue and vice. For an interesting case study, see Megan Vaughan, *Curing Their Ills: Colonial Power and African Illness* (Stanford, Calif.: Stanford University Press, 1991), pp. 129–54. The notion that illness is socially constructed is discussed in Peter Wright and Andrew Treacher (eds.), *The Problem of Medical Knowledge: Examining the Social Construction of Medicine* (Edinburgh: Edinburgh University Press, 1982).

7 See Laura Engelstein, 'Syphilis, Historical and Actual: Cultural Geography of a Disease', *Review of Infectious Diseases*, vol. 8, no. 6 (November–December 1986), pp. 1036–48. This article inspired my discussion of the epidemiology of syphilis in pre-revolutionary Russia.

8 Ibid.

9 Ibid., p. 1038.

10 The view that the Russian countryside was plagued by endemic syphilis was accepted beyond the borders of Russia. For example, the great German venereologist Alfred Blaschko wrote that Russia suffered primarily from endemic syphilis: A. Blaschko, *Hygiene der Geschlechtskrankheiten* (Leipzig, 1920), p. 310. This view which was widely accepted may well have gratified the German sense of superiority vis-à-vis their Slavic neighbours.

11 The leading Russian proponent of this view was Gal'perin. See S. E. Gal'perin, 'K kharakteristike sifilisa sovremennoi derevni', *Vestnik sovremennoi meditsiny*, no. 4 (1926), pp. 20–2; S. Gal'perin 'Bytovoi sifilis', *Biulleten' Narkomzdrava RSFSR*, no. 20 (1927), pp. 49–54; S. Gal'perin, 'Sifilis v russkoi derevne', *Gigiena i epidemiologiia*, no. 1 (1928), pp. 37–41. For the most authoritative foreign statement of this view, see the article 'Endemische Syphilis', in *Handbüch der Haut- und Geschlechtskrankheiten*, vol. 23 (1931), pp. 307–11. M. Jadassohn, who wrote the article, listed parts of Russia and Siberia as classic locations of endemic family syphilis (ibid., p. 307). He made particular mention of Buriat-Mongolia.

12 For example, see V. I. Fel'dman and Ia. O. Gubianskii, 'K kazuistike vnepolovogo sifilisa', *Venerologiia i dermatologiia*, no. 2 (1924), pp. 91–4; Ia. M. Koval'skii, 'K kazuistike semeinykh epidemii sifilisa', *Moskovskii meditsinskii zhurnal*, no. 1 (1925), pp. 53–5.

13 For the pervasiveness of the nurturist assumptions, see Mark B. Adams, 'The Soviet Nature–Nurture Debate', in Loren R. Graham (ed.), *Science and the Social Order* (Cambridge: Harvard University Press, 1990), pp. 94–138. For the use of class analysis in research by Soviet social hygienists on the problem of alcoholism, see Susan Gross Solomon, 'David and Goliath: The Rivalry of Social Hygienists and Psychiatrists over the *Bytovoi* Alcoholic', *Soviet Studies*, vol. 41, no. 2 (1989), pp. 254–75.

14 N. L. Rossianskii, 'Sotsial'nye prichiny polovogo rasprostraneniia venericheskikh

boleznei', *Venerologiia i dermatologiia*, no. 2 (1928), p. 1244. Using data collected by the State Venereological Institute from hospitals and dispensaries, he submitted that whereas in 1914, 56.9 per cent of those registered as having syphilis had admitted to being infected by prostitutes, by 1924, that percentage had dropped to 40 per cent; in 1925 it had fallen to 24.9 per cent.

15 See note 5.
16 See S. E. Gal'perin, 'K voprosu ob organizatsii bor'by s bytovym sifilisom v RSFSR', in *Sbornik posviashchennyi dvadtsatipiatiletiiu nauchnoi i obshchestvennoi deiatel'nosti Prof V. M. Bronnera* (Moscow: Glavnauka, 1926), p. 11.
17 For reports on the fresh outbreak of syphilis, see, for example, I. Z. Talalov, 'Rasprostranenie venericheskikh boleznei i polovoi byt krest'ian Vereshchaginskogo raiona, Permskogo okruga po materialam venotriada', *Venerologiia i dermatologiia*, nos. 9–10 (1928), pp. 1257–8.
18 V. Bronner, 'Venericheskie bolezni', *Bol'shaia meditsinskaia entsiklopediia*, vol. 4 (1928), pp. 640–1.
19 N. L. Rossianskii, *Dispansarizatsiia v bor'be s venericheskimi bolezniami* (Moscow: Narkomzdrav, 1928), pp. 30–1.
20 According to Engelstein, once a geographical area became saturated with non-venereal syphilis, Russian venereologists had declined to consider whether sexual licence might also have played a role in the spread of disease: Engelstein, 'Syphilis, Historical and Actual'.
21 Bronner, 'Venericheskie bolezni'.
22 I. M. Okun', 'Opyt dispansernogo metoda raboty sredi krest'ian', *Venerologiia i dermatologiia*, no. 4 (1925), p. 128. To reinforce this conclusion, the head of the research detachment showed that of the three settlements studied, the three most closely connected to the city showed greater evidence of the urban type of syphilis. He added somewhat wryly that 'the present-day countryside is not the god-forsaken place it once was' (p. 128).
23 Ibid., p. 124.
24 Ibid., p. 132. It should be noted that the onset of sexual life was earlier in the cities than in the countryside for men only.
25 Rossiianskii, 'Sotsial'nye prichiny', p. 1451.
26 Okun', 'Opyt dispansernogo metoda', p. 125.
27 I. Taradin, '"Dosvitki" i ikh vliianie na polovuiu zhizn' krest'ianskoi molodezhi', *Profilakticheskaia meditsina*, nos. 7–8 (1926), pp. 96–104. The evenings were combatted by the Komsomol with only limited success.
28 Ibid., p. 99. Taradin's work is noteworthy because it used interview data to establish the high incidence of sexual relations that occurred on these occasions. Earlier research had inferred this from a higher than average level of births that occurred nine months after the height of the gathering season. For references to the earlier research, see Stephen P. Frank, 'Simple Folk, Savage Customs? Youth, Sociability and the Dynamics of Culture in Rural Russia, 1856–1914', *Journal of Social History*, vol. 25, no. 4 (Summer 1992), pp. 711–36; Barbara Alpern Engel, 'Peasant Morality and Pre-Marital Relations in Late 19th-Century Russia', *Journal of Social History*, vol. 32, no. 4 (Summer 1990), pp. 695–714.
29 See Z. A. Gurewitsch and A. J. Woroschbit, 'Das Sexualleben der Bäuerin in Russland', *Zeitschrift für Sexualwissenschaft und Sexualpolitik*, vol. 18, no. 1 (May 1931), pp. 51–74; vol. 18, no. 2 (June, 1931), pp. 81–110. The custom was described in the

first article, pp. 69–71. The notion of de-sexualized sexuality is examined with respect to prostitution in Elizabeth Wood, 'Prostitution Unbound: Sexuality and Revolution in Russia', unpublished paper.

30 Ibid.

31 P. N. Kraskovskii, 'Sifilis na sele i bor′ba s nim', *Profilakticheskaia meditsina*, no. 2 (1926), p. 79ff.

32 In the mid-1920s, the Russian Commissariat of Health sent similar syphilis detachments to the Kalmyk oblast, the Altai, Dagestan, the Chechen oblast and the Ossetian-Ingush country: S. Gal′perin, 'Sifilis okrain', *Biulleten′ Narodnogo Komissariata Zdravookhraneniia*, no. 3 (1926), pp. 16–21.

33 For a detailed discussion of these research efforts, see Susan Gross Solomon, 'The Soviet–German Syphilis Expedition to Buriat-Mongolia, 1928: Scientific Research on National Minorities', *Slavic Review*, vol. 52, no. 2 (Summer 1993), pp. 205–32.

34 The Soviet team was composed of venereologists associated with the prestigious State Venereological Institute (sometimes called the Bronner Institute) in Moscow.

35 The Russian plan for the expedition filed with the Academy of Sciences in 1927 declared that it was necessary to study not only the progress of the disease, but the social factors which made for its spread: 'Plan rabot sovmestnoi russko–germanskoi ekspeditsii dlia izucheniia sifilisa v Buriato-Mongol′skoi ASSR', Archiv Rossiiskoi Akademii Nauk, fond 2, opis′ 1–1928, delo 58, pp. 16–17.

36 Ibid., p. 80.

37 Throughout the 1920s, Soviet researchers were essaying a variety of methods to tap sexual customs and activity: L. S. Gurevich, 'K voprosu o vyrabotke ratsional′nykh metodov obsledovaniia polovoi zhizni', *Sotsial′naia gigiena*, vol. 7 (1926), pp. 31–53.

38 The questionnaires for women added items on pregnancy and married life.

39 V. M. Bronner, 'Iazyk faktov', *Venerologiia i dermatologiia*, no. 10 (1927), p. 897.

40 Rossiianskii, 'Venericheskie bolezni', *Bol′shaia meditsinskaia entsiklopediia*, vol. 4 (1928), p. 659.

41 I. M. Okun′, 'K metodike i praktike raboty nauchnykh venotriadov sredi malykh narodnostei', *Venerologiia i dermatologiia*, no. 3 (1930), pp. 97–104; I. M. Okun′, 'K kharakteristike sovremennogo sifilisa sredi vostochnykh buriat', *Venerologiia i dermatologiia*, no. 12 (1930), pp. 74–103.

42 Okun′, 'K kharakteristike', p. 76. According to Okun′, the Buriat people knew that their sexual habits were not normal and were seeking a way to reorganize them. In speaking of the heartland, Russia, Vein had tried to say that one could call sexual life disorganized without invoking a moral judgement: M. A. Vein, 'Osnovnye faktory, vliiaiushchie na rost i rasprostranenie venericheskikh boleznei', *Venerologiia i dermatologiia*, no. 6 (1925), p. 134.

43 For physicians' comments on the work of the Komsomol in fighting these deep-seated habits, see Okun′, 'K kharakteristike', p. 82.

44 See A. I. Maiants, G. A. Batkis and L. S. Gurevich, 'Problema pola sredi molodezhi vostoka', *Sotsial′naia gigiena*, no. 2 (1929), pp. 28–64. Throughout the 1920s, students – particularly medical students – were a favourite target of Soviet sex researchers.

45 Maiants, Batkis and Gurevich, 'Problema pola', p. 39.

46 Ibid., p. 38.

9

Abortion and women's health in Russia and the Soviet successor states

CHRISTOPHER WILLIAMS

Introduction

This chapter will analyse the influence which abortion has had on women's health in Russia and the other states of the former Soviet Union. The first section looks at conceptual and methodological problems, while section two analyses the available data on the incidence of abortion by country and according to age, education, marital status and other factors. Section three discusses why women have abortions; the following section explores the impact of abortion on their state of health; section five then examines the nature of the governmental response. Section six reviews female attitudes toward contraception and its impact on abortion levels. A final section considers current and future trends in the post-communist period.

Conceptual and methodological problems

According to the World Health Organization, abortion denotes 'the termination of a pregnancy before the foetus has attained viability, i.e. become capable of independent extra-uterine life'.[1] Viability can be defined in a variety of ways, such as the duration of the pregnancy or the length or weight of the foetus. If weight is used as an indicator, then it is said to be around 1,000 grammes; while if duration is emphasized, viability is attained after 28 weeks' gestation.[2] In this essay, two categories of abortion will be referred to: induced (*iskusstvennyi*) and spontaneous (*samoproizvol'nyi*). The former is generally defined as a 'deliberate' termination of a pregnancy begun voluntarily; while the latter includes all other abortions arising from external causes, such as trauma, communicable diseases and other factors. Spontaneous abortions are also often referred to as a miscarriage (*vykidysh*).[3]

Data availability

The data utilized in this chapter, which may be defective in terms of completeness and accuracy, are the only data available, and must be used with caution. Although all abortions have to be recorded by the authorities, hardly any official data were published prior to 1985. Although the situation changed somewhat during Gorbachev's tenure of office (1985–91), the degree of glasnost prevailing in this area was not as pronounced as one might have expected.

According to Alexander Avdeev and his colleagues, it is possible to distinguish between five stages in the registration of statistics on abortion (*abort*) in Russia and the successor states: first, the period before 1920, when criminal statistics and some clinical data were available but difficult to interpret; second, 1920–5, when some data, based on information from abortion clinics, were available but incomplete; third, 1925–36, when abortion could be calculated from individual cards filed by abortion commission staff; fourth, 1937–55, when abortion data were based on information supplied by abortion clinics and maternity hospitals, and included only those performed for medical reasons; and finally, 1955 to the present, when abortion data have been provided largely by medical establishments.[4]

According to Jones and Grupp, abortion data since 1955 are derived from two types of studies: cohort and clinic studies. The former are undertaken to examine birth histories of a specific cohort of women of a certain age or marital status, while the latter are based on samples of women who require abortions at specific medical facilities.[5] The data provided here relate to clinic studies and refer to the post-Stalin period.

Clinic studies are generally more reliable than cohort studies, but also have some shortcomings, as they are based upon self-reporting, which raises the strong possibility that women in the former Soviet Union, especially in the communist period, might have sought to conceal illegal abortions. As a result, the data given below should only be taken as indicative of the general pattern of abortions in the former Soviet Union. An additional obstacle when using such abortion data relates to the different methods of calculation used in Russia and the Soviet successor states.[6]

Abortion data should be interpreted in the context of the population growth and total fertility rate of the former USSR. Population growth, as Table 9.1 shows, has declined since the late 1950s in the ex-USSR as a whole, and in each of the fifteen countries listed. The rate of population growth has declined between each census, and varies from a low of 23.5 per cent in Ukraine between 1959 and 1989 to a high of 158 per cent in Tadzhikistan. Trends in fertility patterns, shown in Table 9.2, as well as variations in the number of abortions, illustrated in Table 9.3, are two key factors accounting for variations in rates of population growth according to country since the late 1950s.

Table 9.2 shows that the total fertility rate, which indicates the number of children a woman would bear if she survived to the end of her reproductive life under current fertility schedules, has declined for the ex-USSR since the late 1950s, except for a brief increase in the early 1970s. After 1981, however, fertility rates began to recover. There are major differences according to country. Thus most European parts of the ex-USSR fell below the replacement level of 2.1 in the 1960s, sustained a slight upturn in fertility in the early 1970s, but then fell below replacement again for the remainder of the decade. In the 1980s, all European parts of the ex-USSR, except Moldova, experienced rising fertility rates. Since the mid-1980s, however, fertility rates have been dropping again. This has resulted in higher fertility levels in the Baltic states in comparison to other Slavic countries, whose fertility rates have plummeted since 1988. By comparison, the Transcaucasian countries have made a successful transition from the 1950s to the 1980s, enabling Armenia and Azerbaidzhan, for instance, to have fertility rates similar to several European parts of the ex-USSR or contemporary Moldova. In more recent years, though, some Central Asian countries have been experiencing a fertility decline. Thus fertility rates in Uzbekistan, Tadzhikistan and Turkmenistan were lower in 1990 than in the 1970s. If Islamic fundamentalism gains a foothold in the region over the next decade, this trend is likely to be reversed.

The incidence of abortion

One possible explanation for population and fertility decline is the growing number of abortions in the USSR in the period 1954–90. These data are presented in Table 9.3. This table suggests that abortion has been widespread from the Khrushchev years to the end of the Gorbachev era. Notwithstanding the reservations about these data mentioned above, it is evident that from the mid-1960s around 8 million abortions per year were registered. The peak in terms of numbers was reached in 1965 (169 abortions per 100 births, or 122 per 1,000 women of reproductive age, 15 to 49 years). Thereafter a slight, but regular decrease began. For example, in 1970 there were approximately 148 abortions per 100 births; 138 in 1975; 130 in 1980; and 124 by 1990.

It is not possible to compare rural and urban practice on abortion. The statistics supplied only relate to the place where the abortion was carried out and do not refer to the place of residence. Nevertheless, it is true to say that towns are better equipped to perform abortions, so a large proportion of pregnancy terminations by rural inhabitants were carried out and registered in the towns.[7]

It is important to emphasize that women in the former Soviet Union do not necessarily limit themselves to having just one abortion. Many have repeated abortions: one group of medical specialists has argued that a woman in the former Soviet Union has on average up to three abortions during her lifetime.[8]

The data presented in Table 9.4 show variations in abortion levels between states of the former USSR. These figures are tainted by the uneven quality of registration procedures.[9] Bearing this in mind, Table 9.4 compared the national totals (column 2) for each individual country over the last two decades. Using this method, it is clear that the largest number of abortions was carried out in Russia. However, the rapid demographic transition in Central Asia and the absence of modern methods of contraception in these countries have led to a significant change over time. Thus, although Russia ranked first, the countries that follow are Ukraine, Kazakhstan, Belarus and Uzbekistan. (Note, however, that this order corresponds roughly to the countries' descending order of population.) The next group consists of Moldova, Kyrgyzstan, Georgia, Lithuania, Tadzhikistan and Latvia. Turkmenistan, Azerbaidzhan, Armenia and Estonia are in the final group.

Table 9.1. *Population growth in the ex-USSR by country and region, 1959–1989*

Country	Total population (thousands)				Growth (thousands)			Growth rate (per 1,000)		
	1959	1970	1979	1989	1959–70	1970–9	1979–89	1959–70	1970–9	1979–89
USSR	208,827	241,720	262,436	286,717	32,893	20,716	24,281	13.30	9.14	8.85
RSFSR	117,534	130,079	137,551	147,386	12,545	7,472	9,835	9.22	6.21	6.91
Ukraine	41,869	47,126	49,755	51,704	5,257	2,629	1,949	10.75	6.03	3.84
Belorussia	8,056	9,002	9,560	10,200	946	558	640	10.09	6.68	6.48
Lithuania	2,711	3,128	3,398	3,690	417	270	292	13.01	9.20	8.24
Latvia	2,093	2,364	2,521	2,681	271	157	160	11.07	7.14	6.15
Estonia	1,197	1,356	1,466	1,573	159	110	107	11.34	8.67	7.04
Moldavia	2,885	3,569	3,947	4,341	684	378	394	19.34	11.19	9.51
Georgia	4,044	4,686	5,015	5,449	642	329	434	13.40	7.54	8.30
Armenia	1,763	2,492	3,031	3,283	729	539	252	31.46	21.76	7.99
Azerbaidzhan	3,698	5,117	6,028	7,029	1,419	911	1,001	29.53	18.21	15.36
Uzbekistan	8,119	11,799	15,391	19,906	3,680	3,592	4,515	33.98	29.53	25.72
Kazakhstan	9,295	13,009	14,684	16,538	3,714	1,675	1,854	30.56	13.46	11.89
Kyrgyzstan	2,066	2,934	3,529	4,291	868	595	762	31.89	20.52	19.55
Turkmenistan	1,516	2,159	2,759	3,534	643	600	775	32.14	27.25	24.76
Tadzhikistan	1,981	2,900	3,801	5,112	919	901	1,311	34.65	30.06	29.63
European USSR	176,345	196,624	208,198	221,575	20,279	11,574	13,377	9.90	6.36	6.23
Transcaucasus	9,505	12,295	14,074	15,761	2,790	1,779	1,687	23.40	15.02	11.32
Central Asia	22,977	32,801	40,164	49,381	9,824	7,363	9,217	32.36	22.50	20.66

Source: W. Ward Kingkade, 'Demographic Prospects in the Republics of the Former Soviet Union', in Richard F. Kaufman and John P. Hardt (eds.), *The Former Soviet Union in Transition* (London: M. E. Sharpe, 1993), p. 796.

Table 9.2. *Total fertility rates in the ex-USSR by country, 1959–1990*

	1958–9	1965–6	1969–70	1975–6	1980–1	1982–3	1984–5	1985–6	1987	1988	1989	1990
USSR	2.810	2.461	2.389	2.389	2.253	2.367	2.405	2.462	2.532	2.451	2.334	2.263
RSFSR	2.626	2.125	1.971	1.969	1.895	2.050	2.058	2.111	2.218	2.124	2.007	1.888
Ukraine	2.296	1.986	2.044	2.023	1.935	2.037	2.055	2.069	2.035	2.039	2.019	1.902
Belorussia	2.795	2.282	2.298	2.139	2.023	2.092	2.078	2.096	2.051	2.021	1.924	1.844
Lithuania	2.627	2.228	2.354	2.185	1.976	2.026	2.096	2.138	2.166	2.090	1.986	2.044
Latvia	1.938	1.735	1.926	1.946	1.887	2.028	2.071	2.091	2.151	2.112	2.049	2.020
Estonia	1.946	1.920	2.143	2.078	2.029	2.094	2.110	2.102	2.223	2.237	2.211	2.054
Moldavia	3.573	2.683	2.563	2.518	2.403	2.569	2.676	2.770	2.733	2.629	2.464	2.362
Georgia	2.587	2.596	2.616	2.516	2.250	2.245	2.329	2.359	2.295	2.247	2.129	2.203
Azerbaidzhan	5.005	5.271	4.633	3.916	3.227	3.009	2.928	2.936	2.885	2.824	2.791	2.767
Armenia	4.730	3.908	3.195	2.786	2.339	2.352	2.488	2.553	2.544	2.492	2.604	2.827
Uzbekistan	5.044	5.564	5.636	5.660	4.805	4.650	4.653	4.699	4.610	4.309	4.039	4.089
Tadzhikistan	3.926	5.489	5.903	6.313	5.627	5.473	5.492	5.601	5.683	5.376	5.103	5.077
Turkmenistan	5.123	6.039	5.930	5.713	4.920	4.755	4.666	4.725	4.787	4.599	4.300	4.188
Kyrgyzstan	4.320	4.709	4.846	4.850	4.089	4.090	4.140	4.183	4.210	4.005	3.808	3.695
Kazakhstan	4.462	3.503	3.307	3.258	2.911	2.927	3.034	3.081	3.192	3.122	2.804	2.704

Source: W. Ward Kingkade, 'Demographic Prospects in the Republics of the Former Soviet Union', in Richard F. Kaufman and John P. Hardt (eds.), *The Former Soviet Union in Transition* (London: M. E. Sharpe, 1993), p. 804.

The lower level of abortions in some countries compared to others is attributable to different religious traditions, different processes of demographic transition and varying willingness to use abortion as a means of limiting birth. The practice of abortion is far from uniform and does not reflect the level of fertility. It is not a simple question of high versus low fertility, because major differences remain within given geographical areas. For example, in the Baltic states, Catholic Lithuanians retain a reticence toward abortion in relation to the Protestants of Estonia, where it is generally used. In Central Asia and Transcaucasia, the more westernized Azeris have fewer abortions because they have greater access to contraception in comparison with the Uzbeks.

Having considered the overall trend in the USSR as well as abortion incidence by nation-state, I will now examine the characteristics of those women having abortions.

The social characteristics of abortion patients

Surveys conducted between 1958 and 1984 showed that between a fifth and a third of those having an abortion in medical establishments were women aged between 20 and 24. The greatest number of abortions occurred in the 25 to 34 age group, in which two-fifths to two-thirds of women had abortions.[10] But exactly who are these women? Surveys suggest that around two-fifths of women having hospital abortions had only elementary education; between a fifth and two-fifths, incomplete secondary education; a fifth to a quarter, complete secondary education, and a tenth to a fifth possessed higher education.[11] However, A. F. Serenko and his colleagues believe that abortions are 1.3 times more likely among women with a secondary or higher education.[12] The tendency for women to resort to having an abortion is not only influenced by age and educational attainment, but also affected by their marital status. Surveys conducted between 1958 and 1979 show that 5–10 per cent of women who had abortions in medical establishments were single, 80–90 per cent married and 1–5 per cent widowed or divorced.[13]

We have seen, therefore, that women having abortions in hospitals or clinics tend, on average, to be married, aged between 20 and 34, and educated to elementary or secondary level. Many experts also maintain that abortion is common amongst women in all occupations, irrespective of their nationality or place of residence. Surveys conducted in several countries between 1958 and 1979 revealed that a quarter to a half of working women had abortions in the hospital sector, compared to a third of the unemployed and less than 5 per cent of students.[14] The question we must now consider is the motives behind any decision to have an abortion.

Motives for having an abortion

Whether or not a woman's reluctance to have children stems from her desire for personal development, in the form of study, a career or simply a job outside the

Table 9.3. *Abortions in the USSR in the post-Stalin period*

Year	Total number of abortions	Complete legal abortions registered	Spontaneous and criminal (i.e., incomplete) abortions	Abortions per 100 live births	Abortions per 1,000 women aged 15–49
1954	1985302	399046	1586257	7.84	6.84
1955	2598761	600314	1998447	11.92	10.15
1956	4724547	3316632	1407915	65.10	55.40
1957	5338738	3996159	1342579	76.81	66.26
1958	6128871	4844567	1284304	92.24	80.62
1959	6398541	5102306	1296235	96.21	85.79
1960	7038395	5642210	1396185	107.17	96.06
1961	7425507	6006038	1419469	118.39	103.57
1962	7774506	6414217	1360289	132.08	110.19
1963	8023290	6667354	1355936	144.81	114.64
1964	8408408	7021021	1387387	161.30	120.23
1965	8551351	7191686	1359665	169.33	122.46
1966	8337567	7020232	1317336	168.52	118.15
1967	7846354	6623990	1222364	161.94	109.72
1968	7645441	6471055	1174386	158.32	105.25
1969	7460316	6330413	1129903	152.26	101.84
1970	7531270	6406594	1124676	148.99	101.44
1971	7610001	6489481	1120520	147.89	101.07
1972	7497264	6408802	1088462	144.45	98.27
1973	7514765	6439040	1075725	145.48	97.50
1974	7449129	6397731	1051398	139.71	95.89
1975	7471572	6431773	1039798	137.65	95.68
1976	7636191	6588364	1047827	140.09	97.22
1977	7579105	6553674	1025430	138.70	96.22
1978	7497397	6497226	1000171	136.12	94.98
1979	7339566	6374161	965406	131.63	93.21
1980	7333073	6382028	951045	130.49	93.18
1981	7155594	6240562	915032	124.57	91.17
1982	7250355	6336188	914167	120.29	92.13
1983	7085370	6204515	880855	115.07	90.05
1984	7115825	6243572	872253	115.70	89.98
1985	7365852	6475595	890258	118.64	92.77
1986	7116000	6267984	848016	110.62	89.47
1987	6818000	6009655	808345	109.33	85.71
1988	7229000	6469096	759904	124.16	92.42
1989	6974431	6286035	688396	126.89	90.03
1990	6459000	5836823	622177	123.57	84.77

Source: Alexander Avdeev, Alain Blum and Irina Troitskaia, 'L'avortement et la contraception en Russie et dans l'ex-URSS: histoire et présent', *Dossiers et Recherches*, no. 41 (Paris: INED, October 1993), p. 46.

Table 9.4. *Number of abortions registered by Ministry of Health establishments by country, 1971–1990*

Year	USSR	Russia	Ukraine	Belorussia	Uzbekistan	Kazakhstan	Georgia	Azerbaidzhan
1971	6838642	4838749	1155870	190169	156450	382702	49759	64943
1972	6728128	4765589	1129500	185101	148988	383764	54879	60307
1973	6745350	4747037	1140365	193503	143370	387626	77857	55592
1974	6687002	4674050	1143285	194247	151683	377070	83454	63213
1975	6714982	4669940	1145831	194710	160086	390809	95094	58512
1976	6871726	4757055	1196600	199221	161331	395712	102009	59798
1977	6806210	4686063	1186676	202146	161206	406247	102148	61724
1978	6733934	4656057	1170184	201619	158971	392734	91709	62660
1979	6590423	4540440	1153275	203446	158515	380692	88519	65536
1980	6594089	4506249	1196696	201832	160700	378125	88656	61831
1981	6429292	4400676	1145870	202340	166396	359824	94635	59551
1982	6513570	4462825	1172375	198043	169608	364087	82952	63680
1983	6360515	4317129	1159679	207461	175230	362371	81172	57473
1984	6401909	4361959	1166762	210844	185710	349366	69649	57619
1985	6621870	4552443	1178686	200888	199576	367334	69310	53633
1986	6368473	4362110	1166039	171114	211022	332055	74702	51431
1987	6071336	4166196	1068136	158386	223418	329819	75903	49478
1988	6518571	4483856	1073763	217329	258283	362596	78670	44074
1989	6246764	4242028	1058414	250905	226276	358124	68883	42134
1990	5877846	3920287	1045289	259457	210974	355173	61401	25265
1991		3608412						
1992		3265718						

Source: Alexander Avdeev, Alain Blum and Irina Troitskaia, 'L'avortement et la contraception en Russie et dans l'ex-URSS: histoire et présent', *Dossiers et Recherches*, no. 41 (Paris: INED, October 1993), p. 60.

home, or from pressures of material circumstances, has been the subject of intense debate. We need to remember, however, that abortion is an emotional issue, hotly contested by the medical profession, feminist movements and various pressure groups. The former USSR is no exception. Women placed in the situation of having to choose whether or not to have an abortion may have been influenced by any of the aforementioned groups. This fact must be borne in mind when we consider Table 9.5, which presents the results of research in Russia and the other successor states into why women have abortions.

The main reasons cited are poor living conditions, financial difficulties, child care problems and family troubles, usually arising out of a partner's drinking habits.[15] Special mention should be made of the reasons in the 'other' motives category. Many women seek abortions to prevent pregnancies becoming known. This applies in around 25 per cent of cases,[16] and usually includes women who wish to avoid conflicts with their partners, especially if the baby is not his, or if they disagree about starting a family, or about family size.[17]

Lithuania	Moldavia	Latvia	Kyrgyzstan	Tadzhikistan	Armenia	Turkmenistan	Estonia	Year
46679	86959	66122	67167	37849	48138	32313	43682	1971
46723	88649	65223	65901	39331	48813	33202	43917	1972
46288	91450	64117	64943	40039	46654	35095	42665	1973
46658	92018	62451	63442	39650	45869	36105	40723	1974
45582	93394	58786	63963	39396	45483	34124	39641	1975
46718	97619	57692	65025	40320	39647	34893	38922	1976
46384	105808	58617	66503	41653	39136	35235	38499	1977
46485	103263	59565	66052	40504	37022	35819	37370	1978
45896	100484	59208	64351	41542	35745	34858	36779	1979
45189	96283	59909	64957	40135	32604	33762	36157	1980
45551	92432	59067	65291	41832	32105	32453	35569	1981
45183	94461	59190	67555	40482	32004	34817	36827	1982
44098	94840	57426	68690	39556	33158	33106	35139	1983
42481	90398	58708	66227	38624	33385	29266	34615	1984
42026	102703	57873	69382	40656	33896	31139	34844	1985
39245	110011	54511	73802	42441	38116	27793	35749	1986
37783	112426	55391	74060	42321	32587	35882	34713	1987
48556	102747	52058	80809	54490	29149	47444	31395	1988
50117	90860	48957	87212	54494	26141	39068	28428	1989
n.d.	81835	44559	79720	55521	25263	37222	24854	1990

Abortion and health

Most doctors concur that abortion carries high health risks. For example, one specialist declared: 'Abortion is the most serious biological trauma that a woman is ever liable to go through.'[18] While some doctors may exaggerate the risks involved on ethical grounds, there can be no denying that inflammation, haemorrhage, frigidity, sterility, fertility problems, early menopause, increased likelihood of still or premature births and gynaecological diseases can result in cases of abortion.[19] Table 9.6 bears out this claim, showing, for instance, that complications arise in 10–15 per cent of cases, while inflammation occurs in a further 20 per cent. Frigidity and sterility levels ranged from 55–80 per cent; gynaecological problems were also frequent; and finally, fatalities occurred in as few as 2 per cent of cases in Tomsk in 1960–2, but in nearly 40 per cent of cases in the survey taken in Minsk, Belarus in 1977. But why is abortion so disastrous for women's health? Is the operation itself difficult? Is the health service ill-equipped to deal with abortion? Or are the aforementioned risks largely confined to those women

Table 9.5. *Motives for abortion as shown in various surveys, selected times and places (in percentage of total)*

Reason or motive for having an abortion	Vladimir guberniia[a]	RFSFR, 1958–9[b]	Tomsk, 1960–2[c]	Possibly RSFSR, 1962[d]	Aginsk national okrug, 1963–6[e]	Groznyi, 1963–72[f]
Insufficient income or material need	17.0	10.0 (11.2)		14.1	1.9 (–)	8.9
Illness of one or both partners	45.7	5.7 (5.1)	4.5			
Large family already	17.0				29.6 (70.0)	9.1
Social position	20.3					
Insufficient housing or living space		14.0 (4.2)	21.9	14.5		13.2
Child-placement difficulties		11.0 (10.9)				6.1
No husband		5.9 (7.3)			1.1 (5.2)	
Family troubles		4.9 (5.6)				
Unwanted child by one or both parents		33.1 (43.2)	45.6		58.9 (15.6)	
Studies					3.0 (3.7)	
Failure of contraceptive devices						
Presence of small child						
Other	20.3	5.8 (2.0)			5.5 (5.5)	

Notes

1   These are related to the drinking habits of the husband.
2   This category also includes those husbands absent because they were drafted into the army.
3   Namely, insufficient time for bringing up the child.
4   This includes age, and exile to an international setting.
5   Includes study, love of one's job, bad family relations and material difficulties.
6   Levels vary according to the number of children. Hence those with children cite this reason in 64.2 per cent of cases.
7   Also significant are a lack of contraceptives for sale, an unwillingness to use them or a failure to purchase them.
8   Including old age and fear of childbirth.
9   Also includes family difficulties other than those related to spouses' alcohol abuse.
10   Of this sample, 27.9 per cent had a per capita family income of under 50 roubles per month; 36.5 per cent an income of 51–70 roubles; 30.8 per cent an income of 71–100 roubles; 4.4 per cent an income of 101–150 roubles; and 0.4 per cent of this sample had incomes of over 150 roubles a month.
11   This also includes age.
12   Defined as 'everyday familial' factors, which are unspecified, but possibly include material need, social position and so on.

Sources

a   Vladimir guberniia, 1924: A. M. Florinskaia, 'Aborty po vladimirskoi gubernii', *Gigiena i epidemiologiia*, no. 3 (1926), p. 21.
b   RSFSR, 1958–9: E. A. Sadvokasova, 'Nekotorye sotsial'no-gigienicheskie aspekty izucheniia aborta. (Po materialam spetsial'nogo issledovaniia v riade gorodov i sel'skikh mestnostei RSFSR za 1958–1959 gg)', *Sovetskoe zdravookhranenie* (hereafter *SZ*), no. 3 (1963), pp. 47–9. The figures refer to urban and rural inhabitants respectively, with the latter being given in brackets.

Moscow, 1969[g]	Amur oblast, 1969[h]	Moscow, 1969–70[i]	Magadan oblast, 1970–1[j]	Kalinin, 1971[k]	Kalinin, 1971[l]	Kalinin, 1971[m]	Leningrad, 1972[n]	Minsk, 1979[o]
	3.6			4.6	7.5	1.0	7.9^{10}	
	8.8	5.4		5.8	6.1	3.0		5.4
	4.2							2.1^{11}
	7.4	62.0^{5}	23.5	20.2	5.8	20.2	19.6	22.6^{12}
	6.2		7.5^{6}	6.0	12.1	6.1	9.7	
	1.4^{2}		3.6	4.3	2.2	27.3		
15.0^{1}	5.9		5.8^{1}	7.0^{1}	8.0^{1}	8.1^{1}	4.1	3.0
	37.7		72.9	33.4	47.3	21.2	50.2	15.2
	1.2		4.2	8.5	4.7	7.1		1.9
		56.0	10.6^{7}					
	16.0^{3}			3.6	3.5			12.2
	7.4^{4}		4.8^{8}	6.6^{9}	2.8^{9}	6.1	8.5	32.2

c   Tomsk, 1960–2: A. M. Lekhter, 'Opyt izucheniia posledstvii abortov', *SZ*, no. 9 (1966), pp. 23–4.

d   Possibly RSFSR, 1962: A. A. Verbenko et al., 'O sotsial'no-gigienicheskom znachenii aborta', *Zdravookhranenie Rossiiskoi Federatsii* (hereafter *ZRF*), no. 6 (1966), p. 23.

e   Aginsk national okrug, 1963–6: K. I. Zhuravleva and Ts. D. Tsydypov, 'Prichiny i posledstviia aborta', *ZRF*, no. 2 (1971), p. 24. The figures are broken down according to nationality: Russians are given first, and the Buriats in brackets.

f   Groznyi, Checheno-Ingush ASSR, 1963–72: M. T. Inderviev, 'Sotsial'no-gigienicheskaia kharakteristika abortov v Checheno-Ingushskoi ASSR', *ZRF*, no. 5 (1975), p. 26.

g   Moscow, 1969: V. K. Kuznetsov, 'Ob odnom faktore, vliiaiushchem na chislo abortov', *ZRF*, no. 9 (1969), p. 9.

h   Amur oblast, Tambov raion, 1969: A. I. Martov, 'Sotsial'no-gigienicheskie aspekty aborta zhenshchin v Tambovskom raione, Amurskoi oblasti', *SZ*, no. 7 (1973), p. 44.

i   Moscow, 1969–70: S. L. Polchanova, 'Nekotorye sotsial'no-gigienicheskie aspekty rozhdaemosti', *SZ*, no. 5 (1972), p. 15.

j   Far North, Magadan oblast, 1970–1: V. D. Vlasov, 'Nekotorye rezul'taty sotsial'no-demografich-eskikh issledovanii v usloviiakh krainego Severa', *ZRF*, no. 8 (1972), pp. 27–9.

k, l   Kalinin rural population, 1971, abortions for medical reasons only: V. L. Krasnenkov, 'Nekotorye sotsial'no-gigienicheskie aspekty kriminal'nykh abortov sredi zhenshchin g. Kalinina', *ZRF*, no. 5 (1977), p. 23.

m   Kalinin, 1971, criminal abortions only: Krasnenkov, 'Nekotorye sotsial'no-gigienicheskie aspekty', p. 21.

n   Leningrad, 1972: I. V. Poliakov and I. P. Koval'eva, 'Statisticheskii analiz iskhoda beremennostei', *ZRF*, no. 3 (1970), p. 44.

o   Minsk, 1979: I. M. Starovoitov et al., 'Reproduktivnaia funktsiia zhenshchin i motivy abortov', *Zdravookhranenie Belorussii* (hereafter *ZB*), no. 5 (1991), p. 25.

having illegal or criminal abortions? It is to these and other questions that I now wish to turn.

Performing abortions

Whereas the vacuum suction method is widely used in the West, in Russia and the post-Soviet states, even though many doctors are aware of this method, there is a preference for hospitalization in abortion cases. Thus, of the 7.3 million abortions performed in 1988, only 1.2 million utilized the vacuum suction method, with the figure rising to 1.7 million out of 6.5 million abortions performed by 1990.[20] Generally speaking, patients are hospitalized for two to three days, surgical methods are used, such as dilation and curettage, and a general anaesthestic is administered, although not on every occasion.

Many Russian commentators believe that the abortion operation is dangerous in itself.[21] V. M. Orlovskii, for example, points out that even under hospital conditions, the womb may be accidentally perforated.[22] While this may indeed be the case, the performance of abortion in the USSR was made more dangerous than necessary by Soviet medical practice (for instance, the use of 'experimental' methods)[23] and the unhygienic conditions, poor quality of care and shortage of doctors and beds in medical establishments for those undergoing abortions.[24] While all these problems were in evidence during the transition to market principles in the medical sector under Gorbachev, the situation has worsened since the collapse of communism in late 1991, as Narkomzdrav (the USSR Ministry of Public Health) at the all-union level was abolished, and the various health services in the former union republics have been obliged to fight for scarce resources in an uncertain economic and political climate.

As a result of the new frankness permitted under glasnost,[25] which has substantiated earlier claims in western, *samizdat* and émigré sources,[26] public recognition has now been given to the appalling conditions prevailing in abortion clinics throughout the former Soviet Union. It has become clear that the absence of staff and the necessary resources can have dire consequences for any woman in the former USSR who decides to have an abortion and that the health risks associated with this medical practice may be high.

Illegal abortions

These difficulties apply with even greater force to women having illegal abortions performed inside or outside the hospital sector in the former Soviet Union. Data on the number of illegal abortions must be regarded with caution; and only snippets of information have appeared since the advent of glasnost. Thus Inga Grebesheva, president of the Russian Family Planning Association, declared in May 1992: 'More than 10 per cent of all abortions are illegal. Residents of rural areas and teenagers under the age of 17 are most likely to resort to illegal abortions, and they suffer the highest level of complications and mortality.'[27] Similarly,

Nezavisimaia gazeta stated in 1992 that while 3.5 million abortions were performed at state medical institutions, the proportion of abortions performed outside the hospital sector stood at 15.7 per cent (549,500).[28] Anecdotal evidence indicates that the methods used to perform illegal abortions are often primitive. H. Kent Geiger says of the 1920s and 1930s: 'In the villages abortions were performed by a simple village woman thrusting a cobbler's needle into the womb.'[29] While the situation has undoubtedly changed since this time, it is still highly probable that illegal abortions are performed by unqualified persons trying to earn a little extra cash. Thus the health risks involved remain high, as Grebesheva claimed, although 13.3 per cent of those surveyed in the years 1956–62 still maintained that this was not the case.[30] According to Mary Buckley, in 1989 an attempt was made by Narkomzdrav to try and reduce the number of 'backstreet' abortions by extending the legal termination date to 21 weeks.[31] Nevertheless, legal or illegal abortions often result in deaths. E. Sadvokasova points out that the death rate from abortions stood at 2.4 per 100,000 by 1965–6, and the trend appears to have increased since. For instance, in 1990, as we can see from Table 9.3, just under 6.5 million abortions were performed; and in the same year, according to one newspaper source, 276 women died as a result of abortions, or 4.3 per 100,000.[32]

Abortion policy

The former USSR is experiencing a continuing conflict between the resolution of the abortion issue as part of the 'woman question', on the one hand, and demographic dilemmas, on the other.

According to demographic experts, the former Soviet Union has suffered a population crisis since the 1960s.[33] The birth rate only increased slightly from 18.4 per 1,000 in 1965, at the start of the Brezhnev era, to 18.8 per 1,000 by 1988, midway through the Gorbachev interregnum. At the same time, the crude death rate increased dramatically from 7.4 to 10.1 per 1,000 over the same period.[34] The major causes of these trends are changes in the age structure of the former Soviet Union and a rise in the number of degenerative diseases (heart disease and cancer) and other illnesses, such as alcoholism.[35]

However, as we have seen, the increased incidence of abortion (Tables 9.3 and 9.4) has also affected demographic patterns by having a negative impact on the state of health of the female population of the former Soviet Union (Table 9.6). Many Russian authors also believe that abortion has an adverse effect on fertility levels among women in the former USSR (Table 9.2). As suggested by the data provided in Tables 9.3 and 9.4, an 'abortion tradition' seems to have developed in the former USSR, in the sense that many women use abortion in order to regulate family size. Z. Iudina estimates that one-third of all women in the former USSR who abort their first pregnancy risk becoming infertile.[36] The rate of this practice is often high: for example, S. Polchanova argues that in Moscow between 1969 and 1970, 37 per cent of women had aborted their first pregnancy.[37] Various other surveys of the former Soviet Union suggest, in addition, that the ratio of abortions

Table 9.6. *Health status and abortion: frequency of various diseases (in percentage of total) arising from abortion in various regions of the former Soviet Union, 1960–1983*

Disease category	Tomsk[a] 1960–2	Leningrad[b] 1961–70	Leningrad[c] 1969	Cheboksary[d] 1969–71	Krasnodar krai[e] 1969–71	Perm'[f] 1969–71
Complications:	15.0					
miscarriage	0.8					
haemorrhage	14.2					
inflammation			7.1	67.1	67.2	56.6
sepsis	0.8					
other	0.9[1]					
Perforation of the uterus			0.8	0.8	85.5	99.3
Stillbirth		0.26–0.34				
Frigidity and/or sterility						
Menopausal problems						
Menstruation difficulties	2.2					
Extra-uterine or tubal pregnancy	3.2	0.51–0.81	9.1	37.6	30.4	37.7
Gynaecological diseases			14.6			
Fertility problems						
Premature births						
Deaths and fatalities	2.0[2]					
Other						

Notes

1 This figure refers to the influence of peritonitis, which, like sepsis, is the most frequent problem among those having criminal abortions. In this case, the risks were due to the fact that 85.4 per cent of the sample had already had between 1 and 20 abortions.

2 This figure refers to a two-fold increase in the number of fatalities.

3 Of those in this category, 6.0 per cent had cancer and 2.1 per cent had sexual diseases.

4 These results are based on research for a candidate's dissertation of 1975.

5 This figure refers to the complication rate per 100,000 women treated at consultation clinics and other medical facilities.

6 This figure refers to Briansk oblast. Elsewhere in the RSFSR, rates were lower, e.g., in Orenburg oblast the level of gynaecological diseases stood at 6.8 per cent. These differences reflect variations in the availability of staff and resources to treat these diseases.

7 This includes pregnancy toxicosis and chronic somatic diseases.

8 Includes blood pressure, perforation of the uterus and toxicosis.

9 Most of these deaths were caused by sepsis or related problems.

10 In this case, ovarian dysfunction.

11 Namely, very high blood pressure.

12 This category includes internal diseases.

Sources

a   Tomsk, 1960–2: A. M. Lekhter, 'Opyt izucheniia posledstvii abortov', *SZ*, no. 9 (1966), p. 25.

b   Leningrad, 1961–70: N. S. Sokolova, 'Statisticheskii analiz iskhoda beremennostei', *ZRF*, no. 3 (1970), p. 39. The figures refer to the incidence of this disease in Leningrad between 1963 and 1967.

Moscow[g] early 1970s	Moscow[h] mid-1970s	Tashkent[i] early to mid-1970s	RSFSR[j] 1975–80	Noril'sk[k] 1976–8	Minsk[l] 1977	Various[m] late 1970s	USSR[n] 1982–3
14.5	35.7	679.9[5]				40.8	
29.5						6.6–10.0	
					6.0		
					52.0[8]	40–70[10]	38.6[11]
			2.3				
		60–80[4]				55.0	
17.5							
18.4			31.6[6]				
						49.7	
	10.0			36.4			51.3
					39.8[9]		
8.7[3]				33.3[7]			11.0[12]

c   Leningrad, 1969: L. M. Karamova, 'Sotsial'no-gigienicheskie aspekty operativnykh vmeshatel'stv pri ginekologicheskikh zabolevaniiakh', *ZRF*, no. 5 (1974), p. 27. The figures indicate rates per 100,000 women.

d–f Cheboksary, Krasnodar krai and Perm', 1969–71: G. Ia. Tiumina and L. A. Leont'eva, 'Kompleksnye issledovaniia ginekologicheskoi zabolevaemosti (po dannym 3 gorodov)', *ZRF*, no. 12 (1977), p. 29. All figures give rates per 1,000 population.

g   Moscow, early 1970s: N. V. Dorde and T. P. Iakovlev, 'Vliianie bytovykh, semeinykh i professional'nykh faktorov na ginekologicheskuiu zabolevaemost'', *ZRF*, no. 12 (1974), p. 23.

h   Moscow, mid-1970s: O. V. Grinina and N. P. Maskel'skaia, 'O faktorakh, vliiaushchikh na prezhdevremennye rody zhenshchin', *ZRF*, no. 3 (1976), p. 8.

i   Tashkent, early to mid-1970s: I. Katkova and I. Manuilova, 'Iskusstvennye aborty, kontratseptsiia – aktual'nye problemy sovremennogo zdravookhraneniia', in *Nashe zdorov'e* (Moscow, 1983), pp. 29–30.

j   RSFSR, 1975–80: V. A. Alekseeva et al., 'Voprosy organizatsii vyezdnoi akushersko-ginekologicheskoi pomoshchi v RSFSR', *ZRF*, no. 5 (1982), pp. 7–8.

k   Noril'sk, 1976–8: O. M. Novikov and T. G. Zakharova, 'Nekotorye voprosy nedonashivaniia beremennosti v usloviiakh Zapoliar'ia', *ZRF*, no. 6 (1981), p. 15.

l   Minsk, 1977: S. I. Denisevich and L. N. Machulina, 'Faktory riska nedonashennosti', *ZB*, no. 5 (1981), pp. 37–8.

m   Includes RSFSR, 1977, Minsk, 1979, and elsewhere in the USSR in the 1970s: cited in V. F. Volgina, 'Opyt raboty po profilaktike abortov', *ZRF*, no. 12 (1984), pp. 23–4.

n   USSR, 1982–3: A. A. Alekseeva et al., 'O strukture mnozhestvennykh prichin materinskoi smertnosti', *ZRF*, no. 11 (1984), p. 27.

to live births stood in favour of abortion from the 1960s to the early 1980s.[38] In view of the perceived negative impact which abortion has had on demographic patterns in the former Soviet Union, successive Soviet leaderships have sought to address this question.

Soviet policy on abortion has gone through various stages. Abortion was legalized in 1920, made illegal again under Stalin in 1936 because of reduced fertility and negative population growth, then legalized again in November 1955.[39] The 1955 law 'On the Annulment of the Prohibition of Abortion' permitted abortion on request during the first three months of pregnancy, on the condition that it was carried out by qualified medical personnel; criminal abortions remained illegal. At the time of writing, these provisions still apply in most countries of the former USSR in the post-communist period. The only difference is that since the late 1980s payment for abortions has become less secret as a result of the emergence of private clinics performing abortions.

Naturally, the law of 1955, which followed thirty years in which abortion had been illegal, generated a massive increase in the number of abortions (see Table 9.3), which led once again to a negative response from the party leadership under Khrushchev.[40] Campaigns discouraging abortion were called for in the early 1960s, but it was not until a decade later, in the Brezhnev era, that action was eventually taken. The emphasis was not on women's right to choose; instead the health service was urged to launch a health education campaign to combat abortions.

Anti-abortion campaigns

Anti-abortion campaigns have consisted of lectures and radio and television broadcasts in which two main approaches are used. The first approach stresses the physical damage which an abortion might cause.[41] I. Zak, for example, cites the case of a woman who was found unconscious in a taxi, bleeding heavily from a perforation of the uterus after an illegal abortion had been performed.[42] The same author refers to another case of a nineteen-year-old girl who had inserted a primitive instrument into her womb and required a three-hour operation to patch her up.[43] Such horror stories are designed to prevent young women and others from having abortions. By contrast, the second approach expresses moral indignation toward those having abortions. A typical example is an article entitled 'Is Induced Abortion Murder by Experts?', which was published in the Moldovan periodical *Nauka i tekhnika*.[44] The goal here was to get women to think about the unborn baby inside them by appealing to their consciences. However, as Tannahill and Robertson have shown, this tendency to tell people what are 'good' and what are 'bad' forms of behaviour at the expense of skills development, enabling and empowerment, on the one hand, and the provision of better family planning and advice services, on the other, has meant that these campaigns have been largely ineffective.[45]

As a result, although the anti-abortion campaign from the 1970s to the mid-

1980s increased women's awareness of the risks involved and educated them about the need for sexual hygiene, it failed for a number of reasons. There was a lack of suitable health care specialists and facilities to treat abortion patients; the motives for having an abortion were not addressed; the women themselves were not consulted; it was a mistake to take the moral high ground; and finally, the Soviet leadership failed to promote obvious alternatives, such as contraceptives. Many of these problems stemmed from a belief that the 'woman question' had been solved, and from the assumption by policy-makers that abortion was, on the one hand, a medical, not a socio-political problem, as well as being, on the other, the product of psychological factors, attitudes and expectations among women of the former Soviet Union. Thus, instead of addressing the shortages in contraceptives, inadequate housing or poor child care, all of which are major reasons for abortion, successive communist leaders shifted the blame on to career-minded women who were said to lack a responsible attitude toward motherhood.

Searching for alternatives: abortion and contraception

Let us now look at the question of the relationship, if any, between contraception use and abortion. Under communism, condoms were in short supply and men were reluctant to use them.[46] Furthermore, the failure to introduce the pill (*prioral'naia kontratseptsiia*) or IUD on a wide scale has meant that women have tended to rely on other methods, such as the rhythm method, vaginal douche or *coitus interruptus*.[47] Up to the 1980s, the reliability of traditional methods was overestimated, while the value of more modern methods was underrated.[48]

Table 9.7 is based upon a 1991 survey of a sample of 8,059 women for the popular magazine *Health* (*Zdorov'e*). Most of the women questioned were married (87 per cent), with either one child (49 per cent) or two (38 per cent). The large majority were aged between 25 and 39 (52 per cent), although 45 per cent were under 25 and 4 per cent over forty. Fifty-two per cent had attended primary and technical school; 13 per cent, high school; and 35 per cent had a university degree. Finally, most came from Siberia (42 per cent), western Russia, namely Moscow and St Petersburg (35 per cent) or Ukraine (22 per cent).

Of this sample, 41 per cent had had one or two abortions, and although most had used some form of contraception during this period, 18 per cent had failed to use any at all. Of the latter, 40 per cent were aged between 15 and 20, 24 per cent were poorly educated and 22 per cent lived in the countryside. It is also evident that there is still a reliance on traditional and unreliable methods. Thus although 37 per cent 'always' used the IUD, 31 per cent also 'always' used *coitus interruptus* or the rhythm method. Only 10 per cent 'always' used the pill, with 71 per cent remaining very suspicious of it. The younger generation (women under 25) often used modern contraceptives, whereas older women, aged 45 to 50, held the opinion that contraception was more dangerous than abortion (13 per cent) and as a result, they tended to rely more heavily on traditional means, such as the rhythm method, rather than the pill.

Table 9.7. *Types of contraceptive used and attitudes toward them during the Gorbachev era, 1985–1991*

Type of contraceptive device	Usage			Attitude		
	Always	Sometimes	Not used	Convenient	Reliable	Safe for health
	(in percentages)					
Condom	18	51	31	14	28	43
Coitus interruptus	14	46	40	2	8	2
IUD	37	11	52	47	30	20
Rhythm	17	31	52	11	7	19
Vaginal douche	10	19	61	5	3	7
Pill	10	19	71	17	20	7
Chemical	2	14	84	2	1	1
Chemical + condom	1	4	95	1	2	1
Diaphragm	0	1	99	1	2	1

Source: Peter Lehert et al., 'Contraception in the Former USSR: Recent Survey Results on Women's Behaviour and Attitudes', *Planned Parenthood in Europe,* vol. 21, no. 2 (May 1992).

Such trends cannot simply be explained in terms of shortages, with 35 per cent of women stating that condoms were sometimes available and a further 8 per cent noting that they were never available. Poor sex education and ignorance,[49] biased attitudes and fear have also played their part. Concern about the adverse side effects, as Table 9.8 demonstrates, has also reinforced the tendency to judge modern methods harshly. Thus, only 43 per cent thought it was safe to use condoms, and 20 per cent, IUDs (Table 9.7). Whilst Larissa Remennick is optimistic about a gradual shift toward more modern methods,[50] Avdeev and his colleagues are more sceptical, for the following reasons: firstly, the pill is still not widely available (38 million were distributed in 1990 to protect 4.9 million women, or enough for 10 per cent of married women in the reproductive age group, 15–49 years);[51] secondly, there is still considerable mistrust of modern methods among medical practitioners; and finally, a decision was reached on 14 December 1990 to make sterilization easier if women had three children or more and were over thirty years old, or if women were over forty, irrespective of the number of children, or if they were suffering from acute illnesses.[52] It is possible, however, that the fear of AIDS[53] and the growing campaigns against abortion will result in the use of more modern methods, such as condoms, by the end of this century.

The post–communist period: continuity rather than change

Anti-abortion campaigns have continued in the post-communist period.[54] However, by this time the Russian anti-abortion movement has been helped by

Table 9.8. *Side effects experienced by women using various types of contraceptives (in percentage of total) in the former Soviet Union, according to surveys, 1960 to early 1970s*

Side effects experienced by Soviet women using domestic and foreign contraceptives	a[1]	b	c	d	e	f	g	h	i	j	k
Complications:	28.0							23.5			
haemorrhage	10–25			6.7	4.5	2.6					
inflammation				5.4	1.5	1.1					
Pain and discomfort			0.74	7.3	1.5	1.4					
Blood pressure									7.9		
Irregular menstruation		2.7		6.7		6.6	20.2		5.3	40.6	
Nausea							13.2		15.8	43.3	
Vomiting							1.0			5.4	
Reduced libido							2.0		10.5		7.6
Lung or liver complaint		2.7					1.0				7.6
Weight increase or decrease							1.0				0.9
Heart complaint		13.8									
Psychological problems		9.7			0.5						
Infection						1.0					
Other	23.0				85.0[2]		19.2			5.4[3]	0.9[3]

Notes

1 The surveys are listed as letters and then specified in the sources section below.

2 This includes primarily swelling of the breasts.

3 These figures refer to gynaecological diseases.

Sources

a M. A. Petrov-Maslakov et al., *Teoreticheskie i prakticheskie voprosy primeneniia peroral'nykh anti-kontsipientov* (Budapest, 1967), p. 57. This research on condom use is summarized in S. M. Iakovleva, *Sposoby i sredstva kontratseptsii* (Leningrad: Meditsina, Leningradskoe otdelenie, 1970), p. 41.

b Leningrad survey into the use of 'Alkatseptin' conducted between 1960 and 1968, cited in Iakovleva, *Sposoby i sredstva kontratseptsii*, p. 41.

c V. I. Borov, *Ocherki akushersko-ginekologicheskoi neiproendokrinologii* (Moscow, 1968). Research conducted into use of the loop cited in M. A. Petrov–Maslakov et al., *Sovremennye protivozachatochnye sredstva* (Leningrad: Meditsina, 1973), p. 137.

d The use of Soviet IUDs, such as 'LVK-66', is cited in Petrov-Maslakov et al., *Teoreticheskie i prakticheskie voprosy*, pp. 37, 42–3.

e Research into the use of the Soviet IUD, 'PVK-66', given in ibid., pp. 47, 56.

f The side effects associated with the use of two Soviet IUDs, 'LVK-66' and 'PVK-66', cited in ibid., pp. 77–9.

g A case study of the use of the Soviet contraceptive, 'Esliuton', cited in ibid., p. 131.

h Investigation into the use of the Czechoslovak contraceptive, 'Antigest', given in ibid., p. 132.

i Based on a case study of the Soviet contraceptive, 'Steriril', cited in ibid., p. 134.

j An investigation concerning use of the Hungarian contraceptive, 'Infekundin', given in ibid., p. 139.

k 1969–70 investigation of the Soviet contraceptive, 'Euginon', cited in ibid., p. 143.

western pro-lifers. For example, the 'Human Life' international organization of Maryland, USA and the Russian Orthodox Church opened the first anti-abortion conference on 20 May 1994. Five hundred people attended, and speakers came from the United States, Canada, Germany, Poland and Russia. Although they were critical of those having abortions, the organizers stopped short of advocating a ban. As Galina Seriakova of 'The Right to Life' stated: 'We have just freed ourselves from a totalitarian state; to introduce a ban would be stupid. Our society is not ready.'[55] Seriakova was, however, highly critical of current political parties for failing to make abortion a higher priority, especially given the fact that there were an estimated 3.3 million abortions, or 95 per 1,000 live births in Russia in 1993. She was also well aware that western techniques might not work in a Russian context. She stated: 'I do not condone the mass demonstrations and blocking of abortion clinics in which many US advocates engage.'[56]

The role of the revitalized women's movement

Although political democratization since 1985 has enabled the creation of women's groups capable of articulating female interests and concerns, the latter have established themselves slowly, are small in size and until relatively recently have refrained from making forceful interventions in Russian politics.[57] As a consequence, the women's movement in Russia is not yet in a position to influence post-communist policy on abortion. This is hardly surprising, because the rise of neo-fascism and right-wing ideologies in the early to mid-1990s has led to the continuation of conservative attitudes toward women, a hostility to female emancipation and a failure to accord any priority to women's issues. Although feminists succeeded in blocking a proposed new law on the family in 1993,[58] no similar success has yet been registered in relation to abortion. For example, Alessandra Stanley noted in May 1994 that 'while many Russian feminists deplore the extent of abortions and campaign for better contraception and more sex education, they do not regard abortion as in danger of being repealed'.[59]

A full debate on abortion law reform has yet to occur. While most of the blame for this can be attributed to Yel'tsin or an intransigent Duma, the women's movement is also partly to blame for failing to view 'abortion as a necessary condition for the liberation of women', in so far as 'the availability of legal abortion is considered to be a prerequisite for women's equality on the grounds that it gives her the ability to control her own life and body'.[60] Moderates and radicals within the women's movement must, therefore, start to work together.[61] The poor showing of the 'Women of Russia' political movement in the December 1993 elections, when they gained 5 per cent of the vote and approximately 23 seats in the Duma,[62] is a sign of just how far we have to go before women can fight off the current backlash and be in a position to reclaim the abortion issue as their own. The final question we must turn to is how, if at all, all these problems can be overcome in the future.

Abortion in the 1990s: problems and prospects

It's time to declare war on abortions; of course not by banning them. We must educate the population.
Sobesednik (November 1988)

We know that we lead the planet in the number of abortions. We've been writing about it for several years, but nothing changes.
Sobesednik (April 1989)[63]

Future policies and decision-making on abortion will depend upon a number of factors. The first is the ability of the medical profession to continue asserting its monopoly over the female body; the second is the potential role of the women's movement; a third possibility is that the Church might be a major obstacle to change;[64] a fourth factor is the growing influence of western anti-abortion groups fighting for the rights of the unborn child; and finally, and perhaps more importantly, there is the general issue of the fate of Russia and the post-Soviet states as a whole, which are in economic and political turmoil. The continued slow progress toward liberal democracy and a market economy is likely to have a detrimental impact on the position of women, and this situation in turn is likely to affect future abortion patterns well into the twenty-first century.

Notes

I am grateful to University College, Swansea for financing the earlier stages of this research, and the University of Central Lancashire staff development fund for financing its completion. Particular thanks must go to Dr Michael Ryan, Centre for Russian and East European Studies, Swansea and Dr Alastair McAuley of the Department of Economics, University of Essex for their comments on earlier drafts; to Libor Stloukal, Larissa Remennick and Alain Blum and his colleagues for allowing me to cite from unpublished papers; to W. Ward Kingkade and M. E. Sharpe for permission to use the information contained in Tables 9.1 and 9.2; and to Peter Lehert and Planned Parenthood in Europe for permission to reproduce Table 9.7. [Editor's note: A fuller discussion of many of the issues raised in this chapter can be found in Christopher Williams, 'The Political Economy of Health Care in the USSR, with Special Reference to Alcoholism, Smoking and Abortion' (unpublished MSc. (Econ.) thesis, University College, Swansea, 1986), chap. 4.]

1 *Spontaneous and Induced Abortion: Report of a WHO Scientific Group*, Technical Report Series, no. 461 (Geneva: WHO, 1970), p. 6.
2 Ibid.; see also Christopher Tietze, *Induced Abortion: 1979*, third edn. (New York: Population Council, 1979), p. 1.
3 *Spontaneous and Induced Abortion*, pp. 8–9; Tietze, *Induced Abortion*, p. 1; Peter Wingate, *The Penguin Medical Encyclopedia* (Harmondsworth: Penguin, 1982), pp. 2–3.
4 Alexander Avdeev, Alain Blum and Irina Troitskaia, 'L'avortement et la contraception en Russie et dans l'ex-URSS: histoire et présent', *Dossiers et Recherches*, no. 41 (Paris: Institut National D'Etudes Démographiques, October 1993), p. 19.
5 Ellen Jones and Fred W. Grupp, *Modernization, Value Change and Fertility in the Soviet Union* (Cambridge: Cambridge University Press, 1987), pp. 236–9.

6 Avdeev et al., 'L'avortement et la contraception', p. 19. [Editor's note: For further discussion of the unreliability of Soviet abortion statistics, see Mary Buckley, 'Glasnost and the Woman Question', in Linda Edmondson (ed.), *Women and Society in Russia and the Soviet Union* (Cambridge: Cambridge University Press, 1992), pp. 212–14; Larissa Remennick, 'Patterns of Birth Control', in Igor Kon and James Riordan (eds.), *Sex and Russian Society* (Bloomington: Indiana University Press, 1993; London: Pluto, 1993), pp. 47–9.]

7 Avdeev et al., 'L'avortement et la contraception', p. 34.

8 A. A. Verbenko et al., *Aborty i protivozachatochnye sredstva (kliniko-statisticheskie issledovaniia)* (Moscow, 1968), p. 12.

9 Ibid.

10 Christopher Williams, 'The Political Economy of Health Care in the USSR', unpublished MSc. (Econ.) thesis, Centre for Russian and East European Studies, University College, Swansea, 1986, chap. 4.

11 Ibid.

12 A. F. Serenko et al., 'K metodike izucheniia sotsial'no-gigienicheskikh aspektov rozhdaemosti kogort molodykh sem'ei', *Sovetskoe zdravookhranenie*, no. 6 (1973), p. 15.

13 Williams, 'The Political Economy of Health Care'.

14 Ibid.

15 On this see Christopher Williams, 'Old Habits Die Hard: Alcoholism in Leningrad under NEP and Some Lessons for the Gorbachev Administration', *Irish Slavonic Studies*, no. 12 (1991), pp. 69–97.

16 I. M. Avdeeva, 'Izucheniia prichin i uslovii sposobstvuiushchikh soversheniiu prestupnykh abortov i mery po ikh ustraneniiu', in *Voprosy preduprezhdeniia prestupnosti*, no. 2 (Moscow, 1965), p. 74; and A. A. Verbenko et al., *Aborty i protivozachatochnye sredstva*, p. 11.

17 For an example of such disagreements, see the novella by Natal'ia Baranskaia, 'Nedelia kak nedelia', *Novyi mir*, no. 11 (1969), pp. 32–4, 47–9.

18 V. I. Bodiazhina, 'Sokhranite beremennost'', *Zdorov'e*, no. 12 (1977), p. 13.

19 See Verbenko et al., *Aborty*, p. 23; *Spontaneous and Induced Abortion*, pp. 20–9; Malcolm Potts, Peter Diggory and John Peel, *Abortion* (Cambridge: Cambridge University Press, 1977), pp. 179–210.

20 *Vestnik statistiki*, no. 1 (1992), p. 57; Avdeev et al., 'L'avortement et la contraception', p. 46.

21 See, for example, I. R. Zak, 'Abort: eto kak bomba zamedlennogo deistviia', *Zdorov'e*, no. 5 (1973), pp. 14–15.

22 V. M. Orlovskii, 'Srok preryvaniia beremennosti', *Zdorov'e*, no. 11 (1975), p. 17.

23 Avdeeva, 'Izucheniia prichin', p. 75.

24 V. G. Balashova and G. S. Muchiev, 'K voprosam o ratsional'nom ispol'zovanii fonda akusherskikh i ginekologicheskikh koek', *SZ*, no. 5 (1974), pp. 48–52. For the worsening of such problems as overcrowding and competition for beds since the mid-1960s, see Murray Feshbach, *A Compendium of Soviet Medical Statistics* (Washington, D.C.: US Census Bureau, 1985), Table 4, pp. 35–6; Table 13, pp. 56–7; and Table 15, pp. 63–4. I am grateful to Dr Michael Ryan, University College, Swansea, for supplying me with a photocopy.

25 See *Moscow News*, no. 4 (1989), p. 10; for further discussion, see Buckley, 'Glasnost and the Woman Question', p. 208. [Editor's note: On the unchanged situation in abortion clinics up to 1994, see p. 10.]

26 See, for example, G. A. Hobbs, 'Personal View', *British Medical Journal*, 26 November 1977, p. 1413; Bernard Levin, 'If You Ever Thought of Falling Ill in Russia, Read on . . .', *The Times*, 21 July 1978; Tatyana Mamonova, 'The Feminist Movement in the Soviet Union', and Natalya Maltseva, 'The Other Side of the Coin', in Mamonova (ed.), *Women and Russia: Feminist Writings from the Soviet Union* (Oxford: Blackwell, 1984), pp. xix, 115–16.

27 I. Grebesheva, 'Abortion and the Problems of Family Planning in Russia', *Planned Parenthood in Europe*, vol. 21, no. 2 (May 1992), p. 8.

28 *Nezavisimaia gazeta*, 7 October 1992, p. 6.

29 H. Kent Geiger, *The Family in Soviet Russia* (Cambridge: Harvard University Press, 1968), p. 195.

30 Verbenko et al., *Aborty i protivozachatochnye sredstva*, p. 11.

31 Mary Buckley, 'Social Policies and the New Social Issues', in Stephen White, Alex Pravda and Zvi Gitelman (eds.), *Developments in Soviet Politics* (Basingstoke: Macmillan, 1990), p. 198.

32 E. A. Sadvokasova, 'Nekotorye sotsial'no-gigienicheskie aspekty izucheniia aborta', *SZ*, no. 3 (1963), p. 47; *Nezavisimaia gazeta*, 7 October 1992, p. 6.

33 See, for example, Ann Helgeson, 'Demographic Policy', in Archie Brown and Michael Kaser (eds.), *Soviet Policy for the 1980s* (Basingstoke: Macmillan, 1982), p. 123; *Naselenie SSSR v 1988 g* (Moscow, 1989), pp. 333–8; *Vestnik statistiki*, no. 1 (1992), p. 5.

34 These figures are taken from *Narodnoe khoziaistvo SSSR v 1965 g.* (Moscow, 1966), p. 42; and *Statisticheskii-Press Biulleten'*, no. 10 (1989), pp. 5–7.

35 For useful analyses, see John C. Dutton, 'Causes of Soviet Adult Mortality Increase', *Soviet Studies*, vol. 33, no. 4 (October 1981), pp. 548–59; W. Ward Kingkade, 'Health', in Michael Ellman and Vladimir Kontorovich (eds.), *The Disintegration of the Soviet Economic System* (London: Routledge, 1992), pp. 251–71.

36 Z. P. Iudina, 'Abort pri pervoi beremennosti', *Zdorov'e*, no. 4 (1975), p. 17.

37 S. L. Polchanova, 'Nekotorye sotsial'no-psikhologicheskie aspekty rozhdaemosti', *Sovetskoe zdravookhranenie*, no. 5 (1972), p. 15.

38 L. B. Anokhin and L. D. Saraeva, 'Kolebaniia urovni nekotorykh demograficheskikh pokazatelei po raionam oblasti', *ZRF*, no. 1 (1981), p. 23; L. E. Darskii and V. A. Belova, 'Sotsial'no-gigienicheskie voprosy, sviazannye s brakom i rozhdeniem detei v sem'e', *ZRF*, no. 3 (1969), p. 16; and A. A. Popov, 'Mediko-demograficheskii prichiny i faktory iskusstvennogo aborta (obzor literatury)', *ZRF*, no. 9 (1980), p. 26.

39 For more on this, see Libor Stloukal, 'The Politics of Population Policy: Abortion in the Soviet Union', *Working Papers in Demography*, no. 43, (Canberra: Australian National University, Research School of Social Sciences, 1993).

40 On abortion policy under Khrushchev, see David M. Heer, 'Abortion, Contraception and Population Policy in the Soviet Union', *Soviet Studies*, vol. 17, no. 1 (July 1965), p. 77; Alena Heitlinger, *Women and State Socialism: Sex Inequality in the Soviet Union and Czechoslovakia* (Basingstoke: Macmillan, 1979), p. 128.

41 I. M. Starovoitov, 'Reproduktivnaia funktsiia zhenshchin i motivy abortov', *Zdravookhranenie Belorussii*, no. 5 (1981), pp. 26–7.

42 I. R. Zak, 'Abort: eto kak bomba zamedlennogo deistviia', *Zdorov'e*, no. 5 (1973), p. 14.

43 I. R. Zak, 'Kriminal'nyi abort', *Zdorov'e*, no. 3 (1967), p. 14.

44 K. V. Seglenietsye, 'Iskusstvennyi abort – iskusnoe ubiistvo?', *Nauka i tekhnika*, no. 9 (1980), pp. 27–30. For a useful discussion of the moral issues involved, see Joel Feinberg (ed.), *The Problem of Abortion* (Belmont, Calif.: Wadsworth, 1973).

45 Andrew Tannahill and Graham Robertson, 'Health Education in Medical Education: Collaboration Not Competition', *Medical Teacher*, vol. 8 (1986), pp. 1068–71.

46 Dr Mikhail Stern and Dr August Stern, *Sex in the Soviet Union* (London: W. H. Allen, 1981), p. 117; *Meditsinskaia gazeta*, 4 March 1988, p. 4 and 24 January 1992, p. 10.

47 O. Nikonchik, 'Protivozachatochnye sredstva', *Zdorov'e*, no. 2 (1967), pp. 20–1; S. M. Iakovleva, *Sposoby i sredstva kontratseptsii* (Leningrad, 1970), pp. 125–6.

48 Larissa Remennick, 'Continuity and Change in Fertility Regulation Patterns among Former Soviet Women', paper presented to the ESRC Seminar on Women and Gender Relations in Russia, the Former Soviet Union and Eastern Europe, CREES, University of Birmingham, 4 May 1994, p. 5.

49 Christopher Williams, 'Sex Education and the AIDS Epidemic in the Former Soviet Union', *Sociology of Health and Illness,* vol. 16, no. 1 (January 1994), pp. 81–102.

50 Remennick, 'Continuity and Change', p. 5. [Editor's note: For another optimistic view, see Sargeant, p. 28. However, one Russian commentator still stated in 1994 that 'Up-to-date methods of contraception are unavailable to the majority of Russia's women.' See Andrei Baiduzhii, 'What are People in Russia Dying From?', *Nezavisimaia gazeta*, 16 July 1994, pp. 1–4; trans. in *Current Digest of the Post-Soviet Press*, vol. 46, no. 28 (1994), pp. 8–11.]

51 Avdeev et al., 'L'avortement et la contraception', p. 39.

52 Ibid., p. 40.

53 On this, see Christopher Williams, *AIDS in Post-Communist Russia and the Successor States* (Aldershot: Avebury, 1995).

54 The following discussion is based upon Alessandra Stanley, 'In Russia, Abortions Haven, Foes Press the Cause', *International Herald Tribune*, 20 May 1994, p. 2.

55 Cited in ibid.

56 Ibid.

57 Mary Buckley, 'Gender and Reform', in Catherine Merridale and Chris Ward (eds.), *Perestroika: The Historical Perspective* (London: Edward Arnold, 1991), p. 69, and Christopher Williams, 'Women in a Changing Society: Post-Communist Russia in the 1990s', *Northwest Journal of Historical Studies*, vol. 1, no. 5 (1994), pp. 55–63.

58 M. Wyman et al., 'The Russian Elections of December 1993', *Electoral Studies*, vol. 13, no. 3 (September 1994), pp. 254–71; Rosalind Marsh, 'Women after Communism', paper presented to the 20th Annual conference of the Irish Slavists' Association, The Queen's University of Belfast, 8 May 1994. [Editor's note: see also above, p. 18.]

59 Stanley, 'In Russia, Abortions Haven'. [Editor's note: for discussion of the impact of the introduction of fees for abortions, see p. 281.]

60 Joyce Outshoorn, 'Abortion Law Reform: A Woman's Right to Choose?', in Mary Buckley and Malcolm Anderson (eds.), *Women, Equality and Europe* (Basingstoke: Macmillan, 1988), p. 204.

61 Editor's note: There is some evidence that by 1994 this process of co-operation had begun. See p. 293 for the campaign by the 'Women of Russia' movement and the Independent Women's Forum against the charging of fees for abortions.

62 Marsh, 'Women after Communism'. [Editor's note: For further information and a more positive interpretation of this achievement, see pp. 12–13.]

63 Cited in James Riordan and Sue Bridger (eds.), *Dear Comrade Editor: Readers' Letters to*

the *Soviet Press under Perestroika* (Bloomington and Indianapolis: Indiana University Press, 1992), pp. 81–2.

64 For further discussion, see Joni Lovenduski and Joyce Outshoorn, *The New Politics of Abortion* (London: Sage, 1986). [Editor's note: Recent evidence suggests that the Russian Orthodox Church holds conservative views on both abortion and contraception. In a talk at St Antony's College, Oxford, 1 November 1994, Father Gleb Iakunin, a dissident Orthodox priest and Duma deputy, suggested that the Moscow Patriarchate was able to exert considerable influence in this matter on the legislation of Yel'tsin's government.]

10

Sexual minorities: the status of gays and lesbians in Russian– Soviet–Russian society

JAMES RIORDAN

Persecution and torment by no means require persecutors and tormentors; all they need is simply us ordinary folk confronted by someone who is not one of us: a Negro, a wild beast, someone from Mars, a poet or ghost. Such are born to be persecuted.
Marina Tsvetaeva[1]

Introduction

Valentin Rasputin said in an interview with the BBC in early 1991 that homosexuality had been imported into Russia and that if gays and lesbians felt their rights were being violated, they should emigrate. In fact, homosexuality has been known in Russia from ancient times and, indeed, had been treated more tolerantly than it had in the West.[2]

The religious definition of 'sodomy' in ancient Rus´ was even vaguer than in the West, designating both homosexual relations and anal intercourse irrespective of the sex of the partners, as well as deviations from 'normal' sexual roles and positions. Rus´ was certainly more tolerant toward this 'vice' than the West; church penitence for it varied between one and seven years – that is, within the parameters set for heterosexual transgressions.[3]

Lesbianism was normally categorized as a form of masturbation. Bishop Nifont in the twelfth century regarded sexual contact between two juvenile girls as a lesser sin than heterosexual 'lechery', especially if maidenhood remained intact.[4] The Orthodox Church was concerned about homosexuality spreading in the monasteries, yet it was fairly tolerant of its practice, which came as a surprise to foreigners in the sixteenth and seventeenth centuries.

Almost all foreign travellers and diplomats in Russia during the fifteenth to seventeenth centuries (Sigmund von Herberstein, Adam Oleary, Margeret, Collins) remark on the widespread nature of homosexuality in all social milieux and the surprisingly tolerant attitude toward it by European standards of the time.[5] Even Ivan the Terrible, despite his several marriages, evidently enjoyed having young boys dress up in women's clothing, and suspicions went the rounds about his relations with the young effeminate Fedor Basmanov.

156

The Russian historian S. M. Solov'ev wrote, in the moralizing tone typical of the time, 'Nowhere either in East or West did they view this foul, unnatural vice as lightly as in Russia.'[6] This probably came less from conscious toleration than from indifference and a naturalistic-barbaric acceptance of the 'facts of life' (the same existed in the early Middle Ages in western Europe; it was much later that the bonfires of the Inquisition flared up). Whatever the case, homosexuality is neither mentioned nor punished in any Russian legislation, from Iaroslav the Wise to Peter the Great.

The punishment for 'unnatural lechery' – burning at the stake – first appeared in 1706 in Peter the Great's military code, composed on the Swedish model. Yet in 1716, Peter, himself not averse to bisexual relations, watered down the punishment, replacing it with lifelong exile (in the event of the use of violence), and that only for military personnel.

In the latter part of the eighteenth century, with the growth of civilization and extended contacts with Europe, genteel society began to feel uneasy about homosexuality. Amidst the common people it tended to be localized primarily to religious sects. Among the aristocracy, homosexuality sometimes reached scandalous proportions, but not so much in itself as through connections with nepotism and corruption: powerful people settled accounts with their young protégés by high appointments that in no way corresponded to their abilities.

Until 1832 homosexuality was a religious, moral and pedagogical problem, but not a legal one. In 1832 the situation changed. The new criminal code, constituted on the German (Württemberg) model, included Paragraph 995 which outlawed buggery, by which it meant anal contact between men. Buggery was punishable by loss of all class rights and exile to Siberia for four to five years; rape or perversion of a minor (Paragraph 996) was punished by forced labour for between ten and twenty years. This legislation, with minor amendments introduced in 1845, operated until the adoption in 1903 of a New Penal Code that was much more lenient: in line with Article 516, buggery (once again anal contact only) was an offence punishable by imprisonment for a period of no less than three months and, in aggravated circumstances, for between three and eight years.

However, this legislation, particularly in the twentieth century, was rarely applied, at least in regard to the privileged classes, being no hindrance either to their personal lives or to their public careers.[7] For example, only ten people were prosecuted for buggery in 1894.[8] The well-known lawyer, Vladimir Nabokov (father of the writer) proposed decriminalizing homosexuality altogether in 1902;[9] to many the proposal was too radical. Many in society simply turned a blind eye to homosexuality.

A lot of people were aware of the homosexuality of the well-known traveller Nikolai Przheval'skii (1839–88) who always took with him teenage lads as personal assistants. There was no secret about the bisexuality of the ultra-conservative writer Konstantin Leont'ev (1831–91) who lauded the beauty of the male body in his works. Prince Vladimir Meshcherskii (1839–1914), publisher of the *Grazhdanin* newspaper, not only did not conceal his inclinations, he openly distributed high posts to his favourites (he is the man Vladimir Solov'ev once called 'Prince of Sodom and Citizen of Gomorrah'). Some members of the royal family also led an openly homosexual lifestyle, in particular Nicholas II's uncle, Grand Duke Sergei Aleksandrovich – as did Foreign Minister Count Vladimir Lamsdorf.

Intellectuals, too, did not suffer persecution for being homosexual. The poet Aleksei Apukhtin led an openly gay life; he was classmate and friend of Petr Tchaikovsky at the School of Jurisprudence which gained a reputation for such lifestyles. So the legend of the composer's suicide at the sentence of a court of honour made up of his former classmates is patently absurd. The only case of Articles 995 and 996 being applied that the researcher Nina Berberova could locate was a hue and cry over a classics teacher named Langovoi in a private school, who was sentenced to Siberian exile for sex with a thirteen-year-old boy, although he was pardoned after five years.[10]

The poet Mikhail Kuz'min openly appeared in public with what his detractors liked to call his 'little darlings'. The peasant poet Nikolai Kliuev, one-time member of the Khlyst sect, did not hide his homoerotic inclinations. Sergei Diaghilev enjoyed enormous notoriety and provoked universal scandal; he was the founder – together with his cousin and lover Dmitrii Filosofov – of the magazine *Mir iskusstva* and, later, the new Ballet Russe.

Russia also had famous female couples: one of the first Russian feminists, the founder of the literary journal *Severnyi vestnik,* Anna Evreinova, and her lifelong friend Mariia Fedorova; the symbolist poet Poliksena Solov'eva and the wife of a well-known scholar, Natal'ia Manaseina, who left her husband to live with Solov'eva. Marina Tsvetaeva made no secret of her bisexuality. As she herself wrote, even as a young girl, 'I did not fall in love with Onegin, but with Onegin and Tat'iana together (and, perhaps, with Tat'iana rather more). Subsequently I never wrote a single thing without falling in love simultaneously with them both (with her slightly more), not with the two of them, but with their love.' Her romance with another Russian poet Sof'ia Parnok played a considerable part in Tsvetaeva's life.[11]

Lidiia Zinov'eva-Annibal's book *Thirty-Three Freaks* (1907) was the first frank description of lesbian relationships. The actress Vera arranges the wedding of a young woman with whom she is in love. The abandoned groom kills himself, and the two women start living together. But their blissful state does not last long. Vera's friend needs male society and finally abandons Vera who commits suicide. Although the book is superficial, asocial and melodramatic, it does discuss fairly complex problems for the first time in Russian literature.

Russian attitudes toward love and sex were, however, more metaphysical than phenomenological; once the subject turns to real, everyday, earthly enjoyment, it tends to come up against an uncompromising and frightened 'NO!' This timidity, like the interest in androgyny, certainly had its personality origins. People at the time said that Zinaida Gippius's marriage to Merezhkovskii was purely spiritual. Gippius herself was inclined to stress that she was a woman who 'could never give myself to a man no matter how much I loved him'. Yet she also experienced revulsion from the physical side of lesbian love.[12] The non-acceptance and non-embodiment of one's own sexual, above all homoerotic inclinations, typical of the entire circle of late nineteenth- to early twentieth-century Russian intellectuals, engendered an intellectual inconsistency and vagueness in formulations. Abstract philosophical forms enabled them to designate their problems and thereby avoid any tormenting personal self-revelation. As Laura Engelstein justly remarks, 'the open-mindedness of the philosophers was limited by the other-worldly quality of their ruminations'.[13]

Russian society at the turn of the century was not ready for a differentiated perception of these complex phenomena. To the minds of many intellectuals, they formed a single picture of a terrifying 'sexual Bacchanalia', as D. N. Zhbankov called it in an article written in 1908.[14] Relegating sex to one extreme causes moral panic at the other. Sex, and especially 'deviant sex', also acquired importance as a generalized political symbol through attitudes to which people expressed their own moral and political views. Conservative guardians of public morals maintained that 'obsession with sex' undermined the very fabric of the family and public morality; it was engendered by the revolutionary movement and godlessness. The Social Democrats, on the other hand, tried to show that it was the offspring of offensive reaction which followed the defeat of the 1905 Revolution, a consequence of intellectuals' disillusionment with public life and withdrawal into their own private lives.

Probably both were right. Society could not be democratized without a critical review of patriarchal morality, including methods of social control over sexuality; and demands for 'sexual liberation' were an integral part of the social renovation programme and preceded the 1905 Revolution. At the same time, the defeat of the Revolution, which did undermine people's interest in politics, encouraged them to seek compensation in their private everyday lives and, first and foremost, in sex.

For the extreme right, sexophobia and homophobia merged with judophobia and misogyny. Jews and women were equally inimical to creative male principles, perverting men and undermining the rational self-control men required. At the propagandist level of the mass anti-Semitic press, like the paper *Zhenshchina*, this became affirmation that Jews, being themselves sexually restrained and home-loving, were deliberately perverting the Russian people with pornography, prostitution and the advocacy of abortion, contraception and decriminalization of homosexuality. The Black Hundred press claimed that Jews were the owners of all Russian brothels as well as drinking dens, thereby bringing about not only the moral dissipation of Russians, but their physical extinction and reduction in numbers.[15]

On the other hand, populist and Social Democratic critics (Iu. M. Steklov, G. S. Novopolin) were railing against 'erotic individualism' and pornography as products of dissolute bourgeois culture through which the bourgeoisie was trying to infect the naturally spiritually healthy working class. For Novopolin, the literary personages of Kuz´min and Zinov´eva-Annibal were simply 'degenerates perverted through indolence', 'parasites sucking the people's blood and craving for their fat'.[16]

The logic of left and right was, therefore, one and the same: sex and homosexuality were dangerous instruments of the class/national enemy through which it was undermining the spiritual and physical health of 'our side'. The new regime after 1917 inherited both deep-seated attitudes.

Sexual minorities after 1917

The initiative for revoking the anti-homosexual tsarist legislation lay, following the February 1917 Revolution, not with the Bolsheviks, but with the Constitutional Democrats – we have already seen how one Cadet leader, Vladimir Nabokov, had proposed precisely that – and the Anarchists. Once the old Punishment Code had been repealed after the October Revolution, Article 516 also ceased to be valid. The Russian Federation criminal codes for 1922 and 1926 do not mention homosexuality, although the corresponding laws remained in force where homosexuality was most prevalent – in the Islamic republics of Azerbaidzhan, Turkmenistan and Uzbekistan, as well as in Christian Georgia.

During the 1920s, the situation for Soviet homosexuals was relatively bearable and many gays and lesbians (such as Kuz´min, Kliuev and Parnok) played a major role in Soviet culture, although the opportunity for an open, philosophical and artistic debate of the theme, which had opened up at the start of the century, was gradually whittled away.[17] On 17 December 1933, however, the government brought out a bill which became law on 7 March 1934. Accordingly, 'buggery' once more became a criminal offence and this item was inserted into the criminal codes of all the Soviet republics. According to Article 121 of the currently operative Russian Criminal Code, 'buggery' is punishable by deprivation of freedom for a term of up to five years and, in cases involving physical force or the threat thereof, or in relation to a minor, or exploiting the victim's dependent status, a term of up to eight years.

The people's commissar for justice, Nikolai Krylenko, announced in January 1936 that homosexuality was a product of the decadence of the exploiting classes who knew no better; in a socialist society founded on healthy principles there was no place for such people. Homosexuality was, therefore, directly 'tied in' with counter-revolution.[18] Subsequently, Soviet lawyers and medical specialists talked of homosexuality primarily as a manifestation of 'the moral decadence of the bourgeoisie', reiterating verbatim the arguments of the Nazis (such as in the article on homosexuality in the second (1952) edition of the *Great Soviet Encyclopedia*).[19]

Nobody knows the exact number of victims of this inhuman law. According to calculations made by Sergei Shcherbakov, an average of a thousand men fell victim every year. The only official information on the subject was that released after perestroika had begun: in 1987, 831 men were found guilty under Article 121; in 1988, 800 were sentenced; in 1989, 538; in 1990, 497; in 1991, 482; and for the first half of 1992, 227, of whom only ten were actually sentenced under 121.1

(figures for 1991–2 are for Russia only).[20] The victims must have been far more numerous in previous years.

Article 121 was aimed not only at homosexuals. It was frequently employed for dealing with dissidents and augmenting labour camp sentences. Application of the law was selective. If eminent cultural or political figures kept out of trouble (for example, the British spy Guy Burgess or the world-famous pianist Sviatoslav Richter), they enjoyed a kind of immunity and the authorities often turned a blind eye to their homosexual proclivities. But they only had to fall foul of an influential bigwig for the law to move into top gear. That was what destroyed the life of the great Armenian film-maker Sergei Paradzhanov, the Leningrad archeologist Lev Klein and the chief director of the Leningrad *Iunii Zritel'* Theatre, Zinovii Korogodskii.

A gloomy conspiracy of silence intensified even more the psychological tragedy of Soviet 'blues' (homosexuals): they not only feared persecution and blackmail, they could not even develop an adequate self-awareness and comprehend exactly who they were. Medicine offered little help. When in the 1970s the first sexopathological books began to come out, homosexuality was treated as a pernicious 'sexual perversion', a disease that had to be treated.[21] The first and only, at the time, manual on sex education for teachers, by Khripkova and Kolesov, published a million copies in 1982, defined homosexuality as a dangerous pathology and 'a violation of normal principles of sexual relationships'. It went on to say that 'Homosexuality is against both normal heterosexual relationships and society's cultural, moral attainments. It therefore merits condemnation both as a social phenomenon and as a person's mental makeup and behaviour.'[22]

When AIDS appeared in the Soviet Union, those in charge of the state epidemiological programme blamed homosexuals for being carriers of the HIV virus. Even the liberal *Ogonek* published its first article on an AIDS victim (the first Soviet man known to suffer from the disease – a gay engineer who caught the virus in Africa) in tones of unconcealed disgust and condemnation.

All the same, glasnost, together with the threat of AIDS, made it possible to have a more or less frank discussion of sex orientation problems, initially in scholarly, then in popular literature. Igor Kon's *Introduction to Sexology*, which finally came out in 1988 (after a ten-year ban), contained a chapter on sexual orientation, setting out contemporary theories on the subject and demonstrating the harmful and unjust nature of discrimination against gays and lesbians.[23] The book nonetheless had to skirt specific issues concerning homosexuals in the Soviet Union, as well as all the legal problems. The 1989 edition of Kon's book *Adolescent Psychology* (*Psikhologiia rannei iunosti*), intended for teachers and parents, did contain, for the first time in a Soviet publication, a few pages about adolescent homosexuality which looked at it as an aspect of normal psycho-sexual development, rather than as a disease or the result of adults 'perverting' adolescents.[24]

From 1987, the question of exactly what homosexuality was and how one should relate to gays and lesbians – whether to regard them as sick, criminals or victims of fate – began to be discussed extensively in the popular, especially youth, press (*Moskovskii komsomolets, Komsomol'skaia pravda, Sobesednik, Molodoi kommunist, Literaturnaia gazeta, Ogonek, Argumenty i fakty, SPID-info*, the teenage journal *Parus*, and some local newspapers), and on radio and television. Although these publications were extremely diverse in their level and orientation, they were of huge significance. Ordinary people for the first time began to learn from journalistic articles and letters from gays, lesbians and their parents of the crippled destinies, arbitrary police behaviour, court repressions, sexual abuse in prisons, camps and the armed forces, and finally of the tragic, inevitable loneliness of people doomed to live in constant fear and unable to meet people similar to themselves. Each publication provoked a fresh stream of contradictory responses which editors had no idea how to handle.

One fact emerged from the debate: apart from Albania and Romania, the Soviet Union was the only country in eastern Europe (not to mention western Europe) that practised anti-homosexual legislation. A discussion began on the key issue of decriminalizing homosexuality. Although mention of it never made its way into the press, the draft new Russian Criminal Code, prepared by a legal commission in the mid-1980s, had excluded Article 121. Yet discussion and adoption of the new code became drawn out through various political circumstances; meanwhile, disputes on Article 121 spilled out into the popular press and on to the television screens. Three major viewpoints prevailed:

1   To revoke Article 121 completely and not to mention sexual orientation in the Criminal Code, insofar as children and adolescents, irrespective of their gender, are protected by other laws: this stand is taken by a number of lawyers and sexologists (such as Igor' Kon and Aron Belkin).
2   To revoke criminal responsibility for homosexual contacts between consenting adults, but to retain the second part of Article 121 referring to children and minors – the position of many Ministry of Internal Affairs officials.[25]
3   To leave it as it is. This is the demand of right-wing nationalists, some of the hard-line communist and religious organizations.

It was not until early 1992 that some parliaments in the now-independent states of the former Soviet Union debated new penal codes that would decriminalize homosexuality. In both Russia and Ukraine, new legislation was drafted, proposing removal of the infamous Article 121 and reduction of the age of sexual consent for all persons from 18 to 16. For the first time lesbianism came to be recognized in the draft legislation. However, gays and lesbians in the former Soviet Union were concerned that the draft legislation applying to homosexual rape (Article 132 in the draft Russian code) differed markedly from its non-gay counterpart, referring to 'gay male sex, lesbianism, and the gratification of sexual lust in other perverted forms'. The parallel law, which applies to heterosexuals, simply refers to 'sexual relations'.

However, by late 1994 the Russian Duma had not even considered making the draft proposals law, or even discussing them. The political situation would appear to discourage MPs, even given sufficient will, from liberalizing existing legislation. On the other hand, a bill was put before the Russian Duma in mid-July 1994, 'On Preventing the Spread of HIV in the Russian Federation', setting out the rights and duties of Russian and foreign nationals in Russia in regard to HIV. It warned of the real threat of the spread of HIV, but made clear in Article 18 the illegality of any discrimination (at work or study, and so on) against HIV-infected persons. Somewhat paradoxically, given the lack of any mention of AIDS in the 25 articles of the bill, it is intended to replace the law 'On Therapy for AIDS Infection' passed on 23 April 1990.

No matter how radically legislation on homosexuality eventually changes, the position of sexual minorities depends not only on that, but also on the public mood which no one is capable of changing overnight. Irrational fear of homosexuality and hatred of gays and lesbians constitute one of the major problems in present-day Russian sexual culture.

It has to be said that Soviet society has been generally extremely intolerant of any dissident thinking and uncommon behaviour, even that which is entirely innocent. Homosexuals are the most stigmatized of all social groups, according to a number of surveys. For example, according to the nationwide Public Opinion Study Centre, a survey undertaken in November 1989 with a representative sample of 2,600 people from all over the country, the question 'How ought we to treat homosexuals?' produced the following spread of responses: 6 per cent were in favour of providing help, 10 per cent of leaving gays and lesbians alone, 30 per cent of isolating them from society, and 33 per cent of exterminating all homosexuals.[26]

Attitudes toward gays and lesbians are considerably worse than toward any other negatively evaluated social group, even including prostitutes and drug addicts, with whom homosexuality is frequently associated owing to tendentious anti-AIDS propaganda.[27] Many respondents know nothing about gays and lesbians and possibly heard about them for the first time only during the various surveys. Hostility toward them is a particular example of hostility to all that is unknown and alien. All the same, such reasoning is hardly balm to those on the receiving end of hatred.

The right-wing chauvinist media, like *Sovetskaia Rossiia, Den´, Russkoe voskresenie, Nash sovremennik, Molodaia gvardiia, Shchit i mech,* as well as Aleksandr Nevzorov's television programme *600 Seconds,* deliberately whip up homophobia and actively propagate it.

The fascist press methodically and consistently lumps together Bolshevism, Zionism, democracy and homosexuality. Thus, the newspaper *Russkoe voskresenie* ran an article under the title 'Let us defend Russian Orthodoxy against the Yids', in which it wrote, 'Both the Bolsheviks and democratic leaders are of foreign extraction. Both are sexual perverts. You will recall that the first decree issued by the Soviet government was to revoke punishment for homosexuality. Now it's the democrats who are after the same thing. (It was reintroduced by the Russian Orthodox Stalin and his Russian entourage in 1934.)'[28]

During the pre-election campaigns of December 1993, however, reformers gained an unlikely ally. Aleksandr Zhirinovskii, leader of the 'neo-fascist' Liberal Democratic Party (which was to gain more seats than any other party), devoted an hour-long TV election broadcast to sex. During his 'address', he advocated decriminalization of homosexuality and the adoption of children by gay and lesbian couples. At the same time, his explanations for homosexuality (the 'over-mother-ing' of boys, late sexual experience and so on) were unscientific in the extreme. It has to be said that recommendations from such a right-wing maverick as Zhirinovskii are hardly likely to further sexual tolerance for the gay–lesbian cause.

Attitudes toward homosexuality obviously constitute an acute political problem in society today, in all the post-Soviet states. It is not merely a matter of political opportunism or criminal sanctions. Until the end of 1991, gays and lesbians had nowhere to meet in any decent way, to encounter people of their own interests. Of course, big cities have always had well-known places for gays to gather. Yet fear of exposure has made most contacts impersonal, anonymous and short-lived, devoid of human warmth and psychological intimacy.

When most people talk of homosexuality in the former Soviet Union, they have commonly referred to male homosexuality; it is only recently that the popular press has begun to write about lesbians. That has been the same in most male-dominated countries waking up to the realities of inborn sexual behaviour, with females initially excluded from public discussion of homosexual activities, conduct that detracted from their role as producers of children and support for males. Even in the discussion of 'cures for male homosexuality' there has been more than a hint of putting the blame on mothers for turning 'normal' boys into 'abnormal' men through 'excessive maternal love'.

All the same, the position of lesbians has been no better than that of gays. It is true that their relationships have not traditionally fallen within the terms of any criminal code statute, and close relations between women are less open to malicious gossip. On the other hand, a young woman who becomes aware of her psycho–sexual uniqueness will find it more difficult than a young man to find a soulmate. And public attitudes are just as obdurate: ridicule, persecution, sending down from university, sacking from employment, threats to take away children and other sanctions.

Even if the law never recognised lesbianism as a form of homosexuality (women were not mentioned in Article 121) and if virtually all public discussion had ignored lesbianism, it had certainly been described in detail in the scientific literature. For example, the two-volume edition of *Personal Sexopathology*, published in 1983, gives several detailed biographies of lesbians and frank explanations of their means of obtaining sexual gratification, from oral–genital contact to the use of dildos.[29] Further, it emerged in late 1989 that sex-change operations had been carried out in the Soviet Union for over twenty years – not without problems. In 1969, the Latvian surgeon Viktor Kalnbers completed the first Soviet series of operations to transform a woman into a man (who subsequently had a 'happy marriage'). Yet it could not be mentioned at the time, even in a medical paper. Instead, the surgeon was 'given a severe reprimand for carrying out an operation unacceptable in the

Soviet Union and without approval from the Health Ministry'. Questions were even raised in the Latvian Communist Party Central Committee about the surgeon's 'mental fitness' and his 'indulging in debauchery and dissipation'. Although Kalnbers was banned from further operations, his Moscow colleague, Professor Kirpatovskii, did carry out several operations 'to transform men into women'. As Kalnbers commented in *Literaturnaia gazeta* in 1989,

> Our concern for people as a whole has blinded us to the problems of the individual, particularly those concerning intimate relations. A girl who falls in love with another girl and commits suicide is of interest to no one . . . I recall even the Minister (of Health), dismissing my claim that my patient would kill herself, saying 'that's not our concern'. How many tragedies have occurred precisely for that reason![30]

A public discussion of women's sexuality was just starting in 1989. It was launched by a most provocative article (for the USSR) in *Sobesednik* on lesbian love, 'Olia and Iulia', accompanied by a picture of two naked women, one caressing a nipple of the other. While the article's author, Galina Toktal'eva, acted as devil's advocate in expressing society's moral anguish, she gave space to the views of the 25-year-old head of a psychology research unit. Ol'ga, we were told, had once fallen madly in love with a married man; her hatred of all men had stemmed from this failed relationship. Ol'ga and her lesbian friends had formed a 'League of Activists' to spread their creed and encourage female love as well as the rejection (and therefore punishment) of men – 'our society is run by parasitic men'.

Ol'ga's views will be familiar to many western feminists and their supporters: 'Women must defend their right to an existence of equal worth, the right to be a thinking member of society, not a birth-delivery-cum-washing-machine . . . Intimate relations should be a matter of individual choice. The greatest woman poet genius, Sappho, praised female love and friendship . . . Humankind must be punished for the age-old oppression of women, for its humiliation of those who produce life.'[31]

Gays and lesbians fight back

Up to the late 1980s, Soviet gays and lesbians were victims who could only complain about their fate and futilely bemoan their humiliation. True, there were rare exceptions. Some thirty young people in Leningrad, led by Aleksandr Zaremba, came together in 1984 in a 'gay and lesbian' community, set up a 'Gay Laboratory' and established contact with a Finnish gay and lesbian association. They despatched information to the West about the woeful state of Soviet homosexuals and started to conduct therapeutic work on AIDS, which Soviet medicine had completely failed to do. It did not take long, however, before the group caught the eye of the KGB and found itself on the end of political and ideological accusations, threats and repression, as a result of which the group members were forced to emigrate or hold their peace.

During the initial glasnost years 'experts' alone spoke of sexual minority problems in tones of estranged sympathy. But gradually gays themselves broke through into the press, the victims gaining the courage to fight for themselves. Foreign gay organizations and publications offered considerable help in changing their self-awareness.

On the initiative of the Estonian Academy of Sciences History Institute and with the support of several overseas gay communities, the first international conference to be held anywhere in the Soviet Union devoted to 'The Status of Sexual Minorities and Changing Attitudes to Homosexuality in Twentieth-Century Europe' took place in Tallinn between 28 and 30 May 1990. Many eminent foreign scholars, like Jeffrey Weeks and Gert Hekma, took part in the conference, which was very successful and encouraged increased self-awareness and elucidation of the social and psychological identity of Soviet gays and lesbians. The first comparative questionnaire survey into the position and problems of sexual minorities in Finland and Estonia commenced within the framework of the Soviet–Finnish programme for studying social minorities; it had its base in Tallinn under the leadership of the demographer Teet Veispaak. The questionnaire was extended to Russia, but no results have been forthcoming.

In late 1989 Moscow witnessed the establishment of the first Sexual Minorities Association (Alliance of Lesbians and Homosexuals). Its programme underlined that it was 'primarily a legal defence organization with the main purpose of obtaining the complete equality of people of different sexual orientation'. It saw its prime objectives as campaigning to revoke Article 121; changing public attitudes (or, rather, prejudices) toward members of sexual minorities, employing all the opportunities presented by the official press; the social rehabilitation of AIDS sufferers; publishing the newspaper *Tema* (*The Theme*) and other material; assistance to people in their search for friends and soulmates. It considered it important to study homosexual problems, to campaign for safer sex and to gather all available information on gay persecution. It had no formal membership and anyone over eighteen could join.

SPID-info published the association's appeal to the USSR president and the Supreme Soviets of the USSR and the union republics signed by V. Ortanov, K. Evgen'ev and A. Zubov, requesting the removal of discriminatory statutes from the criminal code referring to same-sex sexual contacts between adults, and declaring an amnesty for those convicted under those statutes. At the same time, the authors of the appeal declared 'their resolute condemnation of any attempts to seduce minors and use violence in any form and with regard to persons of any sex and regardless of who actually made such attempts'. They went on to say that 'We do not desire to convert anyone to our belief, but we are what nature made us. Help us to stop being afraid. We are part of your life and your spirituality, whether you or we like it or not.'[32]

Unfortunately, the political climate of Soviet society and the impossibility of having a constructive dialogue with the authorities encouraged a situation where all democratic movements straight away began to split into 'radicals' and 'moderates' who refused to work together. Gays were no different in this respect.

Immediately after the publication of *Tema*'s second trial issue, a split emerged in the association which then actually ceased to exist; in its place there appeared the Moscow Alliance of Lesbians and Homosexuals (MALH) headed by Evgeniia Debrianskaia and the 24-year-old student Roman Kalinin who became the sole editor and publisher of the newspaper *Tema*. The paper was officially registered by the Moscow City Council in October 1990.

The establishment of the Sexual Minorities Association had opened up substantial opportunities to gays. It was an event triumphantly acclaimed in the West. The fact that courageous people had come out openly, demanding civil rights in place of humiliation, was an important moral victory. The question now was how to continue the struggle.

MALH enjoyed political and financial support from American gay organizations; it therefore decided to operate through street meetings and protest demonstrations under trenchant political slogans intended not so much for Soviet citizens as for western correspondents. It was a tactic that found favour with radical gay activists. Kalinin went down particularly well in the United States, was triumphantly received by the mayor of San Francisco, had the date of his arrival in the city proclaimed 'Roman Kalinin Day', was awarded an honorary certificate and won promises to flood the USSR with free condoms.[33]

Funds collected in the USA enabled the International *Tema* Organization to hold an international symposium in both Leningrad and Moscow in the summer of 1991 on gay and lesbian rights and the fight against AIDS. Plenary sessions took place in large conference halls. Simultaneously, the organizers openly showed several gay and lesbian films for the first time in the country. Apart from the plenary sessions devoted mainly to political issues, the organizers arranged several symposia at which specific questions concerning sexual minorities were debated, including their psychological health and culture, AIDS therapy and so on. The participants sensibly decided at the last moment against holding a parade on Red Square under the slogan 'Turn Red Squares into Pink Triangles', confining themselves to a modest protest meeting accompanied by free handouts of condoms.

Sad to say, common features of Soviet–Russian politics began vividly to manifest themselves in the activity of Kalinin and his group: lack of political experience, extremism and unwillingness to consider reality. Demands by the Libertarian Party, of which MALH was a member, to legalize sexual minorities, prostitution and drugs were serious enough taken separately, but to lump them all together and without any argumentation – the press received only bare slogans – just went to reinforce the stereotype that homosexuality, prostitution and drug-taking were all of the same mould and that 'such people' should be given no quarter. Roman Kalinin himself soon left politics for commerce, setting up a gay club in Moscow. His group changed its name to the 'Liberation Alliance', but its publication *Tema*, having attained a declared print run of 20,000 copies in 1991, steadily lost readers and ceased publication altogether in 1993.

The more moderate leaders of the gay movement (Vladislav Ortanov, Aleksandr Kukharskii and Ol'ga Zhuk) were very critical of Kalinin's activities, which had been used as an excuse by conservative local authorities to refuse to register other, more constructive, blue and pink organizations and publications.

After the collapse of the August 1991 coup, the position of sexual minorities somewhat improved. Besides *Tema*, the ARGO-RISK Association (ARGO – *Assotsiatsiia za ravnopravie gomosexualistov* – the Association for Homosexual Equal Rights) officially registered in Moscow and, from 1992, began publishing the paper *RISK* (*Ravnopravie–Iskrennost'–Svoboda–Kompromiss* – *Equality–Sincerity–Freedom– Compromise*), edited by Vladislav Ortanov, which had a circulation of 5,000. The newspaper *1/10* (editor-in-chief Dmitrii Lychev) had a circulation of some 10,000; and yet another 'blue' paper, *Impulse*, was being published by the private information agency of the same name under the slogan 'Power in Unity'.

The *Raduga* (Rainbow) Charity Fund registered in Moscow in July 1992 as 'an independent non-profit-making organization which sets itself the objective of affirming human values, implementing and protecting civil, social and cultural rights and liberties of the individual, affirming the principles of charity and toleration, and proffering psychological, medical, legal and material help to homo-sexuals'. The fund is closely associated with the 'Medicine and Reproduction' Treatment and Diagnostic Centre which has been giving medical and psycho-logical aid since 1990 'to people of a homosexual orientation'. Raduga publishes its own *Information Bulletin* and the illustrated *Gay Digest: Press and Events*.

St Petersburg has the Cultural Initiative and Sexual Minority Defence Fund set up by Ol'ga Zhuk (they were initially not allowed to use Tchaikovsky's name for the fund) and the *Kryl'ia* (Wings) Homosexual Defence Association (whose President is Aleksandr Kukharskii, a professor of physics). *Kryl'ia* was initially called *Nevskie berega* (*The Neva Banks*), then *Nevskaia perspektiva* (*Neva Prospects*), but the city fathers thought these names were 'advocating the homosexualization of the district'. Associations and publications analogous in spirit have arisen in a number of former Soviet republics (Ukraine, Belarus, Latvia, Estonia) and Russian cities (Nizhnii Tagil, Barnaul, Kaluga, Murmansk, Rostov, Omsk, Tomsk and others).

Virtually all these organizations energetically co-operate with medical insti-tutions engaged in AIDS therapy, although in some cases this has to be kept quiet for the sake of respectability and international contacts. In 1994, Moscow had several gay discos (the most expensive belonging to Roman Kalinin); St Petersburg had two or three. A couple of illustrated and fairly serious quarterly journals were in preparation, one being published by the Cultural Initiative Fund, Cultural Initiative and Sexual Minority Defence Fund, the other by Evgeniia Debrianskaia.

Two related St Petersburg journals are the *AIDS, Sex and Health* journal, founded in 1991 and published four times a year, and the *All People Are Sisters* journal published by the feminist group of the same name (*Vse liudi – sestry*).

In August 1993, Moscow was the venue for an international conference on gender issues, leading to the establishment of the umbrella group 'The Russian Association of Gays, Lesbians and Bisexuals – The Triangle' (*Treugol'nik*); it publishes the *Treugol'nik Bulletin*, provides help–lines, contacts and other services.

Like all other post-Soviet groups, gays, lesbians and other sexual minorities suffer from an acute lack of funds and an equally acute inability to collaborate amicably with one another. Their leaders often accuse each other of every mortal sin and demand complete autonomy and authority over the movement.

The newspapers and magazines mentioned are virtually the same in content as those in the West, but, of course, poorer and more primitive. Each issue publishes information about gay and lesbian life, erotic photos (mainly from western journals), translated articles, a contacts service, medical and other advice, advertisements for condoms and suchlike. Female material, not to speak of eroticism, is substantially less than male material. Much is primitive, but the overall level of the publications is steadily rising, especially when one bears in mind how difficult it is to publish at all.

By contrast with national minorities, sexual minorities cannot proclaim their sovereignty and establish their own independent state; their emancipation and socio–cultural integration are two sides of the same coin. There appear to be three paramount tasks facing gays and lesbians:

1   To decriminalize homosexuality as part of the overall process of democratizing the country. No people can be free while it is oppressing social minorities, and gays and lesbians are the most numerous of them, albeit often invisible. This requires the concerted effort of all democratic forces. Political 'happenings' are fine for a community of contented, benevolent people with full bellies; in Russia, however, they may only intensify the overall irritation, frustration and tension. Some gay excesses are reminiscent of enjoying a feast at a time of famine.

2   A no less complex and much more long-term task is to educate the public in a systematic way. As Goethe once put it, 'What people do not comprehend they do not possess.' Homophobia is the result of both ignorance and patriarchal reactionary policies. The mass media, science and the arts have a major role to play here, as do those foreign organizations and individuals willing to offer constructive advice and help when requested.

3   To form a gay subculture, to turn the homosexual ghetto into a normal gay and lesbian community, with its own publications, clubs, advice centres and so on, as in the West.

All three tasks are interconnected, and can only be resolved through co-operation and dialogue with the heterosexual majority.

Recent progress is undeniable. Formerly suppressed and forbidden 'gay sensibilities' and eroticism are gradually being recognized and integrated into élite culture. The most popular theatre director in Moscow is the openly gay Roman Viktiuk; his theatre, where some performances have marked homoerotic overtones, is always full, although the audience is not exclusively or even predominantly gay. In St Petersburg, the classical dancer Valerii Mikhailovskii recently established a first-rate all-male ballet company, and the prominent choreographer Boris Eifman staged a very successful piece about the life of Tchaikovsky in his Modern Ballet Theatre. The problems of gay and lesbian life are often discussed on television and in the mainstream newspapers. A shockingly revealing interview with Boris Moiseev, an openly gay popular dancer, was recently published; Moiseev spoke frankly about his sexual experiences with former Komsomol bosses. Foreign films with homosexual allusions, and even some completely dedicated to this topic, are shown openly in the cinemas and sometimes even on television.

Mikhail Kuz'min's classic homoerotic poetry and his famous novel *Kryl'ia*, as well as novels by Jean Genet, James Baldwin and Truman Capote have been published. A two-volume collection of the works of Russian gay writer, actor and theatre director Evgenii Kharitonov (1941–81) was published for the first time in 1993.

It is not only gay high culture that is available. There are now (mid-1994) four gay discos in Moscow and two in St Petersburg. Moscow gays can meet one another in 'The Underground', a popular gay bar, or in 'The Elf', a café club, or in 'Petrovskii dvorik', a chic gay restaurant that features a special 'blue' show, 'blue' waiters and male striptease. But those who can afford such luxuries are only the very rich, foreigners and male prostitutes.

Many intellectuals are deeply shocked by the fast commercialization and vulgarization of the gay lifestyle, including sexuality. The new gay discos are already monopolized by the *nouveaux riches* on one side, and the male prostitutes on the other. The style of life is expensive, dangerous, aesthetically unpleasing and vulgar. And Russian gay politics is no better than any other kind of post-Soviet politics.

Like almost everything else in contemporary Russia, the advances in gay and lesbian social and legal situations are extremely fragile. Many things available in the capital are still absolutely impossible in the provinces. Political opposition to the legalization of homosexuality is very strong. When the ex-vice president, Aleksandr Rutskoi, was asked in a television interview in June 1993 about his attitude toward sexual minorities, he said with a squeamish gesture, 'In a civilized society there should be no sexual minorities.'

Such attitudes are fairly typical. But if there is no gay community, who will defend gay and lesbian human rights, which are by no means guaranteed in Russia? And who will give them professional social and psychological advice and help them deal with stressful situations?

Gays and lesbians are now finally coming out in Russia as a social and cultural minority, but they still lack a clear self-image. It is not easy to come out into a ruined and chaotic world, where everything is disconnected and everyone is looking for enemies, not friends. If the country takes a radical turn to the right it will be gays and lesbians and their 'sympathizers', along with Jewish intellectuals, who will be the first candidates for concentration camps. But, then, this is a political, not a sexual problem.

At least, a start has been made, 'the ice is on the move', to coin a Russian phrase. The progress in the last few years has been colossal, and Russian gays and lesbians can now count on the firm support of millions around the world to reinforce their gains.

Notes

1 Marina Tsvetaeva, quoted in Oleg Moroz, 'Spravedlivaia li kara?', *Literaturnaia gazeta*, 29 March 1989, p. 11.
2 For detailed information on the history of homosexuality in Russia, see Simon Karlinsky, 'Russia's gay literature and history (11th–20th centuries)', *Gay Sunshine*, nos. 29/30 (Summer/Fall 1976).
3 Ibid.
4 See Igor Kon and James Riordan (eds.), *Sex and Russian Society* (Bloomington: Indiana University Press, 1993; London: Pluto, 1993), chap. 1.
5 See, for example, Adam Oleary, *Opisanie puteshestviia v Moskoviiu i cherez Moskoviiu v Persiiu i obratno* (St Petersburg, 1906); Jurai Krizhanitch, *Russkoe gosudarstvo v pervoi polovine XVII veka*, vol. 2 (Moscow, 1866); George Turbeville, 'To Dancie', in Lloyd Eason Berry and R. O. Crommey (eds.), *Rude and Barbarous Kingdom: Russia in the Accounts of 16th-Century English Voyagers* (Washington, D.C.: Scythian Books, 1968). For a Russian translation, see Semen Karlinskii, '"Vvezen iz-za granitsy . . . ?" Gomoseksualizm v russkoi kul'ture i literature. Kratkii obzor', *Literaturnoe obozrenie*, no. 11 (1991), p. 104.
6 S. M. Solov'ev, *Istoriia Rossii*, 3 vols. (St Petersburg, 1911), vol. 3, p. 750.
7 More detailed information may be found in the works of Simon Karlinsky and Alexander Poznansky. See, in particular, Simon Karlinsky, 'Russia's Gay Literature and Culture: The Impact of the October Revolution', in Martin Duberman, Martha Vicinus and George Chauncey, Jr (eds.), *Hidden from History: Reclaiming the Gay and Lesbian Past* (New York: New American Library Books, 1991), pp. 347–63; Alexander Poznansky, 'Tchaikovsky's Suicide: Myth and Reality', in *Nineteenth-Century Music*, vol. 11, no. 3 (Spring 1988), pp. 199–220; Alexander Poznansky, *Tchaikovsky: A Biography* (New York: Macmillan, 1991).
8 Quoted in Laura Engelstein, *The Keys to Happiness: Sex and the Search for Modernity in Fin-de-Siècle Russia* (Ithaca, N.Y., and London: Cornell University Press, 1992), p. 99.
9 See V. D. Nabokov, 'Plotskie prestupleniia, po proektu ugolovnogo ulozheniia', *Vestnik prava*, nos. 9–10 (1902). This long article is also published in Nabokov's book, *Sbornik stat'ei po ugolovnomu pravu* (St Petersburg, 1904).
10 Quoted in Engelstein, *Keys to Happiness*, p. 99.
11 See Marina Tsvetaeva, *Moi Pushkin* (Moscow, 1967), p. 62. On Tsvetaeva and Parnok, see Simon Karlinsky, *Marina Tsvetaeva: The Woman, Her World and Her Poetry*, second edn. (Cambridge: Cambridge University Press, 1987); see also Sof'ia Poliakova, *Zakatnye ony dni* (Ann Arbor, Mich.: Ardis, 1983).
12 See '"Raspoiasannye pis'ma" V. Rozanova', *Literaturnoe obozrenie*, no. 11 (1991), p. 67. For more detailed information on late nineteenth-century Russian lesbians, see Laura Engelstein, 'Lesbian Vignettes: A Russian Triptich from the 1890s', *Signs: Journal of Women in Culture and Society*, vol. 15, no. 4 (1990), pp. 813–31; Engelstein, *Keys to Happiness*, chap. 3. For a more negative view, see I. M. Tarnovskii, *Izvrashchenie polovogo chuvstva u zhenshchin* (St Petersburg, 1895).
13 Engelstein, *Keys to Happiness*, p. 394.

14   D. N. Zhbankov, 'Bab'ia storona', *Pereval*, no. 6 (1908), p. 26.

15   See Engelstein, *Keys to Happiness*, pp. 304–13.

16   G. S. Novopolin, *Pornograficheskii element v russkoi literature* (St Petersburg, 1909), chap. 10.

17   Detailed information on the lives of Soviet homosexuals may be found in the works of Simon Karlinsky, especially 'Russia's Gay Literature and Culture'. See also Vladimir Kozlovskii, *Argo russkoi gomoseksual'noi subkul'tury* (Benson, Vt.: Chalidze Publications, 1986); this book is much wider than its title suggests and contains data and documents on all aspects of homosexual life-styles and their reflection in literature, diaries, etc. See also Joachim S. Hohmann, 'Zur rechtlichen und sozialen Problem der Homo-sexualität', in *Sexualforschung und -politik in der Sowjetunion seit 1917* (Frankfurt: Peter Lang, 1990); Siegfried Tornow, 'Ruckschritt gleich Fortschritt. Geschichte der Schwulen in Sowjet-Russland', *Siegessaule*, no. 6 (1987).

18   The report on Krylenko's speech is published in *Sovetskaia iustitsiia*, no. 7 (1936), and reproduced in Kozlovskii's *Argo*.

19   See *Bol'shaia Sovetskaia Entsiklopediia*, vol. 17 (Moscow, 1952), 'Gomosexualizm', p. 593.

20   See Alberto, 'Da – ia liubliu parnei: Gomoseksualisty v SSSR', *SPID-info*, 29 November 1989, p. 6. For fuller data, see Masha Gessen, *The Rights of Lesbians and Gay Men in the Russian Federation* (San Francisco: IGLHRC, 1994).

21   See, for example, G. S. Vasil'chenko (ed.), *Obshchaia seksopatologiia* (Moscow: Meditsina, 1977); G. S. Vasil'chenko (ed.), *Chastnaia seksopatologiia* (Moscow: Meditsina, 1984); A. M. Sviadoshch, *Zhenskaia seksopatologiia*, third edn. (Moscow: Meditsina, 1988).

22   A. G. Khripkova and D. V. Kolesov, *Mal'chik–podrostok–iunosha* (Moscow: Prosveshchenie, 1982), pp. 96–100.

23   Igor' Kon, *Vvedenie v seksologiiu* (Moscow: Meditsina, 1988). The book had been published in East Germany and Hungary, approved for publication by two institutes of the USSR Academy of Sciences and backed for publication by many eminent scholars; yet still it had to wait a decade before the public was finally permitted to read it.

24   Igor' Kon, *Psikhologiia rannei iunosti* (Moscow: Meditsina, 1989); it had a print run of 800,000.

25   See, for example, the arguments in *Argumenty i fakty*: the remarks by Moscow police officer V. Kachanov in no. 9 (1990); and the article by Igor' Kon, 'Zakon i polovye prestupleniia', no. 12 (1990).

26   *Vsesoiuznyi tsentr po issledovaniiu obshchestvennogo mneniia*, November 1989; quoted with the kind permission of the Centre. In Central Asia, those advocating capital punishment for gays exceeded 85 per cent of all respondents.

27   See surveys quoted in L. D. Gudkov, 'Fenomen "prostoty". O natsional'nom samoosoznanii russkikh', *Chelovek*, no. 1 (1991), p. 20. Surveys have also been carried out by the Human Values Centre (which remain unpublished).

28   Quoted from Mark Deutsch, 'Uzelki na "Pamiat'"', *Ogonek*, no. 51 (1991), p. 8.

29   G. S. Vasil'chenko (ed.), *Chastnaia seksopatologiia*, vol. 2 (Moscow, 1983), pp. 99–108.

30   Tat'iana Fast, '13 shagov. Rasskaz o serii unikal'nykh operatsii, v rezul'tate kotorykh zhenshchina stala muzhchinoi', *Literaturnaia gazeta*, 20 September 1989, p. 12.

31   Galina Toktal'eva, 'Olia i Iulia', *Sobesednik*, no. 46 (November 1989), p. 11.

32   See *SPID-info*, no. 5 (1990).

33   See *Ogonek*, no. 12 (1991), p. 23.

11

Young women and subcultural lifestyles: a case of 'irrational needs'?

HILARY PILKINGTON

Molodo – zeleno,
poguliat' veleno.[1]

The justification of frivolity amongst young people is not unique to Russian culture, but a common social maxim. It rests on the comparison of the responsibility and obligation of adult life with an earlier period – 'youth' – in which dependency on the adult world is reduced, but the strictures of adult responsibilities have not yet been imposed. The granting to youth of a social space in which to indulge its youthful whims is premised upon the assumption that, when the time comes, young people will take up their attendant responsibilities. It is thus accompanied by the articulation of fears that they might not and sanctions when they do not. This paper focuses on one such fear characteristic of post-Second World War industrialized societies: the *consuming practices* of youth and, in particular, the gendered nature of this debate. Thus the nexus which is being explored is youth–gender–consumption, and the context of the study is not youth in general, but subcultural lifestyles in Russia during the perestroika period (1985–91).

The constraints of space do not allow any thorough theoretical contextualization of this debate; instead the premises from which the ensuing empirical study begins are simply stated.[2] The first premise is that in the West the discourses of both the 'teenage consumer' and 'subcultural resistance' have been deeply gendered. Girls have generally been seen to be located outside, or on the periphery of, subcultural groups and to be the objects of sexual desire or consumption by male members. Where young women have been considered in their own right, it has been largely as the targets of manipulation by gender-aware market creators. In crude terms, postwar, western, industrialized society has been characterized by a 'have fun while you're young' ethos encouraged by lengthening secondary education and a desire, characteristic of the generation growing up during the Second World War, to give young people what they themselves had not had. At the same time, there was a fear that young people would stray so far into their own worlds that they would become unable to relocate themselves in mainstream culture and, consequently, society itself would be swamped by the commercialized anti-culture of youth. In general young women have been peripheral to this debate, but where they have been visible it has been as consumers of fashion commodities manipulated by male desire, or as moral and sexual deviants in a male subcultural environment. However, feminist interventions into this debate have shown that gendered readings of subcultural practice may allow us to see young women's activity as more than purely passive.[3]

The second premise is that the 'teenage consumer' has also been a subject of debate in the Soviet Union from the 1960s onwards. Just as in the West, this was a result of social development which gradually changed the ratio of work to leisure time as well as fostering the rapid development of mass communications. Nonetheless, concerns over the growth of passive cultural consumption were articulated in a culturally specific way. Whereas in Britain, for example, such fears were associated with an 'Americanization' of culture, in the Soviet Union it was a more general 'westernization' or 'bourgeoisification'. This was linked to the popularity of western radio channels broadcasting into the Soviet Union, primarily the BBC and Voice of America, which were seen as the transporters of alien styles and youth cultures to Soviet youth whose political naivety led them to 'imitate' them. Thus there were two aspects of the Soviet teenage consumer which caused concern: young people's tendency to 'consume' rather than 'create' their own entertainment; and the content of that which they consumed, which was perceived as fundamentally opposed to, and subversive of, the socialist personality (*lichnost'*). The problem was dealt with on a theoretical/ideological level by the concept of 'rational needs'. This allowed differentiation between acceptable consumption of spiritual and leisure artefacts (cinema, concerts, theatre and fashion) and 'consumerism' which represented a disharmony between material and spiritual demands and which turned people into the 'slaves of things'. Rational needs were not those based on self-gratification through commodity consumption but those which facilitated the all-round and harmonious development of the individual and, therefore, the progress of society.[4]

Ensuring that Soviet young people filled their leisure time with activities which expressed rational needs was the central task of youth workers (primarily full-time Komsomol workers) and their successes and failures were recorded in youth journals and newspapers. It is from such sources over the period 1985–91 that the following discussion of the youth and consumption debate primarily draws. The gendered nature of this debate is illustrated in three subcultural lifestyles frequently discussed: fandom, 'highlifism' and territorial gang formation.

Fandom

Although young men listen to rock music more than young women – Soviet sociological research suggests that 58 per cent of male respondents listened to Soviet rock and western rock, while only 24 per cent of girls listened to Soviet rock and just 3 per cent to western rock[5] – the young men are not considered to be 'fans'. The term 'fan' in its masculine form (*fanat*) and in its feminine form (*fanatka*) not only distinguishes the sex of the actor, but suggests a completely different activity. The word *fanat* is used of a football fan who is male, aggressive and some-times violent, while the *fanatka* is female, in love with (usually) a male rock star, and, when in a crowd, likely to become hysterical. The debates on youth and music-use have thus been deeply gendered, as can be seen in the separate discussions of the ideological harmfulness of rock music and of fandom.

Rock music was perceived as a western-inspired attack on Soviet youth. Although the perestroika years did not witness anything like the invective of the early 1980s, nonetheless, it was claimed that rock music had been primarily designed 'to help destroy rationality' by inculcating blind consumerism;[6] encour-aged social passivity through a process of gradual 'stupefication' (*effekt oglupleniia*);[7] ruined the brain;[8] and encouraged spiritual primitiveness.[9] The common theme in all these concerns is that rock music threatened *male rationality*, since it induced states where body ruled mind (emotion, dancing, jouisant pleasure). Practical attempts to combat the negative effects of rock music therefore also focused on the need to make it more *mind-ful*. One way to do this was to re-site the consumption of rock to controllable spaces where vulgarity and tastelessness in the practice of music-listening would be prevented.[10] A second was to encourage the critical analysis of lyrics so that people could see what was genuinely good and what was just commercial, rubbish or provocation.[11] Both would enable people to take up a rational position toward the music.

Young women had no place in this debate since, it was suggested, they listened to popular music (*estrada*) rather than rock music.[12] On the other hand, since young women were already governed by emotion rather than rationality, where their music-listening became excessive, they were perceived not only as irrational but as 'fanatical' or even 'hysterical'. Despite the fact that the popular notion of female fans was that of 'hysterical girls' (*isterichnie devitsy*),[13] in fact the mass hysteria associated with fans from the Beatles onwards in the West does not dominate the discussion of fan behaviour as one might expect. Instead the focus is on the individual fan whose behaviour is portrayed as morally degenerate and egotistic. The former includes smoking, having a 'dirty' or 'scruffy' appearance, talking in slang or *mat*, writing graffiti on walls, fighting over souvenirs, drinking, spitting on local children and playing loud music.[14] The latter indicates the effect the behaviour of the fans has on the objects of their fandom; they make abusive and threatening phone calls to their heroes, rob their flats and limit their freedom by mobbing them.[15]

The most extreme form of fandom, however, is that in which the personality of the fan can only be expressed through her relationship with the star. Social psychologist Ol´ga Zaianaia sees these fantasy relationships as the girls' escape from the repulsion they feel for the inadequate world (and the men in it) which they face daily. She is essentially sympathetic to their situation, whilst warning of the danger of the girls becoming 'frozen' in their fantasies and unable to develop their own personalities further.[16] More common, however, is a focus on the ways in which young women try to realize their fantasies by actively pursuing their heroes. Such girls, it is reported, hang around major concert complexes and are prepared to spend the night with anyone, if, as a result, they can obtain the telephone number of their hero. The *fanatka* must be differentiated from other girls who 'take up residence' at the concert halls such as the *tusovshchitsy* (who sleep with influential show-business people in order to advance their own careers) or the *sportsmenki* (who are professional, high-class prostitutes whose clients are the most highly paid stars). The *fanatka*, in contrast, aims to wheedle her way into the star's *tusovka* (circle of friends and groupies), encouraged by stories which circulate about girls who have achieved their dream and married their heroes.[17] Despite her great skill in evading both door ladies and police, however, even the girl who is successful enough to gain access to the star's *tusovka*, and to sleep with him, remains portrayed as a failure. Far from gaining attention and value in the eyes of others through her relationship with the star, it is claimed, the latter soon forgets she exists, and the girl ends up being passed from one member of the group to the other and thus remains the object of male sexual consumption.[18] Indeed, knowing the girls' willingness to do anything to get close to their heroes, other men prey on them, claiming to be part of a particular band or group to persuade girls to sleep with them.[19]

Highlifism

The 'highlifist' has been a much more frequent subject of debate in the press and has precursors in the discussion of the *stiliagi* (Soviet 'teddy boys') and the *zolotaia molodezh'* ('gilded youth') in the postwar period. Both male and female highlifists are seen to prioritize material over spiritual values, but the social implications of their materialistic orientation are evaluated very differently.

Young men's desire for material goods and an extravagant lifestyle are seen as being satisfied by recourse to second-economy dealing or petty crime. As such, their behaviour is considered reprehensible, but comprehensible; after all young men often fall into crime (stealing cars and video films) precisely in order to impress girls and satisfy the latter's materialistic demands.[20] Young women's consumption, on the other hand, is not only of specific goods, but of the 'high life' associated with the underground world of black-marketeering, foreign goods and, especially, prostitution.

The key connection which is made, at various levels of explicitness, is that between girls' frivolous attitude to their maidenly honour and their desire to consume. In an early article discussing black-marketeering by foreign students at a technical institute in Rostov-on-Don, it was noted that a number of girls were happy to be such people's 'girlfriends' in return for clothes and nights out. Spelling out the connection being made between girls' sexual purity and the national pride of the country, the authors asked, 'Have we any right to close our eyes to the fact that in pursuit of the latest foreign "rags", these girls are selling not just themselves but us – our pride, our name and our honour?'[21] Six years later, the same conclusion – that consumption for girls was only possible through men – was drawn on the basis of a study of youth subcultural groups. Girl members of the highlifist group the *mazhory*, claimed Fain, sold their bodies in order to finance the expensive lifestyle of the group. The means by which these girls gained the material prerequisites for entrance into the group, however, also ensured their ultimate exclusion, since they were looked down upon by the male *mazhory*, who sought 'steady relationships' outside the group in order to avoid sexually transmitted disease.[22]

By association, therefore, girls who 'have a good time' are considered to be morally 'loose'. When one young woman wrote to the newspaper *Moskovskii komsomolets* complaining that she was considered to be a 'difficult teenager' just because she enjoyed going out and having a good time,[23] replies to the letter flooded in attacking the girl for the meaninglessness and 'frivolousness' of the way she spent her time. The frequent use of the verb *guliat'* (literally meaning 'to walk' or 'to stroll') was significant for its double entendre (also meaning 'to have a sexual relationship with' or 'to be unfaithful'), since it made the crucial link between young women's participation in 'normal' youth leisure activities and their sexual promiscuity. For girls, then, the social maxim cited at the beginning of this article did not apply. For them to *'guliat''* was not 'part of growing up', but indicative of a moral laxity which was perverting the development of girls into 'real women'.

By the end of the 1980s one could talk of a general cultural stereotype whereby young women were seen to be exchanging access to their bodies for material goods. This attitude had to be confronted daily by young women in Moscow: a sleeveless dress or even overtly imported, foreign clothes could lead to accusations of being a prostitute; going to restaurants with a female friend could mean being forced to prove you had enough money to pay for the meal; having coffee with a foreigner could mean inclusion on the police file of Intourist prostitutes.[24] An article in *Moskovskii komsomolets* in 1990 put this image into words. Professional prostitution, the author argued, was only the extreme of a general tendency – much worse was the fact that tens of millions of girls were involved in hidden prostitution, refusing to get to know men once they found out the size of their pay packets. The reason for this, it was argued, was the perversion of women's 'essence' due to their misguided 'emancipation'.[25]

Territorial gangs

A third subcultural lifestyle inhabited by girls is that of territorial or *dvor*-based gangs which are generally considered to be a breeding ground for delinquent behaviour. Occasionally a strong (Madonna-like) girl in the group is seen to act as the central pillar and source of moral strength for the group.[26] More often, however, girls are portrayed as being lured into them, becoming sexual objects (*obshchie devushki*, or 'common girls') for the male members of the group who have an 'exclusively consumerist' attitude to them.[27] Not surprisingly, then, the same term – *snimat'* – is used for stealing objects and picking up girls.

In the provincial Russian cities situated along the Volga – where territorial gang warfare has been a serious social problem since the end of the 1970s, and an object of media concern since the mid-1980s – rape and other sexual abuse of young women have become a norm of gang practice. Research conducted by criminologists in the city of Kazan´ suggested that in 80 per cent of the city's gangs there were cases of girls being (violently) forced to have sex and in 28 per cent of groups the girls in question were under fifteen years of age.[28] From his own observations in the city of Cheboksary, journalist Vitalii Eremin concluded that no girl was safe and that, 'Girls are now treated like a live good which can be taken, transferred from hand to hand and even sold.'[29] Thus, the only choice left to girls was to become the 'property' of one of the lads, or end up a 'common girl', since not only did the lads group-rape girls, but subsequently circulated rumours that the girl had not been a virgin anyway, thus taking away even her minimal refuge as a 'victim'.

Girls were not only victims of such groups, however. In a 1989 study of *dvor* groups meeting in basements, parks and courtyards in three districts of Leningrad, 30 per cent of the 345 young people interviewed were girls.[30] Girls had their own gangs, called such names as 'The Golden Girls', 'The Sisters of Salem' and 'The Black Foxes', and they engaged in exactly the same activities as the lads (fighting, having fun, drinking, taking drugs, extorting money and petty thieving).[31] In Alma-Ata in the summer of 1989, there were nine such female gangs.[32] Although there is extremely little discussion of girls' active participation in such groups, what there is indicates two 'types' of behaviour.

The first suggests the deceiving or manipulative sexual role of the girl in the group. Thus girls might willingly spend the night with a lad and then demand money from him in order not to 'cry rape'. One such story described a 'basement Emmanuelle' who had the entire local population of fifteen- to twenty-year-old lads in an outlying district of Moscow living in fear of her reporting them to the police for having sex with a minor.[33] According to the journalist, this evidence called into doubt the figures on rape, and such reports undoubtably added weight to claims that many reported rapes were in fact the overzealous continuation of normal flirting games in groups of young people. Hence girls were advised to take less heed of new advice on how to protect themselves (such as self-defence training) than to their immoral behaviour which might be facilitating the rape.[34]

The second behavioural type is the 'frustrated consumer'. The occasion of the trial of one group of girls accused of being involved in a number of attacks on other young women in Cheboksary led a local (female) journalist to the conclusion that the prime motivation of the girls was to steal their victims' clothes (sometimes down to their tights), because their parents were unable to provide the nice clothes they desired. Despite the fact that this practice (known as *obut´*) is common to all gangs (male or female), the explanation developed by the journalist was extremely gender-specific on a number of different levels. First, the motivation for the girls' behaviour was premised on the assumption that the only way for girls to stand out or achieve self-worth was by looking beautiful, and since this required consumer goods which they did not have the money to buy, the accused were drawn into stealing them. Second, the consequence of their actions was, in fact, not to create but destroy their own femininity: the girls are described as 'very aggressive' and 'cynical to the point of insolence'.[35] Finally, the root cause of their deviant behaviour was seen to rest with women; it was above all the double burden borne by their mothers which meant that the latter had insufficient time to spend with their children and thus to keep them out of trouble.[36]

Girls involved in gangs were thus seen alongside female juvenile criminals as being defeminized. By committing crimes, they offended not only society but the laws of nature. As one article published in *Meditsinskaia gazeta* put it, the rise in crime among girls and the increasing 'maleness' of the kinds of crimes they committed was evidence that the contemporary generation of young women had been turned into 'mutants' as a result of the lack of gender-specific education in the family and at school.[37]

What are girls doing in subcultural lifestyles?

The question which must now be addressed is whether girls' subcultural activity can be re-read in order to suggest meanings in that activity other than their desire to consume or men's desire to consume them.

As yet, Soviet academic literature has failed to provide such a re-reading. A gendered analysis of the hippy subculture (*sistema*) is offered by Shchepanskaia, but her study shows precisely how girls are *shut out* of the symbolic system of the group. Western academic literature is also scant. The present author has attempted to show how space has been won by girls in a particular Moscow youth cultural group through a 'good girl' strategy which is implemented at the expense of girls in other subcultural groups who are seen as vulgar, stupid and sexually loose.[38] The subcultural lives of the latter girls remains unexplored, however, and it is this which will form the focus of the rest of this paper. The limited empirical material available to the author means that no real 're-reading' can be offered; the aim is simply to problematize some of the issues already raised.

Fan culture

Fan cultures will not be dealt with at length here, since most of the substantive points about identity-formation through fandom are better drawn from the article cited above. Instead, some of the main misconceptions about female fans will be noted with reference to the Russian youth cultural scene.

First, and most obviously, the image of the female fan in love with a male star falsely simplifies the cultural phenomenon of fandom. More interesting examples of fandom such as the female fans of Alla Pugacheva and 'Bravo' (both following strong female images) are rarely, if ever, discussed. Likewise the popularity of the group 'Depeche Mode', whose lead singers are imitated by male fans in Russia, finds no explanation in the 'fantasy [heterosexual] relationship' model.

Second, fandom is not an exclusively one-to-one relationship or only shared with a close female friend. Many fan groups interact in a wider social environment (*tusovka*) which provides space for positive identity-formation and can be disruptive, if not directly subversive, of dominant gender norms.

Third, even when the relationship is the stereotypical one of female fans and male star, girl fans do not necessarily dissolve their own egos into the 'beloved' and relinquish all control. In fact, not only does the act of fandom help structure leisure time and define one's own identity from those around, but fans firmly believe they have rights in the relationship and are prepared to defend them. When, for example, it was announced that the pop star Iurii Shatunov (of the group 'Laskovii Mai') was to star in a film, the plot of which his fans disapproved, they held a protest meeting outside the editorial offices of the newspaper which had published the news and drew up a resolution (signed by 600 fans) expressing their outrage at the content of the screenplay which did not, as they saw it, represent the true character of their hero.[39]

Fourth, female fans often fail to live up to their image as 'hysterical girls'. Following the death in 1990 of Viktor Tsoi (the lead singer of the Leningrad group 'Kino'), fears of disorder at the funeral proved to be completely misplaced when tens of thousands of fans mourned his passing quietly and respectfully.[40] Nevertheless, fans were prepared to take on the authorities if this was necessary in order to protect the memory of their hero; in Moscow fans took over a wall on the Arbat and covered it with drawings and slogans dedicated to the singer, one of which gave the warning 'Anyone painting over this wall will become our fatal enemy.'[41]

Highlifers

The author's own research did not include extensive interviewing of 'highlifist' groups. The empirical material used here is drawn from letters and interviews in newspapers, as well as from interviews conducted by the author with two young women in Moscow who would certainly not classify themselves as highlifists, but who nevertheless lived a life centred on personal pleasure and fulfilment.

Considering the material available, the first relationship to be problematized is the division between sexual use and abuse. Interviews with sixth-form girls reported in *Moskovskii komsomolets* suggested that for young women virginity was no longer a matter of honour but of embarrassment, and that prestige accrued to those girls who went out with older men (often speculators) who could get them tickets to the Bolshoi Theatre and imported cosmetics.[42] Another letter more clearly spelled out that taking money, clothes and other presents from a number of sexual partners did not constitute prostitution to anyone but 'grannies' and 'failures'.[43] This apparent sexual aggression on the part of the girls was attributed by a male interviewee to girls' fears of being 'old maids' if they were not married by the time they reached the age of twenty, although a female interviewee claimed that it was simply the case that if a girl liked a boy she went out and got him herself, and that it was acceptable to marry someone for his money.[44]

The two girls interviewed by the author (both of whom had begun in *dvor*-based groups, moved on to the punk and hippy subcultures (*tusovki*) and ended up in groups surrounding rock bands, also emphasized the control they had over their own lives. There was, they said, nothing better than 'getting a hit'[45] and 'finding a nice boy to go to bed with'. They freely talked about sex, including sex with other women and group sex, which, they said, was common in these circles. It was also considered normal practice to take presents and money from sexual partners and this was viewed less in terms of 'for services rendered' than part of the reality of living from hand to mouth. The most striking evidence of the choice and control these girls felt in their lives came from their openness about their way of life, and their criticism of some of their male friends who felt the need to pretend they did not use drugs.

Nevertheless, it was clear that the girls also felt that the lifestyle had taken an unwelcome toll. This was articulated in the 'pity' they expressed for each other; both claimed they felt sorry for the other who had lost her looks and become dependent on the drug culture. They both pitied younger people entering this kind of lifestyle because, they claimed, the drugs scene had changed and was now ruled by people who would give you 'bad stuff', get you deliberately hooked and 'get off on your humiliation'. There was also a clear insecurity in their position. They feared being left alone and being let down by friends (especially in times of need). They also feared being outcast, and noted that all girls in subcultural groups were inevitably labelled 'slags'. Above all, though, they feared being revealed as 'dependent'. This was understandable, since the lads with whom they hung out played in rock groups and were centred around their music, while the girls were not centred – except on the lads' music and the drugs which went with it – and thus in down moments they feared the former would disappear and they would be left facing the reality of dependency on the latter.

The transition from choice and use to compulsion and abuse is perhaps most vividly expressed in a letter to the local newspaper from a fourteen-year-old from Novocheboksarsk calling herself 'Siuzanna'. She writes:

> I will recount to you the life of a drug addict, prostitute, 'highlifist', heavy metal fan, *mazhorka*. I am tired of lads taking me without any love in their eyes. I am tired of the daily 'hits' and cruising in a Volga. I am fourteen but my life is over. Everyone writes that whores have a great and carefree time. But it isn't like that. I am fed up of 'free love', of our slogan 'beer and anarchy'. I am what one calls a girl for one night, a common girl . . . [46]

The girl goes on to complain that if she went to visit a friend, within two to three minutes dozens of lads would arrive and if she did not want to have sex with them:

> they use force. I am alone and there are so many of them! . . . I have so many boys but no real, loyal boyfriend. They spend the night and then . . . see if you can find them! On the table there will be a bottle of wine . . . I can't count on support (for what?) or help (me?).[47]

Clearly, for this girl the high life which promised escape and unlimited opportunity had become a prison, in which she had little control over even her body, and from which she could not see a way out.

Territorial gangs

The sexual abuse of girls as part of the ritual of male territorial gangs and the violence to which girls are exposed (see above) is a common theme of letters to the local youth paper of the Chuvash oblast (*Molodoi kommunist*) which is cited above. In another letter to this paper, one girl even recounted how her own boyfriend had done a deal with a group of 'wide-trousered lads' who had stopped them; if he gave her over for them to rape, he would not be beaten up. Fortunately, when the lads realized that she was a virgin and that she had gone with them because she loved her boyfriend and did not want to see him hurt, they let her go without raping her.[48]

If girls' experience is to be re-read, however, it is also important to note the way in which the letters page of the newspaper was used by girls to protest against their rape and warn other girls against walking alone at night,[49] or to avoid having relations with lads from a particular area or town in the region.[50] A number of letters either from individuals or groups of girls showed female solidarity against the abuse, warning particular lads to stop hassling or hitting girls,[51] and some even threatened to take the matter to the police.[52] The answer by one girl to a letter by a lad complaining that girls were no longer afraid of lads showed that girls were prepared to fight back:

> Why should we girls be afraid of the lads? We weren't afraid of you and we won't be afraid, we have our pride as well. You wrote that a girl took your T-shirt – it's a shame she did not take everything else. You shouldn't have been so pushy.[53]

Not all letters were supportive, of course: some accused girls of fabricating rape stories,[54] or of crying rape when they had initiated sexual relations themselves.[55]

Sexual violence has clearly become a norm of youth culture in these cities, but to posit girls as the victims of this culture does not sufficiently explain girls' experience there. There are no clear figures on how many girls participate in the gangs,[56] but according to criminologists, the number is growing.[57] There is also evidence to suggest that their motivations are not based on the desire to consume and to look beautiful, but are, in fact, very similar to those of the male gang members.

Girls join gangs, first of all, to defend themselves. Just as many territorial gangs were first founded by lads of one district in order to protect themselves from an existing aggressive gang, so girls appear to be motivated by personal safety. This often leads them to participate in mixed gangs and join in the organized fights with other gangs. This dependency on the lads for protection from outsiders, however, could lead to them being sexually abused by lads within their own group.[58]

But girls also formed gangs on their own, and the observations of both Eremin and Kuz'mina suggest that they were not motivated primarily by the desire to steal clothes from other girls. The evidence for this is that although they do indeed conduct attacks on girls and steal their victims' clothes, these clothes are not worn, but sold to finance their other leisure habits (drinking, going to dances, smoking dope).[59] In fact, the fashionable clothes they steal are not their style at all. Instead they often reject the primacy of 'Moscow fashions' in favour of the wide trousers or long skirts of the provinces. One letter to the local Cheboksary youth paper asked:

> Why should we follow the example of Leningraders, Muscovites and Kievans? They come and then write that 'it's terrible here, the girls are horrible, the lads completely mad' . . . But everyone should have their own fashion. What difference does it make how wide your trousers are or how long your skirt is? We don't walk around showing our legs off.[60]

Kuz'mina also found significant similarity in the way of life of male and female gangs. The Alma-Ata gang she observed exhibited both the closeness and ruthlessness of male gangs. Like male gangs, girls collected dues from members and could be as merciless as the lads in extracting debts when they needed money. The money was used to finance their lifestyle, which consisted of sitting on roofs, drinking and playing cards, and going to cafés. Gangs were territorially based, members referred to each other as 'sisters' and the most important rule of membership was 'no betrayal'. They often carried knives, and attacks were characterized by risk and competition. Hierarchy in the group was determined according to age (most members being 14–16 years old) and strength (although no special terms were used for younger members, as in the male Kazan' groups). They were well versed in the practice of underground abortion and knew various home remedies for sexually transmitted diseases.[61]

Finally, girls might also join together, or at least act together, in order to assert their sexual access. Letters in the press from groups of girls warned others to back off their lads,[62] or revealed the enmity which emerged between girls if the normal rules of who had access to which lads were disrupted.[63] A similar attitude was revealed amongst girl bikers who participated in gang fights and who joined together in order to exclude new girls brought along by male members of the group.[64]

Conclusion

This chapter has attempted to isolate the relationship between consumption and gender in the discussion of girls in subcultural lifestyles in the perestroika press. This can be summarized as follows:

- The discussion is rooted in the established connection between youth and consumption which had developed already in Soviet ideology and popular consciousness. This was by no means unique to the Soviet Union, but was articulated in a peculiarly Soviet way via a notion of youth as the 'victims of bourgeois propaganda' which posited consumerism as a subversive force infiltrating socialist society from outside.
- The desire to consume is generally portrayed as evidence of a lack of seriousness in one's attitude to life, and since girls are perceived to be

frivolous by nature, the consolidation of this natural trait through consumerism renders it beyond the limits of 'rational needs'.

- A peculiarly negative sexual connotation is attached to 'frivolous' behaviour in the case of girls. In this way, as in the West, the discourse of adolescence ('have fun while you're young') clashes with that of femininity.

- Consuming behaviour reinforces images of women as calculating, scheming and manipulative. While for young men an overnarcissistic attitude might endanger rationality (by giving way to sensual pleasure), this is seen as the result of 'being led astray' either by girls or by the army of western technologies trained on seducing the good Soviet patriot. In contrast, female 'irrational needs' are portrayed as personal deviancy or a product of the 'false emancipation' of women and the failure of Soviet society to socialize its young women correctly.

- Consequently, girls are not seen as consuming 'rationally' but are consumed by their consumption. Their egos (*lichnosti*) became dissolved into the stars they worship, or their bodies are consumed by men. Moreover, self-indulgent consumerism disrupts 'the essence' of femininity which is *self-sacrifice*, and since this notion of womanhood constitutes the basis of the moral order of society, it threatens the very future of that society. In other words, 'rational needs' – those which make self-development compatible with the development of society as a whole – can, by their very nature, exist only for men.

Finally, the paper notes that empirical work on girls' activities in youth cultural groups is extremely limited, but that which is available suggests that the activity of young women in subcultural lifestyles might be re-read. The material drawn on by the author suggests that young women are motivated to join subcultural groups neither by personal nor sexual deviancy, but in order to assert more control over their lives and identities. However, the nature of the subcultural environment often means that there is a fine line between choice and force, sexual freedom and sexual abuse, and it is this line which young women tread.

Notes

1 There is no word-for-word translation equivalent of this saying in the English language, but its sense is 'Enjoy yourself while you're still young.'

2 For a more detailed discussion of the origins of the 'teenage consumer' debate in both western and Soviet academic discourses, see Hilary Pilkington, *Russia's Youth and Its Culture: A Nation's Constructors and Constructed* (London: Routledge, 1994), chaps. 1 and 2.

3 See, for example: Erica Carter, 'Alice in the Consumer Wonderland', in Angela McRobbie and Mica Nava (eds.), *Gender and Generation* (Basingstoke: Macmillan, 1984); John Fiske, *Understanding Popular Culture* (Boston: Unwin Hyman, 1989); Angela McRobbie, 'Settling Accounts with Subcultures – A Feminist Critique', *Screen Education*, vol. 34 (1980), pp. 37–49; Angela McRobbie, *Feminism and Youth Culture:*

From 'Jackie' to 'Just Seventeen', (Basingstoke: Macmillan, 1991); Angela McRobbie and Jenny Garber, 'Girls and Subcultures – An Exploration', in Stuart Hall and Tony Jefferson (eds.), *Resistance Through Rituals: Youth Subcultures in Post-War Britain* (London: Unwin Hyman, 1989), pp. 209–22.

4   A. Kozlov and A. Lisovskii, *Molodoi chelovek: stanovlenie obraza zhizni* (Moscow, 1986), pp. 92–107.

5   S. Kataev, 'Muzykal'nye vkusy molodezhi', *Sotsiologicheskie issledovaniia*, no. 1 (1986), pp. 105–8; N. Meinert, 'Po vole roka', *Sotsiologicheskie issledovaniia*, no. 4 (1987), pp. 88–93.

6   V. Chistiakov and I. Sanachev, 'Troianskii kon'', *Nash sovremennik*, no. 10 (1988), pp. 126–41.

7   N. Sarkitov, 'Ot "khard-roka" k "khevi-metallu": effekt oglupleniia', *Sotsiologicheskie issledovaniia*, no. 4 (1987), pp. 93–4.

8   N. Bekhtereva, 'I Like Dance Music', *Moscow News*, no. 10 (1988).

9   Iu. Bondarev, V. Belov and V. Rasputin, 'Young People: Discarding Flattery And Demagogy', *Moscow News*, no. 6 (1988), pp. 5–6.

10 Iu. Filinov, 'Na konverte pishite "ABV"', *Komsomol'skaia pravda*, 15 January 1986, p. 4.

11 A. Vasilov, A. Kupriianov and I. Cherniak, 'Muzyku zakazyvaet raikom', *Sobesednik*, no. 20 (1986), pp. 8–10; V. Avilov, 'Rok ili urok?', *Komsomol'skaia pravda*, 12 March 1987, p. 2.

12 See Kataev, 'Muzykal'nye vkusy molodezhi', and Meinert, 'Po vole roka'. A further reinforcement of the fact that it was men alone who were threatened by the dangers of rock music was an article which suggested that women's 'natural calling' should be applied to help 'save' young men from the evils of rock music. See A. Chirkin, 'Podrostok, sem'ia i rok-muzyka', *Nash sovremennik*, no. 10 (1988), pp. 141–8.

13 K. Alekseeva and A. Iur'eva, 'Sneg iz-pod sapog', *Moskovskii komsomolets*, 26 October 1990, p. 2.

14 Alekseeva and Iur'eva, 'Sneg iz-pod sapog'; anonymous letter published in *Moskovskii komsomolets*, 30 June 1989, p. 4.

15 D. Shavyrin, 'Tak rebiata, ne poidet!', *Moskovskii komsomolets*, 16 June 1989, p. 4.

16 O. Zaianaia, '"Alen Delon govorit po-frantsuzski" . . . ', *Komsomol'skaia pravda*, 10 December 1989, p. 4.

17 N. Sineusova and T. Romochkina, 'Moia postel' beskonechno pusta . . .', *Moskovskii komsomolets*, 7 March 1991, p. 2.

18 Ibid.

19 A. Maksimov and L. Chebotarev, 'Okhrana trebuet zhertv', *Sobesednik*, no. 50 (1989), p. 3.

20 D. Babich, 'Potomu, chto liubliu', *Komsomol'skaia pravda*, 10 July 1990, p. 4.

21 V. Konovalov and M. Serdiukov, 'Foreign-Made Mirage', *Komsomol'skaia pravda* (1984), 11 January, p. 4; 12 January, p. 4; 13 January, p. 4; 15 January, p. 2; trans. in *Current Digest of the Soviet Press*, vol. 37, no. 5 (1984), pp. 7–8.

22 A. Fain, 'Specific Features of Informal Youth Associations in Large Cities', *Soviet Sociology*, vol. 29, no. 1 (1990), pp. 20–42.

23 See letter in *Moskovskii komsomolets*, 29 March 1985, p. 2.

24 L. Volkova, 'Nebo v alimzakh', *Moskovskii komsomolets*, 31 August 1990, p. 2.

25 A. El, 'Shershe lia fam!', *Moskovskii komsomolets*, 3 February 1990, p. 2.

26 K. Lavrova, 'Vecherom, u pod"ezda', *Komsomol'skaia pravda*, 12 January 1985, p. 2.

27 S. Orlov, 'Osobye primety: glaza naglie', *Komsomol'skaia pravda*, 12 March 1991, p. 2.

28 A. Kashelkin, 'Nasilie kak forma antiobshchestvennogo povedeniia molodezhnykh gruppirovok', in I. Karpets (ed.), *Kriminologiia o neformal'nikh molodezhnykh ob"edineniiakh* (Moscow, 1990), pp. 232–8.

29 V. Eremin, 'Vorovskoi orden', *Nedelia*, no. 13 (1991), pp. 16–17.

30 N. Kofyrin, 'Problemy izucheniia neformal'nykh grupp molodezhi', *Sotsiologicheskie issledovaniia*, no. 1 (1991), pp. 82–5.

31 A. Gromov and O. Kuzin, *Neformaly: kto est' kto?* (Moscow, 1990).

32 V. Kuz'mina, Interview with author, Moscow, 23 August 1991.

33 K. Medvedkin, 'Za prekrasnykh dam prikhoditsia poroi platit' svobodoi', *Moskovskii komsomolets*, 7 February 1991, p. 2.

34 V. Roegli, 'Stat'ia 117, ch. 1, UK RSFSR – Iznasilovanie', *Moskovskii komsomolets*, 15 June 1990, p. 2.

35 V. Ivanova, 'Cheboksarskie "amazonki"', *Sovetskaia Chuvashiia*, 24 November 1990, pp. 2–3.

36 Ibid.

37 L. Sukhareva and N. Kuindzhi, 'Zachem devushke muzhskoe litso?', *Meditsinskaia gazeta*, no. 26 (3 April 1992), p. 11.

38 Hilary Pilkington, '"Good Girls in Trousers". Codes of Masculinity and Femininity in Moscow Youth Culture', in Marianne Liljeström, Eila Mäntyssari and Arja Rosenholm (eds.), *Gender Restructuring in Russian Studies* (Tampere, Finland: University of Tampere Press, 1993), pp. 175–92.

39 'Devichii perepolokh', *Moskovskii komsomolets*, 7 March 1990, p. 1.

40 'Gibel' muzykanta', *Moskovskii komsomolets*, 17 August 1990, p. 1.

41 D. Molchanov, 'Tot, kto pokrasit etu stenu', *Komsomol'skaia pravda*, 31 August 1990, p. 4.

42 O. Boguslavskaia, 'Geroi nashego vremeni', *Moskovskii komsomolets*, 30 September 1989, p. 2.

43 Kison'ka, 'Ia ne prostitutka', *Moskovskii komsomolets*, 12 March 1990, p. 2.

44 Boguslavskaia, 'Geroi nashego vremeni'.

45 Referring to drug-use.

46 Siuzanna, *Molodoi kommunist*, 22 November 1990, p. 11.

47 Ibid.

48 *Molodoi kommunist*, 1 November 1990, p. 12.

49 *Molodoi kommunist*, 13 December 1990, p. 2.

50 *Molodoi kommunist*, 11 October 1990, p. 11.

51 *Molodoi kommunist*, 4 October 1990, p. 12.

52 *Molodoi kommunist*, 27 September 1990, p. 13.

53 Ibid.

54 *Molodoi kommunist*, 4 October 1990, p. 12.

55 *Molodoi kommunist*, 25 October 1990, p. 4.

56 Estimates might be drawn from comparison with other gang structures. Anne Campbell in her study of girls in New York gangs, for example, estimated about 10 per cent female participation. See Anne Campbell, *The Girls in the Gang* (Oxford: Blackwell, 1984).

57 A. Kashelkin and V. Ovchinskii, 'Po nepisannym zakonam ulitsy . . .', in K. Igoshev and G. Min'kovskii (eds.), *Po nepisannym zakonam ulitsy* (Moscow, 1991), p. 325.

58 Iu. Antonian, L. Pertsova and L. Sablina, 'Opasnye devitsy', *Sotsiologicheskie issledovaniia*, no. 7 (1991), pp. 94–9.

59 V. Eremin, Interview with author, Moscow, 28 May 1991; V. Kuz'mina, Interview with author, Moscow, 23 August 1991. Kuz'mina shot a documentary film entitled *Patsanki* in summer 1989 depicting the life of female gangs in Alma-Ata.

60 'Sad April', *Molodoi kommunist*, 8 November 1990, p. 12.

61 Kuz'mina, Interview with author.

62 See *Molodoi kommunist*, 6 September 1990, p. 12.

63 See *Molodoi kommunist*, 27 September 1990, p. 13.

64 A. Lapin, 'Nochnoi eksport', *Moskovskii komsomolets*, 15 November 1987, pp. 2–3.

12

'Full frontal': perestroika and sexual policy

ELENA STISHOVA

This paper's title, which is deliberately couched in very general terms, contains a paradox, if you like, even a challenge. For in my country, which is experiencing the sexual revolution two decades late, there is no sexual policy as such – if you regard a policy as consisting of conscious actions taken on the basis of a well-thought-out conception.

Perestroika, with its aim of creating glasnost and abolishing censorship, did not give rise to constructive ideas. On the contrary, it created a conceptual vacuum. Yet on the other hand, for the first time in the past half-century perestroika made it possible legally to pose the question of sex and sexual relations. And it is this, the legalization of problems which had been forcibly removed from the public consciousness, that gives perestroika its historical meaning. 'We have no sex' – the reply of a Moscow woman broadcast on television during a Soviet–American 'telebridge', which became a well-known saying, gave a spontaneous and absolutely honest snapshot of the public consciousness as it was in 1987.[1] Today, seven years later, even the most smug, sanctimonious hypocrite would not say that. On the contrary, sex is probably the only thing we have in abundance. I have in mind the huge quantity of erotic and even pornographic publications, of a very poor typographical and literary quality as a rule, with which Moscow is virtually swamped, plus the legal showing of contraband erotic and semi-pornographic films in video salons and film theatres, plus Russian mass culture's expansion into the empire of sex, as films and show business win more and more screen time on television.

So it turns out that 'We do have sex.' However, over the years that have passed since the calendar beginning of perestroika – the April Plenum of the Communist Party Central Committee in 1985 – no socially significant ideas about sex or gender have appeared in any of their current aspects whatsoever: from the family and everyday life in society to the mass communication media. Parliament did not accept the law 'For the Protection of the Family', since experts who acted as consultants for the project considered that many of its provisions infringed the United Nations Convention 'On the Liquidation of All Forms of Discrimination in Relation to Women'.

Nevertheless, the absence of a policy is also a form of policy. And the basis of this spontaneously evolving policy is a powerful formative factor – permissiveness, in other words, unbounded legal and moral licence. This is the way that liberty is understood by the masses in our country, where there is a lack of democratic traditions, but on the other hand, the tradition of legal nihilism blooms in profusion; where socialist morality has been abolished along with the abolition of 'developed socialism', and religious morality with its commandments – 'Thou shalt not kill', 'Thou shalt not steal', 'Thou shalt not commit adultery' and so on – does not apply in our atheistic country.

In my opinion, in Russia today the circumstances of our past have conspired to create a unique cultural situation which is of great value to researchers. It is possible to observe in almost laboratory conditions how the collective 'Id', or in Jungian terms the collective unconscious, operates in a society not subject to censorship, and to form a view of the psychological state of society by the deductive method, analysing its signs and symptoms from the pages of newspapers and journals, from video and cinema screens.

But first, by way of contrast, I will give some examples from our 'former life', from the time of total regulation, the climate in which Soviet society took shape. As early as 1924, seven years after the October Revolution, Aron Zal'kind's book *Revolution and Young People* was published, in which one can read such lamentable statements as: 'Sexual life is permissible only in a form which contributes to the growth of collective feelings, class organization, creative, productive or military activity.' Or: 'Purely physical sexual attraction is impermissible from a revolutionary, proletarian point of view.' And further: 'Sexual choice should be formed according to a policy of class, revolutionary, proletarian expediency. Elements of flirtation, courtship, coquetry and other methods of special sexual conquest should not be introduced into love relations.'

The texts cited are not extracts from an anti-utopian novel, but consistent instructions, a projection of Soviet policies on women and sex. Another remarkable illustration is provided by the famous revolutionary in the Leninist galaxy, the commissar for women's affairs Aleksandra Kollontai. In 1921, as the guns of the Civil War were fading, she said in a speech in the Communist Academy: 'The workers' republic approaches women first of all as a labour force, as living units of labour; it regards the function of motherhood as a very important, but supplementary task; and, moreover, not a personal, family task, but a social mission.' The initial consequence of the repressive sexual policy of the era of 'barracks socialism' was sexophobia, both collective and personal. But in our time this forcible control over the individual's personal life has turned into an unprecedented surge of mass interest in eroticism and sex. I will attempt to demonstrate the long-term effects of the repression of sex and individuality through an analysis of post-Soviet cinema, its ideology and mythology.

In making observations and drawing conclusions I am basically relying on film output which more often than not has an anonymous, if not folkloric character – films of this kind possess no clear artistic individuality. It is this sort of low-quality cinema, mass culture of the crudest kind, which most truthfully represents the objectives of mass consciousness, the social expectations of the masses. For, as Berthold Brecht remarked, the 'bad taste' of the masses is more deeply rooted in reality than the 'good taste' of intellectuals.

Among the images rendered taboo by Soviet power, nudity was one of the most prominent. The Soviet cinema was devoid of eroticism, and the spectator was brought up accordingly. At the very beginning of perestroika, before a showing of Rostotskii's film *The Dawns Are Quiet Here*, the television authorities, without the director's permission, cut a most innocent scene at the front which showed the girls washing in a bathhouse, which was, incidentally, artistically very effective. The motive was a concern not to offend public morality.

This continuous process of bowdlerization, or 'selection' over many years bore fruit. I can say from my own experience that when three years ago the Film-Makers' Club showed the controversial film *Empire of the Senses* by the Japanese director Oshima, this was a great test, even for an audience of professionals. We do not know how to look at films of this kind, still less how to make them.

In 1987, as a member of the Conflict Commission of the Film-Makers' Union,[2] I participated in a curious incident, but one which was very typical of that time. *Mosfilm* (the Moscow Film Studio) made the film *Little Doll*, in which a director sympathetic to perestroika put a female teacher in bed with a pupil in the course of the plot. The studio's artistic director sharply objected to this scene, considering that it was sensationalist and its artistic effect nil (I became convinced that this was true after seeing the film). But the majority of members of the Conflict Commission, invited as arbitrators, took the director's part, reproaching the artistic director for authoritarianism and a failure to be receptive to new trends.

I honestly admit that at that time I hesitated over which side to take. It was a time of such great controversy: any arguments 'against', however rational, weighty or conclusive, seemed ideologically reactionary, an infringement of the freedom we had obtained. And only today, when we have already accumulated an experience of freedom as permissiveness, is it possible to take an objective view of that incident. And not on a personal, but a general plane. This is precisely the way that a mentality formed on prohibitions conceives of freedom – as self-will.

This happened before the release of Vasilii Pichul''s *Little Vera* (1988), the film which became a metaphor for perestroika; the actress who played the main role, Natal'ia Negoda, who was photographed topless for *Playboy*, became its sex symbol. The film-makers had to fight for the episode in the film where the sex act was presented very daringly, even for the taste of refined cinema buffs familiar with erotic cinema. This was the last attempt of the dying *Goskino* (the State Cinema Agency) to regulate the film process and influence sexual policy. It is now clear that *Little Vera* was one of the few films of perestroika which bordered on erotic realism. There are also some films in which the problem of sex is presented as an existential problem – N. Khubov's *Body*, P. Todorovskii's *Love* and V. Rubinchik's *Non-Love*. But these films I have mentioned are exceptions to the rule. For the processes occurring in the collective unconscious, the flood of domestic erotic output of a commercial nature is more representative.

Critics do not cease to be amazed at how incredibly rapidly the 'eroticization' of our sexless cinema took place. The erotic high tide swilled over our screens without any opposition from critics or public opinion. In the West during the period of the sexual revolution there were notorious scandals, bans by the censors, lively discussions. In Russia eroticism and sex did not just expand, they advanced like lightning everywhere. There was literally one attempt on the part of the state structures, doomed from the start, to organize a campaign against the 'sexualization' of the screen. And there was a serious discussion in Kiev about the measure of the permissible in contemporary cinema, when philosophers and film buffs expressed quite extreme views. There were no calls for bans – on the contrary, the majority agreed that it was necessary to open the floodgates, and that the removal of taboos on sex and eroticism on the screen was the only way of emerging from a prolonged period of puberty and ultimately attaining maturity.

The legalization of sex in post-Soviet cinema became part of the battle for glasnost and freedom of speech, and what is more, part of the battle for the emancipation of the individual, repressed by total prohibition, and for the emancipation of culture, emasculated by hypocrisy. That is why people in democratic circles, including critics and journalists, take such a tolerant view of this process, for all its sometimes absurd consequences. In the first place, any ban is extremely unpopular today. Secondly, in the highly complex current political and economic situation, such a trifle as the cinema's threat to public morality does not bother anyone. Thirdly, sexual issues are mainly focused on the female image, and this image has a very low status in our society as a result of Soviet policy. Hardly anyone takes seriously the fact that our native erotic output crudely discriminates against women. And this is truly a 'new' form of discrimination – thanks to the censorship and its sexual policy, Soviet power had no problems of this kind.

The process of lowering the female image from its pedestal has been a lengthy one. One of its key points occurred at the beginning of the second half of the 1970s, coinciding with the heyday of the 'period of stagnation' (the Brezhnev era) and the collapse of the ideology of the 'people of the 1960s generation' (liberals whose outlook had been formed by the period of Khrushchev's reforms). That was the time when, one after another, actresses began to disappear from the screen who represented the immemorial Russian type of 'Turgenevan women' (Irina Kupchenko), intellectual heroines (Alla Demidova, Marina Neelova), as well as psychological types related to the world cultural tradition (Margarita Terskhova). Actresses who had been filmed by Tarkovskii and Konchalovskii were no longer in demand. Society had changed its priorities and mythology. This latent process only came to the surface at the beginning of perestroika.

Who would have thought that the favourite heroine of the Soviet people would turn out to be not the 'Beautiful Lady' or the divine Sophia, not the female shock-worker or the heroic partisan defending her Fatherland, not the virago of folklore capable of halting a galloping steed, and not even the working woman? The dream woman has been authoritatively replaced by the prostitute – whether whore, *interdevochka* (hard-currency call-girl) or girl with no inhibitions.

Petr Todorovskii's film *Interdevochka* (*International Girl*, 1989) was the most famous hit of perestroika, a topical sensation produced by our own native film industry. In this film two mythologies intertwined: the literary mythology of the fallen woman, the victim of society, mourned by Russian literature from Dostoevskii to Kuprin, and the latest myth of worldly success, whose vital components are a foreign husband and a smart life abroad.

The epic subject of *International Girl*, which refers back to classical images of women, to Sonia Marmeladova and Katiusha Maslova (the prostitute heroines of Dostoevskii's *Crime and Punishment* and Tolstoi's *Resurrection*) remains unique, and has not been widely reproduced. But a variation of this image has gained currency and become archetypal for the cinema of perestroika. He loves Her, but She is a prostitute. Characters from various sections of society have featured in this heart-rending conflict. Thus, in the film *Upper Class,* a hard-currency prostitute with KGB connections goes by order of her boss to an Intourist hotel in a Black Sea resort where she is supposed to collect compromising material on some VIP – in other words, to seduce this person for the purposes of blackmail.

But the heroine is playing a double game. She has a romance with a respectable foreigner, and her aim is to slip away abroad in order to get legally married to him. For this reason, the *interdevochka* behaves in an unusual way: she lays her cards on the table in front of the man who was supposed to become her victim, whereupon he falls in love with her and helps her to play the game.

In the film *Showboy*, the same archetypal plot is presented in the guise of a melodramatic story about the life of show business sharks who make money out of teenage schoolboys. A rising young pop-star falls in love with a beautiful girl, but she turns out to be a prostitute working for some businessmen (former Komsomol workers, incidentally). They put her in the way of rich foreigners, potential investors, aiming to extract some advantage from them. The 'showboy's' heart is broken; but his dream girl, being no fool, builds a dizzying marital career – she gets married to an investor and flies away with him to Scandinavia . . .

In the comedy *A Brunette for Thirty Copecks*, the mayor of a small town decides to keep up with the times, and opens a brothel in order to increase the municipal budget, and also to transfer free love, which can take the wildest and most unfettered forms, on to a civilized commercial footing. The film contains a scene in which dozens of men storm a women's hostel, reaching their girlfriends through the window on a ladder of knotted sheets, since they are forbidden to enter through the door. However, the mayor's lively wife, who wants to take revenge on her husband for depriving her of her beloved work, since he has confiscated the building of the art museum she directed for the brothel's use, immediately enters the institution. There is nothing left for the jealous mayor to do but to put on a wig, change his appearance and get a job in the brothel as a bouncer, in order to try and keep an eye on his wife.

This vulgar comedy, which parodies and ridicules Soviet views of sex, is interesting for the way that it lets the cat out of the bag: it reproduces a model of relations with women which is typical of patriarchal consciousness, but masked as free thought. By presenting women as the object of sexual or social manipulation by men, the director at the same time paints a vivid portrait of men, and, deliciously, does not notice that he has made a pornographic film. But society does not notice this either . . .

Thus in this series of films the image of the prostitute, if not actually idealized, as in *International Girl*, is certainly not subjected to any moral censure from the authors. Moral and ethical criteria, which are exceptionally important in the Russian cultural tradition, are lacking in this case. This absence is significant, and has various implications. I am emphasizing the ethical implications, since they are obvious and topical. For ethical irresponsibility is the aspect of everyday contemporary consciousness which has clearly appeared in mass culture as a ready-formed phenomenon with its own history and pre-history.

As regards its pre-history, I should like to draw attention to the secret connection between the contemporary film plot about a prostitute heroine and a similar literary subject beloved by authors of the 1860s, including revolutionary democrats. In these novels, He, as a rule a student from the lower classes, enlightened Her, that is to say, the fallen woman, to her true position as a victim of society. She, her eyes opened, became attached to Him, the people's defender, and tried to return to the path of virtue, but sometimes committed suicide.

Today's cinema essentially offers us the other side of the coin, the opposite of the plot regarded as the key to Russian cultural mentality: a humane attitude to the prostitute, or 'charity to fallen women'. It could be argued that the plot about the thinking prostitute, if it does reflect reality at all, reflects the reality of the complexes which tormented spotty students from humble backgrounds who suffered from poverty and were not accepted in high society. Nothing remained for them but to assert themselves at the expense of the 'priestesses of love', putting a *post factum* ideological gloss on their dubious intimate relations. Nevertheless, it did not enter the heads of the revolutionary democrats to declare prostitution a prestigious occupation.

Something similar has happened in the mass consciousness today. Many young female spectators tacitly or explicitly identify with the prostitute heroines. Because they have what simple women in the cinema hall do not have and dream about in vain: dollars, cars, fashionable clothes, good food, cosmetics, relationships, the attention and admiration of men. And the most important thing – the chance of catching a foreign husband. Thus the film *The Night of the Long Knives* by the director Ol'ga Zhukova, presents a prostitute mother with a little daughter who plays, like all children in the world, at 'being mother'. This little girl already knows how to 'pick up' a client, and eagerly demonstrates her skills. In another of Ol'ga Zhukova's films, *Band of Lesbians*, the same girl (here playing the daughter of a brothel madam) demonstrates other ways of working with clients: imitating her mother and her girlfriends, she plays at strangling the manager of an underground brothel . . .

A casual spectator might regard these films as sensationalist and unworthy of attention, as nothing but interference on the airwaves. It could be argued that this kind of market output is a byproduct of civilization which exists in all industrial-ized countries. But the special characteristic of the Russian cultural situation is that these films are representative of social and cultural processes occurring in society.

If we turn to a different kind of film, with pronounced authorial self-consciousness, we will be convinced that this directorial cinema reproduces the same, uncomplimentary view of women (to put it mildly). In the controversial documentary film by Tofik Shakhverdiev, *To Die for Love*, we get to know a respectable wife and mother, with a writer husband, three children, a communal flat and heaps of domestic problems . . . And when in the next episode we see the heroine dolled up and made up, in the company of three men from the Caucasus, we feel a sense of shock when we realize that this comfortable, stout, domestic type of woman has 'picked up' clients and is haggling over the fee in a business-like manner. The husband has the last word: he stands round the corner keeping look-out and feels no qualms about pimping for his own wife and her girlfriends.

The interview which the director has with the couple provides an answer to all possible problems. The woman thinks that her profession is no worse than any other method of earning money in this country. Indeed, it is better, because it is more honest. She sells only what belongs to her personally – her body – whereas others barter with other people's goods. The heroine of the second story is a priestess of love who prefers this way of life to all others. She has a romantic attitude to her profession, and looks very convincing on screen – like a good actress who is playing her part well. In short, the most ancient profession in the world is shown in this film without any personal shame or hypocritical pose – as a business and a hobby.

It cannot be denied that over the last seven years our society has experienced an unprecedented shift in self-consciousness. In this area, apparently, once again 'the sky's the limit'. Sex and eroticism on the screen have been legalized and legitimized. And this seems to be the main result of the process of cultural emancipation. Why should we be surprised that this process has exposed the ulcers of socialism and its complexes, monstrosities and deformations? But we are surprised, because we were not prepared for it. And we are experiencing a culture shock. This is sad, painful and frightening, and gives rise to frustration in society.

The only consolation is that everything passes. And already today there are signs that the public has become satiated with 'porn', that it is ceasing to be an acutely deficit commodity and that it is gradually finding a narrower niche: a market attraction for special categories of spectators.

Notes

1 Editor's note: This was a reply to the television host Vladimir Pozner, who asked the audience to compare the availability of sexually explicit material in Soviet and American society. For an interview with the author of this comment, see S. Shaidakova, 'Ekh, Morozova, v Rossii vse est´, i seks tozhe', *Moskovskii komsomolets*, no. 141 (22 July 1992), p. 4.

2 Editor's note: A 'Commission for the Resolution of Creative Conflicts', chaired by Andrei Plakhov, the film critic of *Pravda*, was established after the Congress of the Film-Makers' Union on 13–15 May 1986 to consider whether previously banned films could now be released.

PART III
Women and work

13
Why be a shock worker or a Stakhanovite?

MARY BUCKLEY

In the 1930s, shock work and Stakhanovism were integral to industrialization and collectivization. Shock work referred to fulfilling obligations over and above work assignments. Stakhanovism (named after the miner Aleksei Stakhanov who hewed fourteen times his quota of coal) was a movement to increase labour productivity to the point of encouraging maximum productivity. Special emphasis was put on individual initiative, on harnessing technology and on learning from the successes of others. The year 1936 was proclaimed 'Stakhanovite Year'.

Western literature

Discussions of Stakhanovism in the West have been dominated by economists and economic historians. For some time, analysis focused quite narrowly on industrial productivity. A central question was whether output increased as a result of Stakhanovite feats, or whether it was disrupted by them. Another issue was the extent to which a privileged caste of industrial workers, a labour aristocracy, was created in a supposedly 'socialist' society, and whether or not, as a consequence, the working class became both divided and demoralized. A third was the connection between Stakhanovism and the need to discipline a rather inefficient and frequently unruly workforce. A fourth concerned the relationship between workers and managers, the extent to which the latter failed to encourage Stakhanovism or instead showed favouritism to Stakhanovites whilst ignoring the general workforce. These areas of debate fed into further questions about the similarities and differences between shock work and Stakhanovism, about how much Stakhanovism was directed in authoritarian fashion 'from above', pushing both workers and managers and sometimes driving a wedge between them, and whether Stakhanovism as a movement had distinct phases, also shaped by developments on the shop floor.[1]

More recently, Lewis H. Siegelbaum's social history of the movement was a welcome addition to our understanding of Stakhanovism's relevance to the 1930s. Siegelbaum broadened discussion to embrace topics of cultural mythology and the making of Stakhanovites, whilst not losing sight of issues of industrial productivity. Important facets of the movement, however, have still not been adequately considered, in particular Stakhanovism's relevance to rural life, social attitudes, resistance to change, ideology, gender, Stalin's cult of personality and popular culture. And, as in many areas of research, it has been male Stakhanovites who have been in the limelight, not female ones.[2]

One can see why scant attention has been paid to female Stakhanovites. Since the focus of Stakhanovism was on triumph over technology, the urban workforce best illustrated this; and most Stakhanovites in heavy industry, the sector prioritized by the regime, were male. The proportion of women Stakhanovites was higher in light industry due to a female preponderance in that sector. In confectionery, leather and textiles, female Stakhanovites outnumbered male.[3] In some rural areas, however, according to Roberta Manning, the majority of Stakhanovites were women.[4] A recasting of central questions giving greater prominence to rural responses to the Stakhanovite movement automatically brings women into the centre of the story. Hitherto in western literature they have been on the periphery.

This relative invisibility of female Stakhanovites in western academic studies contrasts with their noticeable presence in Soviet literature. Young Pioneers and Komsomol members were brought up on socialist realist images of male and female Stakhanovites. Official ideology trumpeted the heroic successes of individual shock workers and Stakhanovites, be they famous men, such as Aleksei Stakhanov, Aleksandr Busygin and Petr Krivonos, or well-known women such as Mariia Demchenko, Praskov'ia Angelina, Dar'ia Garmash, Mamlakat Nakhangova, Evdokiia Vinogradova, Mariia Vinogradova, Vera Nikiforova or Valentina Gaganova. The names of exemplary male and female workers were well known, almost household names (whether hated or loved). Demchenko was instigator of the *dvizhenie piatisotnits* (movement of the 500-ers) dedicated to picking 500 centners of sugar beet per hectare, a record which Demchenko had promised to Stalin at the Second Congress of Kolkhoz Shock Workers.[5] Nakhangova picked cotton at record speed in Tadzhikistan. Angelina and Garmash, affectionately called Pasha and Dasha, were leaders of women's tractor brigades in Ukraine. The two Vinogradovas, usually referred to as Dusia and Marusia, were heroines of the textile industry. Nikiforova worked in the manufacture of shoes.

Shock work did not end in the 1930s, even if the Stakhanovite movement was in some ways discredited. In the late 1950s, the *gaganovskoe dvizhenie* was a movement named after Valentina Gaganova, who, like Stakhanov, had set production records, this time as a spinner in the cotton industry.[6] The *gaganovskoe dvizhenie* encouraged shock workers to join less successful brigades in order to pull their workers up to a higher standard of work.

As far as analysis of shock work per se is concerned, the lack of attention to women is less excusable. According to P. Chirkov, in 1932 shock workers made up 64 per cent of the male workforce and 65 per cent of female workers.[7] Chirkov held that 'It is the most conclusive fact that in labour successes, women did not fall behind men.' But the study of them did lag behind. Similarly, the movement of Stakhanovites' wives has received little more than passing mention, despite the ideological contradictions it generated with official portrayals of female

Stakhanovites.[8] The aims of this movement were to offer support, kindness and encouragement to Stakhanovite husbands, to ask other wives why their husbands were not yet Stakhanovites, and to engage in unpaid labour in factories, schools and canteens in order to promote cleanliness and to challenge corruption.

Future research questions

Behind the success stories of individual Stakhanovites are crucial issues which need further consideration. Why did some women want to be Stakhanovites, whilst others did not? How did female Stakhanovites use their status to their advantage? How did newspapers and journals present to readers the achievements of female Stakhanovites and to what end? How did society react to them? How many forms of opposition to female Stakhanovites were there? And in which respects did they differ from hostility to male Stakhanovites? What was the relationship between Stakhanovism and Stalinism? And also, what was the significance of the movement of Stakhanovites' wives for ideology, production and images of gender roles?

This brief chapter was written at the start of a research project. Thus only preliminary and highly tentative findings are presented here, to be supplemented in future by a much broader reading of archival materials. Here I set out to address two main questions: first, how many forms of opposition did female Stakhanovites encounter?; and second, given hostility to them, why did women seek and/or attain Stakhanovite status? Examples are drawn mainly from agriculture and light industry.

Opposition to female Stakhanovites

Opposition took various forms. These included condemnations behind the women's backs as part of local gossip, direct verbal confrontation (especially concerning inappropriate gender roles), damage to the Stakhanovites' homes, machines or animals, attempts to prevent Stakhanovites from working, threats of violence and physical attacks, often with near-fatal results. Selected examples here illustrate gossip, challenges to changing gender roles, threats and violence.

Gossip and resentment

A clear example of gossip is provided by remarks about Mariia Demchenko after her participation in 1935 in the Second Congress of Kolkhoz Shock Workers. On the Comintern collective farm where she worked in Gordishchensk district, there were people who were 'unfriendly'[9] and those who said:

Just think! Mariika, daughter of Safronov, a most ordinary peasant girl, just like the rest of us, and what has she undertaken! Only the second year that she has been working as a team leader, and she already wants to outstrip everyone.[10]

There was understandable resentment at higher work targets and deep hostility to someone trying to stand out from the others. Four out of the eight workers in her team were offended: 'It seemed to them that they had worked together, they had not worked badly either, but the honour and the presents went to Mariika.' These four young girls left Demchenko's team, not all willing to speak to her any more.[11]

Others simply doubted Demchenko's abilities. There were *kolkhozniki* sympathetic to Mariia, but who 'did not believe in her strength'.[12] And some members of the kolkhoz administration 'did not yet understand that Mariia Demchenko had begun exceptionally important work and did not believe that she could fulfil her promise'.[13] Critics, then, ranged from hostile and resentful co-workers to sympathetic doubters.

Opposition to changing gender roles

Problems frequently arose where work entailed a change in traditional gender roles. Pasha Angelina describes how when she wanted to drive a tractor, 'At first everybody laughed at me.'[14] Later, at the Machine Tractor Station, her comrades jeered and laughed, saying 'She's a woman, what else can you expect of her?'[15] Dar′ia Garmash received a similar reaction from Nikolai, the man she was planning to marry. When she announced that she wanted to enrol in a tractor driving course, Nikolai taunted: 'What are you, a young man, or what?' He insisted, 'It's not for women. It's not for you to poke your nose in there. You'll only be a hill tractor driver, enough to make you a laughing stock.'[16] Nikolai refused to give his permission for her to train to drive a tractor, lecturing that 'It's man's work, understand, man's work. Good tractor drivers cannot be women.'[17] Forced against her will to choose between her tractor and Nikolai, who was 'handsome, tall, slender, broad-shouldered . . . his entire appearance courageous and proud' and whom 'it seemed impossible to love stronger', Dar′ia finally chose the tractor.[18]

Tractor women encountered difficulties before, during and after their training. When in the spring of 1933 Angelina's women's team drove out of the gates of the Machine Tractor Station, a group she had been instructing since January, this first Soviet women's team suffered immediate resistance. On the way to the fields:

> Suddenly, something unforeseen and terrible happened. On the outskirts of the village a crowd of angry women met us. They barred our road and shouted in chorus: 'Turn back! We'll allow no female machines on our fields. You'll destroy the crops!'[19]

Angelina sadly related: 'Here were our own women, women of the collective farm, reviling us.'[20] Opposition was not a simple story of men versus women, but a complex one of different forms of criticism coming from men and women, and also of various forms of support from both sexes. Tradition, cultural values, local superstitions and rituals helped to shape resistance from women and men.

Threats of violence

The next step was the threat of violence. According to Angelina, the women blocking her way to the fields shouted: '"Don't dare move. If you do, we'll pull your hair out and kick you out of here!" We knew that if we did move there would be a scrap.'[21] The situation was defused by Angelina running back to Staro–Beshevo to seek help. She returned with Kurov from the Political Department who ordered the tractor women to start work. Their critics followed them to the fields, after first having laughed at their difficulties in starting the motors. They watched them for three hours before dispersing, finally satisfied that the women seemed to know what they were doing.[22]

Sometimes threats were made to Stakhanovites' parents, especially if the Stakhanovites were young Pioneers or Komsomol members. In Tadzhikistan, men from the *chaikhana* (the all-male tea shop) visited Mamlakat Nakhangova's father. Allegedly, they said: 'You're a fine fellow, Nakhang. Everyone respects you. But your daughter, excuse us, puts us all in a ridiculous position.' Another interjected: 'It makes us look like saboteurs. They could think that we pick little cotton on purpose, that we drag out the harvest.' A third asked, 'What sort of men are we if a little schoolgirl works better than we do?'[23]

Critics tried to put pressure on relatives to make Stakhanovites change their behaviour. Dar´ia Garmash's fiancé, Nikolai, also attempted to dissuade Dasha from her folly by appealing to her mother.[24] But all heroic stories ended either with parents supporting their Stakhanovite children, as in the cases of Mamlakat Nakhangova's father and Dar´ia Garmash's mother, or with children triumphing over their objecting parents, as in the case of Garmash's earlier battle with her mother about joining the Komsomol.

Violence

Sometimes threats of violence were not executed, as was the case with the women blocking Pasha Angelina's path to the fields. On other occasions, they were. Mamlakat Nakhangova was attacked two days after her father had been warned to take control of his daughter.

Nakhangova was returning from the fields when 'they severely beat her'.[25] For three weeks she was unable to get up. But as soon as she did, she returned to the fields. She developed a following among the Pioneers, who subsequently worked with her. But her attackers were undeterred: 'Then they beat her a second time. They beat her within an inch of her life.'[26] Pasha Angelina suffered a similar fate:

> One day, as I was cycling to the fields, I heard the rattling of a heavy cart behind me. I swerved off the road, but the cart swerved too. I turned to the right and the cart turned to the right. I felt that I was being hunted and that in another moment something frightful would happen. Two enormous horses hurled themselves upon me, the heavy cart rolled over my body and then dashed off . . .

I lay bleeding in a trampled furrow for several hours. I was picked up in an unconscious condition and taken to the hospital.[27]

Opponents of Stakhanovism were sometimes out to kill. In this incident, three young men were guilty.[28]

This attack, however, was not Angelina's first experience of violence. In the summer of 1929, when she was sixteen, she was on her way with her brother Kostia and her sister Lelia to a meeting of the Young Communist League in the neighbouring village 'and somebody fired at us from behind with a sawn-off shotgun. And we were only youngsters then.' Lelia was just fourteen.[29] Angelina went on: 'The *kurkuls* [Ukrainian for 'kulaks'] beat my old mother nearly to death only because she was our mother, the mother of communists . . . '[30] In the countryside, resistance to communists affected the lives of some who later became Stakhanovites.

Violence was also one element in reactions to the movement of Stakhanovites' wives. Recollections of members of the wives' movement indicate that, like Stakhanovite women, and despite their very different tasks, their activities were not always welcome. One engineer's wife commented:

At first it was very difficult for me to work, since several workers in the factory looked upon the housewives as people who interfered in other people's affairs 'because they had nothing better to do'.[31]

The wives often had to battle with entrenched behaviour patterns of corruption and immorality. This made their tasks far from straightforward. The same engineer's wife was placed in a children's school, where:

It was especially difficult to put the children's food in order. In the kitchen nepotism reigned. The products supplied were always good and of a sufficient quantity, but the food prepared from them was foul, because the butter, sugar and other products were divided up, put into the kitchen workers' bundles and carried home.[32]

In order to tackle this problem, the engineer's wife arrived at the kitchen very early in the morning to supervise the food. Repeatedly finding hidden jars of food, she immediately used their contents in the children's food. But violence against her ensued:

One day I found butter which had been prepared by the cook to take home. I began to put this butter in the pot with the porridge. The embittered cook pushed me on to the hotplate.[33]

Here the cook was a man. As in the cases cited above, official sources drew attention to male acts of violence against women. However, without more thorough enquiry, one should not rule out the possibility of women attacking women, even if one would expect female violence to pale in comparison with male. Another unanswered question is whether women attacked male Stakhanovites. The answer is, probably not, given the segmentation of the labour force. Increases in norms in jobs performed by men generally affected men. So if anyone was going to be hostile, initially it would most likely have been men. One also instinctively views the Russian male – both urban and rural – as more violent than womenfolk. But this does not exclude the possibility of female violence. There are certainly examples of female hostility to women to prevent them from working. This, and other unanswered questions about violence, await answers from a thorough excavation of archives, including, if possible, those of the NKVD.

What can be concluded with certainty is that to be successful, shock workers, Stakhanovites and Stakhanovites' wives had to rely on commitment, resilience and endurance. They had to be capable of inventive reactions not only to work problems, but also to critics and those likely to inflict harm.

Stakhanovism invariably carried the threat of unpopularity among co-workers for increases in output norms that were feared to result. This applied in all sectors. It is substantiated in memoirs, history books and archives, and was at the time readily brought to the attention of political leaders. A letter to Grigorii Ordzhonikidze, commissar for heavy industry, from a director in the Donbass, noted that one of the reasons for deteriorating work standards was 'unfounded rumours which are circulating among workers' put out by 'enemies of Stakhanovite workers' that 'to meet the anniversary of the Stakhanovite movement norms would again rise'.[34] Cultural resistance, too, to peasants and workers who wished to stand out as different from the collective and to earn higher wages fuelled hostility. Resentment at others for doing better and for reaping obvious benefits not enjoyed by everyone has been a tenacious strand of Russian culture from pre-revolutionary days to the present. Given widespread hostility to Stakhanovites for the pressure their great feats put on others to work harder, what advantages were there in becoming a Stakhanovite? How could they outweigh the unpopularity among co-workers of bearing that status?

The advantages of Stakhanovite status

Given opposition to Stakhanovism, why did women pursue it? Like male Stakhanovites, females enjoyed higher wages and several perks such as better housing, access to education, opportunities for travel and holidays in sanatoria. They also received positive reinforcement at conferences, attained fame through newspaper coverage, biographies and films, were awarded decorations and nominated as candidates for the Supreme Soviet. Moreover, younger women were able to set higher production targets – whether alone or with back-up support – and presumably believed in the importance of doing so. Considering the issue cynically, women may have strived to produce in return for money and status, but it could also have been out of commitment to building communism and/or out of enthusiasm to demonstrate equal abilities with men. Belief in ideology, propaganda and female emancipation cannot be ruled out as possible determining factors. Precise motivations, however, could only be gauged through interviews. But even if the Stakhanovites of the 1930s were still alive, methodological problems would remain. Problems of recall and selective treatment of the past would cloud information. Nonetheless, printed primary sources show a range of relevant factors, even though establishing precise relative weightings is hazardous.

Wages and perks

Higher wages were definitely one attraction. The Stakhanovite Petrova reported in a woman's magazine that 'Before the Stakhanovite movement I earned 200 to 225 roubles, but now 500 and over.' She had progressed from working on one machine to four, then six.[35] Dusia Vinogradova, at the All-Union Conference of Working Men and Women Stakhanovites in 1936, declared: 'I used to earn 180, 200 and 270 roubles a month. But now, working at 144 looms, my earnings amount to 600 roubles. See how I increased my wages!'[36] M. Makarova, a machine operator, told the same conference: 'Comrades, I used to earn 7 to 8 roubles a day, then began to earn from 70 to 100 roubles, which increased to 175 roubles for seven hours. (Applause.) Before I used to fulfil the plan 110 to 120 per cent, but now I am fulfilling it 500 per cent. (Applause.)'[37] Higher wages meant the purchase of otherwise unattainable clothes. Nina Slavnikova told the conference how she puzzled over how to spend her money until a high-earning friend told her: 'I will buy myself beige shoes for 180 roubles, a silk dress for 200 roubles and a coat for 700 roubles.'[38]

Socialist competition also led to higher wages if output increased. With this sometimes came positive reinforcement from the management, invariably noted on the day of the competition by the presentation of a bouquet. Makarova noted: 'When Nina Slavnikova and I competed with each other and earned 175 roubles, they thanked us, called a meeting on the shop floor and brought in bouquets of flowers.'[39] Slavnikova's version coincided: 'On that day we fulfilled the plan 500 per cent! At four o'clock in the afternoon, they called a meeting, presented us with flowers for our good work. That day we earned 175 roubles. (Applause.)'[40]

N. S. Krivitskaia, worker at the Mikoian Cannery in the Crimea, told how factory organizations paid special attention to Stakhanovites: 'They gave us hostel accommodation', and thanks to mass educational work, 'there is not one illiterate person in our shop. There are preparatory courses for higher education and higher schools. The factory has a school.'[41] Krivitskaia went on:

> I also study. I have finished the seven-year school, and the management of the cannery and the trade union committee have promised to help me next year to become a technician. I have promised Party and Komsomol organizations to study for a mark of 'excellent'. It must be said that the management gave me a good room with furniture. In my shift they gave me two apprentices whom I taught. They work with the same methods as I do, and fulfil the norm.[42]

Stakhanovites were often given preferential treatment in housing and education, making daily life easier and the probability of upward mobility higher.

Success in output also brought the perk of holidays. M. Chekunova proudly explained to the conference how as a result of her work efforts, 'I was awarded a prize of a ticket for a resort in the Crimea, at Evpatoriia. I rested there an entire month.'[43] Mamlakat Nakhangova from Tadzhikistan was similarly rewarded by seeing the sea, 'warm, blue and sweet'.[44] The All-Union Pioneer sanatorium 'Artek' hospitably threw open its doors to shock workers of the First Five-Year Plan. Here Mamlakat mixed with other Pioneers of her own age from other republics who had also been given awards. Her experience included meeting young Spaniards 'whose parents were courageously fighting fascists' in the Civil War.[45] Among these children were the daughter and son of Dolores Ibarruri ('La Pasionaria'), the heroine of Spanish communism.

Reinforcement at conferences

Regular conferences brought Stakhanovites together where they received positive reinforcement from political leaders. For example, at the conference held in November 1935 discussed above, Stalin was present along with Ordzhonikidze, Kalinin, Molotov, Kaganovich, Voroshilov, Andreev, Mikoian, Chubar, Zhdanov and Khrushchev.[46] At such gatherings, Stakhanovites talked briefly about their achievements and made pledges to increase their productivity still further. Their speeches often mentioned the benefits of higher wages, as quoted above.

A theme underpinning such events was that shock workers and Stakhanovites were special and deserved acclaim. As well as being showered with praise and requested to perform even better, those in attendance were sometimes rewarded with presents. For example, in his congratulatory speech to a meeting of advanced kolkhoz workers of Tadzhikistan and Turkmenistan in 1935, Stalin announced:

> The government has decided to give a lorry to each collective farm represented here and to make a present of a record player and records to each of the participants of this meeting. (Applause.) And watches: pocket watches for the men, and wrist watches for the women. (Prolonged applause.)[47]

Material benefits were thus received beyond the workplace.

Shock workers and Stakhanovites could use the platforms given to them at such conferences to complain about work difficulties. They frequently alluded to problems of spare parts and repair. At the second oblast congress of kolkhoz shock workers, one delegate declared:

> We raised the alarm. In preparation for the harvest we had a big hitch. On 20 June, out of 104 combine harvesters, only 74 had been repaired. Out of 13,626 horse-drawn threshing machines needing repair, 3,268 had been seen to. Out of 955 intricate threshing machines, 347. Out of 12,285 harvesters and reapers, 4,824 had been attended to. Two hundred and thirty-four sheafers out of 1,252 had been repaired.[48]

And so the list went on. A demand was made to rural organs, directors of Machine Tractor Stations, kolkhoz chairs and brigade leaders to stop this 'neglect' and to promote repairs of 'high standard'.[49] But did this benefit the women involved, or merely serve the regime's end of drawing attention to factors which hindered production? Insofar as the lack of spare parts hampered shock work and plan fulfilment, it directly affected the opportunities for financial gain. Thus it was simultaneously relevant to those aspiring to Stakhanovite status and the regime's priorities. When, however, criticisms were directed at the lack of raw materials for production, which slowed down output potential, often the nature of Stakhanovism itself was to blame. Speed-ups in production inevitably led to imbalances in the plan and to a higher probability of bottlenecks in an already irrational economic planning system.

Fame

Stakhanovite feats invariably brought fame. Whether or not this made Stakhanovism attractive must have varied across individuals. Nonetheless, for those who enjoyed official acclaim in the media, there was a high probability that it would ensue after huge increases in output.

Both shock workers and Stakhanovites were constructed in the media as 'superior' and 'selfless'. For instance, in a greeting to an oblast conference of advanced female collective farmers, the editor of *Krest'ianka v zapadnoi oblasti* (*Peasant Women in the Western Region*) began with 'You, the best of the best', before praising their 'selfless struggle for a good harvest, a high quality of flax and a rise in livestock farming'.[50] The propaganda machine stressed their virtues and attempted to encourage emulation.

One consequence of fame was a stream of visitors. As Demchenko described it:

> People began to come to me here from all over the Soviet Union. Every day five or ten arrived: journalists, photographers, writers and instructors from the district, the oblast and the centre.[51]

Once on the farm, 'one takes my photo, another draws my portrait, a third writes a novel about me'.[52] In Demchenko's opinion, however, this was not necessarily positive, since visitors occasionally picked her sugar beets or trampled on them.[53]

Pasha Angelina, too, acknowledged the fame that she had acquired. In her words:

> Sometimes I hear the word 'famous' or 'celebrated' uttered in connection with my name. The government has conferred high decorations and honourable titles upon me. There is even a Pasha Angelina Street in Stalino; and a ship that plies the Moscow canal is named Pasha Angelina.
>
> I am proud of and cherish all this. To be famous in our country means receiving the people's highest appreciation of one's labour. Such fame is a great, soul-elevating happiness.[54]

Officially, at least, Angelina was not deterred by fame. Mamlakat Nakhangova was much shyer about publicity and public speaking, but nonetheless soon 'got used to it', like other more famous names.[55] Tadzhik and Moscow newspapers gave coverage to her cotton-picking records and a short documentary film was made about her, subsequently shown at an all–Union agricultural exhibition in Moscow and then in cinemas throughout the USSR.[56] Evidence suggests, however, that many Stakhanovites did not strive for this status simply out of a search for fame. Indeed, they did not always anticipate public acclaim and when it ensued did not automatically revel in it. Nakhangova seemed rather overwhelmed and initially felt awkward.

The production records that brought fame were often attained not by individual effort but by a team. Sometimes this entailed intensive support around the clock from co-workers, relatives and well-wishers. The labour feat was thus truly a 'collective' one, true to the communalism of Russian life. According to Demchenko:

> When the digging started, people hardly slept. We lived seventeen days in a tent without a day off. We dug at night, under bonfires. We went to bed at three, getting up at first light. Mum brought flat cakes (*lepeshki*). You know, I really love our flat cakes with fat. Yesterday at five o'clock we dug the last beet (*buriak*) and around us, you cannot imagine what was happening! From all sides people were walking, driving, running. A crowd of people! The equipment of two film crews was whirring.[57]

Just as Stakhanov's records were set with help from back-up workers, the same was true of Demchenko's endeavour to fulfil her promise to Stalin of 500 centners of sugar beet per hectare.

The battle for a bright future: belief, ideology and Stalinism

Whilst material incentives, perks and fame may have been driving factors behind Stakhanovism, one should not assume that they were the exclusive factors. In the context of the propaganda surrounding the five-year plans, many workers were committed to building a new society and to following Stalin. Given the slogans of official ideology, there were workers who enthusiastically engaged in behaviour approved by the party and shaped by Stalinism. Whether out of genuine belief, conformity or unimaginative obedience to party cues, there were millions who strove to work hard and to proclaim loyalty to Stalin, notwithstanding immense problems of labour discipline and general 'hooliganism' in the 1930s.[58] In keeping with historical context, Dusia Vinogradova ended her contribution to the 1935 All-Union Conference of Working Men and Women Stakhanovites with the following, no doubt well-rehearsed, joyous outburst:

> I should like to thank Comrade Stalin and the Central Committee of the Party for the happy life which I now lead. We are now the happiest people in our country! And you, Comrade Stalin, gave us such a life! (Prolonged applause.)[59]

Whilst such oily eulogy makes the western cynic wince with embarrassment at the thought of standing up in public and delivering such lines, however neatly appropriate to a context of personality cult, purges and growing fear, one still cannot automatically assume that they were not at the time believed by the person who uttered them. Many Soviet citizens indeed felt committed to Stalin and to building a glorious socialism, as regular visitors to Russia know from numerous interviews and conversations.

Whereas many believed in socialism and were willing to work hard to set new records, some women amongst them were especially able to do this, either through back-up help, efficient work or youthful energy. Certainly, the media of the 1930s were full of instructions and tips on how to set records more easily. Journals and magazines insisted that good results came from efficient organization. Lessons from success stories taught how to position machines in the factory in order to facilitate speedy walking between them and consequently faster work, or how best to tend animals, be it massaging cows' udders for higher milk production or looking after young piglets to guarantee their survival.[60] Stakhanovite examples were cited to illustrate the techniques, methods and behaviour patterns that would ensure new approaches to work which, in turn, would bring greater efficiency and long-term increases in productivity. The labour force was thus taught how to work better and how to be more hygienic. Descriptions of the activities of Stakhanovites' wives were intended to serve a similar end. Above all, these praises of Stakhanovites and Stakhanovites' wives were 'lessons' in appropriate behaviour for socialist social change. And Stakhanovite innovations were steps down the 'bright path' to communism. Many committed workers endeavoured to take them for normative as well as material reasons.

More complex, too, than previously allowed is the issue of gender politics. Female Stakhanovism was a challenge to deeply embedded attitudes about appropriate gender roles. It was a potential threat to male dominance and to the stability of social relations. Some women Stakhanovites may have delighted in this consequence and many may not have. One cannot make assumptions either way, but must acknowledge the likely variations. One can also note the double irony that by promoting female Stakhanovism, male leaders were unwittingly encouraging instability in gender relations at a time when the Party sought discipline, order, conformity and stability in society at large.

Conclusion

As the USSR disintegrated, many positive images of the past became negative ones. What had once been lauded was now automatically scorned by a crude and uncritical glasnost. Among the new negative images stood 'emancipated woman'. Once acclaimed, she was now a target of abuse. Since the discredited Communist Party of the Soviet Union had drawn women out of the home, put them in dungarees and taken away their femininity, emancipation at the hands of the state must be bad. In their reactions against the 'socialist experiment', many so-called 'democrats' automatically ridiculed images of heroic and supposedly masculinized women. Part of this new attack was a challenge to the official Stalinist ideology of sexual equality in which women were 'side by side' with men, striving 'shoulder to shoulder' for socialism.[61]

One serious implication of this reflex-rejection of 'emancipated woman' is the illegitimacy of equality in the workplace. The notion that women can, or should be, 'side by side' and equal is now challenged. At a time of growing unemployment for women, amounting to over 70 per cent of those laid off in 1992 and 1993, hostility to images of equality (however crude they were in the 1930s) fuels legitimacy for new, similarly crude pictures of an appropriately segmented labour force which includes feminine housewives, entrepreneurial beauticians, industrious homeworkers sewing and knitting and hard-currency prostitutes. Throughout history, in all political systems, periods of recession and unemployment have generated myths of the natural appropriateness of male breadwinners and of sexual inequalities. Such images are disrespectful to women, as they have always been, and in the 1990s are even more hackneyed, as the proportion of single mothers increases in East and West.

When, in this post-Soviet climate, one tells Russian colleagues that one is about to embark upon a study of female Stakhanovism, the responses range from polite surprise to mocking hilarity. Ready suggestions are forthcoming of alternative topics that would be more serious. But given the uncritical nature of many contemporary 'democratic' reactions to the Soviet past, it is imperative that the story of female Stakhanovites be told as fully and as objectively as possible. Notwithstanding problems of the reliability of data, anxieties about 'truth or falsification?' in sources and frustrations of decoding socialist realist jargon and mythology, such reassessments of the past are vital to a fuller understanding of the relationship between society and state in the 1930s, and the extent to which the 'cultural filter' of society reacted to policies handed down to it and subsequently reshaped them.[62]

Notes

I am grateful to those in the audience at Bath who commented upon an earlier draft of this chapter or who put questions to me. They all stimulated further reflection. It must be recorded that this was the most positive, constructive and pleasant conference atmosphere in which I have ever worked. I should also like to thank Bill Rosenberg for his insights.

1 Leonid E. Hubbard, *Soviet Labour and Industry* (London: Macmillan, 1942), pp. 73–82; Alexander Baykov, *The Development of the Soviet Economic System* (Cambridge: Cambridge University Press, 1946), pp. 278–9, 358–62; Maurice Dobb, *Soviet Economic Development Since 1917* (London: Routledge and Kegan Paul, 1966); Donald Filtzer, *Soviet Workers and Stalinist Industrialization: The Formation of Modern Soviet Production Relations, 1928–1941* (London: Pluto, 1986), pp. 179–207; Hiroaki Kuromiya, *Stalin's Industrial Revolution* (Cambridge: Cambridge University Press, 1988); Alec Nove, *An Economic History of the USSR* (Harmondsworth: Penguin, 1969); Solomon M. Schwarz, *Labor in the Soviet Union* (London: Cresset Press, 1953), pp. 193–9; Vladimir Andrle, *Workers in Stalin's Russia: Industrialization and Social Change in a Planned Economy* (Hemel Hempstead: Harvester Wheatsheaf, 1988), pp. 177–201.

2 Lewis H. Siegelbaum, *Stakhanovism and the Politics of Productivity in the USSR, 1935–1941* (Cambridge: Cambridge University Press, 1988).

3 Z. K. Zvezdin, I. I. Belonosov and M. I. Khlusov, *Sotsialisticheskoe sorevnovanie v SSSR, 1918–1964: dokumenty i materialy profsoiuzov* (Moscow: Izdatel'stvo VTsSPS Profizdat, 1965), p. 140.

4 Roberta T. Manning, 'Women in the Soviet Countryside on the Eve of World War II, 1935–1940', in Beatrice Brodsky Farnsworth and Lynne Viola (eds.), *Russian Peasant Women* (Oxford: Oxford University Press, 1992), p. 216.

5 I. Vershinin (ed.), *Mariia Safronova Demchenko* (Moscow: Gosudarstvennoe izdatel'stvo politicheskoi literatury, 1938), p. 5. A centner is 500 kilos. A hectare is 2,471 acres.

6 Zvezdin, Belonosov and Khlusov, *Sotsialisticheskoe sorevnovanie*, pp. 387–98.

7 P. M. Chirkov, *Reshenie zhenskogo voprosa v SSSR: 1917–1937* (Moscow: Mysl', 1978), p. 150.

8 Siegelbaum, *Stakhanovism and the Politics of Productivity*, pp. 238–9, 241–2; Mary Buckley, *Women and Ideology in the Soviet Union* (Hemel Hempstead: Harvester Wheatsheaf, 1989; Ann Arbor: University of Michigan Press, 1989), pp. 115–17.

9 Vershinin, *Mariia Safronovna Demchenko*, p. 7.

10 Ibid., p. 8.

11 Ibid.

12 Ibid., p. 7.

13 Ibid., p. 12.

14 Praskovya Angelina, *My Answer to an American Questionnaire* (Moscow: Foreign Languages Publishing House, 1949), p. 11.

15 Ibid., p. 22.

16 Dar'ia Garmash, 'O samom dorogom', in L. I. Stishova (ed.), *V budniakh velikikh stroek: zhenshchiny-kommunstki geroini pervykh piatiletok* (Moscow: Politizdat, 1986), p. 181.

17 Ibid.

18 Ibid.

19 Angelina, *My Answer*, p. 26.

20 Ibid.

21 Ibid.

22 Ibid., pp. 26–8.

23 Iurii Il'inskii, 'Iunaia stakhanovka', in Stishova, *V budniakh velikikh stroek*, p. 57.

24 Garmash, 'O samom dorogom', p. 182.

25 Il'inskii, 'Iunaia stakhanovka', p. 58.

26 Ibid.

27 Angelina, *My Answer*, p. 43.

28 Ibid.

29 Ibid., p. 16.

30 Ibid.

31 *Udarnitsa Urala*, no. 7 (April 1937), p. 10.

32 Ibid.

33 Ibid.

34 RTsKhIDNI (*Rossiiskii tsentr khraneniia i izucheniia dokumentov noveishei istorii*; formerly TsPA or the Central Party Archive, Moscow), fond 85, opis' 29, delo 701, list 1.

35 *Rabotnitsa i krest'ianka*, no. 16 (1936), p. 8.

36 *Pervoe vsesoiuznoe soveshchanie rabochikh i rabotnits-stakhanovtsev, 14–17 noiabria 1935 g.: stenograficheskii otchet* (Moscow: Partizdat TsK VKP (b), 1935), p. 27.

37 Ibid., p. 275.

38 Ibid., p. 42.

39 Ibid., p. 226.
40 Ibid., p. 41.
41 Ibid., p. 114.
42 Ibid., pp. 114–15.
43 Ibid., p. 72.
44 Il'inskii, 'Iunaia stakhanovka', p. 62.
45 Ibid.
46 *Pervoe vsesoiuznoe soveshchanie*, p. 7.
47 'Rech' tovarishcha Stalina na soveshchanii peredovykh kolkhoznikov i kolkhoznits Tadzhikistana i Turkmenistana', *Bol'shevik*, no. 23–4 (15 December 1935), p. 7.
48 'Obrashchenie 2-go oblastnogo s"ezda kolkhoznikov-udarnikov', *Sotsialisticheskoe zemledelie Urala*, no. 5–6 (May–June 1935), p. 8.
49 Ibid.
50 *Krest'ianka v zapadnoi oblasti* (June 1936), inside cover.
51 Vershinin, *Mariia Safronovna Demchenko*, p. 13.
52 Ibid.
53 Ibid., pp. 13–14.
54 Angelina, *My Answer*, p. 31.
55 Il'inskii, 'Iunaia stakhanovka', p. 63.
56 Ibid.
57 Valentin Kataev, 'Mariia Demchenko', in Stishova, *V budniakh velikikh stroek*, p. 299.
58 B. Shaver, 'Bor'ba s khuliganstvom i khuliganami', *Sotsialisticheskaia zakonnost'*, no. 1 (January 1940), pp. 12–19; P. Sharafanovich, 'Pokrovitelei progul'shchikov i narushitelei trudovoi distsipliny – k otvetstvennosti', *Sotsialisticheskaia zakonnost'*, no. 6 (June 1939), pp. 68–70.
59 *Pervoe vsesoiuznoe soveshchanie*, p. 27.
60 'Kraevoe soveshchanie otlichnikov zhivotnovodstva', *Krasnaia sibiriachka*, no. 3–4 (1936), pp. 14–18; S. Kosaurov, 'Opyt bor'by stakhanovtsev kolkhoznogo svinovodstva za rasshirennoe vosproizvodstvo', *Sotsialisticheskaia rekonstruktsiia sel'skogo khoziaistva*, no. 4 (April 1937), pp. 93–109.
61 For analysis of ideology on women under Stalin, see Buckley, *Women and Ideology*, pp. 108–38.
62 Moshe Lewin, *Soviet Society in the Making* (London: Methuen, 1985).

14

Industrial working conditions and the political economy of female labour during perestroika

DONALD FILTZER

The misery and general social breakdown created by the post-Soviet market economy are now described almost daily in the western press. In many ways women have been especially badly affected, as thousands have lost their jobs, the traditional industries of female employment have sunk further into decline and the collapsing standard of living has made it ever harder to keep the household economy intact. If we are to understand the conflicts and contradictions of emerging post-Soviet capitalism and why (as I believe) it will prove no more historically viable than its Stalinist predecessor, it is important to examine the society out of which it emerged and why that society finally disintegrated. There is now a large body of writing on the position of women in the former USSR detailing the inequalities which they suffered in virtually all walks of life. This article will look at one narrow aspect of women's experience, women industrial workers and their work environment during perestroika, and how the particular nature of their exploitation within production played a major part in destabilizing the Soviet system as a whole.

Perestroika, labour strategy and women workers

Many of the internal strains and contradictions of the policies known as perestroika centred on the Soviet élite's relationship with its industrial workforce. Whatever motivations one ascribes to Gorbachev and the 'reformist' wing of the Soviet Communist Party, central to their strategy was the perceived need to modernize production and bring the economy up to what they believed to be western standards of efficiency. This was not a technical question. It necessarily led the regime to challenge decades-old patterns of work relations within Soviet industry which had long been identified as a major source of the economy's poor productivity and long-term decline. These work relations were characterized by complex patterns of informal bargaining between workers and line managers. Managers routinely intervened to protect earnings from falling below a tacitly agreed floor; tolerated lax discipline, a slow pace of work and the restriction of output; and turned a blind eye to violations of operating procedures and poor quality output. In return they expected workers to co-operate by helping to set right the myriad disruptions and dysfunctions which plagued industrial production, whether it meant working overtime ('storming'), taking time to look for missing parts or tools or rectifying defects in materials or product designs.[1] Historically, these patterns of behaviour had grown up as a response by both workers and managers to the strains placed upon them by the system of hyper-centralized, bureaucratic planning, specifically, the need to deal with constant uncertainties, breakdowns and shortages within a political environment in which independent, organized political expression and activity were overtly suppressed.[2] Perestroika attempted to restructure industrial work practices through a combination of incentives and coercion. The coercion was to come from a reform of the wages system, which would tie remuneration more directly to performance, coupled with the implicit threat of unemployment, as inefficient enterprises would be allowed to go bankrupt.[3] The incentives were to come from a higher standard of living which modernization would allow, and greater political participation by workers in deciding how their enterprises were to be run.[4]

We know now, of course, that all aspects of this strategy failed. The wage reform disintegrated under the pressures of economic collapse; industry, rather than shedding workers, was beset by an ever-deepening labour shortage; the standard of living plummeted on an almost daily basis; and promises of political democracy within the enterprises (as opposed to limited liberalization within society at large) proved hollow.[5] The reasons for the disintegration of perestroika are, of course, numerous and complex, but from the point of view of our present discussion two merit particular attention. First, it proved impossible to modernize the work relations within Soviet industry without totally reforming the *work environment*: no amount of rationalization, reorganization of work routines, or tightening of labour discipline would transform the efficiency of Soviet industry so long as millions of workers continued to face the drudgery of low-skilled, unmechanized jobs carried out under dangerous and unhealthy conditions. Secondly, the Soviet industrial workforce, or working class, was never a homogeneous entity, but was always highly divided, with some groups of workers able to exercise greater leverage and bargaining power on the shop floor than others. In general, this meant that male workers, especially those in skilled trades, could extract concessions from management over work speeds and wages which women workers, young people and rural migrants[6] could not. These two issues are closely connected. For women workers proved to be especially vulnerable to the vicious calculus which made it 'unprofitable' for planners and managers to eliminate the huge number of low-skilled, heavy manual jobs which predominated in Soviet industry, and which were occupied disproportionately by women. The same is true of hazardous and dangerous jobs: the Soviet factory was a lethal environment for men and women alike, but women's weaker political position within the enterprise meant that they, almost exclusively, carried out many of the most dangerous trades.

In general, if we look at the historical position of women workers, we see that they played a distinctive role in the political economy of the Soviet system. On the one hand, they carried out most of the badly paid, hazardous and heavy jobs which men refused to do. On the other hand, 'feminized' industries and occupations – primarily textiles and other branches of light industry, but also including press operators or assembly-line workers in light engineering – were characterized by a higher intensity of labour than those where most workers were men. Work was more strenuous; there were fewer opportunities to lighten the strain through time-wasting; women generally showed better discipline and a far lower incidence of alcoholism; wages were lower; and the revenues generated by these industries were used to subsidize investment in heavy industry. In short, female industries and trades allowed the Soviet élite to regain some of the control over the production, appropriation and disposal of the society's surplus product which it lost in the rest of the economy. Moreover, the two main areas of female industrial employment existed in symbiotic relationship to one another. It was only the existence of the large pool of low-skilled and arduous female jobs which, by narrowing the scope of alternative employment, ensured the steady flow of women into high-intensity branches of industry.

The position of women created serious contradictions within perestroika at two levels. In terms of employment policy, the drive to introduce unemployment into the economy dovetailed with a revival of the 'back-to-the-home' propaganda of the Brezhnev years, itself a confluence of different ideological currents: there were those who believed that such problems as rising crime and juvenile delinquency were the result of a weakening of the traditional family, and that women should therefore spend more time at home; pro-natalists wanted fewer women to work in the hope that the birth rate would rise; and finally, coaxing women out of employment would help introduce unemployment in a way that would be politically more acceptable to men. The early fears of many observers, that women would be the first to lose their jobs in any shake-out of employment, were in this regard by no means unfounded. Yet such a policy, had it been carried through consistently, would have brought crippling bottlenecks to many key areas of production, for, as we discuss below, men simply would not do many of the difficult and taxing jobs which women performed. In the end, it proved a moot point, since mass unemployment did not materialize, and industry was hit with serious labour shortages, as both men and women, skilled and unskilled, left production either to take up better-paying work in co-operatives or to have more time to see to urgent domestic matters, namely standing in queues during a time of worsening shortages.[7]

The relationship between female employment and the inbuilt contradictions of perestroika made itself felt at a still deeper level. Insofar as the élite's power and privileges relied on the maintenance – albeit in a reformed and modernized form – of the Stalinist-type economy, this required the continued relegation of women workers to the subaltern roles outlined above. However, insofar as the long-term success of perestroika required a rise in the standard of living, this demanded a thoroughgoing reconstruction of the very industries in which women predominated, but whose existing conditions of labour and relations of production were crucial to the reproduction of the subordinate position of women upon which the system as a whole depended. In short, two vital conditions of the preservation of the system appeared, under perestroika, to be in irreconcilable conflict with one another. It is in this analytical context that the ensuing discussion of working conditions needs to be seen.

The working conditions of women industrial workers

As with other areas of society, perestroika saw the first relatively open discussions of the problems of the work environment, as labour economists and other commentators began to emphasize the enormous costs which bad working conditions were inflicting upon production efficiency, the workforce and the general environment. The scope of the problem almost defied description. Workers constantly laboured amidst filth, noise, vibration, toxic fumes and dangerous equipment. Safety standards were notoriously lax: as of 1990 the Ministry of Health had issued exposure limits on a mere 1 per cent of all the chemical substances used in industry.[8] Nearly half of all workers were officially listed as working in heavy and hazardous conditions, and a full 35 per cent carried out jobs without the aid of any machinery or mechanical aids,[9] including such key factory operations as transport, warehousing and loading. Even new equipment would be designed and put into production with critical safety faults.[10]

The root causes of the problem lay in the Stalinist planning system. The emphasis on gross plan fulfilment and record-breaking gave managers little or no incentive to introduce safety equipment or ventilation systems, or to monitor and maintain workplace safety. The semi-market reforms of perestroika reinforced these trends, since with enterprises now having to cover increasing proportions of costs and investment funds from sales revenues (as opposed to receiving centralized allocations from industrial ministries), expenditures on labour safety were one of the first budget items to be cut.[11] Moreover, sanctions on managers for violating safety regulations were trivial.[12] But the Stalinist system was culpable at a deeper level. Its essential contempt for those who created its surplus product was reflected in the fact that labour power in the Soviet Union was cheap. Wages were a relatively small proportion of production costs, and for the typical factory manager it was simply far more 'rational' to hire masses of low-paid workers carrying out low-skilled manual operations than to invest in labour-saving machinery. The same was true of safety improvements. Nearly half of all workers earned various benefits – wage supplements, additional leave time, early retirement or the right to free milk or other dietary supplements – for working in hazardous or heavy conditions.[13] Yet it was far cheaper to pay the extra wages involved than to make the large outlays on workplace improvements that would be required to render them safe. This arrangement had a corrupting effect on the workers themselves, who were reluctant to see improvements in conditions if these would cause them to lose these meagre privileges.[14] It was, in effect, an exchange of the worker's long-term health for a slightly higher standard of living. In the end this exchange proved dysfunctional for both the workers and the system. As Nina Kul'bovskaia noted, the country was caught in a vicious circle. Wages were low because labour was inefficient and badly organized. But it was inefficient because people were working in terrible conditions, and so worked unproductively and with bad quality. 'It is a vicious circle. And instead of breaking it with a system of state measures for improving the work environment, we exploit cheap labour power that makes no demands, enticing it with an extra tenner on its wages.'[15]

As accurate as this assessment may be, it ignores one aspect of the problem: a high proportion of the workers in this situation were women, whose hyper-exploitation, as we have already suggested, proved highly rational not just from the point of view of the individual enterprise manager, but from that of the élite as a whole.

The marginalization of women within industrial production has been documented in a number of studies.[16] As in the West, women earned about 70 per cent of what men did.[17] This gap derived from a number of sources. Firstly, women are concentrated in those industries and trades with the lowest wages, primarily food and light industry. Secondly, their wage and skill grades (*razriady*) lag systematically behind those of men, even where women and men work alongside each other in the same occupation. By and large, however, women are concentrated in the less skilled trades: during perestroika they were three-quarters of unskilled workers in industry and 58 per cent of those doing manual labour, both far in excess of their 50 per cent share of industrial workers as a whole.[18] Forty-four per cent of women did manual labour in 1985, as opposed to only 27 per cent of men.[19] Moreover, it has long been the case that when low-skilled, arduous manual jobs are mechanized, women are frequently taken off these jobs and replaced by men.[20] At the other extreme, there have been few women in skilled manual trades, such as tool-setters, maintenance mechanics and electricians.[21]

This marginalization was closely bound up with the notoriously unequal division of labour within the home, which saw women carry out the over-whelming bulk of domestic chores and responsibilities. This meant that women had less free time to upgrade skills and seek better jobs. Perhaps more importantly, these inequalities within the home fed the expectations and attitudes of men and women alike as to the types of jobs and duties women were 'suited' to take on at the workplace. It was indicative that between 1986 and 1990 a mere 17 per cent of women workers in the Soviet Union took courses to raise their qualifications, or just over three per cent a year.[22] In part this was due to women's lack of free time. But it was also due to women's keen appreciation that such efforts were an almost total waste of time. A 1990 survey of working women found that, of those who had improved their qualifications, 65 per cent considered it had brought no change in their work situation. Even more staggering, 90 per cent reported that improving their skills led to neither promotion nor a rise in skill grade, and 81 per cent said it brought no rise in wages.[23]

By official estimates, of the roughly 14.5 million women industrial workers in the Soviet Union in the late 1980s, 3.4 million were deemed to be working in hazardous conditions, including over a million exposed to high levels of dust and toxic fumes; one million working in high or very cold temperatures; and 800,000 working with excessive noise or vibration. Approximately three million were doing heavy physical labour. In all, between 20 and 50 per cent of workplaces employing women did not meet the Soviet Union's already relatively lax safety standards, depending on the branch of industry.[24] Moreover, there is evidence that the situation deteriorated over the course of perestroika: in Sverdlovsk oblast between 1986 and 1990, the number of women workers on heavy jobs in metallurgy and electrical engineering doubled, and in light industry it tripled. Similar, but much more modest increases were reported in certain industries in Belarus.[25]

Regulations imposed in 1982 and 1986 reduced the maximum load which women could lift to 10 kilogrammes for individual items, and seven tonnes cumulative weight over the course of a shift.[26] Not surprisingly, these were routinely ignored. Women in the building materials industry will lift and transport 20 to 40 tonnes of bricks a shift. Women roadbed repairers on the railways must handle sleepers weighing from 100–200 kilogrammes.[27] It is the same with exposure to toxic substances. Women surface workers in coal mining, as well as women in engineering, footwear, textiles and other industries work with acids and caustic substances without adequate protection, suffering not just skin damage, but loss of teeth.[28] In foundries, chemical plants, paint shops and other areas of factory work women are exposed to high levels of toxic fumes, made worse by the poor functioning of Soviet ventilation equipment.[29] Workers were also victims of managerial corruption. Women at the Lytkarino optical glass factory (Moscow oblast) had to clean lenses with ether because managers stole the alcohol intended for this job. In order to cover up the true cause of the substitution, the ether was officially deemed not harmful, and the women received no extra pay.[30] Hazards equally arise from faulty equipment design. The incidence of accidents on textile machinery rose elevenfold in the fifteen years prior to 1989. Textile workers in Kazakhstan used to refer to some of their spinning equipment as 'killer machines'.[31] Moreover, much of the equipment used by women is designed for use by the 'average' man, so that weavers have to stand on tiptoes to reach bobbins, while women crane operators cannot see over the dashboard.[32]

Women also bore the brunt of night work. In 1988 there were 3.8 million women – approximately one in four women industrial workers – doing night shifts, despite the fact that by Soviet law night work for women was banned other than in 'extreme necessity' or as a temporary measure.[33] While it is doubtful that Soviet women worked more night shifts than their western counterparts, they nonetheless did two to three times more night work than men.[34] Although various industries were allegedly attempting to eradicate night shifts for women, one commentator noted that this was proceeding at such a pace that it would take 74 years in the coal industry, 144 years in iron and steel, 90 years in chemicals and 322 years in petrochemicals.[35] The disadvantages of night work are clear. It disrupts family life and leads to greater fatigue, longer illnesses and more accidents. Thus at the KamAZ motor vehicle factory women on night shifts had twice the accident rate as men, a fact the local trade union attributed to the extreme tiredness these women suffered as a result of the need to combine night work and domestic labour.[36] In textile towns, where women – at least until the collapse of production in the post-perestroika period – worked sliding schedules involving nights and weekends, they seldom had days off in common with their families. As the manager of one Ivanovo textile mill commented, 'On Sunday father and children are at the theatre or going for a walk, while mother is at work, at the loom.'[37] At the same time excessive night work among textile workers was blamed for an alleged rise in juvenile delinquency and even male alcoholism, a highly tendentious argument advanced by those wishing to push women out of the workforce and back into the home. However questionable, or even reactionary, these particular conclusions may have been, one underlying point is valid: women doing regular night shifts have even less time to spend with their children than those working days, while losing virtually any possibility of finding free time for study and upgrading their skills.[38]

It is in the textile and garment industries that the problems of unsafe working conditions and a high intensity of labour are most visibly concentrated and systematically documented. The work is often monotonous, highly stressful and requires women to work a majority of the time in uncomfortable positions, subject to deafening noise and vibration, in temperatures often reaching 37–40° C.[39] Probably no other Soviet industry had such a high intensity of labour: equipment utilization in textiles was (and perhaps still is) from 50 to 80 per cent greater than in engineering; over 90 per cent of shift time is spent in productive work, far higher than male-dominated industries.[40] Improvements in equipment, rather than leading to an easing of work loads, were simply matched by higher norms: if in the past a weaver might have tended 8 to 10 looms, she would now tend 20 or 30, walking some ten kilometres over the course of a shift.[41] The work requires intense concentration and agility. A winder on some types of winding machines will replace empty packets over 1,200 times a shift. The process takes 7.6 seconds and requires the worker to bend over some 1,500 times, spending almost half her shift in this position.[42] Quality controllers would inspect cloth passing at a rate of 22 metres a minute,[43] work which is both stressful and probably of questionable value, given the difficulty of detecting flaws at such a speed. Weavers and spinners can spend as much as 75 per cent of their time repairing thread breaks, a job which demands speed and dexterity and which the women carry out in a bent position. The difficulties of this operation are made worse by the poor quality of raw materials – cotton or wool – which increases the amount of breakage.[44]

The impact of these conditions on workers' health is marked. The high noise and vibration levels, microbial contamination of raw materials, and the heightened strain of the work have left textile workers with a wide range of job-induced diseases: hearing damage, respiratory ailments, hypertonia, nervous disorders, heart disease, arthritis, varicose veins, anaemia, skin ulcers, and infertility and a high rate of birth abnormalities. Yet in the USSR none of these were actually recognized as occupational diseases which would have entitled the women to compensations such as higher wages or early retirement, beyond the general provision that women with long years of service in the textile industry could take their pension at age 50, instead of 55.[45] The result was that Ivanovo oblast had one of the highest rates of sickness in Russia, with the average worker losing 10.4 days off work per year.[46]

The combination of bad working conditions, low wages and the financial squeeze on the provision of amenities, in particular housing, led over the years to a long-term exit of women from light industry. Cities such as Ivanovo, which for generations had seen the children of its weavers and spinners following their mothers into the mills, came increasingly to rely on migrant workers from outlying areas and, toward the end of perestroika, temporary workers from Vietnam. As the manager of one weaving factory in Ivanovo commented, 'What mother who has experienced all the "delights" of a weaving or spinning shop is going to send her own daughter there?'[47] According to an official of the Light Industry and Textile Workers' Union, 160,000 workers had fled light industry during the five years 1986–90, this coming on top of a long-term decline beginning in the late 1970s.[48] It has long been the case that few women stay in production trades in textiles past the age of forty or forty-five.[49]

The toll which unsafe conditions take on women workers extends far beyond light industry, however. A 1990 survey indicated that fully a quarter of female urban residents over the age of forty suffered from some form of work-related illness.[50] The life expectancy of Soviet (and post-Soviet) women, as it is for Soviet men, is far below that of other industrialized countries. Before the collapse of the USSR, Soviet women lived on average 67 years, as opposed to 77 years for women in the United States and 79 years in Japan. The maternal death rate was 27 times higher than in Denmark and 10 times higher than in the United States.[51] The birth rate was similarly affected. Women in the rubber, chemical, paint and dye, plastics and synthetic fibre industries were 50 to 100 per cent more likely than the average Soviet woman to suffer complications with childbirth, stillbirths and other gynaecological disorders. Among women in the non-ferrous metals industry the incidence of premature births was four times the Soviet average.[52] Women themselves were painfully aware of what they sacrificed by taking the types of jobs which Soviet society had to offer. In the words of a woman electroplater at the Cheboksary instrument factory, 'Who is going to give us back the teeth that have fallen out, our damaged stomachs? Not to mention the fact that many of us have lost the most precious thing for any women – the ability to become a mother.'[53] Yet, like men, they were equally aware that they had become victims of a system which virtually compelled them to accept these conditions. Perhaps more than men, they were dependent on the extra pay and privileges to which night shifts and work in heavy or unsafe conditions entitled them. If they took other jobs they would be lucky to earn half of what they received in their current employment. Thus the trimmers in the foundries of Moscow's ZiL truck and limousine plant were all women: as of early 1991, that is, before the April 1991 price rises, they could earn 300–350 roubles a month and retire at the age of forty-five. Men simply refused to do this work, because they found it too difficult.[54] Women, therefore, steadfastly resisted attempts to induce them to take other, cleaner jobs, or to accept improvements in working conditions or limitations on night work, for fear of losing their higher wages or their place in the housing queue.[55] Thus women had become the prime victims of the vicious calculus we described above: even if paid their danger money, their labour power was cheap. And so for factory managers and industrial ministries alike, it was economically rational to substitute what seemed like a plentiful supply of female labour for mechanization and improvements.

The crisis in light industry and the collapse of perestroika

The problem of working conditions was rooted in the structural dynamics of the Stalinist economy in two ways. First, women played a highly specific role in the élite's attempt to maintain accumulation and growth in an economy where the social relations of production created a long-term tendency toward stagnation and decline. To this extent, the poor working conditions which confronted women workers were both a product of their subordinate position and a condition of maintaining that subordination and the hyper-exploitation which derived from it. As indicated, this role – and the neglect of light industry which it entailed – was incompatible with the successful implementation of the perestroika reforms, as one commentator perceptively noted:

> The reform, which is based on strengthening incentives to workers, has barely penetrated that branch of industry which has to turn out goods for the materialization of these incentives. The government then has to take measures to limit wage rises, trim back incentives and in essence, trim back the reforms in every industry.
> The logic of things states that it is precisely those enterprises which turn out goods for popular consumption which should be the leaders in the fundamental reconstruction of economic activity, which should prepare the basis for the others. What we now see on the store shelves is a consequence of violating the order in which the reform should proceed, of not knowing how precisely to define priorities.[56]

Secondly, even if the legitimacy of this analysis had been recognized, the long-term decline of the Soviet economy would still have posed a major obstacle to improvement. So much of the economy's stock of means of production was worn out and of outmoded design that it was incapable of undertaking the massive amounts of new investment that would be required to modernize all of the workplaces which required renewal. Indeed, by the time of perestroika the Soviet economy had become characterized by the paradox of a hypertrophied producer goods sector which could not even satisfy the demand for the simple replacement of used equipment, much less produce the machinery for accumulation and growth. Insofar as a reconstruction and expansion of the food and consumer goods sector required the prior construction of plant and equipment which had to be created by heavy industry, the system had become blocked. The renovation and reinvigoration of industry foreseen by perestroika could not proceed without an expansion of consumer goods production, for there was no way to raise the morale of workers within production without a substantial rise in the standard of living.

But this, in turn, could not occur because of the intrinsic weakness of industry itself.[57]

This structural weakness was exacerbated by the conjunctural destabilization caused by perestroika. With enterprises put on cost accounting and self-financing (*khozraschet*), managers abstained from investment in favour of using revenues to meet day-to-day running costs, in particular the need to meet increased wage demands made by workers who threatened to strike or to leave production. As more and more enterprises fell out of the system of centralized allocation of industrial supplies, the distribution network also collapsed: enterprises would no longer honour contracts to deliver to specific customers, but sought the highest bidder; moreover, it was now easier to increase revenues by putting up prices and cutting production. The combined effect of the cut in investment and the difficulties obtaining supplies led to a generalized and accelerating contraction of production, in which light industry was hit especially hard. The standard of living continued to fall, and with it any lingering possibility that perestroika could save the Stalinist system.[58]

We are led, then, to a succinct, but no less inexorable conclusion: if the subordination of women in production was an essential condition of the maintenance of the Stalinist system, this subordination was also a principal factor in bringing about the instability which ended it.

Notes

Much of the material in this article has been adapted from Donald Filtzer, *Soviet Workers and the Collapse of Perestroika: The Soviet Labour Process and Gorbachev's Reforms* (Cambridge: Cambridge University Press, 1994), chap. 5.

1 There are a number of discussions comparing informal bargaining in western and Soviet-type industrial enterprises. See Michael Burawoy, *Manufacturing Consent: Changes in the Labor Process under Monopoly Capitalism* (Chicago: University of Chicago Press, 1979) and *The Politics of Production* (London: Verso, 1985); Vladimir Andrle, *Workers in Stalin's Russia: Industrialization and Social Change in a Planned Economy* (New York: St Martin's Press, 1988); Donald Filtzer, *Soviet Workers and De-Stalinization: The Consolidation of the Modern System of Soviet Production Relations, 1953–1964* (Cambridge: Cambridge University Press, 1992), chap. 8.

2 Possessing only extremely limited possibilities of influencing administrative decisions, and confronted with a ban on strikes and severe sanctions against those who violated them, workers expressed their attitude to shortcomings in production primarily in a non-explicit form: holding back productivity, greater absenteeism, poor technological discipline. The most widespread method of struggling for higher wages, improved working conditions, and social privileges was labour turnover. A. K. Nazimova, speaking at a roundtable discussion, 'Strikes in the USSR: A New Social Reality', *Sotsiologicheskie issledovaniia*, no. 1 (1989), p. 26.

3 Linda J. Cook, 'Brezhnev's "Social Contract" and Gorbachev's Reforms', *Soviet Studies*, vol. 44, no. 1 (1992), pp. 37–56; Filtzer, *Soviet Workers and the Collapse of Perestroika*, chap. 2.

4 David Mandel, *Perestroika and the Soviet People* (Montreal: Black Rose, 1991), chap. 1; Filtzer, *Soviet Workers and the Collapse of Perestroika*, chap. 3.

5 William Moskoff, *Hard Times: Impoverishment and Protest in the Perestroika Years: The Soviet Union 1985–1991* (Armonk, N.Y.: M. E. Sharpe, 1993).

6 The so-called *limitchiki*, who worked in the large cities on temporary residence permits.

7 During 1990 and 1991, large numbers of women did face temporary unemployment, but this was due to the shortage of industrial supplies which forced many factories in light industry to send workers home on unpaid leave. These jobs were not permanently lost, nor were these layoffs part of official policy: on the contrary, they were an unforeseen and unwanted symptom of perestroika's impending collapse.

8 *Ekonomicheskie nauki*, no. 2 (1990), p. 30 (V. D. Roik).

9 *Trud v SSSR* (1988), pp. 63–5, 249; *Znamia*, no. 9 (1991), p. 211 (Evgenii Starikov).

10 *Sotsialisticheskii trud*, no. 1 (1990), pp. 47–8 (M. Begidzhanov, V. Kargashevskii, Iu. Kuz'menko); no. 3 (1990), p. 33 (Z. Molokova, A. Mironenkov).

11 *Sotsialisticheskii trud*, no. 9 (1991), p. 39 (Natal'ia Vladova).

12 *Rabotnitsa*, no. 7 (1990), p. 10 (interview with Nina Karpovna Kul'bovskaia).

13 *Trud v SSSR* (1988), p. 139.

14 *Ekonomika i organizatsiia promyshlennogo proizvodstva* (Siberian Academy, Novosibirsk: hereafter *EKO*), no. 1 (1990), p. 35 (V. I. Shcherbakov); *Sotsialisticheskii trud*, no. 6 (1991), p. 41 (I. Molokanova).

15 *Rabotnitsa*, no. 7 (1990), p. 10.

16 See among others, Alastair McAuley, *Women's Work and Wages in the Soviet Union* (London: Allen and Unwin, 1981); E. B. Gruzdeva and E. S. Chertikhina, 'Soviet Women: Problems of Work and Daily Life', in Murray Yanowitch (ed.), *The Social Structure of the USSR: Recent Soviet Studies* (Armonk, N.Y.: M. E. Sharpe, 1986), pp. 150–69, and 'Polozhenie zhenshchiny v obshchestve: konflikt rolei', in *Obshchestvo v raznykh izmereniiakh* (Moscow, 1990), pp. 147–67; Filtzer, *Soviet Workers and De-Stalinization*, chap. 7.

17 Filtzer, *Soviet Workers and De-Stalinization*, p. 188; *EKO*, no. 8, p. 142 (Tat'iana Boldyreva); Monika Rosenbaum, *Frauenarbeit und Frauenalltag in der Sowjetunion* (Münster, 1991), p. 59.

18 *Sotsialisticheskii trud*, no. 3 (1991), p. 8; Gruzdeva and Chertikhina, 'Polozhenie zhenshchiny', p. 153.

19 Calculated from Gruzdeva and Chertikhina, 'Polozhenie zhenshchiny', p. 154; *Trud v SSSR* (1988), pp. 106, 249. According to *Okhrana truda*, no. 9 (1989), p. 2, there were 4.2 million women in industry working manually without any mechanical assistance, or approximately 30 per cent of women workers (calculated from *Trud v SSSR* (1988), pp. 47, 106). However, this excludes those women doing manual labour in connection with mechanized operations.

20 Filtzer, *Soviet Workers and De-Stalinization*, p. 187; *Trud*, 27 October 1989 (V. Zakharov).

21 Detailed statistical studies of women in skilled trades are available only for the 1960s. Interviews which I carried out in Moscow and Leningrad during the summer of 1991 suggest that the situation had changed little over the ensuing 30 years.

22 *Vestnik statistiki*, no. 2 (1991), p. 54. A 1988 study of workers in the agricultural machinery, iron and steel, non-ferrous metallurgy, electrical engineering and footwear industries, carried out by the State Committee for Labour's Scientific Research Institute of Labour, found that men were three to four times more likely than women

to undergo retraining and acquire new skills: *Sotsialisticheskii trud*, no. 3, 1990, p. 62 (I. Kochetkova).

23 *Vestnik statistiki*, no. 2 (1991), p. 55.

24 *Okhrana truda*, no. 9 (1989), p. 2; *Sotsialisticheskii trud*, no. 8 (1989), pp. 63–4 (L. Shineleva), and no. 3 (1990), p. 33 (Z. Molokova, A. Mironenkov). According to *Okhrana truda*, there were only 275,000 women doing heavy physical labour, but this figure is impossibly low. If women were 44 per cent of workers doing heavy physical labour or working in unsafe conditions, and if just under half of all industrial workers fell into this category, there would have been at least 6.5 million women in this group in the late 1980s. If the figure of 3.4 million in hazardous conditions was even remotely accurate, this would imply another 3 million on heavy work. See *Vestnik statistiki*, no. 1 (1990), p. 41, and *Trud v SSSR* (1988), pp. 45, 139.

25 *Sotsialisticheskii trud*, no. 3 (1991), p. 8.

26 *Sotsialisticheskii trud*, no. 4 (1989), p. 70 (A. Abramova); *Ekonomika i zhizn'*, no. 10 (1991), p. 14. New regulations were to have been drafted during 1991, but to the best of my knowledge they did not reach the statute book: Decree of the USSR Supreme Soviet, 'O neotlozhnykh merakh po uluchsheniiu polozheniia zhenshchin, okhrane materinstva i detstva, ukrepleniiu sem'i', 10 April 1990, *Izvestiia*, 13 April 1990.

27 *Ekonomika i zhizn'*, no. 10 (1991), p. 14; *Izvestiia Akademii Nauk SSSR, Seriia ekonomicheskaia*, no. 1 (1991), p. 66 (V. D. Roik), citing *Rabotnitsa*, no. 3 (1989), p. 10. At the Semiluki refractory materials factory (Voronezh oblast), attempts to apply these limits led to such a fall in the women's wages that the trade union agreed to waive their enforcement: *Ekonomika i zhizn'*, no. 10 (1991), p. 14.

28 *Rabochaia gazeta*, 13 November 1991 (A. Afanas'ev); *Molot* (Lenin factory, Leningrad), 12 April 1990; *Skorokhodovskii rabochii* (Skorokhod Footwear Production Association, Leningrad), 7 August 1990; *Komsomol'skaia pravda*, 1 May 1991 (S. Blagodarov).

29 *Pravda*, 11 June 1988; *Trud*, 7 July 1990 (Khimprom Production Association, Saiansk, Irkutsk oblast); *Rezinshchik* (Sverdlovsk rubber-technical goods factory), 14 August 1990; *Stankostroitel'* (Machine Tool Manufacturing Production Association, Kuibyshev), 17 September 1990; *Sotsialisticheskii trud*, no. 3 (1991), pp. 10–11, 13. At Khimprom in Saiansk, management attempted to cover up the dangers to which women cleaners in its mercury electrolysis shop were exposed by changing their job title to 'deactivators'. When four women protested about conditions and management's generally authoritarian conduct they were fired (with trade union connivance) under the pretext of removing them from dangerous work.

30 David Mandel, interview with workers at the Lytkarino Optical Glass Factory (Moscow oblast), October 1990. I am grateful to David Mandel for permission to use this material.

31 *Okhrana truda*, no. 9 (1989), p. 3; *Sovetskie profsoiuzy*, no. 1 (1991), p. 42 (N. Ermolaeva). In the case of Kazakhstan, the operating manual of the machine in question actually stated that for every 100 spindles 10 runners would fly off. Miraculously, the accident rate on the equipment was surprisingly low, despite its nickname.

32 *Sotsialisticheskaia industriia*, 22 January 1988 (Liudmila Telen'); *Rabotnitsa*, no. 1 (1990), pp. 15–16 (Ada Levina). Women in the paint shop of Kuibyshev's Machine Tool Manufacturing Association made a similar complaint: on some equipment they could not reach the upper areas for cleaning or servicing; on others they had to erect special

trestles to avoid having to crawl around on their hands and knees: *Stankostroitel'*, 17 September 1990.

33 Zoia P. Pukhova, chair of the Soviet Women's Committee, addressing the 19th Conference of the Communist Party of the Soviet Union, 1 July 1988, *Pravda*, 2 July 1988; *EKO*, no. 8, 1988, p. 139 (Tat'iana Boldyreva).

34 *Sotsialisticheskaia industriia*, 22 January 1988 (Liudmila Telen'); *Sotsialisticheskii trud*, no. 3 (1991), p. 9.

35 *Sotsialisticheskii trud*, no. 4 (1989), p. 70 (A. Abramova).

36 *Sovetskie profsoiuzy*, no. 6 (1991), p. 67 (T. Galiev).

37 *Trud*, 14 September 1988.

38 *EKO*, no. 8 (1989), pp. 89–91 (V. D. Roik).

39 *EKO*, no. 8 (1988), p. 139 (Tat'iana Boldyreva).

40 *EKO*, no. 8 (1989), p. 91 (V. D. Roik); *Sotsialisticheskaia industriia*, 22 January 1988 (Liudmila Telen'); *Trud*, 14 September 1988. According to an official of the Russian Light Industry and Textile Workers' Union, workers receive an unpaid dinner break of 30–40 minutes, plus two paid breaks of 10–15 minutes each: Interview with Anatolii Kol'makov, Moscow, 2 July 1991. Of course, the textile industry is not the only one in which women are subjected to such a high intensity of labour. Women rollers in a calendering section of the Sverdlovsk rubber technical goods factory would work an eight-hour shift without a single rest break, despite the large amount of heavy physical labour their jobs involved: *Rezinshchik*, 14 August 1990.

41 *Trud*, 14 September 1988; *EKO*, no. 3 (1988), p. 98 (L. I. Gol'din).

42 *Sotsialisticheskii trud*, no. 9 (1990), p. 27.

43 *Sovetskie profsoiuzy*, no. 1 (1991), p. 41 (N. Ermolaeva).

44 *Trud*, 14 September 1988. Sometimes the problem is caused, or at least exacerbated, by negligence and poor storage facilities, so that raw materials are damaged by exposure to bad weather: see *Zaria* (Lenin Worsted Combine, Ivanovo), 5 April 1991. If anything, the quality of raw materials – especially that of cotton coming from the Central Asian republics – became an even greater problem after the breakup of the USSR: see *Zaria*, 26 March 1993.

45 *Sotsialisticheskaia industriia*, 22 January 1988 (Liudmila Telen'); *Sotsialisticheskii trud*, no. 3 (1991), p. 11; *Sovetskie profsoiuzy*, no. 1 (1991), p. 42 (N. Ermolaeva). According to Soviet pension law, textile workers could retire five years early if they had worked twenty years in industry, at least ten of them in textiles: ibid., p. 43.

46 *Golos Dzerzhintsa* (F. E. Dzerzhinskii spinning-weaving factory, Ivanovo), 26 April 1991.

47 *Trud*, 14 September 1988. On the specific problems of Vietnamese workers in light industry see *Rabochaia tribuna*, 16 August 1990 (E. Seregina).

48 *Trud*, 8 September 1990; *Vestnik statistiki*, no. 2 (1991), p. 39.

49 Filtzer, *Soviet Workers and De-Stalinization*, p. 192; *EKO*, no. 8 (1988), pp. 139–40 (Tat'iana Boldyreva).

50 *Vestnik statistiki*, no. 2 (1991), p. 56.

51 *Sotsialisticheskii trud*, no. 8 (1989), p. 66 (L. Shineleva). These average figures overstate the gravity of the position of urban workers, since living and working conditions in the countryside, and the resulting death rates, are far worse than in the towns. According to Shineleva, the death rate in Soviet rural areas is 20 per cent above that in towns; among children it is 50 per cent higher.

52 *EKO*, no. 8 (1988), pp. 140–1 (Tat'iana Boldyreva); *Sotsialisticheskii trud*, no. 8 (1989), p. 64 (L. Shineleva).

53 *Trud*, 9 August 1990.

54 *Sotsialisticheskii trud*, no. 3 (1991), p. 13. Women painters at the Kuibyshev Machine Tool Manufacturing Association similarly claimed that they could not afford to give up this type of work. *Stankostroitel'*, 17 September 1990. By the same token, the foundry workers at ZiL also pointed out that there were many other trades at ZiL – press operators, painters and furnace operators – which, despite the hazardous nature of the work, were not classified as unsafe and thus earned these workers no compensatory privileges.

55 *Rabotnitsa*, no. 1 (1991), p. 12 (Ol'ga Laputina); *Sovetskie profsoiuzy*, no. 1 (1991), p. 41 (N. Ermolaeva); no. 7 (1991), p. 17 (A. Ivanov); *Sotsialisticheskii trud*, no. 3 (1991), pp. 8–9; *Trud*, 27 October 1989.

56 *Sotsialisticheskaia industriia*, 25 October 1989 (L. Biriukova).

57 For two very stimulating accounts of the contours of this crisis, see the articles by S. Pervushin and B. Lavrovskii in *Voprosy ekonomiki*, no. 8 (1991).

58 For a fuller discussion of the supply crisis and its impact on production, see Filtzer, *Soviet Workers and the Collapse of Perestroika*, pp. 135–47.

15

'Generals without armies, commanders without troops': Gorbachev's 'protection' of female workers

MELANIE ILIC

Under Gorbachev much was revealed about the unsatisfactory conditions of work for female labour in the Soviet Union. The Soviet Labour Code and special decrees for women workers issued in the years immediately following the October Revolution were designed to protect female labour from particular dangers of employment, in view of the perceived delicacy of the female organism and women's important childbearing function. In later years legislation was introduced with the aim of easing women's dual productive and reproductive roles. Glasnost brought to light the limited effectiveness of such legislation in the late 1980s. A number of surveys reported in the Soviet press, journals and magazines revealed the widespread violation of protective labour legislation for female workers. In addition to this, open discussion of a number of Soviet social problems in the late 1980s also partly focused on the dislocation caused in families with working mothers. Simultaneously, the restructuring of the Soviet economy under perestroika threatened to undermine the security of employment for women in a competitive labour market. Proposed changes in the rights of working women and especially in maternity provisions, debated both under Gorbachev and in the post-Soviet period, have attempted to accommodate the withdrawal of women from productive labour by emphasizing their role as mothers rather than as workers.

During the Civil War years and in the 1920s, the encouragement of women to play an active role in the development of the Soviet economy, and the specific conditions of work for female labour became the focus of attention for Bolshevik social reformers in their discussions of the protection of labour and improvements in public hygiene. High levels of miscarriage, stillbirths and infant and maternal mortality, brought about partly by the harsh conditions experienced by women workers in tsarist industries, and the prevalence of poor health and industrial diseases amongst women factory workers were cited as evidence by the Bolsheviks for the introduction of regulations aimed at 'protecting' female labour.[1] Legislation was also introduced to protect the rights of pregnant women and to secure social welfare benefits for new mothers.

Protective labour legislation introduced in the early Soviet period was concerned with hours of work, the physical environment of employment and the transportation of weights and loads by women.[2] In effect, in theory at least, much of this legislation excluded women from certain categories of employment and restricted their participation in other areas of the economy. In reality, however, much of the legislation existed only on paper. The laws themselves were far from being universally applicable, and their implementation was hampered by a shortage of labour inspectors and resistance on the part of both enterprise managers and the workers themselves. These three main categories of restrictions, however, have remained the basis of labour protection for female workers even after the collapse of the Soviet regime.

Despite a number of later retractions, legislation was introduced in the immediate post-revolutionary period to limit the employment of women in over-time work and on night shifts, except as emergency measures or in specified sectors of the economy which were reliant on the employment of women (medical services, telecommunications and so on). Under no circumstances were pregnant women or nursing mothers to be employed in overtime work or at night. It should be noted, however, that such 'protective' measures were not always welcomed by the female workers themselves.

By 1932 the Commissariat of Labour had compiled a long list of jobs in which the employment of women was prohibited because the work involved was considered to be too hazardous or heavy. Women workers were totally banned from underground work in the mining industries except as sanitary or auxiliary workers. Another list was compiled of jobs in which the employment of women should be favoured. By the end of the 1920s, maximum norms had been established for both adult women and young female workers (between the ages of 16 and 18 years) limiting the weights of loads to be transported by hand or in barrows during a single movement or throughout the course of the shift. A maximum load of 20 kilogrammes was established for adult women to carry by hand on an even surface. It is also interesting to note that such was the perceived delicacy of the female organism that considerable debate also took place in the 1920s on the subject of releasing certain categories of female labour from work for two or three days during menstruation.[3]

After the economic dislocation and population losses incurred during both the First World War and Civil War, measures introduced to enhance maternal welfare reflected the Bolshevik concern to draw women into employment, and particularly into the industrial labour force, whilst at the same time encouraging women to fulfil their reproductive capabilities. The new Bolshevik regime attempted to protect the employment rights of pregnant women and the social welfare of new mothers. Pregnancy could no longer be cited as a reason for refusing women employment, nor could pregnant women be dismissed from work. On notification of pregnancy, women could request transfer to lighter work. Pregnant women and new mothers could not be sent on business trips without their consent.

Paid maternity leave of eight weeks before and eight weeks after birth was introduced for industrial workers and six weeks before and after birth for white-collar workers. Maternity leave was not to be counted against a woman's continuous work record. Maternity grants were offered to women to help cover the costs of baby clothes and other essential purchases. Nursing mothers were to be allowed a minimum half-hour break every three hours to feed their babies. Nursing mothers could also request transfer to employment close to their place of residence.

In subsequent years amendments and additions were made to this early legislation.[4] For example, technical developments and progressive mechanization allowed previously prohibited areas of employment to be opened to women. The introduction of safety measures and protective clothing and the encouragement of scientific and technical training also broadened the scope of female employment. Concern for the falling birth rate in the Soviet Union, particularly under Khrushchev and Brezhnev, gave rise to attempts to introduce shorter working days, part-time employment and flexible work patterns for women and to extend the periods of fully paid, partially paid and unpaid maternity leave. Despite these changes, violations of protective labour legislation for female labour became an open area of debate under Gorbachev. A re-emphasis on women's reproductive and domestic roles also gave rise to a significant feminist lobby against social, economic and legal changes which would result in the involuntary removal of women from the labour force.

In the late 1980s, reports began to appear in the Soviet press and in journal literature detailing the conditions of work for female labour and criticizing the widespread ignorance and violations of established protective labour legislation. On the one hand, there were reports of improvements in working conditions for female labour, benefiting on average over one million women every year.[5] On the other hand, the chairs of the Soviet Women's Committee, Valentina Tereshkova and Zoia Pukhova, spoke after the Twenty-Seventh Party Congress in 1986 and the Nineteenth Party Conference in 1988 of the enormous numbers of women working in the Soviet Union in contravention of the Labour Code and established regulations.[6] Pukhova was also critical of judicial reluctance to prosecute for these violations.[7]

In 1988 the popular women's magazine *Rabotnitsa* reported that 3.8 million women were employed on night shifts despite the legal ban on women's night work except as a temporary measure or where there was an identified special need. Many of these women were employed in the light industrial sector. In the textile industry, for example, women were extensively employed at night, starting work at 11 p.m. and finishing at 6 a.m. Some had small children to get ready for school when they arrived home or to look after during the day. One report suggested that at the current rate of reduction of women's night work it would take decades, indeed centuries in some instances, to eliminate such employment totally.[8] In some other areas of the economy, such as the oil and chemicals industries and metallurgy, the employment of women at night was believed to be increasing. In many of the identified sectors the numbers of women employed at night far outstripped the numbers of men.[9] In a number of other branches of the economy, such as textiles, footwear and similar industries, the nature of production often meant that women had to work overtime, sometimes up to eight hours per week, and on their days off.[10]

In 1989 *Argumenty i fakty* reported that, despite the improvements in the conditions of work for many women in recent years, 3.4 million women were still working in conditions considered to be harmful to their health.[11] Many areas of female employment in both heavy and light industry did not meet the requirements for occupational safety or health norms. Factory workers were employed in dusty, polluted and unventilated conditions with high noise levels and unregulated temperatures. These sectors included a number of industries in which women constituted the majority of employees, including textiles, tobacco, chemicals and footwear.[12] There were 275,000 women reported to be working in heavy physical labour, despite the legal prohibition on such work,[13] and 4.2 million women employed in industry and tens of thousands of female workers in the transport sector were reported to be engaged in manual work, despite considerable investment in mechanization of the labour process.[14] In addition to this, women were also widely employed in manual labour in agriculture, where women constituted the bulk of manual workers.

Complaints were also voiced in newspaper reports and journals of the heavy loads which female industrial and agricultural workers were expected to carry during the course of their shift, despite legal guidelines restricting such activities. For example, in construction work and the trading industries, including millions of female sales clerks, women were required to carry heavy loads, the weight of which often exceeded the established norms.[15] Female agricultural workers in particular complained of the heavy loads they were expected to work with, often having to carry these by hand. During the 1980s and in the post-Soviet period attempts were made by the government and trade union organizations to reduce the maximum norm of weights to be carried by female workers, although it is difficult to assess the effectiveness of these regulations in practice.[16] It was also reported that women were still being employed in underground work in certain sectors of the economy, namely metallurgy.[17] Work undertaken by women in all sectors of the economy was often reported to be arduous and monotonous.[18]

In reality there were a number of reasons why women themselves may have chosen to work under such unfavourable circumstances. Employment in the more dangerous and hazardous jobs, and also on night shifts, could offer women higher financial remuneration, a shorter working day, longer holidays and an earlier retirement age than other areas of work. With such benefits available to female labour in these types of jobs, women workers would have little material interest in trying to improve the physical conditions of their employment. Working in heavy industrial sectors was one way in which women could maximize their earning potential in an economy where women's wages were on average 25 to 30 per cent lower than men's. For many women, working in areas where this type of work was a viable option, such employment could prove both convenient and profitable. This has been reported in many instances as women showing a willingness to sacrifice their own health in the short term in order to provide financial security for their families.[19]

In the long run, however, work under these conditions was reported to be detrimental to the health not only of the female employee, but also could possibly lead to higher levels of ill-health and death amongst children.[20] A significant proportion of women reported ill-health in relation to their employment and studies of conditions of work for female labour often noted a range of illnesses suffered by women including, for example, anaemia, arthritis and heart and lung problems.[21] This point was reinforced further in a recent article in *Trud* which suggested that the level of maternal mortality in Russia is four to five times higher than in developed countries.[22] For many women, therefore, the benefits offered by this type of employment may not, in the long term, have compensated for the social consequences.[23]

Despite the benefits available to women working in heavy industrial sectors, female labour constituted the bulk of employees in light industries, where unfavourable working conditions and extensive overtime requirements were also very much in evidence. Women might also choose to undertake unpleasant work in order to secure accommodation, an apartment or other social benefits, including child care facilities. However, once workers found a place to live or secured other benefits, they might seek alternative employment, and this situation contributed to the high levels of labour turnover in some sectors of the economy.[24]

The lower levels of technical and professional qualifications amongst women was cited as an additional reason for the prevalence of female labour in manual occupations.[25] The level of professional qualifications amongst women with small children was reported as being especially low, and the right of these women to be allowed to study during work time, in accordance with regulations introduced in 1987, was widely ignored by managers.[26] The possibility of extended maternity leave was also noted by some commentators as potentially detrimental to women's abilities to raise the level of their professional and technical qualifications.[27] State commitment to improving the conditions of work and the level of qualifications of female labour, therefore, proved to be conflicting and to exist only on paper. In many instances women were reported to be working in conditions which contravened the labour code in ignorance of the legal protection extended to them. In this sense alone the law has proved ineffective in protecting the rights of female labour.

Very often, managers and enterprise administrators were blamed for failing to protect women at their places of employment, despite a legal requirement to do so.[28] It could prove cheaper for enterprises to pay women higher wages to work in unfavourable conditions than to invest in measures which would improve work conditions, labour hygiene and technical safety.[29] Where mechanization of the labour process was taking place this was reported to be benefiting male employees, who were given first priority in access to mechanized equipment, sometimes at the expense of increasing manual labour amongst female colleagues in auxiliary occupations.

Where female labour did have access to machinery and mechanized equipment this was often not designed to be worked by women, and in some instances could prove to be more injurious to labour safety. For example, one report into the construction industry in Odessa cited the inadequate seating arrangements and positioning of windows in cranes, which restricted their use by female employees.[30] Much of the mechanized equipment being introduced into the economy, therefore, was not seen to meet women's physical requirements, and the use of such equipment could prove emotionally and psychologically detrimental to women as well as increasing the risk of accidents at work.[31] One report claimed that 'almost as many women have died at work as did soldiers in the Afghan war'.[32]

The requirements of enterprises to maximize both their output and their use of equipment by retaining a three-shift production pattern (that is, including a night shift), has been cited as a further reason for the persistence of unfavourable working conditions for female labour. Many light industrial sectors, especially textiles, where female labour predominates, have been slow to make changes in their shift patterns since the war. This has resulted in large numbers of women continuing to work at night, despite reports revealing lower levels of productivity for night workers and high levels of social dislocation amongst those families in which women work at night. *Rabotnitsa* cited the limited interest on the part of the government and trade unions to make changes in shift patterns which would reduce the amount of night work undertaken by women.[33] A conflict has arisen between the demands to utilize new technological equipment to the full and to improve the conditions of work for women.

Further resistance was also reported on the part of enterprise managers to the introduction of more flexible work routines and part-time work for working mothers.[34] Such schedules may also have proved disadvantageous to women if they resulted in a reduction in pay allocated either on an hourly basis or according to output. Preferential work schedules for female labour were reported seldom to be implemented in practice, partly because of difficulties arising in administration, and partly because women themselves were often unaware of their rights, especially as mothers of small children, to establish more favourable work regimes.[35] Flexible work schedules may also have allowed more women to enter paid employment. For example, in Uzbekistan it was reported that less than 20,000 women were employed in domestic industries or on a part-time basis when 70,000 women not in employment wished to work under such conditions.[36] Government and statutory attempts to encourage preferential work schedules, part-time or domestic work amongst women are believed, therefore, to have met with only partial success.

Fears were voiced that the radical economic reforms undertaken by Gorbachev would also make women, especially working mothers, more vulnerable to unemployment as enterprises attempted, according to some reports, to resist hiring women with small children or to dismiss women on maternity leave.[37] It was reported also that pregnant women were not always guaranteed the legal requirement of transfer to lighter work or provided with security in employment.

Despite the difficulties faced by female workers in terms of both their conditions of employment and managerial resistance to improving these conditions, for many women having a job remained more than a matter of securing a means of subsistence. The majority of women in one survey said that they would want to continue working, if only part-time, even if their partner received a wage sufficient to support them both.[38] Sociological studies suggested that the percentage of women who would choose to give up work, given a situation of financial security, decreased with rising levels of educational attainment. It is important to note here that far lower levels of dissatisfaction with conditions of work were recorded amongst female white-collar workers, for whom work was most often described as monotonous and tiresome.[39]

Marina Lebedeva reported in *Izvestiia* on a Plenary Session of the Soviet Women's Committee in 1988 where Zoia Pukhova proclaimed that entire branches of Soviet industry would be like 'generals without armies, commanders without troops' if women were excluded from paid employment. Pukhova pointed to traditional female passivity in resisting violations of their legal rights, citing the example of the minister for light industry, V. G. Kliuev, who declared that night shifts were likely to persist in industries under his jurisdiction, despite the fact that the employment of women on night shifts in these industries would automatically contravene article 69 of the Labour Code. The elimination of the night shift, he argued, would result in production being cut by one third. This statement was received at the Nineteenth Party Conference with no open criticism. Pukhova also voiced concern that millions of female manual workers would be made redundant in the following decade.[40]

In March 1989 the official party journal *Kommunist* published an article under the title 'How We Solve the Woman Question'.[41] The authors, researchers at the Institute for Socio-Economic Problems of the Population, outlined four major approaches to the 'woman question' evident in social policy introduced in the Soviet Union.[42] The article is particularly significant in view of the implicit feminist framework adopted in its analysis of sexual inequality in the Soviet Union. In examining 'egalitarian' trends, the article outlined the conditions of work for millions of women in the Soviet Union and pointed to the perceived negative social consequences of widespread female employment. The authors pointed to horizontal stratification in the Soviet labour force and the lower levels of pay earned by women. They pointed also to the large numbers of women employed in heavy physical labour, in conditions not conforming to safety regulations and on night shifts. They called for the elimination of legal norms which resulted in direct and indirect discrimination against women. They also voiced fears that women would be increasingly marginalized under programmes of economic restructuring.

In assessing the variety of reports and the range of debates, which provided evidence of the persistence of harsh working conditions for female labour and the widespread violations of protective labour legislation under Gorbachev, it is clear to see that little was being done to improve the situation of women in the Soviet economy as workers. Sectoral studies suggested that improvements in conditions of work for female labour were proceeding very slowly, if at all. The Council of Ministers and trade union organizations undertook to review protective labour legislation for women workers during 1990-1, in order to update the list of prohibited jobs (last reviewed in 1978) and to establish new norms of loads to be transported by women.[43] It is clear that glasnost gave voice to high levels of dissatisfaction amongst female workers about their conditions of work and low status. But there is little concrete evidence of attempts to improve women's working lives by investing in improvements in the physical environment of their employment, in the mechanization of the labour process in branches of the economy where female labour predominated, or in the introduction of more flexible work schedules which might have benefited millions of women, especially working mothers.

In contrast, debates under Gorbachev and in the post-Soviet period on the need to improve the working conditions of female labour have placed an emphasis on women's role as mothers, rather than as workers. Rather than aiming to enforce or review existing protective labour legislation regulating hours of work, hazardous conditions of employment or weights of loads, changes in legislation affecting female labour came in the realm of extended maternity benefits introduced in 1987, having been announced at the Twenty-Seventh Party Congress in the previous year. In subsequent years a new law was drafted, 'For the Protection of the Family, Motherhood, Fatherhood and Children' which aimed to extend the maternity benefits of working mothers and which would, in effect, have led to the withdrawal of working mothers from productive labour for a prolonged period. In the period following its initial publication, the draft law was openly criticized by a growing feminist opposition, which feared that the fundamental principles embodied in the draft would disadvantage women in the labour market.

In 1987 the period of fully paid maternity leave was extended by two weeks, from 56 to 70 days after the birth of a baby. The period of partially paid maternity leave was extended from one year to eighteen months and the period of unpaid leave was extended from eighteen months to two years. Women were also offered up to fourteen days paid leave each year to care for a sick child. These provisions were introduced gradually, beginning in those regions with the lowest birth rate. Additional benefits to working mothers reduced the total number of hours of work on agreement with the enterprise administration, and with a proportional reduction in wages for women with children up to eight years of age, or with responsibility for caring for a sick family member. More flexible work schedules were encouraged, along with attempts to expand the numbers of women engaged in home working, where levels of pay were notoriously low.[44]

More recently, the draft law 'For the Protection of the Family, Motherhood, Fatherhood and Children' aimed to extend the period of paid leave of absence for the care of new-born children to three years, and this was to be made available to any member of the family. The draft law also proposed to recognize the social utility of child-rearing by the payment of a sum of no less than the minimum wage for non-working parents responsible for the care of three or more children or a disabled child. A reduced work week of thirty-five hours was proposed for working mothers with children under the age of fourteen.[45] The draft proposals, however, in the face of much criticism, failed to pass the second reading in the spring of 1993.[46]

Whilst in theory these proposals opened the way for men to become more involved in child care, feminist opposition to the draft law was significant. It has been argued that the proposed initiatives provided a 'demographic' solution to the current problems faced by female labour by identifying women primarily as mothers. The implementation of the draft law proposals would inevitably have led to discrimination against women as workers. Criticisms of the proposed changes were concerned with the fact that employers would be even less likely to employ women if the period of paid leave for child care was extended even further, and that despite the paternity provisions of the proposed legislation, it is unlikely that Russian men would take up this option. The concept of the 'working mother' rather than 'working parent' in discussions of a reduced work week, it was argued, would also disadvantage women in a situation of competitive employment.[47]

The study of the 'protection' of female workers under Gorbachev and in post-Soviet society gives rise to a number of interesting points of comparison and discussion. In the 1920s and 1930s, when the Soviet Union was experiencing a process of economic reconstruction and rapid industrialization, women were called upon to take an active part in the economic development of the country as factory hands at the bench, as shock workers in labour brigades and as Stakhanovites in an effort to raise industrial productivity.[48] In the 1920s, when the new Soviet state was faced with the population losses incurred during the First World War and the Civil War, female labour was protected and regulated by legislation, in view of the perceived delicacy of the female organism and women's reproductive duties. By the 1930s, in contrast, hundreds of thousands of women were drafted into industrial employment and women were perceived primarily as workers rather than as mothers.[49]

A comparison of the 1980s and 1990s reveals an opposite trend. Attempts were being made by the 1980s, in theory at least, to ease the double burden experienced by female labour by the introduction of more flexible work schedules for working mothers. Under Gorbachev, however, newspaper reports and journal articles openly discussed the unsatisfactory physical and environmental conditions of work experienced by much of the female labour force. These issues were raised at the Twenty-Seventh Party Congress and the Nineteenth Party Conference. Economic restructuring, introduced under Gorbachev, and the emergence of a competitive labour market have made women vulnerable to redundancy and unemployment. In response to this, government policy has been to re-emphasize the role of women as mothers rather than as workers, primarily via the extension of maternity benefits. Feminist campaigners (women at the Centre for Gender Studies in Moscow, for example) have voiced their scepticism of such initiatives. In reality, attempts to progress the latest draft provisions into law seem to have been shelved whilst the Russian government under Yel'tsin attends to more immediate problems. Improvements in the actual conditions of work for female labour are progressing very slowly and are unlikely to bring immediate benefit to most of the women remaining in employment.

The study of protective labour legislation also brings into question the role and function of the law for working women.[50] The role of the law in the regulation of female labour is a long-debated issue, and has given rise to divisions amongst those who would like to secure improvements in the conditions of female employment via the legal system and those who would wish to prevent the exclusion of women from specified areas of paid employment by patriarchal legal structures, thereby allowing women themselves to choose the occupations and conditions in which they work. This division is difficult to resolve. Any legislation designed to bring about an improvement in women's employment conditions, whether in terms of the physical environment of work or concerning job-related benefits, would be welcomed. But if this legislation were to result in women being excluded from jobs, receiving a lower remuneration for their labour or being unable to compete for employment on equal terms with men, it might be regarded less favourably. Improvements in the conditions of employment should benefit female and male workers alike, and should not result in women being relegated to work involving lower pay, skill or status.

Similarly, legislation which aims to allow women more easily to combine paid employment and raising a family can be seen to ease the burden on working mothers. The adoption of extended maternity provisions and employment regulations in European law has been generally welcomed by women in countries of the European Union. It is believed that the incorporation of the rights of part-time workers within these provisions will benefit 285,000 women in Britain alone.[51] However, if such legislation results in women being removed permanently from work or placed at a disadvantage in the labour market, its long-term impact would have to be reviewed. In both east-central Europe and western Europe in recent years, the trend in maternity provision and child care benefits has been to allow either parent to be involved in the raising of children so that nurturing is no longer regarded as an exclusively female function, although this most often remains the case in practice. The fears of contemporary Russian feminists in this respect are, therefore, well founded.

The solution to current economic problems in Russia is unlikely to leave 'generals without armies' or 'commanders without troops', but these armies and troops will almost certainly be differently constituted in respect to the post-Soviet labour force. Criticism of lax adherence to protective labour legislation for female labour in the Soviet Union under Gorbachev came at a time when the introduction of market reforms posed a threat to the continued employment of many working women. It is unlikely that the emerging market economy in Russia will result in legislation regulating the conditions of work for women being more strictly enforced, but it is probable that women will constitute a much lower proportion of the labour force as they experience difficulty in finding work, are made redundant or are persuaded back to their 'purely womanly mission'.[52]

Notes

1 See, for example, S. I. Kaplun, *Zhenskii trud i okhrana ego v Sovetskoi Rossii* (Moscow, 1921).
2 An outline of the legislation introduced in this period is provided in English by Norton T. Dodge, *Women in the Soviet Economy* (Baltimore: Johns Hopkins University Press, 1966). A more detailed exposition is provided in the Soviet literature. See, for example, M. Bukhov, *Kak okhraniaetsia trud rabotnits po sovetskim zakonam* (Moscow, 1925).
3 This provision is noted by Bukhov, *Kak okhraniaetsia*, p. 10. See also Ts. Pik, 'Novie meropriiatiia po okhrane zhenskogo truda. (K voprosu ob osvobozhdenii zhenshchin ot raboty vo vremia menstruatsii)', *Vestnik truda*, no. 2 (17), 1922, pp. 73–7. For the law in practice, see the NKT SSSR decree 'Ob usloviiakh truda zhenshchin-traktoristok i shoferov na gruzovykh avtomashinakh', 9 May 1931, no. 110; extract cited in *Sbornik zakonodatel'nykh aktov o trude* (Moscow, 1977), pp. 629–30.
4 *Trud, sem'ia i byt sovetskoi zhenshchiny* (Moscow, 1990), pp. 58–107, discusses recent changes in protective labour legislation and maternity provision and notes some of the changes currently under review.
5 See for example 'Zhenshchiny v zerkale statistiki', *Agitator*, no. 3 (1988), p. 33, which notes that in 1986 alone 1.2 million women saw improvements in their conditions of work and 'Kak real'no pomoch' zhenshchine', *Argumenty i fakty*, no. 9 (1989), p. 1, which notes that in the past seven years the conditions of work of 9 million women had been improved.
6 *Izvestiia*, 1 February 1987 and 23 October 1988.
7 M. Lebedeva, 'Kogda muzhchiny govoriat . . . ', *Izvestiia*, 23 October 1988, reporting on a plenary session of the Soviet Women's Committee.
8 'Khorosho budet zhenshchine . . . v XXII veke', *Okhrana truda i sotsial'noe strakhovanie*, no. 10 (1988), p. 19.
9 A. Levina, 'Tysiacha i odna noch'', *Rabotnitsa*, no. 4 (1988), pp. 12–15.
10 'Zhenshchiny v SSSR', *Vestnik statistiki*, no. 1 (1990), p. 42.
11 *Argumenty i fakty*, no. 9 (1989), p. 1.
12 For one example, see *Vestnik statistiki*, no. 1 (1990), p. 42.
13 *Argumenty i fakty*, no. 9 (1989), p. 1. A higher figure of 280,000 is cited in *Okhrana truda i sotsial'noe strakhovanie*, no. 10 (1988), p. 19.
14 Ibid.; *Gudok*, 3 December 1989.
15 See, for example, *Izvestiia*, 23 October 1988; *Agitator*, no. 3 (1988), p. 33.
16 On 6 February 1993, a new decree was issued in Russia establishing a maximum norm of 10 kilogrammes for loads to be carried or transported by women twice in one hour if interspersed with other work or 7 kilogrammes if loads are to carried throughout the shift. See 'O novykh normakh predel'no dopustimykh nagruzok dlia zhenshchin pri pod"eme i peremeshchenii tiazhestei vruchnuiu' ('On New Norms for Maximum Allowable Loads for Women for Lifting and Transporting Weights by Hand'), *Ministerstvo truda rossiiskoi federatsii: Biulleten'*, no. 4, 1993 (no. 105). The decree is reprinted in *Okhrana truda i sotsial'noe strakhovanie*, no. 4 (1993). These instructions replaced a previous maximum norm of 15 kilogrammes established in 1982.
17 *Argumenty i fakty*, no. 9 (1989), p. 1.
18 See for example 'Zhenskie igry po muzhskim pravilam', *Chelovek i trud*, no. 3 (1992), p. 13; *Vestnik statistiki*, no. 1 (1990), p. 42; *Vestnik statistiki*, no. 2 (1991), pp. 53–61,

reporting on Goskomstat research conducted March–April 1990 revealing the high levels of dissatisfaction amongst female workers in relation to their conditions of work.

19 See, for example, *Argumenty i fakty*, no. 9 (1989), p. 1.

20 See, for example, *Argumenty i fakty*, no. 9 (1989), p. 1; *Literaturnaia gazeta*, 23 March 1988, reporting on ill-health amongst female tobacco workers in Tadzhikistan; N. Kungurova, 'Ob usloviiakh truda zhenshchin', *Ekonomist*, no. 5 (1991), p. 109, and 'Mladencheskaia smertnost'', *Vestnik statistiki*, no. 4 (1990), pp. 61–3.

21 'Chislo i sostav sem'ei v SSSR', *Vestnik statistiki*, no. 8 (1991), cites 20 per cent of women reporting illness in connection with their work. For reports of ailments suffered by female workers, see, for example, *Literaturnaia gazeta*, 23 March 1988, p. 13; *Izvestiia*, 23 October 1988; *Vestnik statistiki*, no. 4 (1990), p. 62.

22 'Chto edim, chem dyshim', *Trud*, 24 September 1993.

23 Some studies attempted to place the responsibility for juvenile crime and delinquency on the inadequate attention paid to children by working mothers. This issue is discussed by P. H. Juviler, 'No End of a Problem: Perestroika for the Family?', in Anthony Jones, Walter D. Connor and David E. Powell, *Soviet Social Problems* (Boulder, Colo. and Oxford: Westview Press, 1991), p. 198. *Rabotnitsa*, no. 4 (1988), reporting on a 1986 study of three-shift working by the All-Union Scientific Research Institute of VTsSPS (All-Union Central Council of Trade Unions), notes the higher levels of divorce, alcoholic husbands and illness amongst female night workers.

24 E. Tokareva, 'Zhenshchina na rabote i doma: na plechi Mashi', *Izvestiia*, 15 September 1985, which notes concern over the high levels of labour turnover in branches of the economy dominated by manual labour.

25 Kungurova, 'Ob usloviiakh truda zhenshchin', p. 108.

26 '"Eto dlia menia ne zakon!" ili "shtraf za . . . materinstvo": operatsiia "stupeni masterstva"', *Rabotnitsa*, no. 10 (1988), p. 17.

27 N. Rimashevskaia and A. Milovidov, 'O sovershenstvovanii gosudarstvennoi pomoshchi sem'iam, imeiushchim detei', *Planovoe khoziaistvo*, no. 1 (1988), p. 85.

28 See, for example, G. Evdokimova, 'Kogda na rabote opasno', *Pravda*, 19 June 1989.

29 See, for example, *Argumenty i fakty*, no. 9 (1989), p. 1.

30 V. Mikhailiuk and G. Starovoitova, 'Sokrashchenie zaniatosti zhenshchin ruchnym trudom v stroitel'stve', *Planovoe khoziaistvo*, no. 6 (1987), pp. 110–12. [Editor's note: see also Filtzer, p. 219.]

31 See, for example, *Izvestiia*, 1 February 1987; *Agitator*, no. 3 (1988), p. 34; *Pravda*, 19 June 1989.

32 *Soviet Labour Review*, vol. 7, no. 6 (April 1990), p. 12.

33 *Rabotnitsa*, no. 4 (1988), p. 14.

34 See, for example, *Izvestiia*, 1 February 1987.

35 See, for example, *Izvestiia*, 29 May 1986, reporting on initiatives being implemented in Latvia; E. Vasilets, 'Imeiu pravo znat'' o svoikh l'gotakh', *Rabotnitsa*, no. 1 (1988), p. 20; *Argumenty i fakty*, no. 9 (1989), p. 1; *Vestnik statistiki*, no. 2 (1991), p. 57.

36 *Pravda vostoka*, 8 March 1989.

37 *Izvestiia*, 2 June 1988.

38 *Chelovek i trud*, no. 3 (1992), p. 13.

39 *Vestnik statistiki*, no. 2 (1991), pp. 53–6; no. 8 (1991), pp. 62–3.

40 *Izvestiia*, 23 October 1988.

41 N. Zakharova, A. Posadskaia and N. Rimashevskaia, 'Kak my reshaem zhenskii vopros', *Kommunist*, no. 4 (1989), pp. 56–65.

42 The four major approaches to the 'woman question' were classified as 'paternalistic', 'economic', 'demographic' and 'egalitarian'.

43 'O neotlozhnykh merakh po uluchsheniiu polozheniia zhenshchin, okhrane materinstva i detstva, ukrepleniiu sem'i', *Vedomosti S"ezda narodnykh deputatov SSSR i Verkhovnogo Soveta SSSR*, no. 16 (1990), article 269.

44 These initiatives are outlined in 'Zhenshchiny i deti v SSSR', *Vestnik statistiki*, no. 1 (1987), p. 58.

45 The details of the draft law are outlined by L. Osheverova, 'Esli gosudarstvo ne pozabotitsia o sem'e, to nekomy budet zabotit'sia o gosudarstve', *Izvestiia*, 18 March 1992, p. 2.

46 The content and progress of the bill is discussed in more detail in Hilary Pilkington, 'Can "Russia's Women" Save the Nation?: Survival Politics and Gender Discourse in Post-Soviet Russia', in *Interface: Bradford Studies in Language, Culture and Society* (University of Bradford).

47 See, for example, the report by Gabi Liuka in *Nezavisimaia gazeta*, 5 June 1992, p. 6, citing criticisms of the proposals advanced by Anastasiia Posadskaia.

48 This point is noted by Ol'ga Voronina in T. Suvorova, 'Chto takoe feminizm?', *Moskovskaia pravda*, 13 May 1990, p. 2.

49 These issues are discussed in more detail in Melanie Ilic, 'Soviet Protective Labour Legislation and Female Workers in the 1920s and 1930s', in Marianne Liljeström, Eila Mäntysaari and Arja Rosenholm (eds.), *Gender Restructuring in Russian Studies*, Slavica Tamperensia, vol. 2 (Tampere, Finland: University of Tampere Press, 1993), pp. 127–38.

50 Alastair McAuley discusses these issues in the Soviet context in *Women's Work and Wages in the Soviet Union* (London: Allen and Unwin, 1981), pp. 164–5.

51 *Guardian*, 9 March 1994.

52 Mikhail Gorbachev, *Perestroika: New Thinking for Our Country and the World* (London: Collins, 1987; New York: Harper and Row, 1987), p. 116.

16

The return of the family
farm: a future for women?

SUE BRIDGER

In current attempts to re-establish private family farming, Russia has come full circle since the tumultuous events of 1929 when forced collectivization destroyed the ties between the family unit and the land. The decision to promote the peasant family once more to a central position in farming has not, however, been simply a product of Russia's post-communist shift toward a market economy. Though private ownership was not then on the agenda, by 1988 rural families willing to take on personal responsibility for their own land and livestock were already being presented as a model for emulation in the revitalization of agriculture. That this move was fundamentally at odds with the political and economic realities of the USSR's system of state and collective farming was borne out by the sharp conflicts which were to arise as families responded to the Communist Party's calls to lease land. With the breakdown of the USSR, these conflicts have by no means disappeared, whilst the problems involved in setting up a family business on the land have been compounded by Russia's economic crisis.[1] As a result, private family farms are still little more than a drop in the ocean of Russian agriculture and certainly represent a risk which most rural families feel unable to take. Across the country as a whole, the majority of the first wave of family farms were set up by people who had moved from the cities for the purpose: by the time of the USSR's demise at the end of 1991, fewer than 10 per cent of the new farmers in some regions were local rural people.[2]

Given the history of the Russian countryside since 1917, rural mistrust of new initiatives emanating from central government is scarcely surprising. Yet the reasons for rural dwellers' relative lack of involvement in private farming are more complex than this. Whilst economic considerations clearly have a major role to play, there are other issues which are still more fundamental. From the early days of promotion of family farming there had been a tacit acknowledgement that counting on rural families to set up sufficient private farms to feed the nation would be an attempt to achieve the impossible. The demographic situation that has developed across much of Russia over the last quarter-century is unfavourable in the extreme for such a move. Migration into the cities has been draining away the life-blood of the villages throughout this period, despite attempts to reverse the trend. The consequences in a broad belt of regions across the Russian heartland have been severe, leaving farming increasingly reliant on an ageing workforce of people who have already given their best years to the land. Government-sponsored resettlement schemes, both for the USSR and, later, for independent Russia, implicitly recognized that a significant influx of younger, able-bodied families would be needed to provide the new generation of private farmers.[3]

What have manifestly not been considered, however, are the implications for any family of setting up a business together. Where apparently suitable rural families do exist – and they are not yet entirely an endangered species – the assumption appears to be that with support and reasonable conditions anyone can make a success of running a family business. This is not, of course, merely the result of Russia's new-found fascination with the novelties of the market or a lack of experience of its potential pitfalls. It might perhaps be pointed out that Russia is by no means the only society in which the headlong development of small businesses has been presented as the cure for all economic ills. In such a climate, a failure to consider the less palatable realities for the families involved is probably inevitable. Nevertheless, the Russian case offers a particularly curious juxtaposition of events. For just as the massive promotion of the concept of family farming began in the late 1980s, the media was at the same time embarking on an unprecedentedly frank analysis of the pressures and difficulties besetting the rural family. The focus of this chapter is, therefore, the contradiction which lies at the very heart of the promotion of family farming; a contradiction which commentators in Russia have been slow to address, yet which appears particularly glaring when reviewing the media's presentation of rural life from perestroika to the present.

Women in the rural family: old problems, new tensions

As the press began to break new ground following Gorbachev's accession to power, a far more honest approach began to characterize discussions of the rural family. Idealized images of industrious family 'dynasties' began to be replaced by explorations of previously taboo subjects, most notably in the sphere of sexual relationships, and by brutally frank women's letters expressing anxiety at the realities of rural family life. Perhaps inevitably, much of the initial discussion revolved around the causes of family breakdown. The roots of conflict, for many of the women who wrote in to national magazines, were to be found in male irresponsibility and alcohol abuse. In the light of the findings of rural sociologists over the previous two decades, this scarcely came as a revelation. Surveys had habitually reported that alcoholism was most frequently cited by rural women as the source of marital conflict and breakdown. Amongst young people surveyed across a range of Russian regions in the early 1980s, the overwhelming majority of respondents worried about heavy drinking and irresponsible attitudes toward the family in their local communities were women.[4] What was new about the letters which appeared from the mid-1980s was both the level of exasperation with male behaviour which women were expressing, and their criticism of the well-established media habit of blaming women, and particularly women's emancipation, as the source of family conflict.

A flow of readers' letters illustrating both these points was triggered by an article which appeared in *Sel'skaia nov'* in 1987. The article, entitled 'Medea from Pershinka', told the story of Ol'ga, married to the irresponsible and highly egotistical Aleksandr, who ultimately left her with three young children and promptly remarried. In a state of despair, Ol'ga administered an overdose of sleeping pills to each of her children, then, full of remorse, rushed them to hospital before any permanent damage was done. The letters which the magazine subsequently received came overwhelmingly from women, nearly all of whom had experience of a drunken husband and did not appreciate what they interpreted as the attempt of the article's author to condone Aleksandr's behaviour:

> I'm not justifying what Ol'ga did, but you ought to think about what it's like in the village. You can't get out in a crowd to forget about your troubles and relax – it's not like the city. It's much harder to cope with misfortune in the village because everybody's watching you and it's no good expecting help from anywhere. So you just stew in your own juice, chewing over your bitterness and hurt. But then your article blames Ol'ga, not Sasha. It's as if he can't help it, he's just like other men. Don't you think that lets him off too easily? Don't you think it's too easy for men to do exactly what they like? I think this indulgence of men just spoils them.

> Why doesn't the law deal with people like Aleksandr? The only punishment they get is paying maintenance and they even get round that . . . It doesn't matter if they get married ten times and father lots of children because the mothers will bring them up on their own; so that's all right – off you go and enjoy yourself some more, daddy . . . And then the papers tell us that women have only themselves to blame for running after equality – now we've got what we asked for. Equality's not to blame – and, anyway, what equality are we talking about?! It's just that lots of men have completely let themselves go and got used to putting everything on women.[5]

The style of press comment on personal relationships which these women were complaining about was not simply the province of a few chauvinist writers, but had become a thread running through the pro-natalist campaigns from the mid-1970s onwards. In its concern to boost the birth rate, Soviet propaganda sought to encourage women to see themselves first and foremost as mothers. Motherhood, promoted as the highest expression of femininity, was defined not merely as the care of children but also as the physical and emotional support of men. In the wealth of articles which appeared through the early 1980s in particular, women's behaviour was continually portrayed as holding the key to men's sobriety, industry and responsibility toward their children. Women were reproached when their men behaved badly and, at the same time, constantly urged to display patience, understanding and inexhaustible love toward the miscreant. Only this, women were warned, would save the family and ultimately show their husband the error of his ways.[6]

Far from disappearing with the advent of an ostensibly more enlightened administration, the media emphasis on woman as wife and mother intensified as the decade progressed. Legislation introduced from the mid-1980s extended maternity leave and increased provision for part-time work and even for the introduction of homeworking. Both the legislation itself and the considerable amount of discussion on women's roles which accompanied it underscored the notion that a woman's primary responsibility lay not in the workplace but in the home, uniting the family, caring for husband and children. In view of these developments, the chauvinism which had been so frequently expressed in the letters' pages and supposedly 'expert' comment of the national press during the 'period of stagnation' continued to be allowed free rein under perestroika. Newspapers were still to be found printing letters from men outraged that women were failing to look after them adequately. Even in women's magazines, conservative male writers were still being invited to comment disapprovingly on letters from women complaining about domestic inequality.[7] Throughout the period, the message that women bore ultimate responsibility not merely for marital stability and the good behaviour of children, but also for the entire gamut of male activity continued to be remorselessly rammed home in the press and on television.

Yet far from shirking their responsibilities in their pursuit of emancipation, women had consistently been found to be the victims of gross domestic inequality. Throughout the previous two decades, Soviet sociologists had been documenting this phenomenon within both urban and rural families and observing the stress this could place on marital relationships. Studies of the rural family carried out during the 1980s showed little change. The majority of rural newlyweds, though considerably fewer than city couples, declared that they would do housework and budgeting together. In practice, a 1988 study found half the young married women in their survey preparing food single-handedly, whilst around 40 per cent received no help at all with either cleaning or washing.[8]

The attitudes which underpinned these findings were inevitably formed well before marriage. When rural schoolchildren in Orel oblast were asked their views on what made a happy marriage, girls considered 'helping each other', 'home comfort' and 'having the same outlook' to be equally important. Boys ranked 'home comfort' first and placed 'having the same outlook' a distant third. These findings were reinforced by the results of a readership survey on the family run by *Krest'ianka* magazine in 1988. Men who responded to the survey, nearly four-fifths of them under 35, placed 'being a good housewife' top of their list of qualities required in the ideal wife. Interestingly, in view of what one might have expected given rural traditions, older men, and particularly pensioners, were considerably more likely than the young to advocate sharing domestic responsibilities. This response, perhaps more than any other, was indicative of the success the pronatalist campaign had had in polarizing the attitudes of young men and women toward gender roles. Indeed, women writing to the press in recent years commenting on the state of the rural family have sometimes remarked on what they see as a significant change in male attitudes:

Something terrible seems to be happening to our men. They are losing their way. The qualities which for centuries have made the man the family breadwinner are gradually disappearing. My grandfather would turn in his grave if he could see how women have to drag heavy loads and do the digging while their husbands just stand there having a smoke.[9]

Given the structure of employment in the countryside, younger rural women are frequently better educated than their husbands.[10] This may not only aggravate the differing expectations men and women have of roles within marriage, but also provide further grounds for conflict in the face of the realities of family life. Where women come under pressure to fulfil their husbands' expectations that they will carry the brunt of domestic responsibilities, or, indeed, where they believe that this is what they should be doing, sociologists have observed that this frequently gives rise to conflict. Carrying out a full range of domestic tasks almost single-handedly in current rural conditions leaves women with virtually no time to relax. By contrast, their husbands may find themselves with a considerable amount of time on their hands which, unhappily, is often filled with drinking. Commenting on this all too common rural scene well before the arrival of glasnost, one sociologist observed that women's indulgence could not be expected to last for ever: 'many wives are simply not prepared to put up with this and will do anything, including ultimately breaking up the family, to normalize their position'.[11]

Continuing coverage in the post-Soviet press of the problems of the rural family make it plain that there are plenty of rural women who have simply had enough of what they see as the gross selfishness of men within marriage. Where magazines have continued to print articles critical of women considering divorcing egotistical husbands, their authors have received short shrift from women readers, many of them incensed enough to write in to the press for the first time in their lives:

Why is it only ever the woman who is supposed to control her irritation? You can live with a drunkard or a layabout and you're supposed to put up with it all! The woman is Duty while the man is Right and Privilege in the family. Do you think that's reasonable? Women have their dignity too, they're not robots at men's beck and call. Times have changed.

Others, writing in with heart-rending personal stories or simply recounting their own utter exhaustion at being expected to shoulder the entire domestic burden alone, urge the young women seeking advice through the columns of the press not to repeat their mistake of seeing divorce as something to be ashamed of: 'My dear, jack it in and leave him, or else you'll just torture yourself like I have done.'[12]

Journalists commenting in the late 1980s on rural women's letters condemning male drunkenness and lack of responsibility, not surprisingly did not address themselves to the role the media had played in fostering indulgence toward men within the family. Instead, a lack of male role models was deemed to be at the root of the problem, with many of today's married couples growing up in families where fathers and grandfathers had been killed in the war or in Stalin's purges:

> Strange as it may seem, the image of the mother single-handedly bearing the whole weight of family responsibilities may have had a negative influence on the formation of young couples' opinions about roles within the family. The husband demands that his wife should work hard without expecting any of life's pleasures, just as his mother did (or rather was forced to do!). But women today are not in the least inclined to agree to this.[13]

Whilst not wishing to minimize the significance of the traumas endured by the Soviet people, the argument that the postwar demographic imbalance has created such attitudes in young men born as late as the 1960s and 1970s seems rather difficult to sustain. For this generation, the problem seems more likely to be not an absence of male role models, but an absence of suitable ones. As sociological studies from the 1960s onwards testify, the overburdening of women with domestic work and the prevalence of male drunkenness has been around for some time in ostensibly two-parent families. It was on this inauspicious basis that propaganda promoting women's domestic roles and tacitly approving the indulgence of men was fed into the mass media and directly into schools.[14]

If journalists remained unprepared or unable to criticize the effects of past and present policies on the family, the sweeping changes of the late 1980s did at least bring about an attempt to consider how personal behaviour might reflect the state of society at large. In commenting, for example, on rural women's letters asking how men could be unmoved by the effect of their self-indulgence and heavy drinking on their wives and children, the linking of individual irresponsibility with the absence of genuine civic participation in the USSR marked a considerable departure for the press:

> A great deal has been said recently about the fact that, due to various negative factors, individuals have ceased to feel themselves to be masters of the land, of their factory or of the state, and that this has become one of the major brakes on our development. The impact of these same factors has also been to weaken the sense of being master of one's own fate, of one's own family and, ultimately, to weaken the sense of personal responsibility . . . People who come up against contempt for the 'human factor' in their work and in their lives learn to be contemptuous of those around them, and even of themselves, losing the ability to express the most basic emotions such as kindness and sympathy, even for their own children, their partners or their parents.[15]

Whilst this line of reasoning failed to explain how women who were subject to the same 'negative factors' managed to retain their sense of responsibility toward the family, it was at least refreshing to see the Soviet press moving, if only a little, from blaming women to blaming the system. Unfortunately, despite the fact that published letters from the wives of drunken men mentioned beatings, threats and knife attacks, the serious discussion of domestic violence remained a taboo not easily to be broken by the advent of a new policy of openness. With the sponsors of perestroika still firmly wedded to the notion of 'strengthening the family' by well-established means, there was to be no genuine analysis of the nature of male power, or of its abuse, within either the urban or the rural family in the USSR.

If the issue of domestic violence remained clothed in silence, there were other potent taboos to be broken by the advent of reform. The most striking example in the sphere of personal relationships was the discussion of sex which began to appear in the Soviet press during the late 1980s. With the publication of the first articles in youth magazines to broach the subject of sex, the massive postbag received from readers spoke volumes about the levels of misery, anxiety and sheer ignorance which the long-unbroken silence had caused. As a result, an entire wave of articles followed offering both basic information and a discussion of the psychological aspects of sexual relationships.

Throughout the media coverage of sex, a recognition that a lack of knowledge and understanding of sexuality lay at the root of a great deal of inter-personal conflict was particularly prominent. Whilst urban readers could more easily be advised to seek help from a doctor or therapist, the logistical problems experienced by rural people in seeking any form of medical assistance doubtless made advice directly available on the printed page more valuable. Perhaps for this reason the rural press largely concentrated its efforts on psycho-sexual problems and methods of resolving conflict. Likewise, articles appearing in the rural press also offered practical advice on the use of massage and herbal remedies for sexual and gynaeco-logical problems.[16]

Specialists invited to comment on letters from rural readers offered examples from the postbag of families ultimately breaking up through conflicts over sex. Describing characteristic examples of male insensitivity and female ignorance or long-suffering, Lev Gertsik, a specialist in psycho-sexual disorders, laid the blame on sexual illiteracy, an inability to communicate, simplistic notions of male rights and female duties and 'an undemocratic consciousness'. In this unexpected use of political terminology, the author had in mind both a sense of self-respect and of respect for others: 'Democracy in society is impossible unless individuals take account of the rights of others as well as their own. A democratic consciousness is essential in relations between the sexes; harmony is conditional upon it.'[17]

In a subsequent article, Dr Gertsik noted that a third of the readers who had written to him asking for help feared that their marriage would break up if their problems were not resolved. Despite this, virtually all the letters, most of them from rural women, displayed the 'staggering conviction that it was useless even to dream about attaining mutual sexual satisfaction'. Once again, he blamed the 'centuries-old tradition' of emphasizing duties and obligations in family life at the expense of pleasure and enjoyment, together with the prevailing hypocrisy and taboos surrounding the subject of sex. The silence of society, in Gertsik's view, had produced silence within the family, an utter inability even to begin a rational conversation about sexual needs and feelings which provided fertile ground for quarrels and mutual recriminations.[18] By the end of the decade, magazines were publishing readers' letters which made it plain that not only sexual disharmony but also sexual abuse of daughters and step-daughters was by no means unknown in the rural family.

In the absence of reliable data, the prevalence of domestic violence and child abuse in the rural family remains a matter for speculation. What is well documented, however, are the close links between family breakdown and alcohol abuse. In such circumstances it appears not unreasonable to regard the revelations of the press in the late 1980s less as media sensationalism than as the tip of a still-unexplored iceberg. It would, moreover, be remarkable for families in any society to emerge unscathed from the kinds of pressures inherent in the chaotic economic and social conditions of the disintegrating Soviet state. Where obtaining the barest essentials of a family's existence had become a matter of constant struggle, there was little hope of finding peace and comfort in family life, as women's ever more despairing letters showed:

> Living like this, the endless worry and anxiety, the unmanageable workload all send you into a kind of stupor. We don't even have the right to be ill because there's no-one to deputize on the livestock unit. We can't go on strike either because only the innocent animals would suffer. I just don't have any strength left. It's especially unbearable when my four-year-old son asks for just one sweetie every day and I can't give him one. It makes you want to bash your head against the wall! I've become obsessed with the idea of just ending it all – for me, at any rate.[19]

As material conditions become more difficult, living with a husband who feels no obligation to participate in family life inevitably becomes a greater source of resentment. Observing that divorced women in the countryside somehow manage to keep body and soul together, other women may feel that they would lose little materially and gain a great deal psychologically from ridding themselves of a husband who contributes virtually nothing. Commenting in 1992 on an upsurge in divorce in her rural district of Smolensk oblast, a local government official remarked that domestic problems and money worries were increasingly to blame:

> Women have to shoulder the entire burden of domestic life – the shortages, the perpetual attempts to juggle a meagre budget, the worries about finding clothes and shoes for everyone and making meals out of scraps. And the husband often isn't a helper but a burden. The family has ceased to be a support and a refuge in hard times. So when a woman comes to the end of her tether you can scarcely accuse her of egotism and a lack of forbearance and patience. Separation has become the spirit of the age.[20]

When it has become so commonplace for women to express anger and dismay at the results of the polarization of gender roles within the rural family, it is difficult to feel any measure of optimism at prospects for women with the promotion of family farming. Indeed, the issues women raise and the problems they face suggest that this is indeed a major yet unexplored reason for the well-documented rural reluctance to take up private farming. When men are not entrusted with money, as surveys suggest, or their wives even pick up their wages from work to prevent them drinking their income away, the notion of setting up a family business appears laughable.[21]

Whilst it may be reasonable to suppose that the first farming families were amongst the most harmonious in the country, they were unlikely to emerge unscathed from the crisis unfolding in Russia, or to be impervious to the stress which starting up a small business in any society inevitably entails. The promotion of family farming as a mass phenomenon automatically implies the participation of families who will not be so well-adjusted as the model households so celebrated in the press. Yet given the propensity of the media to gloss over or entirely ignore the realities of business for the family, the silence has been deafening on women's attitudes to the development of private farms. In considering, therefore, the issues which may face private farmers in the future, it may be useful to look a little more closely at what was documented of the experience of families involved in leasing in the period just before the USSR's demise.

The effects of farming as a family

From the very beginning of the promotion of family leasing contracts, it was apparent that this type of farming imposed considerable obligations on all members of the families involved. In order to cope with the workload, families would be virtually obliged to involve their children in the work or to obtain assistance from the extended family: adult children or brothers and sisters together with their spouses and families would join in the endeavour to make the family farm viable. Inevitably, a degree of moral pressure would be brought to bear to ensure continuing commitment. It is, after all, no small matter for nuclear families suddenly to join together and begin living and working as an extended family in the traditional peasant manner, especially if the task in hand is often primitive and highly labour-intensive. Reports on leaseholders would sometimes refer to the fact that families which had joined together with great enthusiasm had subsequently split up, but would dwell on the successful resolution of the resulting problems, rather than the causes or the impact of the break.[22] Within the nuclear family itself, the demands of the farm imposed a moral obligation on spouses which, if it was discussed at all, was invariably presented in a similarly positive light – 'a strong farm means a strong family':

> Rina thinks that working on your own farm, on your own land, strengthens the
> family, 'Families are fragile in the city, they'll split up over the least little thing. But
> here on the land, the work itself and the business helps to make a marriage strong.
> Neither I nor my husband could manage the farm without the other.'[23]

Rina Sal´dre, the Estonian author of this comment, was the female half of a partnership which became celebrated in the Soviet press at the height of the leasing campaign as the shape of things to come. A qualified vet, she took on a livestock unit together with her former Party worker and economist husband, Mart. If she, by her own admission and desire, was tied to the farm and, moreover, working an eighteen-hour day in summer, the obligations imposed on her two adolescent daughters were not a great deal less: from a 6 a.m. start both were expected to do a full day at school, complete their homework and help with milking and cleaning in the dairy unit, finishing the working day at around 9 p.m.

Rina's view of the effects of all this on her daughters, as it was reproduced for public consumption, was that they were going through such 'universities of labour' as no formal system of education could ever provide.[24]

The implication in this style of reporting was that genuine peasant work, as manifest in the new family farms, was of a qualitatively different order to any other, capable of imbuing children with moral values which would make them the backbone of any future society. Needless to say, the opinions of the children them-selves were never canvassed, yet it was clear that, given women's prevailing attitudes to manual farmwork, not all rural mothers were impressed by the notion of 'universities of labour':

> Your article touched on the question of family leaseholding. It was as if you were saying that any family could take on a contract if they had more than one child. Well, I've got three under school age, so you think I should take them out into the fields and make them work? I don't seem to recall hearing anything about city people teaching their children this kind of 'love of hard work'. But it's obviously another story when it's country people![25]

By the same token, specialists commenting on the impact of family farming on the rural family were liable to espouse opposing views. Some sociologists felt that the benefits far outweighed any possible problems and appeared primarily to be echoing the archetypal city view of rural life: 'Fresh air, fresh food, space, closeness to nature, work alongside their parents and mutual help are all factors which are extremely beneficial in a child's upbringing.'[26] Others feared that the sheer demands of making small-scale peasant farming viable in prevailing conditions could not help but lead to the exploitation of child labour. As an experienced family lawyer commented:

> Manual labour is being reinforced. Is this really the path we want to follow as we approach the twenty-first century? Is this move toward family contracts being backed up by concern for proper leisure or for cultural provision for country people? Are we seeing an improvement in schools or in health or in the service sector? Or is the only concern the same as it's always been – how to squeeze the maximum amount of agricultural production out of the rural family? All this will produce in the end will be new negative phenomena.[27]

Certainly, as private farming has developed in Russia, it has become apparent that new farming families are continuing to rely heavily on the contribution of their children. At the Second Independent Women's Forum held in Dubna in November 1992, for example, one of the principal demands of the women from family farms was that their children be excused from school attendance during sowing and harvesting. They clearly saw no potential problems or tensions in this position, simply stating, 'they can't go to school then' as their rationale. The Russian government, moreover, effectively gave its approval to this state of affairs with a proposal in 1993 to recognize fourteen-year-olds as full members of family farms.[28]

If the Soviet media of the late 1980s presented the decision to start a family business as a straightforward matter for the adults involved, the approach to the question of the children's future was no less simplistic. For the most part it was simply assumed that children who engaged in farmwork from an early age would automatically become committed to it for the rest of their working lives. As Mart Sal'dre commented, 'A master of the land is someone who knows that the land will be given to his children and that they will work on it if their father has taught them a love of work and of the land.'[29] In a similar vein, another of leasing's pioneers, Anatolii Churin, described local attitudes toward his adolescent son:

> Our neighbours feel sorry for him. 'You ask too much of Shurik', they say, 'all we ever hear is "Shurik, come here quick, Shurik, bring that!"' But why should he grow up to be lazy? I understand now why peasant families in the old days used to hope for a son so much. They are a real help to their father! All my hopes are on my son.[30]

Interestingly, even in these early years of family farming and in the context of largely uncritical media reporting, there already appeared to be a predictable difference of perspective between the men and the women. Whilst the men were quoted extolling the virtues of inheritance, the women were either silent on the subject or expressed a different opinion. As ever, women's views of rural life were more inclined to the sober analysis of its realities. In both the Churin family and that of their partners on the farm, for example, the women both expressed the dissenting view, wanting something different for their daughters. On the new peasant farms, even in the best of families, the combination of heavy manual labour and chronic lack of rural services were already making themselves felt and posing problems for women that would not be easily overcome in the future.

Market reform, women's response

In the process of rapid economic change which characterized Russia's first two years as an independent state, agriculture's downward spiral has been particularly marked. Inflation and financial constraints have led to a significant decline in farm output, major cutbacks in livestock herds and job losses. Over 70 per cent of the new rural unemployed are women, the majority under thirty with young children. As in industry, many of those still in work have been subjected to protracted periods without wages. The significant difference, however, is that agricultural wages, never as high as those in industry, have now slumped substantially to around half the far from generous industrial level.[31]

In the process of wholesale farm privatization, farm workers have opted primarily for restructuring involving the least degree of change to the former state and collective farms and continue to display little enthusiasm for family farming. Reforms may continue to remove controls on private land ownership, but the practical difficulties private farmers face still deter the majority. As a result, small independent farms are increasingly the preserve of former state and collective farm managers and specialists together with former city dwellers. Nevertheless, even with the contacts and experience such farmers can presumably command, private farms as a whole continue to suffer from severe under-mechanization and insufficient utilities. By the end of the 1993 season there were some 270,000 private farms in Russia occupying approximately five per cent of agricultural land. Around 14,000 private farms had gone out of business in 1993. The Russian government was no longer looking to this type of farm for the future of food production, as agriculture minister, Viktor Khlystun, acknowledged on launching the 1994–5 agrarian reform programme, 'to think that private farmers would become dominant in farming is wrong'.[32]

Without a radical change in rural conditions, it is difficult to see how family farming can offer women anything more than the arduous life which the younger rural generation has for more than two decades been so comprehensively rejecting. Indeed, as long as it remains so overwhelmingly reliant on manual labour, what it demands is likely to be significantly worse. As matters stand, it is not easy to envisage how anything but a sense of personal obligation would induce the daughters of Russia's new farming families to remain on the land which should be theirs and create the peasant families of the future. For the majority of women in the countryside, setting up an independent family farm simply does not present itself as an option. Noting that a vast amount of newsprint had been expended debating 'why the peasant won't take on the land', one journalist writing in late 1992 observed that this was the wrong question. In villages across the country, he remarked, it was the women who ran the home, planned the family finances and had the last word in any serious decision. The question that should be asked, therefore, was more precise – why won't peasant women take on the land?:

> And women have a short answer to this: 'I haven't got the strength.' Because women really do spend an enormous amount of energy keeping the house in order, looking after the plot and feeding and clothing the children. It's the woman who repairs and decorates the house, it's her savings that pay for the television, the fridge and the furniture, she's the one who makes sure there's a piglet grunting and hens clucking in the shed, that potatoes are stored in the cellar, there are jars of cucumbers, tomatoes and preserves and that the children are fed and clothed. But the husband . . . ! I don't know how many bitter stories and complaints I've had to listen to! He doesn't care about the house, he's always in a temper, he comes home drunk, he treats the place like a hotel. How is a woman supposed to develop a farm, put up buildings and work dozens of hectares of land when her small plot takes up the last ounce of her strength?[33]

If the 'sickness' in the rural family, as this writer described it, ever more visible with the ending of press censorship, had been acting as a substantial brake on the development of private farming at this stage, there could be little hope of improvement as the economic crisis deepened. By the summer of 1993, inadequate or disappearing farm wages were provoking a major retreat into subsistence farming as more intensive cultivation and increased livestock on their plots had become increasingly crucial in keeping rural families afloat. In this burgeoning of activity on the former private plots, women inevitably had a major role to play, a role requiring more strength and more commitment from the already exhausted and disenchanted. In circumstances such as these, women who have rejected formal routes to independent small businesses on the land are having 'family farming' in its most basic form thrust upon them. Whether, in the current state of play in rural families, this will genuinely represent a family effort appears, however, to be a matter for debate. More likely, as so often during the decades of communist rule, rural women in the new Russia will be presented with little choice but to sacrifice themselves for their family's survival.

Notes

1 Following price liberalization the costs of setting up a new farm have spiralled, whilst obtaining adequate long-term credit remains highly problematic.
2 *Krest'ianskaia Rossiia*, 14 September 1991, p. 3.
3 In 1992, the Russian government set up a new state agency for resettlement with the aim of attracting former rural inhabitants, demobilized army officers and refugees from former Soviet republics to set up private farms. The agency had an initial target of 10,000 families per year and was offering substantial index-linked financial incentives.
4 V. I. Staroverov, *Sotsial'nyi oblik sel'skoi molodezhi* (Moscow, 1985), pp. 200–1; Susan Bridger, *Women in the Soviet Countryside* (Cambridge: Cambridge University Press, 1987), pp. 142–7.
5 Galina Ronina, 'Chernoe i beloe', *Sel'skaia nov'*, no. 1 (1988), p. 28.
6 See Bridger, *Women in the Soviet Countryside*, pp. 133–8.
7 See, for example, *Pravda*, 17 October 1987 and 19 February 1988; *Krest'ianka*, no. 2 (1987), pp. 30–2.
8 Staroverov, *Sotsial'nyi oblik*, p. 167; M. G. Pankratova, *Sel'skaia zhenshchina v SSSR* (Moscow, 1990), p. 99.
9 *Sel'skaia nov'*, no. 1 (1992), p. 39. The school survey is in Staroverov, *Sotsial'nyi oblik*, p. 110.
10 The rejection of manual farmwork by young rural women has produced an increasingly segregated female workforce in the countryside. Whilst middle-aged to elderly women labourers and livestock workers form the overwhelming majority, the young predominate amongst the significant minority of both agricultural and non-agricultural specialists. Young men, meanwhile, have the option of skilled manual work operating agricultural machinery, an avenue effectively closed to women. See Bridger, *Women in the Soviet Countryside*, p. 159.
11 A. A. Petrakov, *Sel'skaia sem'ia i deti* (Izhevsk, 1983).
12 Maiia Pankratova, 'Plokh on – ia khorosha', *Sel'skaia nov'*, no. 6 (1991), pp. 38–40; Maiia Pankratova, 'Ekh, zhizn' nasha . . .', *Sel'skaia nov'*, no. 1 (1992), p. 38.
13 Ronina, 'Chernoe i beloe', p. 29.
14 The pro-natalist campaign of the late 1970s and early 1980s relied heavily on images of femininity and domesticity to persuade women to bear more children. The course on 'The Ethics and Psychology of Family Life' which was subsequently introduced into Soviet schools stemmed from the discussions and debates of this period.
15 Ronina, 'Chernoe i beloe', p. 30.
16 See, for example, *Krest'ianka*, no. 7 (1988), supplement, or the extremely detailed series of herbal remedies printed in *Sel'skaia molodezh'* in 1991.
17 L. Gertsik, 'Nevidimye miru slezy', *Sel'skaia nov'*, no. 2 (1989), pp. 47–8.

18 L. Gertsik, 'Gde ty, zolotoi kliuchik?', *Sel'skaia nov'*, no. 10 (1989), pp. 37–8.
19 *Sel'skaia nov'*, no. 9 (1989), p. 22.
20 Liubov' Mironikhina, 'Semeinyi koshelek', *Sel'skaia molodezh'*, no. 6 (1992), p. 22.
21 Pankratova, 'Plokh on – ia khorosha', p. 38; Mironikhina, 'Semeinyi koshelek', p. 21.
22 V. Somov, 'Nelegkaia sud'ba arendy', *Sel'skaia nov'*, no. 8 (1989), p. 7; *Sel'skii chas*, Soviet Television, Channel 1, 7 August 1988.
23 I. Vladimirovna, 'Rina i Mart – sovetskie fermery', *Krest'ianka*, no. 1 (1989), p. 9.
24 Ibid.; also Iu. Govorukhin, 'Stepen' svobody', *Sel'skaia nov'*, no. 2 (1989), p. 15.
25 *Sel'skaia nov'*, no. 9 (1989), p. 22.
26 G. Ronina, 'Bedy nazvany. Chto dal'she?', *Sel'skaia nov'*, no. 11 (1988), pp. 18, 20.
27 Ronina, 'Bedy nazvany', p. 18. A similar view was expressed to me by the eminent rural sociologist, Ivan Slepenkov, in a personal interview in Moscow in May 1988.
28 *Moskovskaia pravda*, 13 August 1993, p. 1.
29 Vladimirovna, 'Rina i Mart', p. 9.
30 N. Korina, 'Vybiraem, chto nam po dushe', *Krest'ianka,* no. 6 (1989), p. 14.
31 Vladimir Terekhov, 'Rossiiskie selianki odni nivu ne podnimut', *Nezavisimaia gazeta*, 12 August 1993, pp. 1–2.
32 *Business World Weekly*, no. 28 (1993), p. 12, and no. 12 (1994), p. 2; *Segodnia*, 10 February 1993, p. 3; *Moscow Times*, 1 April 1994, p. 7.
33 Viktor Konov, 'Reshaet-to khoziaika . . .', *Sel'skaia nov'*, nos. 11–12 (1992), pp. 8–9.

17

The post-Soviet woman in the move to the market: a return to domesticity and dependence?

LYNNE ATTWOOD

Despite their clashes over political and economic policy, there is one thing on which the current leaders of Russia seem to agree: the market has a male face. It is the antithesis of socialism, of the 'nanny state' (to borrow Margaret Thatcher's clearly female image of state welfare provision), whose pampering over-protectiveness is now said to have stifled personal initiative and entrepreneurship. In contrast, the market emphasizes traditionally masculine qualities – aggression and rationality, independence, competition, the willingness to take risks. In this chapter I will be arguing that the move toward a market economy has been accompanied by a celebration of masculinity, both literally and metaphorically, and the denigration of the strong and capable woman worker glorified in the first decades of Soviet history. Attempts to return women to a more domestic mode of life, and the proliferation of images of violence against women which abound on cinema screens and the press, can be seen as two sides of the same coin: this could be termed the aggressive re-masculinization of post-Soviet Russia.

Even before the advent of Gorbachev's reforms and the subsequent rejection of socialism, concern was being expressed that however well-intentioned it had been, socialism had brought about a number of negative consequences in the sphere of gender relations. From the middle of the 1970s, Soviet writers were arguing that women's high level of involvement in the workforce had led to a distortion both of female and male personality. Women had been forced to develop personality traits more appropriate to the workplace than the home, and while their independence and self-confidence had increased, their propensity to nurture and concede had contracted. This had produced a range of alarming social and demographic problems. Children were abandoned to the impersonality of state crèches and kindergartens, and neglected children ultimately turned into teenage delinquents. Men were robbed of the traditional masculine role of breadwinner, and became weak, apathetic and alcoholic. The divorce rate was up and the birth rate down. A mass of concerned articles appeared in the popular press with titles like 'Where are the Real Man and Woman?' and 'The Bitter Fruits of Emancipation'.[1]

At that time the problem was seemingly intractable. Women constituted 51 per cent of the workforce; their participation was essential, and their mass withdrawal inconceivable. All that could be done was to encourage a shift in the balance in their lives. Accordingly, a propaganda campaign was launched to persuade women to place the family in the centre of their lives and relegate work to second place. The educational reforms of 1984 included the introduction of a school course called 'The Ethics and Psychology of Family Life', which contained a large element of gender socialization and was clearly aimed at ensuring that the next generation of adults adopted more traditional gender roles. There was also a series of measures aimed at enabling women to work part-time or from home, though lack of co-operation on the part of enterprise managers rendered these largely unsuccessful.

The move to a market economy has radically altered the situation. The labour shortage of the past has been replaced by the prospect of widespread unemployment, and what Jan Adam has described as a tacit 'social contract' between rulers and ruled has come to an end.[2] Before, the bulk of the population refrained from openly challenging the system, and did without certain rights and freedoms in exchange for a package of social welfare provisions, including a job, a relatively egalitarian distribution of income, health care and stable and affordable prices for basic requirements. This egalitarianism is now held responsible for the appalling state of the economy. It is said to have stifled personal ambition, bred resentment against those who tried to rise above the mass and assured the lazy that however little they worked, they would still be as well off as their neighbours.[3] The new system is based on competition and profit, both on a corporate and an individual level. Those who work hard will, at least in theory, earn enough to be able to buy back the services they once received as a matter of course. Those who do not will fall by the wayside.

Women, especially those with young children, are clearly at a severe disadvantage in the new Russia. In a society based on competition, their additional domestic and maternal responsibilities make them seem less reliable and efficient, and so prime candidates for redundancy. Already under Gorbachev, women began to bear the brunt of the negative consequence of economic reform. The introduction of *khozraschet*, or self-accounting, meant that unsuccessful enterprises could no longer rely on government bail-outs but had to ensure their own profitability, and the first employees to lose their jobs were inevitably those deemed the least effective members of the workforce; for the most part, these were women.[4] When labour exchanges opened on 1 July 1991 and began to register the numbers of newly unemployed, women turned out to constitute between 70 and 80 per cent of the total.[5] Accordingly, the image of women and men as partners in the building of socialism began to be replaced by that of the traditional functionalist family in which men and women have different but supposedly complementary roles: a single male breadwinner battles with the world of work, and comes home to the loving care of a wife who devotes herself to home and children. The perceived economic needs of the new Russia thus coincide neatly with the desire first expressed in the 1970s, to return to more traditional gender roles. While the attempt to resurrect the 'real' man and woman was not feasible at that time, the move to a market economy and the onset of unemployment have made it not only feasible, but highly desirable.

The sociologist Igor' Bestuzhev-Lada has long been a protagonist in this campaign to return women to the home, though the reasons he has given in its support have altered in accordance with economic changes. Initially he stressed the demographic problems which resulted from the high level of female participation in the labour force – the low birth rate leading to an imminent labour shortage, and the difficulty that this reduced workforce would have in providing for an ageing population. If women devoted themselves less to work and more to the family, he argued, the birth rate, and hence the pool of future workers, would inevitably increase. With the onset of perestroika it became clear that there would not be a labour shortage, but, instead, a labour surplus. Bestuzhev-Lada now talked enthusiastically of the higher productivity which would result from perestroika, which would allow for a smaller workforce and for women to choose whether to work or to stay at home with their children. Since women only thought they wanted to work because of decades of erroneous upbringing, however, once this was reversed most would opt to stay at home. Bestuzhev-Lada predicted that the typical woman of the future would 'have paid leave for six months before the birth, and will spend the whole of it in a sanatorium in order to give birth to a healthy child . . . After birth comes another three years' paid leave . . . Then for another seven years – until the child becomes a teenager – she will work part-time.'[6]

When the initial optimistic phase of perestroika had passed, it became clear that instead of a 'rationalization of the economy' there would be mass unemployment. With what must have been a touch of irony, the magazine *Rabotnitsa* interviewed Bestuzhev-Lada on what could be done to alleviate the high level of female unemployment. His response was that women could not be considered unemployed since they had families to look after: 'the workplace for a woman is with her children. She is not without work – children are her work.'[7] His implicit suggestion was that women had no right to take jobs from men, since the latter did not have such useful distractions and so psychologically suffered more. Work, it seemed, was primarily a way of filling time.

Elsewhere Bestuzhev-Lada did acknowledge that work also brought important financial rewards, and that women engaged in 'maternal work' should receive a government grant. Although he has continued to adhere to this principle, it has gradually been scaled down in accordance with economic realities. In 1988 he argued that if a woman was simply looking after her own children, this would be sufficient return for society's money.[8] By 1992 he had decided that in order to earn this grant she would also have to undertake compulsory part-time service as assistant at a Child Consultation Centre or the local school.[9] In 1988 he insisted that the grant should be sufficient to ensure women's financial independence;[10] by 1992 he envisaged women having to supplement it by engaging in some form of cottage industry – doing paid knitting or macramé, selling home-made pies, taking other people's children for walks. 'Women often do not realize that they have the possibility of earning money at home', he argued, pointing with approval at the large number of home workers in the United States,[11] and failing to note that these are among the most exploited members of the workforce: underpaid, lacking job security and excluded from the normal range of workers' benefits.

Bestuzhev-Lada's cosy vision of the patriarchal family restored to its former pre-eminence in a free market society found its concrete expression in the draft bill 'For the Protection of the Family, Motherhood, Fatherhood and Children', which was under consideration by the last Russian parliament and received its second reading in February 1993. Despite the inclusion of the word 'fatherhood' in its title, the bill was concerned solely with motherhood, and how this related to a woman's work outside the home. At first glance the bill seemed like a positive piece of legislation, which would have promoted women's interests by putting pressure on employers to protect the health and welfare of their female workforce. However, in practice it would have exacerbated a situation in which women were already, as the economist Zoia Khotkina put it, 'excessively burdened by social privileges'.[12] The bill demanded, for example, that an employer pay a female employee on maternity leave no less than twice the minimum pay, and if he was unable to transfer her to light work or allow her to work from home throughout her pregnancy, he would have to release her from her job while continuing to pay her the average wage. The bill also stated that employers could not allow women with children under the age of fourteen to work more than thirty-five hours per week, a first step toward establishing part-time work as the norm for women. Furthermore, if a family had three children, the mother could not be considered unemployed: she could not register at the labour exchange, receive unemployment benefit or appear on any lists of people seeking work.[13] This last clause was a clear echo of the views of Bestuzhev-Lada, who was apparently one of the government's advisers on the bill.[14] Various aspects of the bill did provoke controversy, and it had not been passed before the confrontation between Yel'tsin and Parliament in October 1993.[15] If it had been, it would have served to enshrine in law women's dependence on their husbands. The fact that many women do not have husbands and have to struggle to bring up children on their own has received scant attention.[16]

Yel'tsin's wife, Naina, might be seen as the model of post-Soviet woman. In a rare interview, published in the newspaper *My* (*We*) in August 1992, she declared that 'I am not the first lady, I am simply the wife of the Russian president . . . Everything is just as it was before for us. I've remained a housewife . . . I choose his ties, I take care of his shirts and suits . . .' She admitted that unlike Raisa Gorbacheva she undertook no public or social work, but this, she said, was because she had no power to effect any real change: 'All I can do is to ask the President for help. But there is an unbreakable rule in our family: I must never ask my husband about anything that relates to his work.'[17] This vision of woman as wife and servant to the newly empowered Russian male is something that has united politicians virtually across the political spectrum. Yel'tsin's greatest political adversary in the last parliament, Ruslan Khasbulatov, noted approvingly in his book

The Struggle for Russia that the market was creating the conditions which would allow 'the man [to] feel himself the head of the family'.[18]

Alongside this rather dismal development of post-Soviet gender relations, there has been a second and still more disturbing image of women propounded by the media: as the passive victim of male violence. Its most obvious vehicle has been the pornographic press, one of Russia's biggest growth industries. Sheila Jeffrey, an anti-porn crusader in the West, has described pornography as 'the eroticizing of [women's] subordination',[19] a label that could well be applied to the Russian variety. Throughout, the emphasis is on male power and female passivity. A quantitative study of the visual images in eight pornographic tabloids published in 1992 – *Venera, On i ona, Krasnaia shapochka, Mister Eks, Eshche, Iskusstvo liubvi, Fortuna* and *SPID-info* – reveals the following breakdown. The greatest number of photographs, fifty-six in total, were of nude women or semi-nude women. If their faces were visible, they generally wore expressions of passive welcome. Often the faces were not visible, or were in the shadow, and hence emphasis was placed on the 'important' bits for the purposes of male sexual gratification – the genitals and breasts. A further eighteen pictures dispensed completely with the rest of the body and consisted only of breasts, legs or sexual organs. In other words, the woman was reduced to nothing but her sexual parts. One cover of *SPID-info*, for example, showed a pair of disembodied female legs sitting on a chair.[20] The next issue of *Mister Eks* went still further and had a pair of legs bound to a chair, so combining dismemberment with bondage.[21]

Seven pictures showed a clothed man with a nude woman, which served to emphasize the woman's vulnerability in relation to the man. In a further three pictures there was one clothed man and two nude women, in one of which the women were sprawled on the floor clinging pathetically to the man's legs. This emphasizes not only the women's vulnerability, but the man's virility; he has the power to command not just one woman, but women in general. The same idea is communicated by another picture of a man having sex with two women.

There were thirteen pictures of nude couples; but whereas the woman's genitals were fully revealed, either the man's body was in shadow or his genitals were concealed because of the positioning of the woman's body. Clearly these images were aimed at providing men (at least heterosexual men), not women, with visual pleasure. Finally, five pictures showed or hinted at violence against women: there were suggestions of bondage, torture and in one case, of murder.

Of course, there is nothing specifically Russian about these images; they are the staple of pornography in any culture. More alarming, then, is the fact that such images are not only found in the pornographic press in Russia but have wandered into popular mainstream publications. The current affairs magazine *Stolitsa*, for example, illustrated the back cover of one issue with a full-page photograph of a slinkily clad woman putting a gun to her mouth, an apparent metaphor for oral sex.[22] Portraying the penis as a weapon is an obvious metaphor of male power over women, and once again the woman, in holding the gun to her own mouth, is acquiescing in this threatened violence. *Sovershenno sekretno* had a front-cover photograph of a clothed man pulling the hair of an apparently naked woman (only her head and naked shoulders were visible), and from her sultry expression it seems as if she is enjoying this treatment. This is particularly alarming because the picture was illustrating an article on rape.[23] The pages of *Ogonek* are replete with female nudes. The youth newspaper *Sobesednik*, a weekly supplement to *Komsomol'skaia pravda*, is one of the worst offenders, containing frequent images of naked women and bits of women, women being tied up in ropes, women being hauled out of the sea in nets.

Cinema screens have also hosted a spate of images depicting male violence against women.[24] Savva Kulish's *Tragedy in the Rock Style* (1988) and Sergei Snezhkin's *Extraordinary Incident on a Regional Scale* (1989) both include scenes in which women are forced into sex, and emphasize the passivity of the victims: both are clearly miserable, but neither puts up any resistance. In films which do show women trying to defend themselves, their efforts prove futile. In Viktor Sergeev's *The Assassin* (1990), the protagonist, Ol'ga, hires a mafia gang to punish four men who have sexually abused her. Her revenge backfires when she falls in love with one of the four and tries to call the gang off, but is unable to do so. Although she sets the violence in motion, then, she loses control of it and becomes its victim. Nor is it any coincidence that the first punishment the mafia carries out is the gang rape of the teenage daughter of one of Ol'ga's attackers. Rather than avenge the original offence, the mafia has repeated it in relation to another woman. The message is unmistakably that women should not even attempt to challenge male hegemony. That Ol'ga falls for one of her attackers is also an implicit suggestion that women might not be entirely averse to rough treatment.

Pavel Lungin's *Taxi Blues* (1990) expresses a similar view. The film is primarily concerned with the development of an unlikely friendship between two men, a tough body-building taxi driver called Ivan and an alcoholic Jewish musician called Lesha. As with so many films of the glasnost era, the frustrations of Soviet life are channelled into acts of aggression, which are directed at men no less than women. However, they take on a sexual connotation in relation to women and are clearly perceived as an acceptable part of male sexuality. After Ivan's girlfriend has been drunkenly flirting with Lesha, Ivan punishes her with violent sex; her angry yells soon subside and instead she starts clinging to him lovingly. The normally effete Lesha finds the strength to attack his estranged wife, but she also forgives him and they end up locked in embrace. The status women occupy in men's lives is symbolized by the present Lesha brings back to Ivan from New York – an inflatable rubber woman. Women are the passive objects of male lust: men's only meaningful relationships are with one another.

In Abai Karpykov's *Blown Kiss* (1990), female acquiescence in male sexual violence is represented in an entirely symbolic form. Nast'ia is confused and frustrated when her fiancé refuses to sleep with her until they are married, and finds consolation in the arms of a patient in the hospital where she works, a racing driver injured in a high-speed crash. The affair unsettles her to the extent that she toys with the idea of killing herself, and the only weapon she can find is a hunting rifle. This, like the racing car driven by her new lover, is clearly a phallic symbol, a point emphasized when Nast'ia, attempting to find the best position in which to carry out the deed, points the rifle up between her legs. Later, having abandoned the suicide attempt, she is reconciled with her fiancé after he confesses to having once raped a woman, which seems to convince Nast'ia that he is a real man after all. In the final scene, the couple is seen racing along a new road on a motor-bike; Nast'ia is imploring her fiancé to slow down, but he ignores her. They crash, and she is killed – but before she dies, she enfolds him in what seems like a grateful embrace. This, it could be argued, is a symbolic depiction of rape – and, once again, the woman apparently enjoys it.

Ivan Dykhovichnii's *Moscow Parade* (1992) explores the connection between sex and violence in a historical context, that of the privileged Stalinist élite of the 1930s. One handsome young NKVD officer is so quintessentially Soviet that he has been chosen as the model for a sculpture of the New Soviet Man, but he has a secret penchant for handcuffing the wrists of young women and raping them. One of his victims blames her mild-mannered husband for failing to protect her, but it is unclear whether she really wanted protecting. As psychologist A. Nemtsov notes in his analysis of this film, she frequently urges her husband to develop some sexual aggression of his own: 'Take me! Take me!', she repeatedly demands.[25]

Sex can be used as a way of humiliating women, of putting them in their place. Georgii Branev's *To See Paris and Die* (1992) is set in a communal flat at the start of Khrushchev's 'thaw', when the old fears have not subsided and suspicions still abound. No one is sure who is spying on whom, and one of the flat's inhabitants is particularly nervous, since she has much to hide. Her husband was not, as she claims, a surgeon killed during the war, but is a jail-bird who is still alive; and despite her apparent anti-Semitism, she is herself Jewish. When a new tenant in the flat learns of her secrets by intercepting her post, he demands a curious price for his silence: she is forced to prostrate herself before him and perform oral sex.

Throughout this motley assortment of films, a number of consistent features emerge. These are the linking of sex and violence, the contrast between male aggression and female passivity, and the suggestion that women enjoy their subordination. Indeed, in some cases women seem enthusiastically acquiescent in their own humiliation. Nemtsov uses the film *Moscow Parade* to support his thesis that despite the image of the strong woman promoted in the Soviet Union's past, women are in fact naturally more passive than men, and their sexuality is to a significant degree masochistic. A number of psychologists, he reports, believe that women enjoy being tied up during sex; the restricted mobility heightens their pleasure, and their inability to control the situation means that they have no need to feel any guilt for what happens.[26] In other words, women enjoy being deprived of autonomy. It is just a short step on from this to conclude that women like being raped.

In the West there have been heated debates over whether a causal connection exists between pornography and rape. Such a discussion lies beyond the scope of this chapter. The figures for rape in Russia certainly show a marked increase since perestroika,[27] but this could have at least as much to do with greater awareness of the problem and hence willingness to report the crime, or simply improved detection methods. More pertinent for our purposes is the way in which rape and violence against women are tackled by the media. Although the mainstream press generally adopts an appropriately concerned tone, there is a strong tendency to emphasize women's vulnerability, and even to hint at their culpability.

In *Sovershenno sekretno*, for example, Elena Svetlova cites uncritically the opinions of a number of male 'experts' on rape. They give the distinct impression that 'boys will be boys', and that men simply have these strong sexual feelings that need to find an outlet. In fact it turns out to be women, rather than men, who are the real cause of the problem. One expert argues that 'women are generally brought up to be potential victims. They learn to be continually prepared for the possibility of assault. Girls grow up with a feeling of fear, with a guarded attitude toward the world, in anticipation of danger.' A person who seems so afraid, he continues, will actually provoke assault. Conversely, another expert argues that women are asking for trouble if they appear too friendly and trusting of men; in other words, they provoke assault if they do not have a sufficiently guarded attitude toward the world. A third holds that there is no way that a woman can be safe other than driving round in an armoured car with an escort of bodyguards, and laments the fact that there are still women who work on night shifts 'and have no choice but to come home late'.[28] The implication is that working the night shift is the only acceptable reason for women to be on the streets after dark. In short, women cannot win. If they are fearful of attack, they are asking for trouble; if they are not fearful enough, the result will be the same.

Mariia Musina, writing in *Rabotnitsa*, has offered a more sophisticated analysis of the causes of male violence against women, but she, too, inadvertently comes close to blaming women for their own fate. She notes that psychologists working with rapists have found that they generally perceive women as hostile and aggressive; they imagine that they have always been under the control of women and have been made to feel dependent and inferior, and rape is a way of reversing their positions. It has nothing to do with sexual need or sexual attraction, then, but is the result of 'a desire to humiliate and suppress women'.[29] In this article she makes no attempt to explain why men should come to have this perception of women, but in a later article about a serial killer she links the man's hostility toward women with a sense of abandonment by his mother. His parents had separated when he was five years old and he went to live with his father. Then, by chance, his mother's new family moved into the same apartment block, and although he regularly passed her in the lift or the corridor she would never acknowledge that she knew him, in case his father disapproved. When the man began murdering women, he was symbolically punishing his mother.[30]

Aleksandr Poleev, a psychotherapist writing in *Nedelia*, similarly blames mothers for male hatred of women.[31] Misogynists are the products of two unfortunate types of family, he explains. In the first type, the head of the family is a strong and demanding woman who dominates both her son and her husband. The son grows up hating his mother's power and strength, and by extension the strength of all women. His overriding aim in adult life is to humiliate women in turn for what his mother did to him. In the second type, the head of the family is the father, who is himself either a misogynist or a misanthropist. Still the fault lies with the mother, however. She is incapable of standing up to her husband, and even tries to protect herself by diverting his anger on to the son. So the boy comes to resent not his father's strength, but his mother's weakness.

Once again, the woman cannot win. If she is strong and the father weak, the boy resents her strength. If she is weak and father strong, the boy resents her weakness. Judging from Poleev's advice to women trapped in relationships with misogynistic men, the only type of woman of which he approves is one who is weak but totally self-sacrificing. If the woman places the preservation of her family above her personal well-being, he argues, she may be able to cure her husband. She needs to gain a full understanding of the cause of his misogyny by building up a picture of his childhood, and, in particular, *what kind of mother he had*. Then she can set out to reform him with a combination of 'tact, delicacy and a loving heart', and, presumably, a willingness to endure all the abuse he subjects her to in the meantime. This is a clear reflection of the images we discussed earlier, of women coming to love their tormentors and acquiescing in their own abuse.

In seeking the cause of this anti-female attitude, we come back to the argument outlined at the start of this chapter. It was noted that from the mid-1970s the Soviet press had begun to express considerable concern about the negative consequences of female emancipation. Women had given work such a central role in their lives that they were said to have developed a range of masculine characteristics required in the workplace, such as independence, rationality and unemotionality, and had ceased to pay sufficient attention to caring for their husbands and children. In his book *Love, Marriage and Friendship in the Soviet Union*, the émigré Russian sociologist Vladimir Shlapentokh even included a section called 'The Aggressiveness of Soviet Women'.[32] It could be argued that the visual images of male violence against women which abound in the press and on screen, and the way in which experts almost justify the phenomenon in real life, is a backlash against this 'aggressive', 'masculinized' Soviet woman.

It has taken this long for the backlash to occur, although the supposed masculinization of women has been causing concern for more than two decades, because only now is the economic and political climate ripe for it to do so. As we have noted, when discussions on the subject began there was little which could be done, since women were such an essential part of the workforce. This is no longer the case. Furthermore, we have noted that the switch to a market economy has been portrayed as a male phenomenon, with the market characterized by traits traditionally associated with men. Accordingly, it has been accompanied by a display of aggressive masculinity which requires as its counterpoint a passive femininity. Withdrawing women *en masse* from the workforce will not only ease the unemployment crisis, but it will also serve to bolster this resurgent patriarchy by rendering women dependent on, and hence subordinate to, men.

It is possible to draw some tentative parallels with other cultures and other historical periods. Ironically, Elizabeth Waters has made some similar observations about the early years of the Soviet regime. The Revolution was, she has argued, 'largely a male event, and those virtues the Bolsheviks admired – singleness of purpose and strength of will – were traditionally understood as male attributes'.[33] As socialists, the Bolsheviks had an obligation to put women's rights on the agenda, but they were given a far from prominent position: 'Bolshevik Marxism viewed change first and foremost in terms of production; the worker and the factory took the centre of the revolutionary stage.'[34] Indeed, the supposed emancipation of Soviet women rested on nothing but their mass participation in the workforce; ideology on women's rights merely provided *post hoc* rationalization for policies enacted on economic grounds. What is happening today is not dissimilar, though there are a few essential differences. Change is now viewed in terms of the male entrepreneur and the market. The collapse of socialism means that it is no longer necessary even to pay lip-service to the notion of women's equality, which allows commitment to the patriarchal family to be revived with impunity. Once again, however, this new ideology neatly dovetails with perceived economic need.

Turning to the West, we can find similar examples of a male backlash against women who have appeared to be getting above their station. Scholars have noted that in the United States, for example, in the wake of the Second World War, men returned to civilian life to find a world that was very different from that which they left behind. Women's mass entry into the workforce while the men were at the front, and their assumption of the 'male' role of head of the family in the absence of their husbands, challenged, as one commentator puts it, 'the sense of any natural supremacy of the masculine'.[35] The result for men was a sense of social dislocation, not dissimilar to that apparently experienced by the 'feminized' Soviet male. Determined attempts were made to get women to give up their jobs, either by force or persuasion; by November 1946 two million American women had been thrown out of work, while magazines expressed alarm at 'the increased incidence of juvenile delinquency during the war' which they attributed solely to maternal neglect.[36] American film-makers reflected these social attitudes and solutions, just as Russian ones are doing now. A spate of tough *film noir* thrillers showed independent, ambitious female protagonists who began by challenging male hegemony, but were ultimately rendered harmless either by being killed off or married off. In this way patriarchy managed to reassert itself. All the same, we should note with optimism that it ultimately did not prove as easy to turn back the clock in real life as it did on screen.

In conclusion, it has been argued in this chapter that the domestication of women and the images of violence against women are two sides of the same coin: an attempt to reassert male dominance in post-Soviet Russia after decades of concern that women were challenging male supremacy. At the risk of over-stretching the metaphor, we can also posit that the social, economic and political changes currently under way have created ideal conditions for the minting of such a coin. We can only hope that in the long term it fails to become legal tender.

Notes

1 For a more detailed discussion, see Lynne Attwood, *The New Soviet Man and Woman: Sex-Role Socialization in the USSR* (Basingstoke: Macmillan, 1990; Bloomington: Indiana University Press, 1991).

2 Jan Adam, 'Social Contract', in Jan Adam (ed.), *Economic Reforms and Welfare Systems in the USSR, Poland and Hungary* (Basingstoke: Macmillan, 1991), p. 2.

3 Walter D. Connor, 'Equality of Opportunity', in Anthony Jones, Walter D. Connor and Donald Powell, *Soviet Social Problems* (Boulder, Colo.: Westview Press, 1991), p. 140.

4 See, for example, N. Zakharova, A. Posadskaia and N. Rimashevskaia, 'Kak my reshaem zhenskii vopros', *Kommunist*, no. 4 (1989), pp. 56–65.

5 Personal interview with Zoia Khotkina from the Moscow Centre for Gender Studies, Moscow, August 1992.

6 I. V. Bestuzhev-Lada, 'Net detei – net i budushchego u naroda', *Nedelia*, 15–21 August 1988, p. 21. Bestuzhev-Lada repeated this to me virtually word for word in an interview conducted in Moscow in August 1992.

7 Interview with I. V. Bestuzhev-Lada conducted by A. Levina, '"Iarmarka" vakansii, ili 5 sposobov bor'by s zhenskoi bezrabotitsei', *Rabotnitsa*, no. 2 (1992), pp. 10–11.

8 Bestuzhev-Lada, 'Net detei'.

9 A. Levina's interview with Bestuzhev-Lada, '"Iarmarka" vakansii'.

10 Bestuzhev-Lada, 'Net detei'.

11 Levina's interview with Bestuzhev-Lada, '"Iarmarka" vakansii'.

12 Personal interview with Zoia Khotkina from the Moscow Centre for Gender Studies, Moscow, August 1992.

13 See Elena Averina, 'Pri chem tut zhenshchiny?', *Stolitsa*, no. 27 (1992), pp. 39–40.

14 This is what he told me in a personal interview, August 1992.

15 Indeed, I was told in 1993 by members of the Centre for Gender Studies in Moscow that a copy had been sent for comment to the European Human Rights Commission. [Editor's note: For the bill's eventual failure to pass, see above, p. 18.]

16 Editor's note: For further discussion of this problem, see p. 270.

17 Naina El'tsina, 'Ia ne pervaia ledi, ia prosto zhena prezidenta Rossii', *We/My* (Russian edn.), no. 11 (August 1992), pp. 1, 9, 14.

18 Quoted in the *Guardian*, Section 2, 30 March 1993, p. 9: mini-review by Neil Parody under heading 'Easily Missed'. The book was published by Routledge, London, 1993.

19 Sheila Jeffrey, *Anticlimax: A Feminist Perspective on the Sexual Revolution* (London: Women's Press, 1990), p. 43.

20 *SPID-info*, no. 7 (1992), front cover.

21 *Mister Eks*, August 1992, front cover.

22 *Stolitsa*, no. 23 (July 1991), back cover.

23 *Sovershenno sekretno*, no. 2 (1992), front cover.

24 For a more detailed discussion, see Lynne Attwood (ed.), *Red Women on the Silver Screen* (London: Pandora, 1993); Lynne Attwood, 'Sex and the Cinema', in Igor Kon and James Riordan (eds.), *Sex and Russian Society* (Bloomington: Indiana University Press, 1993; London: Pluto Press, 1993), pp. 64–88.

25 A. Nemtsov, 'Rabfak i Marsel'eza', *Iskusstvo kino*, no. 11 (1992), pp. 13–17.

26 Ibid.

27 The figures are as follows:

	Soviet Union as a whole	RSFSR
1987:	16,765	10,902
1988:	17,658	11,560
1989:	21,873	14,597
1990:	22,469	15,010

Source: *Zhenshchiny v SSSR* (Moscow: Finansy i statistika, 1992), p. 771.

28 Elena Svetlova, 'Sindrom zhertvy', *Sovershenno sekretno*, no. 2 (1992), pp. 16–18.
29 Mariia Musina, 'Zhenskie strakhi', *Rabotnitsa*, nos. 2–4 (1992), pp. 24–5.
30 Mariia Musina, 'Chuvstvoval sebia zagnannym zverem', *Rabotnitsa*, no. 1 (1993), pp. 16–17.
31 Aleksandr Poleev, 'Liubliu – no strannoiu liubov'iu', *Nedelia*, no. 7 (1991), pp. 10–11.
32 Vladimir Shlapentokh, *Love, Marriage and Friendship in the Soviet Union: Ideals and Practices* (New York: Praeger, 1984), p. 202.
33 Elizabeth Waters, 'The Female Form in Soviet Political Iconography, 1917–32', in Barbara Evans Clements, Barbara Alpern Engel and Christine D. Worobec (eds.), *Russia's Women: Accommodation, Resistance, Transformation* (Berkeley and Oxford: University of California Press, 1991), p. 228.
34 Ibid., p. 232.
35 Frank Krutnik (citing the work of Pam Cook), *In a Lonely Street: Film Noir, Genre and Masculinity* (London: Routledge, 1991), p. 64.
36 Maxine Margolis, *Mothers and Such: Views of American Women and Why They Changed* (Berkeley: University of California Press, 1985), p. 216.

Feminism and politics in Russia and Ukraine

PART IV

Feminism and politics in Russia
and Ukraine

18

The 'woman question' and problems of maternity in post-communist Russia

ELENA SARGEANT

The main purpose of this chapter is to analyse contemporary views on the effect of perestroika on women in Russia, to explore the changes which have occurred in women's functions and roles in society in the years 1991–4 due to the political turmoil of the transition period from socialism to capitalism, and to discuss the problems created by these changes. It will focus in particular on the themes of motherhood, demography and infant mortality in Russia, then explore possible economic, legal and political solutions to the problems of Russian women.

During the seventy years of Soviet power, women were not liberated, but mobilized as a workforce for the construction of communism, and obliged to carry a double burden of duties.[1] They acquired a certain degree of financial independence, but at the same time they were used to fill mostly unskilled and low-paid jobs, rarely gaining promotion to well-paid, decision-making posts, including political ones.[2] In this context, the opinion of Marina Pankova, a journalist from the newspaper *Nezavisimaia gazeta,* that by 1993 the political and economic changes in Russia were reducing women's social status more and more and prompting the growth of 'discriminatory processes', sounds very unconvincing.[3] The fact that in 1993 the average real pay in the country was one-third lower for women than for men, and that women's pensions were accordingly only 70 per cent of men's, was equally true of the pre-perestroika period. The reason Pankova gives for this situation, that there is 'a gap in the level of skills and training, since for women, as a rule, the most active years of professional development coincide with the period of motherhood'[4] was relevant for the communist period too. Her statement that 'women at present [referring to the post-perestroika period] have very little influence on the political decisions of men – women make up only 5 per cent of the Russian Supreme Soviet, and [in 1993] only the Russian Federation Ministry of Social Protection is headed by a woman'[5] – sounds as if earlier, during the communist period, women had some political influence. However, women in pre-perestroika Russia never played any significant role in politics. In fact, those women who were 'elected' to the Supreme Soviet were formally appointed and were puppets, destined only to raise their hand in unanimous approval rather than to express an independent opinion. Such a delusion, in my opinion, is due to the communist propaganda slogan of the 1930s which is deeply implanted in the minds of the majority of the population of the former Soviet Union – that the 'woman question' in the country had been resolved once and for all and that Soviet women enjoyed complete equality with men. In fact, that was one of the numerous lies propagated by the state.

Discrimination against women in all areas of life, albeit in latent form, always existed in Soviet society. This was the crux of the so-called 'woman question' in Russia. It is therefore impossible to agree with a popular Russian poet, Larisa Vasil'eva, that 'There are not and cannot be any "women's problems." They were dreamed up by bureaucratic minds.'[6] Her statement that 'all the problems that women experience are social problems, for they affect men as well as women; we are inseparable',[7] is inadequate, although true to a certain extent. In my view, the distinctive nature of women's issues in Russia is that it is only women, and not men, who are associated with everything concerning families, children and reproduction.

At present we are witnessing an utterly contradictory phenomenon in Russian society.[8] Before perestroika woman's main role was proclaimed to be that of worker and active builder of communism; but after perestroika she was urged to fulfil her traditional function as a housewife,[9] in order to prepare society psychologically for massive female redundancies. As a result, according to Academician Tat'iana Zaslavskaia, the former president of the Soviet Sociological Association, in 1988, 40 per cent of all working mothers would have left their jobs if their husbands' earnings had been high enough to ensure an adequate standard of living for their families. But as Zaslavskaia indicated, most Soviet women have no choice but to work, either because their husbands' salaries are insufficient to make ends meet, or because they themselves are heads of households.[10] Furthermore, women who do not accrue the requisite twenty years of service in the public sector are ineligible for old-age pensions.[11] Therefore, notwithstanding the current fantasy about traditional female roles, 90 per cent of women, exhausted by 'emancipation', have to work.[12] And when women are faced with forced unemployment due to staff reduction, the majority of them feel absolutely terrified. Moreover, the image of a perfect housewife sitting at home, expecting her husband to earn enough to keep their family, was not and is not applicable to about 10 million Russian single mothers who have only themselves to rely upon. In any case, since there are 9.2 million more women than men in Russia, not every woman is able to find a man to support her.[13]

Many young people cannot afford to start a family life at all. At present we are witnessing a significant decrease in the number of marriages. Whereas in 1987 1,443,000 marriages were registered in Russia, in 1992 there were only 1,054,000.[14] The trend toward a decrease in the number of marriages continued to intensify in 1993 and 1994, although the number of marriages between young people aged between fifteen and nineteen increased in 1993. But at the same time they are the most likely to get divorced before reaching the age of twenty.[15] One out of eight registered marriages per thousand members of the population ends in divorce, and one-third of divorces involve young couples. As a rule, increasing difficulty in creating the normal conditions for family life is the main reason for divorce.[16]

Compared with 1991, in 1992 the number of divorces increased by 4,000, or by 7 per cent in a single year, and amounted to almost 640,000 for the whole of Russia, as opposed to 580,000 in 1987. As a result of family break-ups in 1992, 569,000 children under eighteen in Russia were left without one of their parents. Over 4 million children, 12 per cent of all children under eighteen, currently live in incomplete families.[17] Thus the perestroika vision of a return to 'a purely womanly mission'[18] seems implausible and unrealistic.

Some demographers, however, consider that women's unemployment – women amounted to 80 per cent of all the unemployed in 1993[19] – has its advantages, because it causes women to stay at home to devote themselves completely to their households, which could be beneficial for population growth. On the other hand, an unstable financial situation and a permanent threat of losing her job cause many a woman to postpone indefinitely or completely abandon any plans of having a baby. This, however, does not seem to apply to the majority of women in the 19–22 age range. According to statistics, the birth rate of first-borns among that group of women remains virtually unchanged, because among them the desire to have a baby prevails over economic considerations.[20]

There is a steady increase in out-of-wedlock births among adolescent girls and among women over thirty. In 1987, they accounted for 13 per cent of all births; by 1992, the figure was 17 per cent.[21] Both ages, though for different reasons, are not favourable to the birth of healthy babies, and the circumstances usually provide such women with worse social and economic conditions than married couples. Nevertheless, the aforementioned tendency of postponing or abandoning completely plans of giving birth has already caused a considerable drop in the birth rate in the European regions of the former Soviet Union.[22] The number of babies born in 1992 was 11 per cent less than in 1991. There were about 100 abortions per 1,000 women, which is more than twice the number of births. Only 90 per cent of women in 1992 carried their pregnancies to term, and there were complications in 40 per cent of births. Women are giving birth to fewer healthy babies every year. Whereas in 1985 every tenth or eleventh baby was born sick, in 1989 the figure was one in eight, in 1991 it increased to one in six, and in 1993 to one in five.[23] One of the reasons for this was malnutrition and poor health among women.

Of every 100 newborns in Russia, 6 to 8 infants have birth defects as a result of chromosomal mutations in human cells caused by contamination and poisoning of the environment. The number of spontaneous abortions due to the same reason doubled over the period of ten years. The situation in rural areas is as bad as in large industrial cities, because of the treatment of 144 million hectares of cultivated land out of 160 million with pesticides. The effect of mutagenic factors is intensified by unbalanced diets, a lack of the optimal quantity and variety of food, and an acute shortage of vitamins, many of which are anti-mutagenic.[24] The obvious solution to this problem seems to me to be a reduction in the contamination of the environment. Since it is not possible to reduce pollution quickly and at once all over Russia, the easiest way would be to grant more economic freedom to entrepreneurs who produce ecologically clean products.[25]

The demographic situation in the country, which has been steadily deteriorating since 1988, has become a matter of concern for the whole of Russian society. In 1992, for the first time in Russia's recorded history, a natural population decrease of almost 220,000 people was recorded in the country.[26] In 1993, the number of births declined by 200,000, or 13 per cent, while deaths increased by 330,000, or 18 per cent.[27] According to a report published in May 1994 by the Russian Federation State Statistics Committee, a decline in population is observable in 49 regions of the country out of 89 (in 1992 this figure was 41, and in 1991 it was 33), where 90.2 million people, or 61 per cent of Russia's total population, currently live. The most noticeable decreases in population in 1993 occurred in Chukotka okrug (9 per cent), Magadan oblast (6 per cent), Kamchatka oblast (3.7 per cent), Murmansk oblast (2.3 per cent), Sakhalin oblast and the Komi republic (2.1 per cent), St Petersburg city and the republic of Chechnia (1.4 per cent), the republic of Ingushetia (1.3 per cent), and Sakha (formerly Yakutia; 1.2 per cent).[28] In spite of the overall decline in population, Kalmykia, Dagestan, Kabardino-Balkaria, Karachay-Cherkessia, Tuva republics and Tiumen' oblast were still registering positive population growth in 1993.[29] This same source also states that Chechnia, Ingushetia, Chukotka okrug and Sakha, in contradiction to the article cited above, also showed an increase in population in 1993. This discrepancy may indicate the unreliable nature of current data.

Some experts consider that the drop in the standard of living due to the aggravation of the economic situation, the political instability, and the destruction of the social infrastructure caused by the transition to a market economy did not directly cause the decline in the birth rate. Instead, in their view, these factors only influenced it in negative ways and aggravated it, since there would be a decrease in population even without the economic crisis.[30] They consider that the beginning of this process occurred in 1988 as a direct consequence of the drop in the birth rate in the late 1960s, which was in turn a direct result of the low birth rate during the war years. Moreover, Iurii Poliakov, the director of the Centre for the Study of the History of Russia's Territory and Population within the Institute of Russian History, maintains that at present we are still facing the consequences of the Civil War of 1917–22, when the country's population dropped by 13 million people.[31] The demographer Viktor Perevedentsev considers that the reduced number of those born during the Second World War was not the only reason for a sharp drop in the birth rate in the 1960s. According to him, it was mostly caused by the Soviet government's policy aimed at involving women in economic production. The proportion of women employed in the country's economy increased from 46 per cent to 52 per cent, but the birth rate dropped dramatically too.[32]

During the last five years, the number of women aged between twenty and twenty-nine, that is, the group of the highest fertility, has declined by 1.7 million, or nearly 15 per cent, because that was the period when daughters of the very scarce generation born just before, during, or just after the Second World War reached child-bearing age.[33] Another reason for the current drop in the birth rate, according to A. Demin, an expert on President Yel'tsin's staff, was:

> the measures to assist families with children that were implemented from 1982. These measures were undertaken on the upswing of a demographic wave, when the birth rate was already relatively high, and led to an artificial elevation in the last birth rate peak in 1987. The increased birth rate during this period stemmed primarily from changes in the planned timing of the birth of children in families, and not from a reconsideration of the planned number of children. Whole generations of women carried out their life plans ahead of schedule. Now the majority of these women are of childbearing age, but they have already borne not only their first children, but generally their second and even third ones as well.[34]

This is an arguable point. It is not clear why women should have reconsidered the planned timing of their children, as Demin maintains, and hurried to have all their children at once in the first half of the 1980s. Were they afraid that later all their benefits would be taken away, and that they should therefore take advantage of them as soon as possible? The measures were meant for the long term, and in my opinion, are not an adequate reason for women to bring forward the timing of their family.

Boris Sergeev, an expert at Moscow State University's Centre for the Study of Population Problems, insists, on the contrary, that the root causes of the catastrophic fall in the birth rate and the increase in the excess of deaths over births are 'the impoverishment of part of the population, the mass incidence of disease and malnutrition'.[35] The journalist Azer Mursaliev, however, considers that the current birth rate drop in Russia is not directly related to socio-political reasons, and, I would add, economic ones. He argues that 'if a decline in the birth rate in Russia is caused by a harsh drop in the standard of living, why then is there a birth rate decline in rich Sweden and Denmark, and, on the contrary, a rise in the birth rate in Afghanistan, Iraq or Bangladesh?'[36] It is common knowledge that the more babies people have in countries with a low standard of living and high infant mortality rate, the greater the chances there are for some of their children to survive. At the same time, the higher the well-being and the standard of living, the lower the birth rate. Mursaliev considers that this tendency can be explained by L. N. Gumilev's theory that humankind is a part of nature, living according to its laws, and that therefore peoples as well as individuals are born, grow old and then die.[37] This sounds very pessimistic and fatalistic. The belief that Russia is naturally dying, and therefore all measures to reverse this tendency would be hopeless, seems far-fetched, although titles like 'Is Russia Dying?' have started appearing in the Russian press.[38]

More optimistically, Yel'tsin's adviser A. Demin considers that 'Despite the complexity of the current demographic situation, it would be wrong to consider the situation hopeless or to speak of a catastrophe.'[39] He predicts that 'Some increase in Russia's birth rate can be expected as early as the second half of the

1990s, when the quite large generation of girls now 14 to 18 years old will reach the age of intensive child-bearing.'[40] Other observers consider that under the current unfavourable conditions, it is unrealistic to think that this would completely alter the demographic situation.[41]

Although fear may not be the major reason for a drop in the birth rate, it nevertheless plays a significant role. 'Women in Russia are afraid to give birth and do not want to go through it', maintains the journalist Elena Shafran, 'because of their distrust of doctors, women's clinics and maternity hospitals.'[42] Most clinics and hospitals are not equipped with up-to-date diagnostic and operational equipment and the most essential medicines. They are dirty and old, and their staff are usually unattentive and rude. Women go through pregnancies with undetected and untreated diseases, and, along with terrible complications and infections, they produce infected, sick babies. About 15 per cent of newborn babies in Russia on average come into the world with congenital defects for the reasons mentioned above. For example, of every 10,000 women who gave birth in 1992, 1,225.9 were anaemic; 1,139.7 were suffering from toxaemia; 385 had diseases of the circulatory system; 581.8 had diseases of the genito-urinary system; and many had inflammatory intra-uterine infections.[43] A sharp increase in fatalities during childbirth can be observed in contemporary Russia. In 1987, 49.3 mothers died per 100,000 live births. In 1991 the number was 52.43, while the average European level was 22, and in Denmark it was 3.6, in Austria 4.6, in Great Britain 5.9 and in Norway 5.6.[44] The death rate among Russian mothers is even higher in regions beyond the Urals. For instance, whereas in Russia as a whole there is an average of 50.8 maternal deaths for every 100,000 births, in Kemerovo oblast, in particular, there are 106.[45]

Women's illnesses, complications and deaths connected with pregnancy and childbirth could be prevented in 60 per cent of cases if they were able to eat a proper amount and variety of food, to live in a healthy environment, and if they were correctly diagnosed, which does not occur in 80 per cent of cases, and were given qualified medical treatment.[46] Unfortunately, these basic things continue to be out of reach for most Russian women, and motherhood continues to be very dangerous in Russia. Thus it seems reasonable to regard the declining birth rate as a manifestation of the many problems that women face in contemporary Russia, rather than as a separate phenomenon.

In the unfavourable demographic situation, the problem of increasing infant mortality becomes very acute. Whereas in 1991, according to the journalist Andrei Baiduzhii, the number of babies who died before the age of one was 16.8 per 1,000, in 1992 it increased to 17.1.[47] Boris Brui, a consultant for the Russian State Statistics Committee's Administration of Demographic Statistics, quotes slightly different figures: the infant mortality rate averaged 17.4 per 1,000 newborns for the whole of Russian Federation in 1990, 17.8 in 1991 and 18.0 in 1992.[48] Despite the discrepancy in figures, the calculations cited above vividly demonstrate the trend toward an increasing death rate among newborn babies.

The infant mortality rate differs significantly among the republics and provinces of the Russian Federation. In 1992, for instance, the lowest rates were in Orel oblast, and the highest were in the republics of Altai and Tuva. In 1993, a decline in infant mortality was recorded in St Petersburg city; in Leningrad, Orel, Tula and Astrakhan´ oblasts; and the republics of Buriatia and Dagestan. In many other areas, such as, for example, the republics of Udmurtia, Khakassia and Adygeia and Altai krai, as well as in Ul´ianovsk, Kaluga, Pskov and Kamchatka oblasts, the rate increased.[49]

Searching for ways of increasing the country's population, the Russian authorities have turned their attention to the proper care of premature babies, whose number has a tendency to increase with each passing year because 'ecology, chronic stress, malnutrition among women, irregular diet, the general psychological and emotional state of Russian society and a large number of abortions (6.5 million per year) are starting to have a negative effect in various regions'.[50] As a rule, premature babies in 14 per cent of cases are unplanned, out-of-wedlock offspring of teenage mothers. In three years the number of fifteen-year-old mothers, for whom the risk of giving birth to premature, unhealthy babies is especially high, has increased by 50 per cent.[51] Every year 4,000 to 7,000 babies in the latter category alone are born in Russia. Only 27 to 28 per cent of them survive. In the developed countries the figure is 60 to 80 per cent.[52] In general, 'the weight of newborns in Russia dropped by an average of 10 per cent, and a normal baby from a normal family weighs no more than 2,600 to 2,700 grammes'.[53]

President Yel´tsin issued a decree on sustaining the lives of infants weighing 500 grammes or more and the registration of newborn infants in accordance with the criteria of the World Health Organization which became operative from 1 January 1993. According to these criteria, babies who weigh at least 500 grammes, have been carried to a term of 22 weeks, and have at least one of the signs of life in the absence of breathing – that is, heartbeat, pulsation of the umbilical cord or muscular contractions – are considered to be alive, and doctors are obliged to do everything to sustain their lives. This decree is of enormous importance, because if the Russian state starts recognizing a child's right to life as of the moment the foetus becomes viable, it would be obliged to work out the means and conditions for saving its life, and to pay pre-natal and post-natal leave and monetary benefits to mothers of premature babies. But in spite of the decree, the Russian State Statistics Committee continues to register only babies who were born weighing at least one kilogramme, who had been carried for at least 28 weeks and who can breathe on their own.[54]

Many doctors who are specialists in the care of very young children express their profound concern that this decree can hardly be carried out in Russia because of a lack of special equipment and experience. Moreover, without special treatment, under-weight babies of less than one kilogramme in weight could be mentally and physically impaired.[55] The construction of up-to-date special maternity hospitals that would handle premature deliveries and the training of medical personnel is needed. This would require huge funds and will take a great deal of time. Unfortunately, the presidential decree did not stipulate measures for implementing the resolution. In the meantime, the introduction of world criteria in Russia has been regarded as leading to an increase in the figures for infant mortality from 17.4 to 25 per 1,000 births.[56]

The complex socio–economic situation in Russia causes fatal consequences not only with respect to the falling birth rate but also to the babies who are born. The number of parents who abandon their newborn children because they cannot afford to feed and keep them has increased considerably during the last few years. In 1991, there was an increase of 10,000 abandoned children in comparison with 1990. Of all children in children's homes, 97 per cent have parents who are living (and therefore only 3 per cent of them do not have parents living).[57] The most disturbing fact is that 'Children are no longer seen as something of absolute value to society; even totally normal parents are ceasing to see them as something of value. Families living in poverty that is an insult to their humanity have come to view the birth of a child as an "extra mouth", as a burden.'[58] Many people justify their unwillingness to have children with reluctance to procreate misery and poverty. Bitter statistics prove this point. At the end of 1992, 42 per cent of families with children under eighteen were living on the brink of poverty or below the poverty line; for families with one child the figure was 34 per cent; with two or more – 47 per cent, and with three or more – 72 per cent.[59]

During perestroika, foreigners acquired permission to adopt abandoned babies from the former Soviet Union. According to I. Volodina, deputy head of the Department of Social Protection of Children, during 1991 and 1992 among 25,000 adopted children, 578 were adopted by foreigners.[60] Russian public opinion has an ambivalent attitude toward this practice, despite the fact that foreigners are permitted to adopt abandoned babies only of a certain category, that is, those with abnormalities in their development. According to negative public opinion in Russia, adoption by foreigners is considered to be the 'sale of national property' and the 'non-regulated export of babies for their use as transplant donors'.[61] On the other hand, international adoption of handicapped babies is considered to be the last and only chance to save children's lives and to improve their health, since well-off foreign parents are able to provide them with the medical treatment and care they require. Russian boarding homes, on the contrary, cannot provide the means for expensive multiple operations, treatment and a decent way of life for these children.[62] According to the journalist Ella Maksimova, 'The fact is that educators who have been working in the field of adoption for many decades cannot remember a case in which Russian citizens took a disabled or deformed child into their family.'[63]

Moreover, even those Russian parents who adopted healthy children before the economic turmoil of perestroika encounter great difficulties in bringing them up. The Russian journalist Natal'ia Davydova cited a letter to the popular Russian magazine *Ogonek* from a lonely woman who had decided to share her distress with the editorial board. She wrote that several years ago she had adopted two children from a children's home, but that she had recently taken them back because she had no food to feed them.[64]

In December 1992, the Russian Federation Supreme Soviet adopted the resolution 'On Urgent Measures to Regulate the Adoption of Children who are Citizens of the Russian Federation by Citizens of Other States', which is in effect pending the drafting of a law. Proclaiming its fundamental provision that 'Every child who has lost his parents should end up in a family, and Russian citizens have priority in adoptions', it stipulates that foreigners may adopt children only in 'exceptional cases' when Russian citizens cannot or do not want to take the child. It was proposed that all abandoned children would be registered at the Ministry of Education 'with the aim of transferring them to other areas and regions of the Russian Federation for adoption'. They would be permitted to leave the country when the possibilities had been exhausted throughout the whole of Russia. Information on the children would be put into a nationwide data bank, from where it would go to the republics, oblasts and okrugs.[65] Implementation of this plan to create a national data bank seems unrealistic, because of the poverty and backwardness in Russian society.

There are two points of view on whether perestroika managed to bring any improvements in the solution of women's problems. According to T. N. Nikolaeva, who delivered a report to the United Nations Committee on the Elimination of Discrimination Against Women in early 1989, Soviet women had made 'revolutionary progress' thanks to M. Gorbachev's reforms.[66] This speech reflected the official point of view of the Soviet Communist Party which ruled at that time. On the other hand, according to Annette Bohr, 'the vast majority of Soviet women do not believe that perestroika has made their daily lives any easier, either by alleviating food and housing shortages or by improving the supply of consumer goods and services'.[67] Instead, perestroika introduced new problems which naturally changed with the economic and political development of events in the country. In 1989, when perestroika started to bear its first fruit, Larisa Vasil'eva noted new tendencies in the everyday lives of Russian women:

> Outdated and inaccurate ideas have been abandoned, but new problems have arisen
> . . . sugar is rationed, soaps and detergents are in short supply, women have to stand
> longer in queues. At work everything is chaotic due to the transition to economic
> accountability. At home, a woman's husband is irritated over the success of the
> co-operatives. Or if he is a co-operative worker, he's upset about the tax system.
> Children are sceptical and don't believe anything any more.[68]

In the post-perestroika period, one of the main causes of concern for women became the constant price rises in addition to the problems already mentioned.

The St Petersburg feminist Ol'ga Lipovskaia commented in March 1989 that perestroika had given women nothing but the opportunity 'to let off steam'.[69] However, it is worth noting that even acquiring an opportunity to 'let off steam' could be considered a great achievement. During perestroika, women of various occupations and interests gained an opportunity to get together in order to discuss various questions and to make informal decisions, which were brought to the attention of the press, legislative and governing bodies. Among such women's groups several worthy of mention are a women film-makers' union, a women journalists' club, a council of women writers, an international association of 'Grandmothers for Peace', an association of women employees of internal affairs agencies and many others.

The Russian women's movement became energetic and enthusiastic after obtaining freedom of speech and political activity after the collapse of the communist regime. It focused its attention on legislation, in order to elaborate new post-communist laws on social protection for families, women and children. At the end of 1992, a Group of Gender Expertise consisting of fifteen independent experts was formed within the Supreme Soviet of the Russian Federation. Its aim was to help Russian parliamentarians and law-makers create laws which would take into account the specific interests of both sexes. This intention was very important, because all Russian laws had previously been non-gender-specific. One of the first acts of the group was its work on new labour and family laws. The experts of the group criticized and forced the reconsideration of a new labour law, because it could have placed women in a situation in which they would have had to choose whether to work or to have children, as it envisaged that all maternity benefits would be paid by employers. In such circumstances they would have preferred to employ men rather than women.[70]

The experts of the group also rejected a new draft of the family law 'For the Protection of the Family, Motherhood, Fatherhood and Children' which had been drawn up in 1992 by the Russian Supreme Soviet's Joint Committee on Women's Affairs and the Protection of the Family, Mother and Child. Two reasons in particular were given for this. Firstly, the main functions of the family were stated as being reproductive and economic ones, which could have meant that if a husband and a wife did not want or could not have children, they would not have been defined as a family. Secondly, in the article of the draft law 'On the Protection of Working (Student) Mothers', it was envisaged that, irrespective of organizational and legal rules, employers should establish a working week of not more than thirty-five working hours for all working mothers with children up to the age of fourteen.[71] Although this appears to be a good means of creating better conditions for combining motherhood with work, such a provision under the circumstances of competition for employment in the market system would undoubtedly have made a woman an unprofitable worker for any employer, and would have caused an increase in women's unemployment.

Another women's organization, the Liberal Women's Foundation, plans to participate in the political process and in law-making. It was created in February 1994 by such well-known women as Irina Khakamada, leader of the 12 December Alliance Deputies' group; former minister of social protection Ella Pamfilova; Galina Sidorova, political adviser to the Russian Federation minister of foreign affairs; public affairs writers Liudmila Saraskina and Evgeniia Al'bats; and others. The main purpose of the foundation was proclaimed to be 'to assist women in their professional undertakings in any field from the creation of their own businesses to involvement in politics'.[72] According to its creators, the main difference between the foundation and other women's groups is that it will not ask or expect the government to provide any help but intends to carry out projects on its own. The first independent act by the foundation was to disseminate in the news media advertising intended to promote a softening in people's behaviour.[73]

Unfortunately, not all projects can be carried out by women's organizations on their own, even by the Liberal Women's Foundation, without governmental and societal assistance. Although the President's Commission on Women, Family and Demography, together with the International Foundation for Safeguarding the Health of Mothers and Children, organized the Russian Federation Assembly on 'Protecting the Health of Mothers and Children' in January 1994, with discussions of the quantitative and qualitative parameters of the demographic crisis in Russia and how to combat it, they cannot change anything without a purposeful and organized policy and government funding. One example of a successful state demographic policy can be found, not in the distant past, but in 1982 when, after the adoption of measures aimed at an increase in the birth rate, for instance, granting mothers of babies younger than one year old a partially paid maternity leave, there was a considerable upsurge in the number of births. Unfortunately, no state policy on improving the demographic situation has been adopted since the end of the 1980s, when the birth rate started decreasing again, although some social protection measures have been introduced, for example from 1 February 1993, when the government increased allowances and payments to families with children.[74] However, these measures were inadequate.

One woman on her own, even at the highest level of power, cannot influence the co-ordination of social policy either, as in the case of Ella Pamfilova, former minister of social protection for the Russian Federation. She resigned from her post in February 1994 because, according to her, even as a minister she could not do anything for people who need social support because 'the functions of ministers have been reduced to the level of dispatchers' functions. All serious political decisions are made behind the scenes, by a narrow group of advisers close to the Prime Minister [Chernomyrdin].'[75] She complained that she was not even able to gain access to Chernomyrdin, and that journalists were instructed not to publicize her criticism of the situation in the state executive bodies.[76]

Under the pressure of women's organizations, on 4 March 1993 President Yel'tsin issued Decree No. 337, in which he outlined state policy on immediate objectives for women: the provision of conditions for women's real participation in the design and implementation of state policies; the creation of organizational, economic and legal guarantees for the realization of women's right to work; the establishment of women's competitiveness in the labour market; the gradual elimination of the historic lag in budget payments for fields in which mainly women are employed, and others. The decree ordered the Cabinet of Ministers to prepare proposals to include a programme for 'Russian women' in the list of the most important problems due to be worked out at the federal level in 1993. It also instructed the Cabinet to submit proposals based on the National Report on the Implementation in Russia of the Convention on Elimination of All Forms of Discrimination Against Women by 1 January 1994 for subsequent submission to the United Nations Organization, and recommended that the local executive bodies within the Russian Federation design and approve regional programmes for improving the position of women. The presidential decree established a Public Commission responsible for the problems of women, families and children attached to the president's staff, with the purpose of carrying out state policy in this respect. Control over implementation of the decree was placed with the chief of the president's administration.

However, a degree of scepticism is in order about the possibility of this decree, as well as many others, being carried out. It resembles a set of slogans, because it does not oblige anyone actually to do anything; it uses phrases such as 'to improve', 'to eliminate', without clarifying what concrete measures could be taken in order to carry out these proposals. No penalty is envisaged for those who do not follow the decree. In view of the situation in Russia, where people have become accustomed to ignoring laws and government decrees, this would be a very useful provision.

Even if people want to implement a government directive, in real life it is virtually impossible to do so because of a lack of means and facilities. Hence decrees naturally fall into oblivion. One of the numerous examples is a resolution 'On Urgent Measures to Improve the Situation of Women and the Family and the Protection of Mothers and Children in the Countryside', adopted by the Russian Federation Supreme Soviet in 1990. In spite of the proclamation and its various, very beneficial, norms for the improvement of women's life in the countryside, nothing changed. The shortage of mechanized equipment, fuel and lubricants obstructed and still obstructs the reduction of manual female labour – one of the main problems for women in the countryside. On the contrary, it is increasing, especially in livestock farming, in which women continue lifting and carrying multi-kilogramme milk cans and vegetable sacks.[77] This can irrevocably damage their health. By the beginning of 1994, the government had drawn up about thirty different programmes and decrees on the protection of mothers' and children's health, but all of them remain unimplemented because of a lack of funding and co-ordination.[78]

The president's decree 'On Measures of Social Support for Families with Many Children' is not effective either, because it does not envisage anybody being responsible for its implementation. One mother of a large family complained to a journalist from *Argumenty i fakty* in June 1993 that although the decree stipulates that the local authorities should give plots of land to large families, only a small fraction of the families finally get them. Banks justify their unwillingness to give loans at no interest to large families, as is stipulated in the decree, because of a lack of money, while at the same time giving loans to businessmen at 200 per cent interest. The decree allows large families to obtain medicines on prescription free of charge, but, as a rule, pharmacists say that they do not have the medicines, although they find them for those who pay.[79] It is possible to adduce many other examples of this kind of anecdotal evidence which gives the Russian people grounds to consider that in the nascent Russian market economy many directives concerning measures for protecting mothers and children are ineffective.

It is thus becoming obvious that it is virtually impossible to solve women's problems merely by issuing laws and decrees. The only means of changing the situation for the better seem to be the development and establishment of a legal mechanism ensuring the implementation of laws aimed at improving the situation of women,[80] and the creation of a strong material and financial base for their realization.

On the other hand, the state's demographic measures should be more thoroughly thought out before putting them into practice, not afterwards, to avoid the inevitable discrepancy between good intentions and bad consequences. Bureaucratic directives issued by the government in March 1994 to increase the birth rate and reduce abortions by removing most abortions from medical insurance coverage, thereby introducing fees on them, will undoubtedly have unforeseen consequences. Women are hardly likely to bear children because of abortion fees, but will instead opt for illegal abortions which are already the cause of death of many women. Nor is it likely that the quality of fee-paying operations will increase in comparison with free abortions. It is, moreover, immoral to force a woman to pay for her so-called 'pleasure' and simply for being a woman. The government could achieve its intention of decreasing the number of abortions by intensifying publicity about preventive methods of contraception and by investing in the pharmaceutical industry and health service. Another proof that by limiting the availability of free abortions it is impossible to force women to opt for giving birth is the fact that, although the quantity of abortions is already falling (in 1992 there were 3 million registered abortions, compared with only 2 million in 1993), the ratio of 3 to 1 between abortions and births remains the same.[81] It seems that women have started avoiding both childbirth and abortions and using contraceptives.

Although some people, such as Deputy Health Minister N. Vaganov, think that it is impossible to increase the birth rate by any means, others are convinced that it is possible. The demographer Viktor Perevedentsev, for example, suggests a number of measures in this respect: first, the introduction of home-purchase loans for newlyweds with a provision to write off certain parts of the loan after the birth of each child; secondly, the recasting of marriage and family law concerning the amount of maintenance for children on separation or divorce, with a view to increasing it. Perevedentsev considers that many women do not want to give birth to a second or third child because they are afraid that in the case of divorce they would suffer financial difficulties, because the existing norms for alimony which were adopted in the 1930s (the fixed amount of maintenance for one child is a quarter of the absent parent's income, a third for two children, a half for three, and so on) are out of date. Perevedentsev's third proposal is the state financing and protection of free crèches and kindergartens for children.[82]

In conclusion, I would argue that women's lives and the country's birth rate (they are naturally interconnected) could be improved considerably, depending upon how quickly Russia is able to overcome the profound crisis that has affected all areas of life, how quickly and successfully people will adapt to the unfamiliar conditions of the market economy and how effective the measures taken to provide the population, especially young families, with social protection will be. Hope lies with the young women's movement in post-communist Russia, which should be encouraged to become strong and unified in order to be able to explain to public opinion the very important role of women in society, and to demonstrate that a country can not be considered democratic if it ignores the problems of its women and children. It should influence Russian legislators to take women's specific problems into consideration, because the very existence and survival of a society depends upon their solution.

Notes

1 For further discussion, see Mary Buckley, 'Social Change and Social Policy', in Stephen White, Alex Pravda and Zvi Gitelman (eds.), *Developments in Soviet and Post-Soviet Politics*, second edn. (Basingstoke: Macmillan, 1992), p. 229; Gail Warshofsky Lapidus, *Women in Soviet Society: Equality, Development and Social Change* (Berkeley: University of California Press, 1978), p. 338.

2 See N. Zakharova, A. Posadskaia and N. Rimashevskaia, 'Kak my reshaem zhenskii vopros', *Kommunist,* no. 4 (1989), pp. 56–65.

3 Marina Pankova, 'Alevtina Fedulova: "Women Are People Too"', *Nezavisimaia gazeta,* 6 March 1993, p. 6; trans. in *Current Digest of the Post-Soviet Press* (hereafter *CDPSP*), vol. 45, no. 10 (1993), pp. 23–4. [Editor's note: For a more positive view of this article, see above, p. 13.]

4 Ibid.

5 Ibid. [Editor's note: The subsequent resignation of Ella Pamfilova, minister of social protection, in 1993 is discussed above, p. 279.]

6 Larisa Vasil'eva, 'Post-Congress Reflections on Women's Role in Society', *Pravda,* 24 June 1989, p. 3; trans. in *Current Digest of the Soviet Press* (hereafter *CDSP*), vol. 41, no. 25 (1989), pp. 33–4. [Editor's note: For a more positive view of this article, see above, p. 24, note 43.]

7 Ibid.

8 On other problems facing contemporary women, see Kathleen Mihalisko, 'Women Workers and Perestroika in Ukraine and Belorussia – a Problematic Relationship Unfolds', *Radio Free Europe/Radio Liberty Bulletin,* no. 14 (1989), p. 31.

9 T. Khudiakova, 'Women Are Leaving the Political Scene. Is This Compatible with Democratizing Public Life?', *Izvestiia,* 23 October 1991, p. 2; trans. in *CDSP,* vol. 43, no. 43 (1991), pp. 22–3.

10 Interview given to TASS by Tat'iana Zaslavskaia, 9 June 1988; cited in Annette Bohr, 'Resolving the Question of Equality for Soviet Women – Again', *Radio Free Europe/Radio Liberty Research Bulletin,* no. 14 (1989), p. 12. [Editor's note: Zaslavskaia is now director of the Institute of Public Opinion in Moscow.]

11 Aaron Trehub, 'Social and Economic Rights in the Soviet Union', *Survey,* vol. 29, no. 4 (127) (1987), pp. 24–8.

12 Andrei Baiduzhii, 'Demographic Catastrophe Has Become a Reality', *Nezavisimaia gazeta,* 2 February 1994, p. 1; trans. in *CDPSP,* vol. 46, no. 5 (1994), pp. 18–19.

13 Elena Ivanova, 'There Are More Women in Russia Than Men', *Rossiiskie vesti,* 7 July 1992, p. 3; trans. in *CDPSP,* vol. 44, no. 28 (1992), p. 22.

14 Boris Brui, 'While Politicians Argue, Russia Is Degenerating', *Nezavisimaia gazeta*, 23 September 1993, p. 6; trans. in *CDPSP*, vol. 45, no. 41 (1993), pp. 21, 32.
15 Elena Abashkina and Elena Semenova, 'Deti ne v mode?', *Argumenty i fakty*, no. 17 (April 1994), p. 13.
16 Lidiia Osheverova, 'Esli gosudarstvo ne pozabotitsia o sem´e, budet nekomu pozabotit´sia o gosudarstve', *Izvestiia*, 18 March 1992, p. 2.
17 Brui, 'While Politicians Argue', p. 21.
18 Mikhail Gorbachev, *Perestroika: New Thinking for Our Country and the World*, (London: Collins, 1987; New York: Harper and Row, 1987), p. 116.
19 Pankova, 'Alevtina Fedulova', pp. 23–4.
20 Andrei Demin, 'Foundations for Drop in Birthrate Were Laid Fifty Years Ago', *Izvestiia*, 22 April 1993, p. 4; trans. in *CDPSP*, vol. 45, no. 16 (1993), p. 26.
21 Brui, 'While Politicians Argue', p. 21.
22 Inna Voitko, 'Lord, How Tired I Am of Living!', *Pravda*, 23 October 1991, p. 2; trans. in *CDSP*, vol. 43, no. 43 (1991), p. 22; see also Ivanova, 'There Are More Women', p. 22.
23 Pankova, 'Alevtina Fedulova', pp. 23–4; Lidiia Ivchenko, 'A Quarter of a Million Russian Citizens Die of Unnatural Causes', *Izvestiia*, 3 March 1993, p. 4; trans. in *CDPSP*, vol. 45, no. 10 (1993), p. 23.
24 Brui, 'While Politicians Argue', p. 21.
25 Ibid.
26 Ibid.; see also Andrei Baiduzhii, 'The Demographic Situation in Russia is Getting Worse', *Nezavisimaia gazeta*, 26 January 1993, p. 1; trans. in *CDPSP*, vol. 45, no. 3 (1993), p. 29; Voitko, 'Lord, How Tired I Am of Living!', p. 22.
27 '148.4 million People Live in Russia. The Population Continues To Decline', *Nezavisimaia gazeta*, 5 May 1994, p. 6; trans. in *CDPSP*, vol. 46, no. 18 (1994), pp. 9–10.
28 Ibid.
29 Brui, 'While Politicians Argue', p. 21.
30 Ibid.; see also Viktor Perevedentsev, 'Nas v Rossii vse men´she', *Moskovskie novosti*, no. 25 (19–26 June 1994), p. 8.
31 Boris Stanishnev, 'Drama pod nazvaniem "Perepis´ naseleniia"', *Argumenty i fakty*, no. 27 (July 1994), p. 5.
32 Perevedentsev, 'Nas v Rossii', p. 8.
33 Demin, 'Foundations for Drop in Birthrate', p. 26.
34 Ibid.
35 Boris Sergeev, 'Is Russia Dying?', *Nezavisimaia gazeta*, 24 November 1993, p. 1; trans. in *CDPSP*, vol. 45, no. 47 (1993), pp. 17–18.
36 Azer Mursaliev, '"Staryi Svet" prodolzhaet staret´', *Moskovskie novosti*, no. 25 (19–26 June 1994), p. 9.
37 Ibid.
38 Sergeev, 'Is Russia Dying?', p.17.
39 Demin, 'Foundations for Drop in Birthrate', p. 26.
40 Ibid.
41 Ivchenko, 'Quarter of a Million Russian Citizens', p. 23; see also Baiduzhii, 'Demographic Catastrophe', pp. 18–19.
42 Elena Shafran, 'Expulsion of the Foetus', *Izvestiia*, 26 January 1994, p. 8; trans. in *CDPSP*, vol. 46, no. 4 (1994), pp. 23–4.

43 Ibid.
44 Liubov' Piatiletova, 'Motherhood Is a Dangerous Profession', *Pravda*, 3 September 1993, Moscow supplement, p. 3; trans. in *CDPSP*, vol. 45, no. 35 (1993), pp. 26–7.
45 Baiduzhii, 'Demographic Catastrophe', pp. 18–19.
46 Ibid.; Tat'iana Khudiakova, 'We Could Turn into a Country of Pensioners', *Izvestiia*, 2 February 1994, p. 3; trans. in *CDPSP*, vol. 46, no. 5 (1994), p. 19.
47 Baiduzhii, 'Demographic Situation', p. 29.
48 Brui, 'While Politicians Argue', p. 21.
49 Andrei Demin, 'Infant Mortality in the Russian Federation for the First Ten Months of 1992', *Izvestiia*, 11 January 1993, p. 2; trans. in *CDPSP*, vol. 45, no. 3 (1994), p. 29.
50 Nadezhda Efimova, 'Corpse with a Beating Heart', *Meditsinskaia gazeta*, 4 December 1992, p. 9; trans. in *CDPSP*, vol. 45, no. 3 (1993), p. 30.
51 Larisa Saenko, 'U vas ne rebenok, a vykidysh', *Moskovskie novosti*, no. 5 (31 January 1993), p. 12.
52 Baiduzhii, 'Demographic Situation', p. 29.
53 Piatiletova, 'Motherhood Is a Dangerous Profession', pp. 26–7.
54 Ibid.
55 Svetlana Tutorskaia, 'We Will Produce Subhumans', *Izvestiia*, 21 January 1993, p. 6; trans. in *CDPSP*, vol. 45, no. 3 (1993), p. 29; see also Efimova, 'Corpse with a Beating Heart', p. 30, and Saenko, 'U vas ne rebenok', p. 12.
56 Efimova, 'Corpse with a Beating Heart', p. 30.
57 Grunicheva, '*Kukushonok* ishchet gnezdo', *Moskovskie novosti*, no. 1 (2 January 1993), p. 3.
58 Voitko, 'Lord, How Tired I Am of Living!', p. 22.
59 Brui, 'While Politicians Argue', p. 21.
60 L. Grunicheva, 'Deti na eksport', *Argumenty i fakty*, no. 13 (April 1993), p. 8.
61 See Natal'ia Davydova, 'Kak vy tam v Amerike?', *Moskovskie novosti*, no. 51 (20 December 1992), p. 5; Ella Maksimova, 'Diana Who Can't Leave', *Izvestiia*, 4 March 1993, p. 5; trans. in *CDPSP*, vol. 45, no. 10 (1993), pp. 24–5.
62 Irina Volodina, 'Eto byl edinstvennyi shans', *Moskovskie novosti*, no. 51 (20 December 1992), p. 5.
63 Maksimova, 'Diana Who Can't Leave', pp. 24–5.
64 Davydova, 'Kak vy tam v Amerike?', p. 5.
65 Maksimova, 'Diana Who Can't Leave', pp. 24–5.
66 Cited in Mihalisko, 'Women Workers and Perestroika', p. 31.
67 Bohr, 'Resolving the Question of Equality', pp. 10–16.
68 For the new problems faced by women under perestroika, see Larisa Vasil'eva, 'Post-Congress Reflections', p. 33; for further discussion, see Mary Buckley, 'Introduction: Women and Perestroika', in Buckley (ed.), *Perestroika and Soviet Women* (Cambridge: Cambridge University Press, 1992), pp. 1–13.
69 Interview given to Radio Liberty by Ol'ga Lipovskaia, 22 March 1989; cited in Bohr, 'Resolving the Question of Equality for Soviet Women', p. 16.
70 Interview given by Elena Ershova to Natal'ia Kraminova, *Moskovskie novosti*, no. 5 (31 January 1993), pp. 10–11.
71 Ibid.
72 Gleb Cherkasov, 'New Challenge to Russian Traditions: Liberal Women's Foundation is Created', *Segodnia*, 15 February 1994, p. 2; trans. in *CDPSP*, vol. 46, no. 7 (1994), p. 17.

73 Ibid.
74 L. Iur'eva, 'Komu chto prichitaetsia', *Moskovskie novosti*, no. 11 (9 March 1993), p. 4.
75 Galina Valiuzhenich, 'Why Ella Pamfilova Resigned', *Argumenty i fakty*, no. 5 (February 1994), p. 3; 'Ella Pamfilova Really Is Leaving', *Izvestiia*, 17 February 1994, p. 1; trans. in *CDPSP*, vol. 46, no. 7 (1994), p. 18.
76 Valiuzhenich, 'Why Ella Pamfilova Resigned', p. 18.
77 Professor Vladimir Terekhov, 'Russia's Farm Women Can't Raise the Crops on Their Own', *Nezavisimaia gazeta*, 12 August 1993, pp. 1–2; trans. in *CDPSP*, vol. 45, no. 32 (1993), pp. 25–6.
78 Khudiakova, 'We Could Turn into a Country of Pensioners', p. 19.
79 V. Kurganova, 'Buket iz "tsvetov zhizni"', *Argumenty i fakty*, no. 23 (June 1993), p. 5.
80 Terekhov, 'Russia's Farm Women', pp. 25–6.
81 Sof'ia Shishkina, 'Kakie uzh deti zdes' i seichas?', *Moskovskie novosti*, no. 25 (19–26 June 1994), p. 8
82 Perevedentsev, 'Nas v Rossii', p. 8.

19

The Russian women's movement

Anastasiia Posadskaia, the Dubna Forum and the independent women's movement in Russia

ROSALIND MARSH

Anastasiia Posadskaia's speech at the Second Independent Women's Forum in Dubna in November 1992 should be seen in the context of her contribution to Russian feminist thought,[1] and of the significance of the Independent Women's Forum in the Russian women's movement as a whole.

The modern feminist movement in Russia began in 1979, when an unofficial journal, *Woman and Russia*, began to circulate in Leningrad, edited by Tat'iana Mamonova.[2] The dissident women discussed issues forbidden in the Soviet press at that time, and not even considered by dissident men: the discrepancy between articles of the constitution guaranteeing equality for women and the difficulty of realizing it in practice; discrimination against women in politics; the abuse of women in prisons; the appalling conditions in maternity hospitals, abortion clinics and child care centres; the increasing incidence of rape in Soviet society; and the brutal behaviour of men toward women in backward areas of rural Russia. The *Woman and Russia* anthology revealed that the women's movement consisted of two divergent strands, which are still represented in Russia today. At the end of 1979 a split occurred between Tat'iana Mamonova and Natal'ia Mal'tseva, who were liberal feminists on a western model, and some of their former associates, Tat'iana Goricheva, Iuliia Voznesenskaia and others, who espoused Russian Orthodoxy, and produced another *samizdat* journal, *Mariia*, which advanced more traditional values inspired by the ideal of the Virgin Mary.[3] For the 'Mariia' group, the roots of Russian feminism were spiritual, not political; but they also advocated a more civilized domestic life for women, discussing such subjects as the double workload of Soviet women – eight hours at work followed by five to six hours queueing for food; the horrors of communal kitchens; and the need to do the entire family wash in a hand basin. The limits of official tolerance for feminist writings in Brezhnev's time was demonstrated by the arrest of several leaders of the movement, some of whom (Mamonova, Goricheva and Voznesenskaia) were forced to emigrate in 1980. Subsequently, in 1982, the new leader of the 'Mariia' group Natal'ia Lazareva was arrested and imprisoned for 'anti-Soviet propaganda'.[4]

Contemporary Russian feminists do not acknowledge any particular debt to their precursors, although they are aware of their activities.[5]

When Gorbachev came to power in 1985, he took a more active interest in women's issues than any leader since Lenin, and it was hoped that women's lives would be made easier. Many commentators were very optimistic at the beginning of perestroika: the *Guardian* correspondent Martin Walker, for example, claimed in 1986: 'In material terms, as regards the quality of daily life, women stand to be the greatest beneficiaries of the Gorbachev reforms.'[6] The greater emphasis laid by Gorbachev on the consumer and services side of the economy, the measures introduced to strengthen the family, the turn toward 'socialism with a human face' – all seemed to point to the movement of Soviet society toward a world in which women's views were more central. However, the inception of glasnost initially led to no serious discussion of gender issues, while in the years 1987–9 the media regularly represented women, not as the victims of social evils in Russian society, but as their cause.[7] Social problems such as crime and drug-taking, not to mention the general spiritual malaise of Russian society, were frequently ascribed to family break-up and working women's neglect of their children. Thus when propaganda claims about the Soviet regime's 'emancipation' of women came to be challenged in the late 1980s, it was the validity of the goal itself which was called in question, rather than the illusory nature of Soviet-style 'emancipation'.

Despite his good intentions, Gorbachev's views on women proved to be reactionary, similar to those which had been voiced in Russia by political leaders since the mid-1970s. In his book *Perestroika* (1987) he made the now infamous statement about the need to return women to their 'purely womanly mission' involving 'housework, the upbringing of children and the creation of a good family atmosphere', which, he felt, had suffered on account of 'the sincere and politically justified desire to make women equal with men in everything'.[8] Gorbachev did, however, also advocate increasing political representation for women, although he regarded the main forum for women's political expression as the official women's councils (*zhensovety*).[9] During the perestroika period, the two opposing camps which had formed within the predominantly male Russian intelligentsia – 'democrats', who believed in western pluralism and the market economy, and 'patriots',[10] who advocated a return to traditional Orthodox values – were both agreed that women should be encouraged to devote more time to home and family.

In the Gorbachev era, women did not immediately respond to the opportunities of glasnost, perhaps because they were weighed down by their 'double burden' of work and domestic responsibilities, and because the prevailing ideology did not encourage them to participate in public life. However, by the late 1980s, because they had lost faith in the will of male politicians and media figures to consider their problems, unofficial women's organizations began to form spontaneously, attracting women from a variety of ethnic, social and professional backgrounds.[11] Feminism also began to revive among small intellectual circles in the main cities. In 1988, in Leningrad, Ol′ga Lipovskaia began to edit a *samizdat* feminist journal,

Zhenskoe chtenie (*Women's Reading*);[12] in Moscow, the economist Anastasiia Posadskaia, who was engaged in research into problems of women's employment, along with three women with a feminist background which she herself lacked[13] – Ol'ga Voronina, from the Moscow Institute of Philosophy, Valentina Konstantinova, a specialist on the women's movement in Britain, and Natal'ia Zakharova, an economist from the Institute of Mathematics – decided to form the 'Lotos' group ('League for Emancipation from Sexual Stereotypes'). Members of the group began to rise to public attention in 1988–9 for their articles analysing the patriarchal nature of Soviet society and advancing proposals to improve the social position of women.[14] A major breakthrough was achieved on Women's Day, 8 March 1989, with the publication of the article 'How We Solve the Woman Question' by Anastasiia Posadskaia, Natal'ia Zakharova and Natal'ia Rimashevskaia, director of the newly formed Academy of Sciences Institute for Socio-Economic Problems of the Population,[15] which advocated the replacement of patriarchal relations between men and women by a more egalitarian approach, based on a mutual complementarity of the sexes. The article aroused the interest of Maeva, head of the Women's Department of the Council of Ministers, who said that she was interested in co-operation.[16] Because of their article and their contacts with the Council of Ministers, and perhaps, due to the protection Rimashevskaia enjoyed from Gorbachev (they had been contemporaries and friends at the Moscow University Law School in the 1950s), Posadskaia, Zakharova and Rimashevskaia were asked to produce a position paper for the Council of Ministers. Toward the end of 1989, they took the opportunity to ask the government to support the establishment of a special Centre for Gender Studies within Rimashevskaia's institute. The Centre was set up in May 1990 with five researchers under the direction of Anastasiia Posadskaia.[17]

The year 1989 proved to be a watershed for the women's movement. When quotas for women's representation in parliament were partially lifted, thus halving the number of women elected to the USSR Congress of People's Deputies in March 1989, it was finally brought home to many Soviet women that the socialist state's alleged success in achieving equality of the sexes had been largely symbolic. Women at last realized that they could not depend on the state to act on their behalf, but would need to work for change on their own initiative.

By 1990, a great number of unofficial women's groups had emerged in the former USSR, which, notwithstanding their diversity, can be conveniently divided into four main categories.[18] The first consists of political groups, including women-only groups which formed within broader political movements during perestroika, such as Sajudis in Lithuania or Rukh in Ukraine; or independent political organizations, such as the United Party of Women established in Leningrad by Vera Kuril'chenko and the Women's Party of Sovereign Russia from Tomsk. In the post-communist period, the most influential example of this category is the 'Women of Russia' political movement. The second type is feminist groups devoted to consciousness-raising, which try to break down traditional gender-role stereotypes and to disseminate feminist literature. These include the Moscow

Gender Centre, the group associated with Ol'ga Lipovskaia (who in April 1993 established the St Petersburg Centre for Gender Problems), the Moscow club 'Transfiguration' (*Preobrazhenie*), the lesbian group within the Association for the Protection of Sexual Minorities, and an independent organization called 'Ariadna', which promotes gender research and conducts training programmes to help women in business, political leadership and other endeavours. The Liberal Women's Foundation, formed in 1994, belongs to this category, although it may also be able to wield some political influence. The third category comprises professional associations of women writers, film-makers, academics, workers in the defence industries, lawyers, teachers in secondary and higher education and support groups for those in business and management. The fourth and most numerous group is composed of grass-roots women's movements, particularly those associated with perceptions of women as mothers, which have protested against the infringement of their rights. The best known is the Committee of Soldiers' Mothers, which by June 1990 had formed an all-Union committee called 'Women's Heart'. There are also many groups in different geographical locations whose aim is to protect women and children under the new conditions of privatization and rising unemployment, societies to help refugee families fleeing ethnic unrest and associations of women with large families or sick children.

In March 1990, Ol'ga Lipovskaia and Natal'ia Filippova made the first open attempt to launch an independent women's movement in the USSR when they convened a meeting of representatives of many small women's groups, which in May 1990 formed an organization called SAFO (*Svobodnaia Assotsiatsiia Feministskikh Organizatsii* – the Free Association of Feminist Organizations), which provided support and psychological counselling for women.[19] In July 1990, the group associated with the Moscow Gender Studies Centre expanded when the Centre held an open seminar on 'Women in politics and policy for women'. Those who attended, including Ol'ga Lipovskaia and a number of women from the KamAZ truck factory in Naberezhnye Chelny, established a new organization, NeZhDI (*Nezavisimaia Zhenskaia Demokraticheskaia Initsiativa*, or the Independent Women's Democratic Initiative), an acronym which also means 'Don't Wait!'[20] This name reflected women's impatience with the slow pace of change under Gorbachev and their desire to organize themselves, to discuss the problems that concerned them and act positively to change their situation.[21] They produced a document outlining an interpretation of human nature that corresponded to western feminist ideas, contradicting essentialist Soviet ideas about the innate difference between men and women.[22] In January 1991 NeZhDI moved on to a wider political arena, openly expressing its opposition to Gorbachev's move to the right by issuing a document attacking the shootings in Lithuania and Latvia and calling for acts of civil disobedience. Yet although the women of the Centre demonstrated in favour of the people of Lithuania, and later in support of Yel'tsin during the attempted coup of August 1991,[23] its members were generally critical of the new democratic parties' lack of interest in women's rights.[24]

The most important venture undertaken by these women's groups was the First Independent Women's Forum, held in Dubna, north of Moscow, on 29–31 March 1991, which took as its slogan 'Democracy without women is not real democracy.' The significance of this Forum, which the KGB tried to prevent on the grounds that lesbianism was to be discussed,[25] was that it was the first independent women's conference in Russia since the All-Russian Women's Congress of 1908. It brought together 172 women from 48 organizations and 25 cities, and proved to be a great success.[26] The Forum achieved its principal aim, which was to raise the profile of the independent women's movement, demonstrating that women's organizations were no longer being set up on orders from above, but were being established on the initiative of women themselves. Lesbianism was only one of the many themes discussed, which also included 'Violence against women', 'Women in patriarchal culture', 'Women and the market economy', 'Problems of the independent women's movement' and 'Women in politics'.[27] There was an atmosphere of tolerance and companionship; women danced together and exchanged addresses and telephone numbers. The Final Document, drawn up by the participants, referred to the many forms of discrimination against women under Soviet socialism, both before and after perestroika. The main theoretical results of the conference were a definition of discrimination against women based on the United Nations Nairobi Declaration, partially ratified by the USSR in 1981, and a declaration of intent to co-operate and unite, independent of any parties or the official Soviet Women's Committee.[28] It is possible that the Forum may have exerted some influence on Gorbachev, who by 1991 was eager to increase his flagging support, since, ironically, the last draft reform programme of the Communist Party of the Soviet Union, published just before the attempted putsch of August 1991, actually contained some reform proposals of benefit to women. However, by that time it was irrelevant, as Soviet socialism had already been discredited.[29]

The Second Independent Women's Forum, held in Dubna from 27 to 29 November 1992, was a much more ambitious undertaking which attracted more than 500 participants, at least a hundred more than the organizers had expected.[30] The information network established at the First Forum had succeeded in spreading news of the conference all over the former USSR; delegates attended from as far away as Vladivostok, and from several countries of the CIS. More western women were also present than at the First Forum, notably from the United States, UK, the Netherlands, Germany, Scandinavia and Australia. The vitality of the grass-roots movement made it necessary to change the conference programme, as hundreds of women queued up to speak about the new organizations which they had formed.[31] The Forum enabled these different organizations to establish contact with each other, to learn how to obtain funding and make their work more effective, as many had encountered considerable difficulties in their dealings with bureaucracy. The Second Forum was a watershed in that it proved that a genuine and widespread 'women's movement' now existed in Russia and the post-Soviet states, consisting of many different strands and representing a variety of viewpoints, which have been usefully defined by Valentina Konstantinova as 'democratic, feminist, traditionalist reform, undemocratic and radical'.[32]

Anastasiia Posadskaia's introductory speech at the Second Forum is interesting, because it provides a concise, but penetrating analysis of Soviet women's history from the beginning to the end of Soviet rule and a clear statement of the problems facing women in the post-communist era, while at the same time establishing an ambitious agenda for the burgeoning women's movement. It is particularly notable for its clear-sighted rejection of the argument that women's problems will be automatically solved if political and social reforms are introduced. Her insight is extremely important, since this was the central myth which dominated seventy years of Soviet policy toward women, and is also largely accepted by democratic political parties and anti-feminist women in Russia today. Posadskaia's aim is to persuade the political authorities to treat problems of concern to women not as unimportant or as automatically soluble in the wake of social reforms, but as a vital and integral part of the reform process itself.

Another significant point is the emphasis Posadskaia lays on the failure of Soviet government policy toward women in both the 'socialist' period (1917–85)[33] and the perestroika period of Soviet history (April 1985 to December 1991). In a striking phrase, she argues that Soviet socialists attempted 'liberation of the female sex without liberation of the individual', whereas perestroika attempted the reverse, 'liberation of the individual without liberation of the female sex'. Implicitly in this speech, and more explicitly in her later writings, she suggests that the revival of feminism in Russia in the late 1980s cannot primarily be ascribed to women's angry reaction against the campaign to return them to the home, but to women's belated acknowledgement that neither 'real socialism' nor perestroika had brought them the vaunted 'emancipation' it claimed. In Posadskaia's view, the main aim of Russian feminism is to effect a synthesis of the two emancipations: emancipation of the individual *and* emancipation of the female sex.[34]

Posadskaia sets great store by the 'independence' of the women's movement, since, after decades of manipulation by a totalitarian political system, Russian women have no desire to be in thrall to any political party. She is very concerned that the Forum should not claim to speak in the name of all women, but to provide a public arena for any women's organization or any individual woman who wishes to express her own views. Some Russian feminists see only the positive aspect of this approach: Ol'ga Lipovskaia declared 'Let a thousand flowers bloom.'[35] However, my experience of the Second Women's Forum suggested that such tolerance and pluralism embody both the strength and the weakness of the independent women's movement. Although the desire to avoid enforced 'unification' from above is understandable after women's experience of manipulation by the Soviet regime,[36] it may be necessary for liberal Russian women to attain greater unity and solidarity before they can develop a cohesive movement which has an opportunity of wielding genuine influence in contemporary Russia.

Posadskaia's charismatic speech provided an excellent opening to the Forum, but the main work of the conference took place in the many workshops discussing a great variety of women's issues.[37] A heated session on 'Women in politics' discussed the problems experienced by women in first getting nominated, then elected and, after election, in promoting the causes they espoused; it was agreed that there was a need for more high-quality women candidates, more training to take part in politics, and a better strategy for getting women candidates elected. Western delegates shared their experience of working in family planning clinics, rape crisis centres and women's refuges; others contributed information on sex discrimination, equal pay legislation and practical advice to women farmers, and issued a warning against attempts to promote low-paid home work for women. At a fascinating session on 'Feminism and the problems of the women's movement', it became obvious that there was a huge gulf between ordinary Russian women who ask: 'What is feminism? What can it do for me?' and such sophisticated theorists as Tat'iana Klimenkova of the Moscow Institute of Philosophy, who employs concepts derived from Foucault, Lacan and other French feminist thinkers.[38] The experience of this session suggested that it will be a long time before western-style feminism takes hold in Russia, if indeed it is appropriate at all. Other important subjects discussed at the Forum included the fate of women caught up in ethnic and national conflicts; problems associated with women's work, education and unemployment; and the special problems of rural women, elderly women and those in defence industries converting from military to peacetime production. The most popular session was 'Women in business', which attracted over a hundred people, suggesting that many women have adapted to the new conditions of the market, or are eager to learn. Many Russian businesswomen do not want to fit into the patriarchal economic system, but acknowledge women's social responsibility at a time when the market is assuming barbaric, uncivilized forms. They recognize the urgent need for female employers to create jobs for other women and to offer help to the disabled and unemployed, although they admit that women are often hindered by the finance laws, and by bankers who discriminate against them.

All in all, the Second Forum of 1992 proved to be a chaotic, though exhilarating experience. Its slogan was 'From problems to strategy', suggesting that its main aim was to suggest specific methods of combating the many problems confronting women in the post-Soviet states. The summary document prepared by the Gender Studies Institute contained many concrete proposals addressed to the political authorities at all levels; but, unfortunately, few of these have yet been implemented. Perhaps because the Forum had grown too large for only a small group of women to organize, or because of the political crisis in October–November 1993 and the approach of the December elections, no Forum was held in 1993; although, according to Posadskaia, a third is planned.[39] In the wake of the Second Forum, a women's information network (ZhISET) was established; and the economic section held its first seminar in May 1993. The Independent Women's Forum has now emerged out of the two national conferences as an open, public women's organization.

In a statement issued by the Women's Forum at the beginning of the

December 1993 parliamentary election campaign, the accent was again placed on the movement's independence. Organizers of the Forum complained about the undemocratic haste with which the elections were being prepared, and the threat of violence against those who raised controversial issues, but felt it was essential to take part in the first parliamentary elections called under Yel'tsin's presidency. They did not support any particular party, but appealed to members to support women candidates from any party. However, the Forum refused to join the Russian Women's Union (the renamed Soviet Women's Committee which became part of the 'Women of Russia' electoral bloc) when directly approached by Ekaterina Lakhova, Yel'tsin's adviser on women and the family, although it was prepared to co-operate with them in order to support women candidates at the local level. The feminists who run the Forum are suspicious of the conservative views of the 'Women of Russia' movement and wary of being manipulated, as the Russian women's movement has been in the past.

In December 1993, Anastasiia Posadskaia herself, along with Ol'ga Lipovskaia, stood for election to the Duma for the Iavlinskii–Boldyrev–Lukin bloc, a democratic movement led by the economist Grigorii Iavlinskii, Gorbachev's adviser during the late perestroika period. However, no candidates from the Independent Women's Forum achieved election. It cannot be denied that the majority of Russian women feel closer to the more conservative views of the 'Women of Russia' movement than to the Independent Women's Forum.

Nevertheless, the Gender Centre and the Forum have continued to wield some influence outside parliament, helping to get the 1992 draft law 'For the Protection of the Family, Motherhood, Fatherhood and Children' dropped, and campaigning alongside 'Women of Russia' to prevent abortion becoming fee-paying.[40] Thanks to a grant from the German Fraueneinstiftung, the Centre now employs fifteen researchers and has an information centre with a database of women's organizations and a unique library of feminist writings, many donated by western sympathizers. In the four years of its existence, the Centre has undertaken a number of research projects, such as 'Woman and the market', 'Women and politics' (1991), an oral history project on 'What was it like to be a Soviet woman?' and 'Gender aspects of emigration from the former USSR' (1992). Researchers from the Centre have also prepared an alternative submission to the UN Commission for the Convention on the Elimination of All Forms of Discrimination Against Women, collected data on women's wages and set up business courses to teach entrepreneurial skills to women. Most recently, the Centre has been commissioned by Ekaterina Lakhova to produce a report on women's situation in Russia today.[41]

Posadskaia declared in 1991 that the Centre aims 'to do everything': to operate not only as a research unit, but also as a teaching, methodological and information centre.[42] On the academic side, its objective is to develop into a fully fledged Institute of the Russian Academy of Sciences. In the political sphere, members of the Centre are willing to give support to journalists prepared to speak out against sexism and discrimination against women in the media. In the future, it is possible that Posadskaia and other Russian feminists will co-operate with the Liberal

Women's Foundation, founded in 1994 by democratic deputies such as Ella Pamfilova and Irina Khakamada.[43] The next major event for which feminists from Russia and the other post-Soviet states are eagerly preparing is the United Nations Fourth Congress on Women to be held in Beijing in September 1995.[44]

Notes

1 For further information about Posadskaia, see the interviews with her in Elizabeth Waters, 'Finding a Voice: The Emergence of a Women's Movement', in Nanette Funk and Magda Mueller (eds.), *Gender Politics and Post-Communism: Reflections from Eastern Europe and the Former Soviet Union* (London and New York: Routledge, 1993), pp. 290–302; Anastasia Posadskaya, 'Self-Portrait of a Russian Feminist', in Posadskaya (ed.), *Women in Russia: A New Era in Russian Feminism* (London: Verso, 1994), pp. 183–201.

2 Tatyana Mamonova (ed.), *Women and Russia: Feminist Writings from the Soviet Union* (Oxford: Blackwell, 1984); for further discussion, see Alix Holt, 'The First Soviet Feminists', in Barbara Holland (ed.), *Soviet Sisterhood* (Bloomington: Indiana University Press, 1985), pp. 237–65; Iuliia Voznesenskaia, 'Zhenskoe dvizhenie v Rossii', *Posev*, no. 4 (1987), pp. 41–4.

3 On the divisions in the movement, see Holt, 'First Soviet Feminists', pp. 242–51; Voznesenskaia, 'Zhenskoe dvizhenie', pp. 41–4; Rochelle Ruthchild, 'Sisterhood and Socialism: The Soviet Feminist Movement', *Frontiers: A Journal of Women's Studies*, vol. 7, no. 2 (1983), pp. 4–12.

4 *Mariia: Maria Journal du Club féministe Maria, Leningrad* (Paris, 1981). For the constant torture by cold and hunger which Lazareva was subjected to in a punishment cell, see Irina Ratushinskaya, *Grey is the Colour of Hope*, trans. by Alyona Kojevnikov (London: Hodder and Stoughton, 1988).

5 They are not mentioned, for example, in Anastasiia Posadskaia's account of the history of the independent women's movement, 'Women as the Objects and Motive Force of Change in Our Time', in Posadskaya, *Women in Russia*, pp. 8–13. Ol'ga Voronina, 'The Mythology of Women's Emancipation in the USSR as the Foundation for a Policy of Discrimination', in ibid., p. 55, note 1, refers to the 'marked eclecticism of feminist and patriarchal views' in the *Woman and Russia* anthology. Those who had emigrated lost influence in their homeland: for example, a message of support from Tat'iana Mamonova read out in English at the Second Dubna Forum in 1992 was not particularly well received.

6 Martin Walker, *The Waking Giant: The Soviet Union under Gorbachev* (London: Michael Joseph, 1986), p. 186.

7 For a notorious example of this approach, see Karem Rash, 'Vsekh tsarstv dorozhe', *Pravda*, 22 February 1989, p. 3, who argues that 'A woman at work means the disintegration of the family and a low birth rate.' Posadskaya, 'Self-Portrait of a Russian Feminist', p. 193, relates that a long article she gave *Moscow News* in 1989 on the media's distorted approach was cut, except for a fleeting reference to 'men's liberation'. Elizabeth Waters, '"Cuckoo-Mothers" and "Apparatchiks": Glasnost and Children's Homes', in Mary Buckley (ed.), *Perestroika and Soviet Women* (Cambridge: Cambridge University Press, 1992), pp. 123–41, suggests that by 1989–90 censure of single mothers who had left their babies in children's homes had given way to criticism of the

government and the 'system' for allowing women to live in poverty instead of creating the prerequisites for a decent family life.

8   Mikhail Gorbachev, *Perestroika: New Thinking for Our Country and the World* (London: Collins, 1987; New York: Harper and Row, 1987), pp. 116–18; see above, p. 237. On the more positive aspects of Gorbachev's policy, see Mary Buckley, *Women and Ideology in the Soviet Union* (Hemel Hempstead: Harvester Wheatsheaf, 1989; Ann Arbor: University of Michigan, 1989), pp. 196–200.

9   For further discussion of the women's councils in the 1980s, see Buckley, *Women and Ideology*, pp. 209–17; Genia Browning, 'The Zhensovety Revisited', in Mary Buckley, *Perestroika and Soviet Women*, pp. 97–117.

10   These terms are used by V. Toporov, 'Dnevnik "Literatora"', *Literator* (Leningrad), no. 21 (May 1991), p. 7.

11   For fuller discussion, see Mary Buckley, 'Gender and Reform', in Catherine Merridale and Chris Ward (eds.), *Perestroika: The Historical Perspective* (London and New York: Edward Arnold, 1991), pp. 70–80; Ol'ga Lipovskaia, 'New Women's Organizations', in Buckley, *Perestroika and Soviet Women*, pp. 72–81; Solomea Pavlychko, 'Between Feminism and Nationalism: New Women's Groups in the Ukraine', in ibid., pp. 82–96; Valentina Konstantinova, 'The Women's Movement in the USSR: A Myth or a Real Challenge?', in Annie Phizacklea, Shirin Rai and Hilary Pilkington (eds.), *Women in the Face of Change: The Soviet Union, Eastern Europe and China* (London: Routledge, 1992), pp. 200–17. The best sources of contemporary information about women's groups in the former USSR are the newsletter *Women East–West*, edited since 1987 by Mary Zirin, and the journal *Women's Discussion Club: Women's Movement in the Ex-USSR*, edited by Nina Beliaeva, and published by Interlegal USA, New York.

12   For more information, see Rosalind Marsh, 'Olga Lipovskaya and Women's Issues in Russia', *Rusistika*, no. 5 (June 1992), pp. 16–21; Susan Hardy Aiken and Adele Barker, 'Afterword: Histories and Fictions', in Aiken, Barker et al., *Dialogues/Dialogi: Literary and Cultural Exchanges Between (Ex) Soviet and American Women* (Durham, N.C. and London: Duke University Press), pp. 359 and 384, note 6. On the plans of the Petersburg Centre for Gender Issues to relaunch *Zhenskoe chtenie* in 1994 as an open publication, see Olga Lipovskaia, 'Petersburg Center for Gender Issues', *Women East–West*, 31 (January 1994), p. 9.

13   Posadskaya, 'Self-Portrait of a Russian Feminist', p. 190, states that two of her colleagues in 'Lotos' (presumably Konstantinova and Voronina) had written their theses on western feminism, but, as was common in the pre-glasnost era, had been obliged to write '"critiques" of ideas they actually found very appealing'.

14   See, for example, Ol'ga Voronina, 'Muzhchiny sozdali mir dlia sebia', *Sovetskaia zhenshchina*, no. 11 (1988), pp. 14–15; Voronina, 'Zhenshchina v "muzhskom obshchestve"', *Sotsiologicheskie issledovaniia*, no. 2 (1988), pp. 104–10.

15   Rimashevskaia was one of only two female directors of a Moscow research institute in 1988 (the other was the well-known Tat'iana Zaslavskaia, head of the Russian Centre for Public Opinion Polls, which was partly associated with the trade unions). For Rimashevskaia's isolated position and the prejudice she encountered from male academics, see Posadskaya, 'Self-Portrait of a Russian Feminist'; Rimashevskaia, 'The New Women's Studies', in Buckley, *Perestroika and Soviet Women*, pp. 120–1.

16   Natal'ia Zakharova, Anastasiia Posadskaia and Natal'ia Rimashevskaia, 'Kak my reshaem zhenskii vopros', *Kommunist*, no. 4 (1989), pp. 56–65; for further information,

see Waters, 'Finding a Voice', p. 289; Posadskaia, 'Self-Portrait of a Russian Feminist', p. 191; see also Marsh above, p. 10.

17   Waters, 'Finding a Voice', pp. 289–90; Posadskaya, 'Self-Portrait of a Russian Feminist', pp. 191–2; Rimashevskaia, 'New Women's Studies', pp. 121–2.

18   This analysis to some extent follows the divisions proposed by Mary Buckley, 'Political Reform', in Buckley, *Perestroika and Soviet Women*, pp. 62–6.

19   *Guardian*, 19 March 1990; Lipovskaia, 'New Women's Organizations', pp. 77–8; Valentina Konstantinova, 'No Longer Totalitarianism, But Not Yet Democracy: The Emergence of an Independent Women's Movement in Russia', in Posadskaya, *Women in Russia*, pp. 57–73.

20   For further information on NeZhDI, see 'Women in Action, Country by Country: The Soviet Union', *Feminist Review*, no. 39 (1991), pp. 127–32.

21   Posadskaya, 'Introduction', p. 1.

22   For an English translation of this document, see 'Feminist Manifesto', *Feminist Review*, no. 39 (1991), pp. 127–32.

23   Posadskaya, 'Introduction', pp. 1–2.

24   Marsh, 'Olga Lipovskaya', p. 18; Posadskaya, 'Introduction', p. 3.

25   Marsh, 'Olga Lipovskaya', p. 19.

26   Interview with Ol'ga Lipovskaia, March 1991.

27   For a report on the conference, see Cynthia Cockburn, 'Democracy Without Women Is No Democracy', *Feminist Review*, no. 39 (1991), pp. 141–8.

28   See the 'Concluding Document of the First Independent Women's Forum, Dubna, 29–31 March 1991', *Women East–West* (September 1991), p. 17.

29   Posadskaya, 'Introduction', p. 3; but for a critique of this programme, see Posadskaya, 'Women as the Objects and Motive Force of Change', p. 12. It is to be hoped that this Communist Party document will not be seen with hindsight as analogous to the Provisional Government's ill-fated declaration giving women the vote in 1917.

30   Anastasiia Posadskaia, personal letter, February 1993. The full proceedings of the Forum are published in Olga de Haan-de Vogel, Gien Tuender-de Haan and Anne van de Zande (eds.), *From Problems to Strategy: Materials of the Second Women's Forum, Dubna, 27–29 November 1992* (Hilversum, Netherlands: Ariadne Europe Fund, 1993).

31   Some new women's organizations represented at the Forum are mentioned in Rosalind Marsh, '"From Problems to Strategy"? Impressions of the Second Independent Women's Forum in Dubna', *Rusistika*, no. 7 (June 1993), p. 17. For a full list of participants, see Lidiia Skoptsova et al. (eds.), *Directory of Participants: Second Independent Women's Forum, Dubna, Russia, 1992* (Hilversum, Netherlands: Ariadne Europe Fund, 1993).

32   Konstantinova, 'No Longer Totalitarianism', p. 65.

33   Posadskaia uses this term to denote '*real* socialism', the regime that actually existed in the USSR in the years 1917–85: see Posadskaya, 'A Feminist Critique of Policy', p. 164.

34   Posadskaya, 'A Feminist Critique of Policy', p. 169.

35   Ol'ga Lipovskaia, personal conversation, Dubna, 1992.

36   For a sympathetic western attitude to this approach, see Kate Clark, 'Translator's Preface', in Posadskaya, *Women in Russia*, p. xi.

37   See the document produced by the organizers of the Forum: 'II Nezavisimyi Zhenskii Forum: "Ot problem k strategii", g. Dubna, 27–29 noiabria 1992 goda: materialy Orgkomiteta II Nezavisimogo Zhenskogo Foruma' (Moscow: Tsentr gendernykh

issledovanii Instituta sotsial'no-ekonomicheskikh problem narodonaseleniia Rossiiskoi Akademii Nauk, 1992). For highly personal accounts of the Second Forum, see Marsh, '"From Problems to Strategy"?', pp. 16–19; and the articles by Ulana Trylowsky and Diane Farrell under the rubric 'The Second Independent Women's Forum in Dubna, November 27–29, 1992: From Problems to Strategy', *Women East–West*, no. 26 (January 1993), pp. 6–10.

38 For an example of her style, see Tat'iana Klimenkova, 'What Does Our New Democracy Offer Society?', in Posadskaya, *Women in Russia*, pp. 14–36.

39 Posadskaya, 'Introduction', p. 7.

40 See above, pp. 278, 281.

41 Waters, 'Finding a Voice', pp. 291–2, 300; Posadskaya, 'Self-Portrait of a Russian Feminist', p. 192.

42 Waters, 'Finding a Voice', p. 290. Several paperback volumes of essays by scholars from the Gender Centre have been published, notably Ol'ga Voronina, *Feminizm: perspektivy sotsial'nogo znaniia* (Moscow, 1992); Z. A. Khotkina (ed.), *Zhenshchina i sotsial'naia politika (gendernyi aspekt)* (Moscow, 1992); and N. M. Rimashevskaia (ed.), *Zhenshchina v meniaiushchemsia mire* (Moscow: Nauka, 1992).

43 See Sargeant, pp. 278–9.

44 I am grateful to Nijole White for information that women's groups in Lithuania and Latvia are already engaged in preparations for this event.

The feminine dimension of social reform: from one Forum to the next

ANASTASIIA POSADSKAIA

(Co-chair of the Organizing Committee of the Second Independent Women's Forum)
Introductory speech on behalf of the Organizing Committee of the Second Independent Women's Forum, Dubna, November, 1992

I have the great honour of saying a few words to the participants of the Second Independent Women's Forum in Dubna.

At the First Forum, which took place in Dubna from 29 to 31 March 1991, it was most important for us to see that an independent women's voice existed in the country, that women's organizations and initiatives were emerging which were spontaneous, not created by a decision 'from above', and to understand that 'Democracy without women is not real democracy.' In the Final Document of the Forum, its participants established that various forms of discrimination against women had existed, both in the period of state socialism and during perestroika.

The slogan of the present Forum is 'From problems to strategy'. Our emphasis is on the need for concrete actions, the formulation of resolutions which will allow us to change the situation, to alter policy and public awareness so that women's problems will be regarded not as secondary problems which will automatically be solved after the situation as a whole has been transformed, but as an essential, integral and extremely important component of the general process of social reform.

When we emphasize the need to develop strategies, we have in mind strategies at many different levels: at the level of state policy – and today we have invited representatives of state power and members of Parliament – at the level of individual regions and towns, different branches and sectors of the economy, and at the level of enterprises, institutions and local organs of power. And the most important thing is that we should leave this Forum feeling stronger as individuals, conscious that we ourselves and our own problems are part of the global female community, which has a right to its own voice in the period of the construction of the new world order.

It is often asserted that there is no women's movement in our country. I think that this is probably a result of ignorance, for which we ourselves must first and foremost bear the responsibility. There are a great number and variety of women's organizations (and today we have the opportunity of confirming this) which, however, know very little about each other, and which few people know anything about. Therefore the main task of the women's movement, in my opinion, is to become socially visible. In this connection, the work of the Women's Information Network (ZhISET) is only the first step. But this is mainly an exchange of information *within* the movement. The main thing is to transform the range of social information available about women and their position. This objective must be achieved on several planes.

- It is necessary to secure regular publication of nationwide information about the position of women in the press, which will enable social monitoring to take place.
- It is necessary for similar information to be collected by local government authorities and to be made available to local women's organizations.
- It is necessary to support those organs of mass information and those journalists, both male and female, who oppose discrimination against women, including sexism in the mass media.

We appeal to society to fulfil these objectives. But, now that we have gathered at the Forum, we can and must learn more about ourselves. As a result of the past Forum, a Women's Information Network (ZhISET) has been created, and many of you have regularly received the journal *You and Us* (*Vy i my*), produced by our American friends on the 'Women's Dialogue' programme.[1] However, it is abundantly clear that the mere dissemination of information from some centre is a totally inadequate means of ensuring the proper functioning of the network. The network must live. In order to achieve this, it is imperative to develop a model for its effective operation: to establish a procedure for joining and financing the network, its basic rules, a method of renewing it periodically, a means of providing information to non-members of the network, and so on. It is essential for us at the Forum to take a definite organizational decision on all this.

Second, it is vital to achieve regular publication of the collection *Who's Who in the Women's Movement*. We need not only information about organizations, but information about *individuals*. How did each of us become aware of women's problems, and what does it mean for us to be in the women's movement, to be concerned with women's issues? I think this personal aspect is very important.

Third, we need regular publication of the collection *Women's Organizations in Russia*, which should include all grass-roots women's groups, initiatives, educational programmes and publications. It is vital that this should be not merely a list of statutory regulations which appear to have been copied, but information about concrete actions, programmes and problems. The Centre for Gender Studies has already established a method of producing a collection of this kind, and we need to continue this work at the Forum.

Fourth, the papers, arguments and information about the situation of women in various towns or regions which you have brought to the Forum, as well as the process of discussing the problems proposed in the sections, afford unique material, since this is a rare occasion when women *themselves* are speaking about their own and general social problems, and are *themselves* suggesting ways of solving them. On the basis of all this material, an Alternative National Report on the situation of women will be prepared, which will be a form of public monitoring of the social status of women.

The accomplishment of all these projects may mark the beginning of a transformation in the amount of information available about women and their situation. It will be good if we at the Forum manage to prepare the ground for their implementation.

When we were planning the Forum, we were often asked if it had any political orientation. I think that today, when not a single political party or group has a fully fledged, workable programme for improving the social status of women, when women are in practice excluded from the process of political decision-making at all levels of power, when illusions about the *automatic* improvement of the social position of women in the periods of socialism, perestroika and post-perestroika have been shattered, it would be a mistake to be associated with any particular political force. Women must learn how to make use of the existing political structures to achieve the aims of their social programme. It is unfortunately true that the many years when women's public activity was politically manipulated have engendered among women an aversion for politics, which they do not regard as a worthwhile sphere for their endeavours. But we must acknowledge that a radical change in the macro-social situation is impossible unless we do enter the political structures. The problem is how to overcome both this internal barrier and the external barrier of the stereotyping of women as unsuitable candidates for a political career. The question of how, when we have entered the political structures, we can change them, is quite a different matter; how we can turn them into a forum for solving social problems and not for achieving personal or political ambitions. We need to create a new type of political culture and political activist, to create an ethically integrated policy which will be implemented by people who are concerned not with acquiring and retaining power at any price, but with solving social problems. The situation at present is such that we cannot even speak of an ethically integrated policy. We can see how dubious methods of political struggle are used not only by representatives of opposing groups, but also by politicians on the same side. We did not write the rules of the political game, but we must realize that, unless they are revised, no real change can be expected simply by increasing the representation of women in the power structures. This conclusion is graphically illustrated by the example of the socialist period, when women were allocated 'from above' up to one-third of the seats in the national parliament, yet power remained repressive and totalitarian. This does not mean that we should not look at our problems *from a political viewpoint*. We are not *outside* politics, we are outside *that kind* of politics.

We are often asked why we call our Forum 'independent' – independent of what, and of whom? After all, a monopoly by one political party no longer exists; the entire situation has changed since the First Forum was held. We think that the word *independence* as applied to the women's movement in our country (and, perhaps, in other post-totalitarian countries too) is the key to an understanding of its essence. After decades in which they were puppets, politically manipulated and totally integrated into the totalitarian state system, women have decided to organize themselves, to discuss problems that concern them, to inform society that they can *see* discrimination against women and *understand* its consequences, and are prepared to *act* to change this situation. At the same time, and this is particularly important, the independent women's movement does not attempt to speak in the name of *all* women, does not abrogate to itself the authority of an all-Russian women's organization, but presents an open forum for any women's organization and any woman who seeks *her own* answer to 'the woman question'.

We are also asked to whom we are addressing our concern about the position of women: the government, Parliament, the political parties or men in general? Perhaps my answer may appear banal, but first and foremost we are addressing ourselves, for without a change in our own consciousness and the acknowledgement that *our problems are not simply women's problems, but social and political problems*, we will not attain the level on which they can be resolved: the level of social action.

Today, as at the First Forum, members of the western women's movement are present. Their experience is important for us, since they began their struggle significantly earlier, in a period when in our country structures of women's and other social groupings organized from above were dominant, and there was no question of their having an independent voice. The women's movement in the West over the last twenty-five years has been able to overturn or cast doubt on many conventional social stereotypes relating to the position of women in society. One of these is that 'women's' problems can automatically be resolved after the necessary economic and social conditions have been created in society. In our view, the experience of the western women's movement demonstrates that only an independent strategy formulated by women themselves and not *for them* can really change the position of women in society, and thus humanize society itself. Otherwise there will only be a movement from one form of patriarchy – a society based on the subordinate, secondary position of women – to another. However, it is not, and cannot be simply a matter of copying other people's experience, but rather of realizing that without a knowledge of the history of the worldwide women's movement, including the history of the pre-revolutionary women's movement, we cannot devise our own contemporary strategy.

There is one more question which I think we need to discuss at the Forum – the question of feminism and its prospects in our country. Over many years a negative, stereotyped attitude toward feminism became established in our country. I think that this was a result of the prolonged isolation of our country from world culture, as a result of which many women say 'I am not a feminist', without having any idea of what feminism is. At the same time, feminism is one of the achievements of civilization which, at the very least, people should know about, before rejecting it. That is why it is very important to discuss issues relating to the future of feminism in Russia and other countries of the former USSR, and its links with the women's movement.

If we turn to our own country, then we can already review the experience of solving the 'woman question' not only in the period of 'real socialism', but also in the period of perestroika and the post-perestroika reforms.

At the First Forum we said that socialism had not brought any true emancipation to women and men, that patriarchal gender relations had been reproduced at the level of society as a whole. This was mainly a result of the conceptual flaws in socialism's emancipation programme (the attempt to liberate the female sex without the liberation of the individual, the attempt to emancipate women without emancipating men, the lack of any idea of creating equal opportunities in the social sphere). However, the need for women's emancipation was an integral part of that social programme.

What has happened in our country in the course of the last six and a half years has led to a radical transformation in the economic, political and cultural values of its national populations. The political transformation of the one–party totalitarian system, as it passed through the stage of glasnost, has led to the formation of a multi–party system and an embryonic civil society. At the same time it has become blindingly obvious that the democratization of society has proved to be a *male project*, in which woman has been allotted, in an overt or covert form, the role of object, not subject of social reform. This finds expression in the following tendencies:

- in politics, the ousting of women from the structures of legislative and executive power;
- in the economy, greater discrimination against women in payment for work, in hiring, firing and promotion; the feminization of poverty; an increase in job segregation;
- in the cultural sphere, on the one hand, an intensification of propaganda promoting patriarchal relations between the sexes – the so–called ideology of women's 'natural destiny' – and, on the other hand, the mass exploitation of sexuality based on the commercialization of the female body.

All this enables us to draw the conclusion that:

- perestroika, a programme intended to increase the sphere of individual freedom (a movement toward political and economic pluralism), in the sphere of *gender relations* represented a *period of post-socialist patriarchal renaissance* – which, incidentally, is also typical of *all* the former socialist countries; and
- the attempt to liberate the individual *without the liberation of the female sex* is just as futile as the socialist programme of liberating the female sex without the liberation of the individual.

Today the situation is beginning to change. We can see political parties and movements gradually 'waking up'; it has become fashionable to have a woman spokesperson, a women's section or a women's programme. Unfortunately, in a country without any tradition of an independent women's movement, this 'fashion' may lead to the substitution of one type of political exploitation of women for another. We must be aware of this danger, and not allow any party or move-ment to form its policy and win our votes by manipulating women's problems to its own political advantage. Only a political structure which *actually* includes women in the decision-making process *in practice* can count on women's support in return.

The dream of the organizers of the Forum is to turn it into an annual meeting of old and new women's organizations, so that it can become a real resource for the burgeoning women's movement. Every day new women's organizations, groups and projects are springing up. Many of them have the sad experience of searching for like-minded people, of applying in vain to bureaucratic bodies who, in the main, want nothing to do with them. I would very much like the Forum to give these organizations the opportunity of an annual open platform; it should exist for them, not they for it. Within the Forum specific subsections can be established: a political and economic section, sections for the discussion of issues arising from the conversion of defence industries to peace-time production, sections for women writers and so on, which will gather for their own meetings and co-ordinate with the large annual Forum. Will we succeed in putting this idea into practice? After all, we are all very different. Yet I think that an acknowledgement of the *reality of this diversity* possesses a no less general democratic significance than the acknowl-edgement that we can have strategies in common, developed in the course of the intersection between our diverse individual experiences and our collective experience.

In conclusion, I should like once again to emphasize the important questions to which, among many others, this Forum will seek answers:

> Why is over half of Russia's population not taking an active part in Russia's opportunity for democracy?

> Does the independent women's movement have any chance of success in the Russia of today?

> What changes are there in policy on women and the institutions responsible for its implementation?

> How is contemporary society's image of women changing?

> What does privatization mean for women?

> Who is the 'new woman' nowadays: unemployed or entrepreneur; guardian of the domestic hearth or 'call-girl', short-lived object of the affections of the new Russian businessman; young 'model' or domestic servant in the homes of the nascent middle class?

> What opposition can women offer to the policy of using violence to resolve national conflicts? What is the position of women refugees?

> Is there any feminine dimension to the army reforms and the conversion of industries to peacetime production?

What prospects are there for young women, and what remains to be done by those who have already lived most of their lives?

What organization can we establish in opposition to the harsh hierarchical structures?

Our Forum is an attempt to answer these questions.

Note

1 Editor's note: *Vy i my* is a Russian-language newspaper for women published under the auspices of the National Council for Research on Women, intended for both Soviet and American women. It contains information on such subjects as the development of the US women's movement, health care, reproductive rights, the family, education and the acquisition of organizational, managerial and communication skills.

20

Feminism in post-communist Ukrainian society

SOLOMEA PAVLYCHKO

Feminism emerged in Ukraine in the 1880s, as an ideology, an organized women's movement and a mature feminist cultural tradition. This is a well-known fact of Ukrainian intellectual history. However, in 1900, some fifteen years later, Lesia Ukrainka, a woman who became a national cult figure during her lifetime, made an interesting remark. Analysing the work of Ol'ha Kobylianska, the author of two feminist novels, she argued that Kobylianska lost interest in feminism in her later work because 'the actual concept of women's equality did not need theoretical proof'.[1]

In other words, for Lesia Ukrainka, as for the majority of *fin de siècle* Ukrainian intellectuals, especially those from western Ukraine (at that time part of the Austro-Hungarian Empire), feminist theory was an integral part of the programme of the progressive democratic movement. (Ukrainian intellectuals of that period were primarily concerned with another question: the conflict between populism and 'art for art's sake'.) That did not mean that the ideas of John Stuart Mill, Henrik Ibsen or their Ukrainian proponents such as Natal'ia Kobrynska and Ol'ha Kobylianska were acceptable to the philistine provincial middle class, not to mention the backward, uneducated rural community. However, for the main-stream of the intelligentsia, the idea of women's equality was accepted as conventional wisdom.

Today a comparatively narrow circle of the intellectual and cultural élite with its traditionally numerous component of women writers, scholars, scientists and artists is more or less familiar with feminist ideas, whether of the western European, eastern European or indigenous varieties. The rest of society, from the over-whelmingly male political leadership to the mixed strata of so-called intelligentsia (such as teachers, medical workers, engineers and office workers), and the predominantly female class of underpaid workers (such as road builders and dairymaids on collective farms), does not have the faintest idea about the long and dramatic history of feminist ideology in this or any other part of the world.

Thus, if a piece on feminism occasionally appears in a journal or a newspaper, it is often polemical in style and followed by a question mark. The sociologist Ol'ha Ivashchenko, for example, entitles her article in the popular Ukrainian journal

Ukraina: 'Do We Need Feminism?' She is sure that we do need it, but she is also sure that she is provoking a discussion, and she addresses its opponents, not its supporters.[2] Moreover, the general title of this journal column is 'To be or not to be', which further emphasizes the controversial nature of the issue.

Ukraine (like most of the former Soviet colonies) missed the twentieth century in a very profound sense. Feminism provides a poignant example of this. Arguments which did not require theoretical proof a hundred years ago have to be elaborated once again. Moreover, those same arguments are passionately rejected, not by uneducated people, but by educated individuals with high official status in society – very frequently by women and quite frequently by former dissidents and political prisoners who sacrificed their own freedom for the liberties of today.

Conscious anti-feminism and subconscious sexism can easily be explained by the lack of democratic traditions, the underdevelopment of civil society and the low political culture of contemporary Ukrainian society. That society is usually characterized as post-colonial, post-communist and post-totalitarian. Some analysts would like to add two more epithets to this list – post-industrial and postmodern – even though the first three 'posts' are just catchwords. Complex and contradictory social processes which often have no analogies even in neighbouring countries with a more or less similar past cannot be reduced to scholastic definitions.

It is evident that after the collapse of communism and the Soviet empire, an ideological and cultural void has appeared which has to be filled with some new content. A society of great social contrasts and political and ideological eclecticism, in the throes of a terrible economic crisis, painfully seeks new ideas in two spheres: its historical past, which until recently was banned; and, of course, the West, which is subject to no less of a ban.

During the last seventy years, the notion of women's emancipation formed part of a highly unpopular socialist or communist totalitarian ideology, which was, moreover, of foreign (Russian) origin. Such ideas as the communist feminism of Aleksandra Kollontai, female emancipation and equality of the sexes were totally discredited by their Soviet practice, even though this equality existed only on paper. Feminism and emancipation are now political dirty words.

While a new (non-Soviet) attitude toward women is being formed in Ukraine, patriarchal mythology of all kinds is being revitalized in the course of the so-called national revival. At the same time, there is an invasion of mass culture from the West: Barbie dolls, mediocre video films and beauty contests, all with their well-known gender stereotypes. These two utopias, local and imported, these two neighbouring worlds, do not intersect, although they have similar double standards and a similar misogynistic message.

Since December 1991 the USSR has been dead and Ukraine has existed as an independent state, but 'Soviet reality' and '*Homo Sovieticus*'[3] are still alive. A civil society cannot develop overnight. People break their habits and superstitions only with great difficulty; and at least two-thirds of those in positions of authority are former communists and members of the *nomenklatura*. Communism has formally been overthrown, the power of the Communist Party and the KGB has been abolished, the pristine confines of censorship no longer exist and the Moscow centre no longer rules Ukraine. But there are numerous reminders of Soviet rule, such as efforts to breathe new life into the Communist Party or Komsomol, demands that the private ownership of land should never be permitted, monuments to Lenin, and the position of women.

Totalitarianism is still alive in the system of social prohibitions and restrictions, in political behaviour and certain cultural stereotypes. Our internal passport with its *propyska*, which authorizes an individual's movements from one place to another, is a most vicious totalitarian device, and so is the exit visa (permission from the official authorities to leave your own country). Totalitarianism is alive in the thinking and phraseology of certain political leaders ('We are not going to let foreigners criticize our country'), totalitarianism is alive in official cultural policy ('We won't let anybody criticize our classics') and even in the cult of the mother.

Totalitarianism implied not only the dictatorship of the party and a profound social stratification of society, but also the reduction of the citizenry to an 'atomized . . . and structureless mass':[4] a gigantic labour force; a mob of isolated, heterogeneous, but uniformly loyal individuals; a mob which is a fertile medium for totalitarian consciousness presumably has no gender.

But a bread queue can easily turn into a mob. Queues in food shops – a typical phenomenon of Soviet and post-Soviet existence – consist predominantly of women, angry, brutal, disillusioned and frustrated women who long for the pre-perestroika past of cheap prices for sausage, and are prepared to rush and storm the Parliament, the Cabinet of Ministers or any body which may be responsible for their misery. These queues could easily be ignited into a mob by the slogans of any demagogic ideology, communism included. It is therefore not surprising that the co-chair of the newly formed Ukrainian Communist Party is a woman.

Despite all the political changes in the official understanding of the role of women, nothing has changed. New governments adopt new programmes with familiar titles. The one adopted in 1992 was called 'A Long-Term Programme for the Improvement of the Position of Women, the Family, the Protection of Motherhood and Childhood'. The government's policy can be clearly understood from the title: women's problems are motherhood, child care, home and family. The same interpretation is borne out by the name of the Parliamentary Commission for Women's Problems, the Protection of the Family, Motherhood and Childhood in the Ukrainian Parliament of 1990–4. The new Ukrainian Parliament elected in March 1994 abolished the Commission altogether, provoking considerable criticism from women. Official decrees of the government or Parliament dealing with women are rarely regarded as socially important documents. And if they attract any comment at all (which happens quite rarely), they are usually criticized by angry women, mainly because their rights as mothers are not sufficiently protected, and only occasionally from a more or less feminist viewpoint.

The official celebration of International Women's Day on 8 March has turned into an annual anti-feminist ritual. Women are praised for their good looks and fine female qualities. In actual fact this is the most important male holiday, when women annually reassert themselves as passive, submissive creatures, eager to accept male domination and power.

In 1990 I wrote about the first women's organizations which emerged in opposition to the Ukrainian Soviet regime and the Ukrainian communist *zhensovet* [Women's Council].[5] Now the latter has a new title – the Council of Ukrainian Women (*Spilka Zhinok Ukrainy*) – and a new programme, but is still under the old leadership. It was the only women's organization greeted by President Leonid Kravchuk on the occasion of its Congress.

Radical changes have occurred since that time. Ukraine became an independent state in 1991.[6] The Women's Community of Rukh (*Zhinocha Hromada Rukhu*) and the Union of Ukrainian Women (*Soiuz Ukrainok*) – the most active in the national movement of 1990–1 – remain the largest women's organizations. The Women's Community split from Rukh and now operates independently. The Committee of Soldiers' Mothers, established in September 1990, remains the most serious political force in Ukrainian society.[7] Each of Ukraine's three ministers of defence, appointed from 1991 to 1994, began their job by consulting the leadership of this organization.

There are some new women's groups. Two worth mentioning are 'Lybid', the Ukrainian International Charitable Women's Organization, which has a narrow, but important objective: to help women establish their own businesses; and the Ukrainian Christian Women's Party from L'viv headed by Ol'ha Horyn. While 'Lybid' is a non-political club for businesswomen, the Women's Party is strongly political. The objectives of its programme are very close to those of the Union of Ukrainian Women and the Women's Community. Ukraine's independence, state-building, protection of the Ukrainian language and support for national schools are far more important for the party than either traditional or feminist women's issues.

The Women's Party was established in L'viv in July 1992 and remains a regional organization. Its main aim is to rouse women from political and social passivity, to make them active participants in political events in Ukraine in this crucial period of their nation's history. The Party's Programme is quite eclectic. It demands 'real equality for women, their participation in political life and state administration',[8] and its first major event was a conference held in L'viv in November 1992 on 'The role of women in nation-building'. At the same time, the Programme is typical of every national-democratic women's group in regarding women first as mothers, then as citizens, and in demanding the protection of women in their traditional role. In actual fact, however, women become conscious citizens when they *are* concerned mothers. On the one hand, the Party promotes Christian values as a moral foundation for its activities; on the other, it is open to women of all religious denominations.

A special paragraph of the Programme is devoted to ecological issues. In its concern for the environment, the Women's Party is close to the Green Party. Its goals are to fight against society's ignorance of ecological matters, to restructure environmentally dangerous enterprises, to monitor the construction of new enterprises with a view to their ecological safety, to conserve and gradually close down all nuclear power stations, to assert permanent control over ecological issues and to establish the responsibility of individual officials for the conscious or subconscious violation of ecological norms. The Women's Party is trying to become a pressure group influencing central and local government on ecological issues, as the Committee of Soldiers' Mothers has become in relation to military issues.

In June 1994, on the eve of the presidential elections in Ukraine, President Kravchuk met the leaders and representatives of twenty-three women's organizations. He was indirectly asking women – the majority of the country – to support him in his campaign, which he lost a couple of days later.[9] However, even if the activists of these twenty-three organizations had been united in their desire to support one of the candidates, they would not have been able to do so. Most of them have a small membership; their printed materials, if published, have a very low circulation; and they are isolated from the majority of women, who are under great stress from the general economic crisis and their traditional double burden, and threatened by unemployment and poverty. Besides, Ukrainian women's organizations are very isolated from each other. Attempts to unite all women's organizations in an umbrella organization collapsed because of their political differences. The Council of Ukrainian Women regards itself as the co-ordinating body for other women's organizations. However, it mostly attracts politically neutral groups, such as the Association of Mothers with Many Children or women's charitable groups. The organizations with a strong political agenda remain independent. In the course of the parliamentary election campaign of 1994, their political polarization became even more visible and irreconcilable. On the one hand, there are the 'old' women's groups which emerged in the course of perestroika and subsequently in the period of national revival and state-building; on the other, groups of the new communist wave, such as 'Women of Crimea' (*Zhenshchiny Kryma*), with its anti-Ukrainian and communist orientation. They emerged on to the political stage in the course of the elections to the parliament and regional legislatures.

The groups of the national-democratic wing have their own disagreements. In 1994, the two largest women's groups, whose orientation is more political than feminist, Women's Community and the Union of Ukrainian Women, separately celebrated the centenary of the first feminist organization in Ukraine, the Union of Ruthenian Women in Stanislaviv, established in 1884 in Galicia.

The women's organizations which emerged in 1990 as part of the Ukrainian movement for secession from the USSR are now in crisis. This is partly the same crisis experienced by the whole democratic movement, which has to rethink its agenda in the period of state-building. However, women's organizations also have to re-articulate their agendas on political, social and gender issues.

Patriarchal values and attitudes have not yet been challenged by the Ukrainian women's movement. Moreover, the programmes of Ukrainian political parties do not mention women's concerns and problems other than the protection of mothers and children.[10] New women's voices, or women's voices in general, are not heard in politics. The March 1994 parliamentary elections brought only thirteen women to the highest state legislative body, most of them members or supporters of the left, communist and socialist factions. In the meantime, the political influence of women and women's organizations remains quite small. They predominantly consist of women in their forties or older. The younger generation is still silent.

But rethinking of the agenda is inevitable, and it has started, if only slowly. The organizations with a national orientation, Women's Community, the Union of Ukrainian Women and the Ukrainian Christian Women's Party, all stress their concern for state-building. The 1992 conference of the Ukrainian Christian Women's Party and the 1993 conferences of Women's Community and the Union of Ukrainian Women had as their respective themes 'The role of women in nation-building', 'Women and state-building' and 'Women and democracy'. So, like it or not, they are taking subconscious steps toward a feminist understanding of the role of women in the new Ukraine. On the other hand, Atena Pashko, the head of the Union of Ukrainian Women, tends to regard western feminism as something totally inapplicable to Ukrainian conditions. She has stated: 'We cannot copy any models of western women's organizations. We have to create our own model.'[11] The fact that three separate conferences were held on a near-identical theme is characteristic of the current state of the women's movement in Ukraine.

Only Women's Community managed to publish papers from its conference.[12] This publication reflected the old, familiar contradiction between feminism and nationalism. Half of the papers were devoted to all aspects of the national 'revival' – schools, culture, language, spirituality and religion. Some of them had nothing to do with women at all, but about half had quite a strong feminist orientation. More-over, feminism as an ideology or critical approach is emerging in Ukraine outside women's organizations. The word itself is mentioned more often in newspapers, the mass media and academic discourse than in the discourse of women's groups. Two examples will illustrate this. In June 1993 the Institute of Sociology of the Academy of Sciences of Ukraine organized a conference on 'The young family in a troubled social environment', at which some issues were discussed from a feminist perspective. In 1994 the journal *Ukraina* published extracts from Simone de Beauvoir's *The Second Sex*, the full text of which was released by Osnovy Publishers at the end of 1994. This was the first major publication in Ukrainian of the classical western feminist text. Along with the papers from the conference of Women's Community, *Women in State-Building*, it marked one more step toward the establishment of a fully fledged women's studies.[13] However, the path to women's studies as an academic discipline looks long and difficult. The first serious journal for women, *Piata pora* (*The Fifth Season*), which offered, instead of cookery recipes or embroidery tips, analysis of the situation of women in economics, the social environment, art, history and politics, attracted the best-known Ukrainian women writers and scholars, but went bankrupt after the publication of two issues in 1993.

While I am a fervent supporter of Ukrainian independence, I cannot help but note that the so-called national revival is a revival of masculine culture. One of its aspects is a kind of new mythology which has been produced and developed by some writers and pseudo-scholars of a populist persuasion. The central image of this mythology is a woman, usually called *Berehynia*, the Hearth-mother, who is either a Ukrainian pagan goddess or a stalwart peasant. She is the perfect Ukrainian woman, the spirit of the Ukrainian home, the ideal mother, who played an important role in national history, the preserver of language and national identity. This fantasy of Ukrainian matriarchy, which allegedly existed in some prehistoric past, has been developed in a novel by the formerly dissident author Vasyl' Ruban with the same eloquent title, *Berehynia*,[14] a somewhat ridiculous attempt to build a 150,000-year-old matriarchal Ukrainian myth.

By restructuring and idealizing this patriarchal myth, which centres on the universal woman – warrior, mother, worker, artist and artisan – Ukrainian culture is responding in part to the culture shock of post-totalitarian freedom which has destroyed all former taboos.

Pornography and the sex trade, the first fruits of western freedom, have been accompanied by a new wave of Russification. Ukrainian book production is experiencing its greatest crisis period of the twentieth century, because paper is not manufactured in the country. However, street bookstalls are full of third-rate books, usually translated from English into Russian and published abroad in Russia, Belarus, Moldova or at home, by numerous co-operatives. Meanwhile, the middle-class fantasies of American and Latin American soap operas are widely propagated by Ostankino, the Russian-language television channel.

There are two typical responses to these foreign innovations. The first is to fence the national culture off from low-grade foreign influences, to isolate it and develop genuine national values: Ukrainian music, Ukrainian poetry and Ukrainian folk culture. Unfortunately, national mythologies or past utopias, including the matriarchal utopia, primarily demonstrate the insecurity or inferiority complexes on the part of both men and women, and have little chance of winning the competition with aggressive newcomers.

The second response is to assimilate so-called western 'freedoms' and imitate so-called western 'cultural values'. Thus we now have Ukrainian pornography, Ukrainian beauty pageants and mail-order brides, providing a brutal response to those idealists who claim that such things can occur anywhere but in Ukraine. No group in the wide political spectrum, no intellectuals or leaders of the women's movement feel brave or qualified enough to marshal any resistance to the new mass culture of either type.

Of course, a Ukrainian woman as the perfect incarnation of virtue or of traditional Ukrainian feminine spirituality exists only in the dreams of male nationalist ideologues. Real life leaves little room for utopias.

The time of radical economic reform in Ukraine is still somewhere in the future;[15] economic crisis in Ukraine is the unpleasant reality. The majority of the population lives below the poverty line. Mass unemployment is imminent;

women are likely to be, and already are, the first to become unemployed. This is typical of all the former Soviet states. The 'feminization of poverty' is society's most immediate prospect. And women, according to Halyna Lytvynova, editor-in-chief of the newspaper for women *Ia, ty, my* (*I, You, We*), have already become 'the majority who are discriminated against'.[16] Women's organizations and society as a whole will soon face this problem.

In view of the current discussion on market reform, it will be useful to provide a brief discussion of this issue. The business class and the private sector of the economy is a relatively new phenomenon in Ukraine. And, of course, in this new milieu, which is half-opposition, half-underground and yet democratic, women have attained certain positions which they are unable to achieve in traditional spheres of society. The emerging business class has some peculiar gender distinctions, certain exclusively male and female groups.

Former speculators and black-market dealers, owners of trading co-operatives, commercial shops, street 'kiosks' and casinos, and unofficial currency-changers probably constitute its most visible part. This colourful crowd of young men has its own modes of behaviour, body language and fashions. Another group also consists of men, but older men with the solemn style of the former *nomenklatura*. These are the directors of big enterprises, communist bosses of all kinds who understood the slogans of *perestroika* in their own way, and rushed into business, preserving good contacts within the bureaucracy and developing a mutual support network.

Women have some specialities of their own. At the lower level, there are *babushkas* in food markets: sellers of meat and groceries, who have outlived all political regimes. Another overwhelmingly female group of younger, urban 'tourists' to Europe who are brutal in manner also operate at the lower level of the private sector. With the advent of perestroika, thousands of tourists of this type rushed to Polish, and later Turkish markets with weird goods: from nails to primitive wooden souvenirs, cigarettes and vodka. Cheap goods bought in Europe are sold by the same people at flea-markets, which for some time have been the most frequently visited places in Ukrainian towns.

In such a paradoxical country as post-communist Ukraine, women do nearly all the accounting work in savings banks and enterprises at all levels. Wherever you turn in Kiev, you can see an advertisement for a bank or a stock market, and you would be surprised to learn how many women work there. The reason is simple. In the very recent past, universities and institutes gave diplomas to so-called 'economists'. This qualification embraced a multitude of different skills: from an expert in the political economy of socialism to a *tovaroved*, a person responsible for the inventory in a warehouse, most of them women and most of them seriously underpaid.

In banks, old and new, state and commercial, there are a large number of women on the staff, and even on the boards of directors. One interesting develop-ment is that departments of short-term credit, capital construction or personnel are mainly female, while newly formed departments, which reflect recent economic trends such as factoring transactions, securities and investments or futures trading, consist mainly of younger men.

You can meet women at the highest level of Ukrainian business. Lidiia Pokrasion, for example, is the director and owner of the Ometa Business Kiev insurance company, which prepares documents and insurance policies for newly formed small businesses in Kiev and its vicinity. The company is flourishing, and, naturally, Mrs Pokrasion is often asked to share the secrets of her business success. In one of her interviews she announced that femininity is the most important feature of the modern woman, including the businesswoman, as if trying to mislead all the men who rule society, to prove to them that she is not threatening their power, or even to gain some advantage from the fact of being a woman. This statement is typical of a successful woman in a patriarchal country without any articulated feminist social agenda.

However, women are increasingly contemplating independent careers in the professions, politics and business. Ukrainian women are ready to work hard and take responsibility. In the very near future they will undoubtedly play a greater role in the Ukrainian economy.

In the West, it is fashionable to refer to a backlash against feminism and the casualties of the women's movement.[17] New types of misogyny require new responses from feminist writers and theorists. The backlash against feminism in the West is sometimes mentioned even in our part of the world to demonstrate the negative consequences of the whole movement.

In Ukraine we are experiencing an even greater backlash. Women's views are not represented, their needs are not met, their problems are not addressed, their rights are not implemented. In the very near future, it is imperative that women should voice their opposition to a society ruled by old men in dark suits and grey ties, to their mythology and misogyny. Otherwise, a democratic civil society in Ukraine will remain an impossible dream.

Notes

1 Lesia Ukrainka, *Tvory v 12-ty tomakh*, vol. 8 (Kiev, 1977), p. 69. [Editor's note: Lesia Ukrainka (pseudonym of Liaryssa Kosach, 1871–1913) was a writer of prose and drama who was actively engaged in the Ukrainian struggle for national autonomy. The writer Ol'ha Kobylianska (1863–1942) in her novels, *Tsarivna* (*The Princess*, 1895) and *V nediliu rano zillaia kopala* (*She Gathered Herbs on Sunday Morning*, 1909), depicted women who strove for education and enlightenment, and wished to become independent members of society.]

2 Ol'ha Ivashchenko, 'Chy potriben nam feminizm?', *Ukraina*, no. 9 (1994), pp. 2–3. [Editor's note: For further discussion of this article, see Rubchak below, p. 325.]

3 Editor's note: This term is taken from a book by the former Russian dissident Aleksandr Zinov'ev, *Homo Sovieticus*, trans. by Charles Janson (London: Victor Gollancz, 1985).

4 Hannah Arendt, *The Origins of Totalitarianism*, revised edn. (London: Allen and Unwin, 1967), p. 318.

5 Solomea Pavlychko, 'Between Feminism and Nationalism: New Women's Groups in Ukraine', in Mary Buckley (ed.), *Perestroika and Soviet Women* (Cambridge: Cambridge University Press, 1992), pp. 72–96.

6 For further information, see Bohdan Krawchenko, 'Ukraine: The Politics of Independence', in Ian Bremmer and Ray Taras (eds.), *Nation and Politics in the Soviet Successor States* (Cambridge: Cambridge University Press, 1993), pp. 75–98.

7 Bohdan Piskyr, 'Materi dlia bat'kivshchyny Ukrains'ka derzhavnist', materynstvo ta natsional'na bezpeka', *Suchasnist*, no. 6 (1994), pp. 70–82.

8 *Prohrama i statut Ukrains'koi khrystyians'koi partii zhinok* (L'viv, 1992), p. 4.

9 Editor's note: There is no evidence that the new Ukrainian president elected in 1994, Kuchma, holds less conservative views than Kravchuk on the position of women.

10 For details, see Lidiia Kononenko, 'Zhinotstvo v politychnykh partiiakh Ukrainy', in *Zhinka v derzhavotvorenni. Materialy mizhnarodnoi naukovoi konferentsii (Kiev, 29–30 travnia 1993 roku)* (Kiev, 1993).

11 Atena Pashko, 'Druhe krylo – zhinotstvo', *Ukrainka*, no. 1 (1992). See also below, p. 324.

12 *Zhinka v derzhavotvorenni.*

13 For a less positive view, see Rubchak below, p. 325.

14 Vasyl' Ruban, *Berehynia* (Kiev: Ukrains'kyj pysmennyk, 1992).

15 Editor's note: This process appears to have begun in October 1994, with President Kuchma's new radical reform programme.

16 Halyna Lytvynova, 'Torishnii buket. Tochka zoru na deiaki "dribnytsi" derzhavnoi polityky shchodo zhinok', *Holos Ukrainy*, 27 February 1993.

17 Susan Faludi, *Backlash: The Undeclared War Against Women* (London: Vintage, 1992) and the review of this book by Pamela Wells, *The Times Literary Supplement*, 19 June 1992.

21

Christian virgin or pagan goddess: feminism versus the eternally feminine in Ukraine

MARIAN J. RUBCHAK

As a newly independent post-colonial society strips away layer upon layer of accumulated colonial baggage, it begins to rediscover its historical memory and reconstruct its identity. The process starts with the repudiation of the pseudo-myths of identity, and the false perceptions which have been imposed upon it by the former colonizing centre. In post-emancipation Ukraine people are striving to reclaim their lost heritage – their cultural, linguistic and spiritual traditions – by reviving the national myths and ancient rituals in which their social values are seen to be encoded. They have made the restoration and revitalization of their historical traditions a conscious programme as a way of authenticating their collective being.

In any newly emerging state such a resurrection of tradition invariably accompanies the recovery of the traditional woman. 'One of the first things that new nation states do', writes Akhil Gupta, 'is write the history of the "nation". . . stretching into the distant past', where 'women are generally recognized only in their role as producer of citizens and are thus precariously positioned as subjects of the nation'.[1]

Contemporary Ukrainians perceive many of the values and symbols being resurrected as authentic representations of an ancient matrifocal, indeed matriar-chal, Ukrainian culture. During the process of recovering the memory of their archaic society, the Ukrainians stress their 'matriarchal heritage'.[2] Ancient symbols and values are projected on to a new, culturally determined female stereotype. They are used as the basis for recreating a 'metanarrative' of the woman's natural domain (which, of course, is not natural at all, but socially constructed). By doing so, however, Ukrainians create a new pseudo-myth of identity, and forestall the development of an authentic feminist consciousness. Such a recreated 'meta-narrative' encourages women to view their proper contribution to society not as equal partners in a contemporary age, but rather as women whose roles are enshrined in what is today regarded as the 'traditional', and therefore presumably genuinely Ukrainian symbolic structure and central cultural values.

We therefore proceed from the assumption that in the past Ukrainian women lived in a society in which the sexes had complementary roles of roughly equal value, that they enjoyed 'equality in difference', so to say.[3] Thus women could be certain that their 'natural' female roles were highly regarded, and that their equality in difference vouchsafed them respect and prestige. This status stemmed from a condition that characterizes many agricultural societies, which tend to be organized along egalitarian lines. In such societies 'women have traditionally played socially recognized and valued economic and social roles. The latter were viewed as being parallel to those of the men, and a meaningful place was thus created for each sex.'[4] Women in ancient Ukraine took pride in their equal (although not identical) status. Within marriage they were not looked upon as inferior beings, but instead enjoyed full and equal partnership with the men.[5] This is no longer the general rule, however, because former cultural values do not apply. Yet, inasmuch as the master narrative refers to these ancient values as embodiments of the Ukrainian women's authentic identity – not only as women, but also as Ukrainians – they have been incorporated into the ideology of the liberation of Ukraine from its colonial cultural dependency.

What does such a recovery mean for the contemporary Ukrainian woman? To begin with, Ukraine is no longer an agricultural society, therefore the old agriculturally based values have lost their viability. And the former complementarity of gender roles in Ukraine – the basis of the 'separate but equal' relations between women and men – began to erode in eastern Ukraine when it passed to Russian control in the middle of the seventeenth century. This turn of events introduced an entirely new set of values to much of Ukrainian culture. Although the difference in function remained as before, this difference no longer connoted equality. As a newly-imposed patriarchal culture penetrated eastern Ukrainian society, the position of its women deteriorated accordingly. This process spread throughout Ukraine during the Soviet era, when all of Ukraine ultimately came under the cultural influence of the Russian-dominated centre.

In newly independent Ukraine the concept of a 'God-given' or 'natural' predisposition to motherhood and domesticity endures as before, but iconographic depictions of Ukrainian motherhood have been recoded away from the recent Soviet matrix, and have increased in intensity with their incorporation into the nationalist discourse. Seemingly Ukraine's quest for a legitimate, well-defined national identity cannot be separated from woman's traditional role as mother and nurturer; these are the attributes that characterize the quintessential Ukrainian female, and embody her authentic being in that society. Moreover, the same qualities that traditionally conveyed so much esteem in the private life of Ukrainian women now flow easily into the public realm, where they no longer carry the same value. Regardless of the sphere of their public activities, however, women still define themselves primarily in traditional terms. Here is an interesting example from everyday Ukrainian political life: during the recent elections to the city council in Kiev (1994) a successful female candidate distributed her campaign leaflet, which emphasized her qualifications for office as 'a woman, mother and citizen of Ukraine'. Only then were her professional credentials presented, an impressive list that included physicist and mathematician. To my knowledge not one of the sixty-nine male deputies advertised any but his professional achievements.[6] Moreover, once they begin to play a public role, no matter how impressive, Ukrainian women themselves move into a public agenda that allegedly corresponds to their so-called 'natural' (read 'feminine') inclinations. This, in its turn, has the effect of 'feminizing' their public undertakings, and as such significantly altering the value of such efforts.

Because Ukrainian women subscribe to the newly recreated metanarrative, they insist upon the application of an old system of values to what they perceive as their natural maternal and domestic obligations. A variety of cultural overlays, however, has diminished the traditional prestige attached to such obligations, notwithstanding the fact that the metanarrative continues to extol their virtues. The very fact that women are as likely as men to reject the need for any change in prevailing attitudes toward women in Ukraine illustrates the widespread hostility to the very concept of an authentic feminist consciousness in Ukraine. In their support of cultural regeneration, Ukrainian women today continue to uphold the division of labour 'along sexual lines . . . as fundamental principles' of their womanhood,[7] and thereby willingly perpetuate their own inferior status.

Throughout this essay a number of questions will be posed. How is the national revival in Ukraine affecting both the private and the public roles of its women? Is there any potential for reconciling the national struggle for cultural independence and the development of a genuine feminist consciousness? As the Ukrainian people struggle to transform themselves into a fully sovereign nation, what sort of prospects exist for equal female participation in public life within that context?[8] And finally, in a post-colonial society such as Ukraine, is it even possible to challenge freely the patterns of exploitation, or will women's own historically shaped perception of themselves as women inevitably get in the way?[9] To put the last question another way, in an attempt to reconstitute their idealized traditions, are Ukrainian women themselves destined to promote a romanticized (even mythologized) vision of their status in society, which would stand in the way of challenging the current forces of opposition to their emancipation?

Numerous Ukrainian intellectuals have argued (and the opinion appears to be widespread among the general populace as well) that the urgency of state-building compels the Ukrainian people to subordinate such movements as women's liberation to the task of constructing a fully modern, fully independent country. Oksana Sapeliak, president of the Ukrainian Association of Women in L'viv, put it quite succinctly when, in 1990, she declared that before she and her Association sisters start liberating women, they must first liberate the nation.[10] Indeed, such ordering of priorities has a well-established tradition in Ukraine – one which goes back a hundred years or more. In her discussion of Ukrainian women in the Austro-Hungarian Empire in the late nineteenth century, Martha Bohachevsky-Chomiak reminds us that in general 'women's liberation was less important than national emancipation'.[11] More illustrative still is her reference to the fact that 'patriotism became an important theme of all [women's] organizations. The stress [was] on family, self-sacrifice, and the importance of defending national tradition'.[12] This same sentiment was echoed more recently, during a joint congress of the Union of Ukrainian Women and the World Federation of Ukrainian Women's Organizations, which took place in Kiev in August 1993. A resolution was passed which calls for Ukrainian women to save their nation by revitalizing its moral spirit. They are enjoined to resurrect the finest of the Ukrainian traditions to aid them in their great mission.[13]

Ukrainian independence was finally achieved in 1991, but the task of state-building has scarcely begun. Insofar as the national struggle for liberation is a continuing, and (in theory) never-ending process, to say that society will address the problem of women's liberation after the nation itself has achieved de facto sovereignty is to postpone all feminist issues indefinitely. Moreover, because one struggle does not exclude the other, the temporal sequence of the two processes is in fact artificially established. Under the circumstances, one is tempted to speculate that the postponement itself is in reality an unconscious excuse for avoiding an issue that is highly problematic in Ukrainian culture. By incessantly insisting that cultural regeneration, with all it entails, is their first priority, Ukrainian women are exerting themselves to perpetuate their own traditional roles, while at the same time accepting their contemporary public roles as a parallel set of obligations.

When analysing the position in which contemporary Ukrainian women find themselves, it is important to understand that, as Michelle Rosaldo reminds us in a different context, 'woman's place in human social life is not in any direct sense a product of the things she does, or even less a function of what, biologically, she is. It is, rather, the meaning her activities have acquired through concrete social interactions.'[14] Various anthropologists have pointed out that all 'notions of "motherhood" and "domesticity" are historical and ideological rather than "natural" constructs'.[15] In Ukraine, the symbol of motherhood and the connection between women and the hearth (often the burial site of clan or family members in Ukraine, underlying the metaphor of generational continuity) have remained in the foreground of the Ukrainian consciousness as presumably a biologically driven phenomenon, which has nothing whatever to do with social constructs. This is so much the case, in fact, that the entire idea of renewing the nation, or building a young state – with its concomitant revival of ancient customs – has paradoxically been perceived by society as inseparable from the implicit reversal (in effect the 'antiquation') of the role of its women, as a way of getting back to the essence of what it means to be Ukrainian. Thus a direct connection is established between restrictions of female activity – such as holding high public office, for example – and the process of state-building.

A striking example of the extremes to which attitudes by and toward women can be taken in contemporary Ukraine is offered in an article by Kateryna Motrych, which was prominently featured in the monthly magazine *Zhinka* (*Woman*)[16] in January of 1992. Entitled 'To you, the women who stand next to the cradle of the nation, my message', the article is strategically positioned below a photograph of President Kravchuk, hand on heart, and looking like a benevolent *pater familias*. Its references to woman as the nation's mother, protecting it at the cost of her own personal concerns, aptly encapsulates (although the article itself, notwithstanding its sincere intent, borders upon parody) many of the prevailing attitudes and the 'feminine discourse' in Ukraine today. The author writes:

> The Ukrainian woman has a responsible mission (she is perhaps the only woman in the world, emancipated from her very inception, who never waged a battle for equal rights with her husband, but always fought instead for the equal rights and liberty of Ukraine. . .). Like the Blessed Virgin, the Ukrainian woman must give birth to the Ukrainian Saviour . . . And it is up to us all to create the conditions within which she can once again be herself, the *Berehynia* [pagan goddess-protectress] of the nation. In a free and democratic Ukraine, the first thing that we must do is to liberate women from heavy and debilitating work, and provide the means that will enable them to devote themselves to child-rearing for the first seven years of the child's life. So commands the Almighty God. Our ancestors knew well that during these initial seven years it was the mother's biosphere that protected her children from disease, and healed them . . . The salvation of our nation is – Woman. The Mother, and the grandmother of the human race . . . To her we must return her sacred mission, encompassing that of the Blessed Virgin and the *Berehynia*. In her hands we must once again place the cradle that rocked the [all-male] *Zaporizhs'ka Sich*,[17] the hetmans, the geniuses, the philosophers and the food producers.

Within the elaborate structure of what are now perceived to be the ancient symbols of authentic Ukrainian womanhood (symbols that conveyed its special status) two goddesses are being invoked to create an idealized and 'overdetermined', or overinvested, pseudo-cultural quasi-myth of Ukrainian femininity, or simply the *kitsch* of eternal womanhood. Through the concept of the eternally feminine, this 'myth' is meant to serve the fetishism of motherhood, and hence the idealization of the Ukrainian family (which we actually know to be victimized by contemporary Ukrainian circumstances). Sadly enough for women, this myth has become an essential element in the creation of a contemporary national awareness. Although the awareness is subject to continual reconstruction in various social, economic and political sectors, throughout its many permutations the symbol of an ideal Ukrainian femininity persists. It illustrates thereby not only the enduring strength of ancient Ukrainian myths, be they diminished or not, but the extent to which gender asymmetry has penetrated the consciousness of the Ukrainian people without them being aware of it.

Ukrainian women today are seemingly content with the benevolent paternalism which has superseded the concept of equal status that once characterized their ancestors. Drawing upon the traditional view of respect for 'woman's work', and continuing to refer to it as a status symbol, paradoxically enough, as we have already seen, they are the ones most likely to encourage each other to subordinate their personal interests to the higher national cause, as well as to their 'sacred' mission as mothers. The Ukrainian woman's God-given mission, like that of the Virgin Mary, is constantly affirmed to be one of giving birth to saviours, that is to say the geniuses, philosophers and military leaders of the nation. There is, of course, no thought of such outstanding individuals being female. For her part the *Berehynia,* whatever her origins,[18] has actually come to mean many things to contemporary Ukrainians – protectress of the nation, guardian of the domestic hearth (the traditional heart of Ukrainian life) and the generational fire, and the image of woman's domesticity. Thus blended, the two symbols from disparate cultural spheres – the Christian Virgin mother and the pagan deity – are invoked by female authors such as Motrych (she is by no means atypical) to remind Ukraine's women of their proud heritage as females, and their proper feminine priorities. Together, the two symbols have been blended into a new metasymbol of Ukrainian femininity as a divinely ordained entity, with its own biologically determined essence, implicitly fortified by images of 'biosphere', 'persona', 'aura', 'genes' and so on. A pagan deity assumes Christian functions in conjunction with her 'sister', the Christian Virgin. What is extremely interesting in this process of cultural construction or preservation,[19] is the way in which the functions of the two mythologems – Christian and pagan – have merged, demonstrating the confusion that results when a pagan goddess is invoked to bestow her blessing upon Ukraine, thereby carrying out the function of a Christian deity. Such an invocation becomes a pseudo-religious, quasi-metaphysical attempt to validate concrete societal processes by the Virgin Mother and the pagan deity alike. This combined metasymbol has created its own discourse, which rhetorically perpetuates a romanticized vision of an artificial, mythologized, quintessential Ukrainian woman. The power of this metasymbol is amply illustrated by the very fact that both genders subscribe to it. As the subject of literary works, the performing and applied arts and popular sociology, each of the two elements of the metasymbol variously embodied is used to construct a new cultural heritage.

What accounts for the remarkable persistence of this cult of motherhood and family? Why is it that even Ukrainian women themselves are so reluctant to separate the issues of feminism and state-building, and instead treat them as separate and presumably sequential developments? Why is it that they do not see the way in which the Christian and pagan elements – as they are embodied in the above example – are invoked to illustrate the allegedly 'natural' female inclinations, or their biologically determined proclivity for 'woman's work', even as they conspire to impede the formation of a genuinely feminist consciousness?

To appreciate more fully this devotion to a romanticized past, it will be useful to examine the manifestation of what is so often represented as Ukraine's matriarchal heritage. I will stress the high status that the women of Ukraine enjoyed, from its very beginnings to the middle of the seventeenth century, when the country became a colony of Russia. I should also reiterate that such stature stemmed from the Ukrainian conception of the household as embodiment of the complementarity of male and female labour. And it bears repeating that it is precisely the same social values that governed Ukrainian households in the past, and determined the high regard that women enjoyed in Ukrainian society, which paradoxically became important elements in their later subordination. Taken together, the traditional cult of mother and protectress of the hearth, along with the 'natural' contributions that Ukrainian society expects of them in both the public and the private spheres, have become the most significant factors to impede the formation of a genuine feminist consciousness in contemporary Ukraine. What Susan Kay has attributed to all Soviet women, when she described them as being 'oppressed by mythologies [that is, Soviet mythologies] which dominate the culture in which they live',[20] also characterizes post-colonial Ukrainian women, except of course that their mythologies go back much further in time. They have inherited not only the oppressive patriarchal culture of Soviet society, but also the mythology of ancient Ukraine, itself subsequently perverted by the dominant culture of the colonizer, and in conflict with contemporary reality which now oppresses them in its own special way.

As previously mentioned, among the early Slavs who populated Kievan Rus´ (the ancestral home of modern Ukrainians), there is strong evidence for a matrifocal order[21] which accorded women considerable influence and prestige.[22] For example, the controversy that surrounded the introduction of Byzantine Christianity to the Kievan state reflects this. From the outset, its women vigorously opposed what was an essentially masculine faith, rooted in the principles of patriarchal authority.[23] They remained intractable and continued to ward off the incursion of a misogynistic clergy by resisting Orthodox Christianity. This occurred 'not only because they feared losing their power, but also because of the church's denigration of the feminine in dogma and rite'.[24] Churchmen resorted to various stratagems in an effort to draw women into the patriarchal Byzantine Church, but the women were adamant in their preference for pagan cults. Demands on the part of the Byzantine clergy that the father act as head of the family also met with little success: 'The continued centricity of the mother could not be overcome.'[25] It is this legacy that Ukrainian women have inherited.

The high esteem that females enjoyed in ancient Rus´ was particularly evident in the marriage rituals. According to one eleventh-century charter, no marriage could take place without the consent of the woman, and it was not unusual for young females to seize the initiative in courtship.[26] This tradition persisted in Ukraine into the early modern period of the country's history, at which time prospective brides still enjoyed considerable freedom of choice in husbands.[27]

By way of an interesting contrast, whereas ancient Ukrainian women had been able to resist actively the authority of the Orthodox Church because they belonged to a society that was accustomed to strong and highly valued women, no such general precedents existed for women in Muscovy.[28] Muscovite Russian society was founded upon, and evolved along, authoritarian principles. First, the Muscovite grand dukes, then their successors, the Russian tsars, rested their claims to legitimacy on a patriarchal conception of the ruler as the divinely ordained father, or *batiushka,* of his people.[29] The tsar exerted his authority over his subjects in much the same way that a typical Russian father dominated his biological family. Or, as Barbara Alpern Engel has described it, 'The authoritarianism that characterized Russia's autocratic political system also shaped family relations.'[30]

An excellent example of the way in which this worked is to be found in the sixteenth-century *Domostroi* (*Household Regulation*). This handbook reflects the already well-established nature of gender relations in Muscovy-Russia. Implicitly supported in this by both Church and state, it mandates the subordination of women through corporal chastisement. Specifically, a husband is expected to resort to the lash to punish his erring wife, although at the same time he is enjoined to administer such punishment in private, in a 'careful and controlled way, albeit patiently, painfully and fearsomely'.[31] The main virtues of a good wife are docility and obedience. In Ukraine, *Domostroi* does not seem to have been widely used, because Ukrainian women were reared in a different environment from their Russian counterparts.[32] The reader is also reminded of the ancient Kievan law against both wife and husband beating.[33] Wife beating became a widely established practice throughout Muscovite Russian society but, except for some small pockets – the Boyko region in the Carpathian mountains comes to mind – it was not a widely accepted custom in Ukraine. Moreover, Ukrainian women never experienced the seclusion of the *terem* (women's quarters in élite households), in which Muscovite women were isolated. Such factors, among others, reflect some very different formative experiences for women in the two countries.

After much of Ukraine passed to Muscovite control in the seventeenth century, and subsequently became part of the Russian Empire, Russian imperial culture began to exercise its power over the Ukrainians.[34] Muscovite influence introduced so many new elements into Ukrainian culture that its traditional paradigm became distorted, contributing to an eventual inversion in women's status. The prolonged period of Muscovite Russian colonization of Ukraine caused a gradual patriarchal-ization of its society. Ukrainian women lost much of the prestige that they had earlier enjoyed as women, although it must be stressed that their condition was never fully reduced to that of their Russian counterparts. The reasons for this were first, that the tradition of Ukrainian women's dignified status could not be fully eradicated, and second, that the symbols of exalted motherhood were thoroughly internalized by Ukrainian women and remained securely lodged in their consciousness as paradigms of their womanhood. However, the authoritarian patriarchal Russian society to which Ukraine was joined in the second half of the seventeenth century did impose a new cultural order, within which the status of the empowered Ukrainian woman began to change. Such changes should be regarded as symptomatic of the position of inferiority into which Ukrainian women were ultimately forced. This was both exacerbated and reinforced by the fact that Ukraine itself occupied a similarly inferior, peripheral position within the Russian Empire, as a result of which Ukrainian women became doubly marginalized.

The new round of colonization, this time by the Russo-centred Soviet regime, perpetuated Russia's cultural imperialism, thereby reinforcing its patriarchal authoritarianism. Contrary to the Soviet leaders' assurance of a better life for women in a communist state, this promise was never realized. The Soviet era witnessed the intense propagation of a perverted socialist ideology, as a means of forcing compliance with directives relentlessly imposed by the political centre upon the various nations which made up the Soviet Union. The experience of Ukrainians, especially the deteriorating status of Ukrainian women, in Soviet society 'is particularly revealing of the connection between colonization and the deterioration of interpersonal relations'.[35]

Notwithstanding its declared commitment to gender equality, rooted in the Marxist theory that calls for the socialization rather than the equalization of domestic responsibilities,[36] the sorry record of the male-dominated Soviet regime on the issue of women's rights is all too well known. Instead of addressing the requirements of the entire society – women and men alike – the regime subordinated gender-specific needs to its male-controlled political and economic agendas. Its projected reforms, which would have somewhat ameliorated the condition of women (at least in their prescribed domestic sphere) never specifically addressed the established pattern in the sexual division of labour. Ultimately, contrary to the much-vaunted sexual equality proclaimed by Marxist dogma, a typical response to the question: 'What does being modern mean to you?' became: 'It means being first and foremost an ordinary mother! Being a good wife, a loving daughter. Our emancipation never liberated us from this great female duty and never deprived us of its great joys.'[37] Or the following: 'A woman remains a woman, and her great strength is probably that, whilst on a par with men at work [which she cannot possibly have been in such a society!], she reserves for herself alone that area of women's affairs which makes her the custodian of the family hearth.'[38] Such responses simply underscore the shrewd application by the Soviet hierarchy of familiar patriarchal symbols to reinforce the women's acceptance of their so-called 'biologically determined functions', which allegedly dictate their 'natural' private and public roles. So persistently and effectively was the strategem applied that women themselves – having been conditioned to their socially prescribed roles – became its most aggressive proponents. They subscribed to the image of the new Soviet icon of 'femininity' – a combination of the tractor-driving heroine of socialist labour and the fertile mother breeding healthy children for the socialist utopia soon to come, thus legitimating the very regime that oppressed them.[39] In contrast to their Russian counterparts, however, Soviet Ukrainian women fused this Soviet icon with their own collective memory of the empowered matriarch.

One striking example of the recalled past of strong Ukrainian women can be found in the reminiscences of the mother of Serhiy Koroliov (a prominent scientist, inventor and builder of the spaceship), Mariia Koroliova, who lived in Nizhyn during the early Soviet era. Describing herself as a descendant of the Ukrainian Cossacks, she recalls: 'The Moskalenkos and the Lazarenkos are my forefathers . . . They showed their courage and strength on the field of battle, but at home turned over all authority to the women. As far as I remember, matriarchy ruled at home.'[40] Mariia had preserved a genuine connection with her Ukrainian past, but can the same be said of contemporary Ukrainian women? They are so intent on reconstructing the symbols of an authentic past, yet they produce only surrogate symbols which assume an illusory reality, and whose original meaning has long since faded.

To underscore the impact of the Soviet mentality with respect to feminism upon Ukrainian women, let me briefly return to the Ukrainian women's magazine

Zhinka. Instead of addressing the issue of feminism in Ukraine, it concentrates on criticizing the extremes in feminism and promoting its own Ukrainian ideal of 'happy slavery'.[41] Then, the very title of the first newspaper for women only to appear in Ukraine, *Charivnytsia (The Sorceress)*, is yet another indication of the total absence of a feminist consciousness in that country.[42] There *was* one self-styled 'feminist journal', *Piata pora: zhurnal dlia zhinok (Fifth Season. A Journal for Women)*, the first issue of which was published in Kiev in January 1993, but in spite of its stated mission it too failed to deal with feminist issues.[43] Despite a promising beginning, its contents were reduced to mostly conventional materials, aimed at the typical female readership in Ukraine. They dealt primarily with such things as the various roles which women have played in Ukrainian history and their age-old concerns as wives and mothers. And even more indicative of the prevailing attitudes toward women in Ukraine were the comments on this new publishing venture from its well-wishers – eight of Ukraine's prominent male writers. They effectively demonstrate just how much work remains to be done before the average (and not-so-average) Ukrainian can even begin to conceptualize sexual equality. To give but one example, the well-known author Oleh Chornohuz writes: 'I want only one thing from women – a smile.' He considers that a woman's smile exemplifies peace and well-being in the family, the state and the entire planet, and calls upon the women of the world – to smile! Only thus, Chornohuz asserts, will the men be disarmed and conflicts be resolved, even those in government! The fact that these comments are an obvious parody on the Marxist dictum 'Workers of the world, unite!' simply underscores the frivolous attitude toward feminism which prevails throughout Ukrainian society. Parody or not, Chornohuz has aptly highlighted the prevailing Ukrainian stand on women, one that has thoroughly penetrated the contemporary Ukrainian consciousness.

A statement made by the first president of the recently reactivated Association of Ukrainian Women, Atena Pashko, sums up the typical *female* attitudes and priorities very well. According to her, the greatest hope of the Association is to become part of a united national effort that will produce caring mothers for the nation. Thus, for the time being most Ukrainian women seem content to cling to ancient gender-specific roles, personified by the Virgin Mary and the *Berehynia,* the Madonna and the pre-Christian goddess, seeking in them their worth as women in the dynamic of their contemporary existence. If such ideas were only infrequently expressed there would be no need to dwell on the issue. However, examples such as I have given abound in Ukrainian publications and discourse.

Somewhat divergent and more hopeful in tone is the position adopted by a very talented writer-scholar in Ukraine, Valerii Shevchuk. In a recent interview, which appeared in issue 8 (1994) of the weekly journal *Ukraina,* he affirmed the right of Ukrainian women to equal treatment in all of society, including the domestic sphere. The title of his interview is: 'I Would Like to See Women as Human Beings and not Simply as Friends of Human Beings'. It promises much, and in many respects the interview lives up to that promise. One is at a loss, however, to explain the accompanying photographic insets. On one side we have the author's picture, portraying a smiling, dignified face; on the other is the portrait of a naked young woman with pendulous breasts, ostensibly representing the eternally feminine. Is *she* meant to convey the image of the liberated Ukrainian woman? Or does she represent the classic *Berehynia* – the pagan goddess – herself? It is difficult to say.

It will be instructive to follow the evolution of the policy on feminism in this journal. In issue 6 (1994), prior to Shevchuk's interview, it began publishing in serial form a translation from the French of Simone de Beauvoir's *The Second Sex*, by Natal'ia and Pavlo Vorob'ev and Iaroslava Sobko. The intent is obvious – a dialogue on western-style feminism appears finally to have opened up – but what is even more deserving of our attention at this juncture are the photographic insets that accompany each segment. The first contains a picture of a dreamy-eyed young woman alongside some flowers, suggesting a nineteenth-century romantic pose of the model female. Yet another segment of *The Second Sex* is published in issue 9 of *Ukraina,* only this time it includes a photograph of a young lady flanked by two men. All we have is a rear view of them leaning over a city wall. The men are dressed in business suits and the woman in a tailored dress, but a gust of wind has whipped up her skirt to reveal a nicely-shaped bottom clad in white panties. This conveys a mixed message, but it just might be that the photograph is meant to convey precisely what *The Second Sex* is writing against. If this is indeed the case, then we can argue for some real progress in the thinking on feminist issues among Ukrainians. A second article in this issue addresses the problem of feminism in Ukraine. Written by a sociologist, Ol'ha Ivashchenko, it is entitled: 'Do We Need Feminism?' The photograph which accompanies the article shows a peasant woman, of indeterminate age, raking a shabby, overgrown yard, and aptly portrays the hard lot of the average Ukrainian woman. To my knowledge, this is the first attempt by a Ukrainian scholar to discuss feminist consciousness and its application to Ukraine in such a serious way. This is an excellent beginning to what is hoped will become an important area for study in Ukraine. It is worth emphasizing that the journal appears to have begun to move in the right direction. What remains now is to see how well it resolves the question of whether or not Ukraine truly believes that it needs western-style feminism.

Having noted the above, it is still an obvious fact that, with only a few exceptions, Ukrainian women seem content to live in a system designed and dominated by males. They cling to gender-specific roles, as exemplified in various configurations of symbols – various metasymbols – in the images of the Virgin Mary and the *Berehynia*. As the representations of an ancient, mythologized and 'overdetermined' reality are resurrected to become the building blocks of a newly emancipated state and its society, Ukrainians are seemingly unaware that such antiquated vestiges are often applied haphazardly (perhaps with the unconscious intent of compromising any kind of feminist movement), and thus misapplied to the new and quite different structures which characterize contemporary Ukrainian reality in our postmodern world.

There is, of course, no question that countless ancient rituals and symbols –

many of them, like the Virgin Mary, banned by the Soviet colonizer – need to be resurrected in order to remind the people of their cultural legacy. But it would be a mistake to look upon such symbols as exact representations of today's reality, to 'treat the present as if it were an intact remnant of the unchanged past'.[44] Among other factors, the transformation of Ukrainian society has been mediated by a master narrative imposed by the colonizer. Inscribed upon the colonized, it has yielded a colonial subtext that has altered the contents and significance of the old symbols. Henceforth, colonization must be reckoned with in all analyses of Ukrainian society, because some of its effects will never be erased. That whole experience too has become a part of the total process of Ukraine's becoming. Ukrainians can no longer assume that there is an essential and unbroken continuity between a pre-colonial Ukrainian past, and a post-colonial Ukrainian present. In such a new context, Ukrainian women need to recognize that a return to the past, and a traditional reinterpretation of its symbols, is impossible, if only because their colonial experience has forever changed both the symbols and the women themselves. Now, in order to move beyond that experience, as many of their Russian counterparts have done, for instance, it is up to Ukrainian women to reassess their priorities, to 'reinvent' their history as contemporary females in a free state, to create a new discourse that will respond to women's issues today by investing the symbols of their past with new and authentic meanings – authentic for our own time. What is required for this to occur is a psychological transformation which will enable the members of the fledgling state to recognize and deal with the imprint of foreign distortion, mediated by the special interests of an alien political centre. In order to overcome it they need to develop a sufficient awareness of its impact upon their development, even as they utilize the inevitable traces of that colonial past for their own growth.

Because there were no imperatives of state-building to distract them when the Soviet Union collapsed, Russian women were the ones who were most prepared to address the challenges of feminism directly. Insofar as they had always been in the cultural mainstream, Russian women were not encumbered by a perceived need to link their cultural priorities to any political agenda directed toward achieving cultural and political sovereignty. It should also be mentioned that feminist ideas were already familiar to them, because feminism had begun to filter into the USSR as early as the 1970s, although it was confined to the two principal cities of the dominant Russian centre, never being allowed to cross over into the other republics. What is more, Russian women were not confused by a legacy of highly valued female roles in society, as Ukrainian women were. This circumstance made it possible for them to view themselves as age-old victims of a misogynistic society who needed to struggle against their traditionally subordinate status. The gender-specific roles that accorded women a highly valued position in traditional Ukrainian society simply did not obtain in the case of Russian women. The former Soviet state, however, was a great leveller, and the traditional female centrality in Ukraine did become a thing of the past. Ukrainian women should be aware of this transformation as they seek to resurrect the ancient symbols.

The present discourse of national revival falsely encourages them to view themselves as members of a society which always has recognized, and continues to uphold female centrality. This discourse is a serious impediment to the formation of a genuine feminist consciousness. Contemporary Ukrainian women have yet to appreciate that they are subjects not only of a new state, but of a radically different state from the one from which they have drawn the elements of their womanhood. They must resolve the contradictions between the new and the old in such a way as would enable them to function as whole human beings and not, in the words of Shevchuk, as helpmeets of whole human beings.

Notes

1 Akhil Gupta, 'The Song of the Non-Aligned World: Transnational Identities and the Reinscription of Space in Late Capitalism', *Cultural Anthropology*, no. 7 (February 1992), pp. 70–2.

2 The existence of matriarchal societies is still a problematic issue in scholarship. Heide Göttner-Abendroth, *The Dancing Goddess: Principles of a Matriarchal Aesthetic*, trans. by Maureen T. Krause (Boston: Beacon Press, 1991), marshals much convincing evidence to show that a matriarchal age, long suppressed in the public mind, was the real foundation of later patriarchal societies. In the case of Ukraine, the numerous and persistent references to its matriarchal tradition testify to a past in which its women apparently played a dominant role.

3 For discussion of this doctrine of equality in difference, see Karen Offen, 'The Second Sex and the Baccalaureate in Republican France, 1880–1924', *French Historical Studies*, vol. 13 (1983), pp. 251–86.

4 Mona Etienne and Eleanor Leacock (eds.), *Women and Colonization* (New York: A. J. F. Bergin, 1980), p. 6.

5 For a good treatment of this relationship, see Nataliia Polons′ka-Vasylenko, *Prominent Women of Ukraine* (Winnipeg, Canada: Soiuz Ukrainok Kanady, 1965). The author refers, for example, to a list of what constituted crimes during the Kievan Rus′ period of Ukrainian history over which the ecclesiastical courts held jurisdiction; among them are wife *and* husband beating. Examples of the strong Ukrainian woman are to be found not only in historical documents and memoirs, but in various artistic expressions as well. The opera *Cossack Beyond the Danube* by Hulak-Artemovsky comes to mind. It is set in seventeenth-century Turkey, where the Cossack Karas has been taken captive along with his wife Odarka. He despairs over his Turkish captivity and lives in terror of his wife who beats him every time he comes home drunk.

6 We must, of course, take cognizance of the fact that it would be political suicide for a woman to campaign on feminist issues. Referring to herself as a woman and a wife, however, would be perceived as not presenting a threat to the male deputies. It would also be acceptable to women voters who still thought of themselves and other women, even those in public life, in traditional terms.

7 Feminism in late nineteenth-century France is characterized in this way in Karen Offen, 'Depopulation, Nationalism and Feminism in Fin-de-Siècle France, 1880–1924', *American Historical Review*, vol. 5, no. 89 (June 1984), p. 667.

8 A list of the one hundred most influential people in Ukraine today indicates just how far women have yet to go to achieve any kind of parity in public life. Published in *News*

from Ukraine, no. 20 (13–19 May, 1993), p. 1, the list includes the names of ninety-nine men and one woman.

9 This same question is posed in a discussion of Third World women by Chandra Talpade Mohanty, 'Under Western Eyes: Feminist Scholarship and Colonial Discourses', in Chandra Talpade Mohanty, Ann Russo and Lourdes Torres (eds.), *Third World Women and the Politics of Feminism* (Bloomington and Indianapolis: Indiana University Press, 1991), p. 58.

10 See *News from Ukraine*, no. 5 (1990), for the full text.

11 Martha Bohachevsky-Chomiak, *Feminists Despite Themselves: Women in Ukrainian Community Life, 1884–1939* (Edmonton, Canada: Canadian Institute of Ukrainian Studies, 1988), p. 87.

12 Ibid., p. 97.

13 As reported in 'Ukrainka i demokratiia', ('The Ukrainian Woman and Democracy'), *Literaturna Ukraina* (*Literary Ukraine*), 5 August 1993. Indeed, it is not unusual for newly emerging states to enlist the support of their women by appealing to them as the traditional bearers of ethnicity, which is so vital to the nation's survival. For a discussion of this, see Elzbieta Matynia, 'Women after Communism: A Bitter Freedom', *Social Research*, vol. 61, no. 2 (Summer 1994), pp. 352–3.

14 Michelle Z. Rosaldo, *Knowledge and Passion* (Cambridge: Cambridge University Press, 1980), p. 400.

15 Chandra Talpade Mohanty, 'Introduction: Cartographies of Struggle: Third World Women and the Politics of Feminism', in Mohanty et al., *Third World Women*, p. 31.

16 The magazine was originally published as *Radianska Zhinka* (*Soviet Woman*).

17 The nucleus of the Ukrainian Cossack host (*Sich*) was established in 1553–4 in the Dnipro (Dnieper) basin to obstruct Tatar raids on Ukraine. Because the precise location was Khortytsia island just below the Dnipro rapids (known as *zaporizhia*) the *kozaky* (Cossacks) became known as the *Zaporizhs'ki kozaky* (Zaporozhian Cossacks). In 1578, King Stefan Bathory of Poland granted *de jure* privileges to the *Zaporizhs'ki kozaky* by enrolling some of them in the official registers. This accorded them privileged status. By the early seventeenth century the Ukrainian Cossacks fell into three major groups or categories: the 'registered' Cossacks – primarily town dwellers, and the 'unregistered' Cossacks, who were subdivided into the Zaporizhs'ki, who had not received official status and lived beyond the pale of the Polish–Lithuanian Commonwealth, and the vast majority of frontier Cossacks without any designation. By this time the frontier territory in eastern and south-eastern Ukraine was controlled by the Ukrainian Cossacks.

18 Solomea Pavlychko, 'Between Feminism and Nationalism: New Women's Groups in the Ukraine', in Mary Buckley (ed.), *Perestroika and Soviet Women* (Cambridge: Cambridge University Press, 1992), pp. 82–96, states that in her opinion the name *Berehynia* itself is a relatively new one in Ukraine. Needless to say, however, similar goddesses are polygenetic and they abound in ancient Ukrainian mythology.

19 The metasymbol has actually evolved from the function of preservation into something new, and potentially dangerous to women.

20 Susan Kay, 'A Woman's Work', *Irish Slavonic Studies*, no. 8 (1987), p. 115.

21 Joanna Hubbs, *Mother Russia: The Feminine Myth in Russian Culture* (Bloomington: Indiana University Press, 1988), p. 91.

22 Dorothy Atkinson, 'Society and the Sexes in the Russian Past', in *Women in Russia* (Stanford, Calif.: Stanford University Press, 1977), p. 4, supports the notion of a

powerful feminine presence in ancient Ukraine (which she mistakenly calls southern Russia, instead of using the correct term Rus'), by noting that 'a number of excavations have revealed weapons in ancient female graves'. Joanna Hubbs, *Mother Russia*, p. 13, refers to traces of a matrilinear society among the Rus' (whom she erroneously calls Russians).

23 Hubbs, *Mother Russia*, p. 90ff.

24 Ibid., pp. 87, 92.

25 Ibid., p. 99.

26 Ibid., p. 81.

27 The aggressive role of women in courtship rituals is reflected, for example, in numerous Ukrainian songs, folk sayings and so on.

28 The typical Russian woman, according to L. R. Lewitter, 'Women, Sainthood and Marriage in Muscovy', *Journal of Russian Studies*, vol. 37 (1979), p. 5, 'probably did not set eyes on her future husband until the wedding day'.

29 This kind of absolutism should not be confused with the later and more complex notion of the divine right of kings.

30 Barbara Alpern Engel, *Mothers and Daughters: Women of the Intelligentsia in Nineteenth-Century Russia* (Cambridge: Cambridge University Press, 1983), p. 3.

31 Carolyn Johnston Pouncy (ed.), *The Domostroi: Rules for Russian Households in the Time of Ivan the Terrible* (Ithaca, N.Y. and London: Cornell University Press, 1994), pp. 143–4; Engel, *Mothers and Daughters*, pp. 9–10; Lewitter, 'Women, Sainthood and Marriage', p. 4.

32 Bohachevsky-Chomiak, *Feminists Despite Themselves*, p. xxii.

33 See note 5 above.

34 This was accomplished in a variety of ways. For example, 'through its cognitive dimension: its comprehensive symbolic order which constituted permissible thinking and action and prevented other worlds from emerging', as the situation of women in Nigeria is described in Helen Callaway, *Gender, Culture and Empire: European Women in Colonial Nigeria* (Urbana: University of Illinois Press, 1987). Such an assessment can apply with equal validity to Ukrainians.

35 The point was developed in a discussion of Indian societies in South America: see Etienne and Leacock, *Women and Colonization*, p. 18.

36 Susan Bridger, *Women in the Soviet Countryside* (Cambridge: Cambridge University Press, 1987), p. 124.

37 Although the present example is taken from an interview with Ada Rogovtseva, published in *Krest'ianka*, no. 4 (1980), p. 30, Soviet women had long since become habituated to such responses.

38 Bridger, *Women in the Soviet Countryside*, pp. 135–6.

39 In her discussion of women working outside the home in post-communist societies, Elzbieta Matynia, 'Women after Communism', p. 359, takes as her examples a variety of eastern European women. Of Czechoslovak women, for example, she says: 'The working woman was popularized to serve the ideological objectives of the Communist Party system.' She goes on to point out that many Czech and Slovak women voiced a desire to retreat from the world of work because they considered themselves 'overemancipated'. What this overemancipation amounted to was the well-known double burden, which glorified the woman who combined her work in the public sector with traditional female domestic and child-rearing obligations. Such sentiments are now frequently heard among women in Ukraine, who are exhausted by their

double burden. Seeking a way out, they concentrate upon returning to the private sphere. Very few appear to be looking for alternative solutions, such as shared domestic duties. And even when such burdens are in fact divided, it is rare for the women themselves to admit that household chores and child-rearing are anything but their responsibilities.

40 There is a description of Koroliova, and other examples of empowered women in Ukraine's past, in Oles' Kozulia, *Zhinka v istorii Ukrainy* (Kiev: Naukova Dumka, 1993).

41 This expression was used to describe the condition of contemporary Ukrainian women in *Ukrainian Weekly*, 8 August 1990.

42 Its inaugural issue, published in western Ukraine, was announced in the Ukrainian–American daily *Svoboda*, 18 December 1991. At present, *Charivnytsia* appears only sporadically.

43 Editor's note: For further discussion of *Piata pora* and its subsequent bankruptcy, see Solomea Pavlychko above, p. 310.

44 Etienne and Leacock, *Women and Colonization*, p. 5.

Index